Ravi Takhar

How to Build a Bank

The Moorad Choudhry Global Banking Series

Series Editor
Moorad Choudhry

Ravi Takhar

How to Build a Bank

A Guide to Key Bank Regulations, the License Application Process and Bank Risk Management

DE GRUYTER

The views, thoughts and opinions expressed in this book represent those of the author in his individual private capacities, and should not in any way be attributed to any employing institution, or to the author as director, representative, officer, or employee of any affiliated institution. While every attempt is made to ensure accuracy, the author or the publisher will not accept any liability for any errors or omissions herein. This book does not constitute investment advice and its contents should not be construed as such. Any opinion expressed does not constitute a recommendation for action to any reader. The contents should not be considered as a recommendation to deal in any financial market or instrument and the author, the publisher, the editor, any named entity, affiliated body or academic institution will not accept liability for the impact of any actions arising from a reading of any material in this book.

ISBN 978-3-11-110055-5
e-ISBN (PDF) 978-3-11-110154-5
e-ISBN (EPUB) 978-3-11-110291-7
ISSN 2627-8847

Library of Congress Control Number: 2023942322

Bibliographic information published by the Deutsche Nationalbibliothek
The Deutsche Nationalbibliothek lists this publication in the Deutsche Nationalbibliografie; detailed bibliographic data are available on the internet at http://dnb.dnb.de.

Cover image: Nikada/E+/Getty Images
Typesetting: Integra Software Services Pvt. Ltd.
Printing and binding: CPI books GmbH, Leck

www.degruyter.com

To my beautiful Billy the Cat. All my love. I miss you every moment of every day! And to Tayin, thank you my sunshine.

Bede.

1st May 2023

Contents

Foreword

Banks come in very many different shapes and sizes.

In 2024 there are banks that offer a sophisticated digital-only service with not just financial products accessible via their “app” but also the goods and services of partner firms in different industries. At the same time, there are banks that do not offer any kind of digital service via desktop internet or app at all, and whose customers continue to interact with it via physical branch, post and/or telephone. Innovation is the preserve of only some banks.

This considerable variation amongst banks in size, business model, product suite, customer franchise and customer interaction notwithstanding, there are one or two things that all banks in the world have in common. One of these is regulation. Banks are heavily regulated corporate entities, and banking is a heavily regulated industry. Naturally this regulation is the responsibility of a central government authority, usually (but not always) the country’s central bank. All banks are regulated.

‘Twas not always thus. Modern banking as one would recognise it today dates from the 15th century (there is at least one bank in Europe conducting business today that can trace its origins back to the beginning of the 16th century), yet a formal supervision process for banks would be observed in only nascent form from the late 19th century onwards. The Bank of England, formed in 1694, was not nationalised as a public sector entity until 1946. There was a long period of time when banking was conducted, and conducted successfully, without any formal supervision or regulation being in place.

Like corporate entities in any industry however, during this time there were bank failures. And when a bank fails, the “knock-on” effect on the rest of the country can be, and frequently is, considerable. Hence the need for regulation (not that that prevents banks failing; large-scale bank failures this century are clear evidence that regulation may be a necessary, but is certainly not a sufficient, condition to prevent banks failing).

Today banks are heavily regulated beasts. The supervision process is highly prescriptive and onerous. One might even go so far as to call the process burdensome. And that is certainly the case for new banks. A group of stakeholders wishing to set up a new bank today, in more or less any jurisdiction, must expect to spend considerable time, effort, resources and expense as they work their way through the banking license approval process. It is not so much a complex process, rather a very detailed process with many steps along the way before completion.

Which is why this book deserves a very wide readership amongst any of said stakeholders. Start-up shareholders, aspiring fintechs, board directors, indeed anyone involved in the process of creating a bank will benefit from reading this text. There is not just a detailed, step-by-step description of the approval process, there are also really rather useful templates that the reader can take away and apply to his or her own bank startup project. Addressing regulatory requirements satisfactorily, and in a timely

https://doi.org/10.1515/9783111101545-203

manner, is the absolute key to a successful bank license application. This book will assist greatly in achieving this.

Early on in the text the author writes,

> I believe banks are the single most important business institution in any developed economy.

Spot on 100%, although I would go further and remove the word “developed”. Banks are vital to economic development in any country. Which is why this book is such a welcome addition to the practitioner literature on banking.

How to build a bank. Absolutely . . . read it, and then hopefully go and do it!

Professor Moorad Choudhry
Surrey, England
November 2023

1 How to Build a Bank

1.1 What is a Bank?

In its simplest form the essential difference between a bank and any other business is that the key creditors of a bank are guaranteed to be paid back all the money they have lent to the bank by the government of the state in which the bank operates.

The government guarantee enables the creditors of the bank to sleep in peace secure in the knowledge that no matter what the bank does, the creditors will get their money back.

The government guarantee is also the backbone of the modern world economy. Without the guarantee, the world would not have enjoyed the unparalleled growth in economic wealth that it has benefited from over the past 100 years.

So who are a bank's creditors? That, my dear reader, would be you and me and all the other millions of people around the world who deposit our hard-earned money into banks. Certainty that the money you have worked hard for is always safe in a bank and that you can always get it back is a fundamental human right.

1.2 The Guarantee

The fact that the clever people in banks can take your money and then provide loans to enable people to buy their homes or businesses, again another fundamental human right, shows how a simple government guarantee can help ensure economic growth and prosperity.

The government guarantee is a precious privilege enjoyed by the banking sector. State privileges do not come without a cost. This cost or in other words the requirements of a government, usually through its appointed Regulator, to enable a business to operate as a bank is the key topic of this book.

The Regulator's requirements, although specific to the banking sector have a great deal of relevance to any business. Fundamental requirements for the safe and successful operation of any business can be found in the rules relating to obtaining a bank licence.

This book uniquely and in unprecedented detail will provide a breakdown of the core documentation required to operate a banking business.

1.3 How This Book Helps

The book will start with the core document for any business, the Business Plan. Any good business plan should contain a number of key pieces of information. For a bank, the Regulator has helpfully set out every piece of information that it believes is essen-

https://doi.org/10.1515/9783111101545-001

tial to ensure that a business is viable. This book will set out and review every key requirement for a good business plan. As stated, these requirements are applicable to any business, not just the business of banking.

The book will then review the plan, which sets out how much capital will be required to achieve the business plan. For banks this document is called the Internal Capital Adequacy Assessment Plan or ICAAP for short. Academics have written huge volumes on the subject of capital. The ICAAP is an excellent summary required by a Regulator, which in one document encompasses all you will ever need to know on the subject of capital requirements for the operation of any business.

The book will again provide a breakdown of each section of the ICAAP document and the methodology for the calculation of the capital required to operate a banking business.

A well-worn phrase in business lore is that businesses do not fail due to lack of capital but a lack of liquidity. This is particularly true for banks. A bank may have all the capital required for the effective operation of its business, but if there is any fear that it does not have sufficient liquidity, people will be queuing up outside its doors for their money back and the bank will fail. The Regulator therefore requires banks to produce a plan, which demonstrates that they have adequate liquidity, known as the Internal Liquidity Adequacy Assessment Plan, or ILAAP for short.

Again, the discipline required to complete an ILAAP will benefit any business. The ILAAP sets the liquidity that will be required at all times to ensure the effective operation of a bank.

Bank regulators are also keen for banks to set out how they will recover from difficult financial and economic conditions. Where a Resolution is not possible the Regulator will want to see a full step by step plan of how the bank will shut its business down in an orderly manner. Again, these disciplines are beneficial to the operation of any business.

This book sets out in a manner that is completely unprecedented all the requirements for the core documentation essential for the operation of a bank and will be required reading for anyone who wants to operate a safe and well-run business, banking or otherwise. Each chapter is dedicated to the Regulatory Business Plan, the ICAAP, the ILAAP, the Recovery Plan and the Resolution Plan. If all the documents are complete and their detail implemented, a Regulator in any jurisdiction should be able to grant that business a licence to operate as a bank.

1.4 Templates of Core Documentation

Each chapter of the book – again, uniquely and for ease of reference – sets out actual templates of a Regulatory Business Plan, ICAAP, ILAAP, Recovery Plan and Resolution Plan (in their original format, structure and layout). Where it was not deemed necessary to reproduce them (since every situation will require its own specific tables to be created), some tables have been left out in the templates but their location has been marked with captions as prompts. These can be simply adapted to create the core documentation for a bank licence application in any jurisdiction.

I believe banks are the single most important business institution in any developed economy. Every other business relies on them to a lesser or greater degree. If they fail the whole economy fails. I hope this book will begin to simplify a very complex area of regulatory law and rules to enable a better understanding of the banking sector and hopefully a better understanding of the key requirements for a successful long-term banking business.

2 The Regulatory Business Plan

2.1 Outline of RBP

A business plan is simply a document that sets out how the company that is the subject of the business plan will be profitable. Historically, a business plan was a document designed for investors to determine whether it would be worth them putting their money into the business to achieve their return aspirations. Investors develop an expertise in being able to spot a weak business plan and are materially and personally interested in making sure they make the right decision. A wrong decision means that they will either lose their hard-earned money or the hard-earned money that has been entrusted to them by their clients.

This is what makes me smile about the Regulators looking at Regulatory Business Plans (RBPs). They are not going to lose any money, whether the RBP makes sense or not. They don't care about that and quite frankly do not have the business expertise to be able to determine whether a business plan will be successful or not. They are Regulators; they are not business people. In fact, they are as far removed from business people as you could possibly get.

For bank application purposes, therefore, the RBP is not so much a proof of the business concept as an exercise in ticking regulatory boxes. That is the simple reason why most RBPs will look very similar and an advisor will be able to charge a huge fee for making sure that an applicant's RBP looks like all the other RBPs approved by the Regulator. I repeat again the Regulator and indeed the advisors are not business people.

As the RBP is a tick box exercise, let's make sure we get each of those boxes ticked.

What are the boxes?

- Ownership
- Business viability
- Financial resources
- Non-financial resources
- Governance
- Risk
- Implementation Plan

2.2 Ownership

Who is the owner of the business? There is a fundamental difference between how an investor would look at a business and a Regulator.

As an owner is not strictly the executive management of the business and investors are in most cases investing with or diluting down the holding of the founding owner, the owner in isolation is not a fundamental investor point. This is of course caveated by the

https://doi.org/10.1515/9783111101545-002

obvious, i.e., the owner should pass simple character and identity checks, but these are relatively straight forward to satisfy.

From a Regulator's perspective however, ownership is one of the most fundamental questions. Not only who is the owner, but what are his or her motives in obtaining a bank licence. This has become a very big issue for the Regulator. There are, as you would expect, historic examples of the Regulator getting this completely wrong. The Regulator has often failed to identify whether an owner of a bank is in fact suitable. There are many examples of this failing.

Let's start with my own experience of this failing, Pensions Bank and Antonov.

Pensions Bank was created by an insurance broker and someone whose company I have very much enjoyed: Geoffrey Pointon. Geoffrey and I enjoyed having lunch together.[1]

I will always recall the brilliantly simple way he obtained a bank licence in the 1970s for Pensions Bank.

Geoffrey, in his insurance business, began taking money deposited with him by customers for safe keeping. Geoffrey would invest that money or just hold it on deposit on behalf of his customers.

He got a call from the Bank of England to come in for a meeting. At the Bank, Geoffrey was informed that he was taking deposits from his customers, for which he needed a bank licence. Geoffrey agreed that he should have a licence and the Bank gave him a licence. That was it. A new bank was born, Pensions Bank.

Geoffrey was then approached by a Russian businessman, Vladimir Antonov, whose family owned Portsmouth Football Club, and who liked sports cars (and cars in general) and who also wanted a UK bank to add to his collection of trophy assets.

The Antonovs created huge banking empires in Russia and Latvia, and a UK bank was an ideal platform for their international business aspirations.

The Regulator was informed that Geoffrey was going to sell his business to Antonov. The Regulator approved the transfer to Antonov.

The Antonovs' love of cars is legendary. As well as creating a new sports car, the Spyker, Antonov was keen on buying the highly regarded Swedish car manufacturer Saab. Saabs have always been regarded as superb cars and had a loyal and fanatical worldwide fan base. Ford acquired the company and it became a little unloved and started a downward spiral. Antonov wanted to buy it from Ford. In summary, the

1 My favourite was always at Tamarind, a wonderful restaurant in Mayfair, which was the first Michelin star Indian restaurant in the UK. It is still regarded by some as the best Indian in the UK, but there are so many good Indian restaurants in London at the moment that I could not say this anymore. As an aside and as you would expect, you cannot get better Indian food than in Delhi (Indian accent). Same goes for Italian food in Rome (Roscholi) and kebabs in Istanbul (Zenga). Strangely Dubai matches nearly the best food in the world for all important food countries. Well done Dubai. The best Indian restaurants at lunchtime in London are without a doubt the best places to eat in peace and privacy. Geoffrey was a wonderful conversationalist, but not so good at eating Indian food with his hands!

US government had to approve the sale of Saab, but for reasons that are unclear, the consent to Antonov was not obtained.

At the same time, questions were also being asked about the Antonov family's other banking interests in Russia and Latvia.

Again, without any detail of the particulars, the Regulator then decided that it was prudent to stop Antonov taking any active part in the management or operation of Pensions Bank even though it was his bank.

The Regulator therefore, after permitting the transfer to Antonov, decided that in fact Antonov should not be able to own or manage a UK bank.[2]

2.3 Business Viability

Regulators and business plans. How is the Regulator or indeed any investor ever going to know whether a business is viable? The simple fact is that unless a business is proven, i.e., has been operational for a number of years and through those years produced a constant and stable cashflow, profit and steadily growing balance sheet, you cannot tell whether it is viable. Business plans are exactly that – plans. There is no certainty that they will be realised. Indeed, I am sure that the Regulator, investors and a number of other stakeholders are scratching their heads and wondering why the 200 plus page business plans of a number of the challenger banks have not been realised. They are not realised as they are simply bad.

So, the best way for a Regulator to determine whether a business plan is viable is to be able to point to another plan that it has approved and, on that basis, approve the plan that is in front of it. The advisors have picked up on this and so for huge amounts of money they will produce a business plan for a challenger bank applicant that resembles all the others that have historically ticked all the boxes for the Regulator. Most of those business plans will point to a market where the big banks are not active, usually something to do with small and medium size businesses ('SMEs'), and concoct a plan to lend to that market.

---

2 I met Antonov on a beautiful sunny day in London. His offices were just next to the Bank of England. As you would expect everything was luxuriously appointed, wood-lined walls, sumptuous leather chairs, leather-lined and heavy desks and fine art accenting each room. Geoffrey Pointon kindly arranged the meeting.Antonov seemed to be a fun-loving, rich, sports car and jet plane owning magnate, wonderfully handsome, young and surprisingly and pleasantly humble. I told him I understood the situation at Pensions Bank and that I would like to buy the bank from him. He there and then agreed in principle that he would sell the bank for its current net asset value. Deal done.I left Antonov's office with a great feeling of joy. At last, I had the opportunity to buy a bank. My next question was how was I going to get the money.

After 20 years of lending in our market, it was nice, if a little patronising, to be told by the Regulator that our business, Orchard Funding Group PLC, was viable.

2.4 Financial Resources

This is a big section in the RBP. Please note however that, here, it is just the outline of a much more detailed and interrogative analysis of financial resources that takes place in two documents that we will be discussing in more detail in later chapters, the ICAAP and the ILAAP.

The key financial resources of a new applicant are like the key financial resources of you and me – cash. For new applicants, cash will be invested by investors for the purposes of the operation of the business and the bank licence application process. For existing businesses, financial resources are the capital of the applicant.

We will analyse this in more detail in the ICAAP section, but at this stage you need to be aware that the Regulator will want to see that the applicant has the capital or in other words cash, now, to operate its business and operate as a bank. This is despite the fact that the applicant may not need the capital immediately and will only need the capital once it has received the licence.

Many people have considered the minimum amount this capital has to be. Regulations point to minimum capital requirements of £5 million for a bank. There are some European regulations which suggest that this can be even lower for certain banks. The fact is that no one is going to get through the application process without at least £20m of capital. The Regulator historically did not insist on this capital being demonstrated before a bank applicant went into the mobilisation process. This has now changed. An applicant must demonstrate it has the capital to operate a bank before it goes into the mobilisation process. This has effectively killed applications from a number of potential new bank entrants and in turn will in the future drastically reduce the number of new banks. Most of the existing challenger banks would not have been able to satisfy this requirement when they were making their applications.

The requirement to post cash is a difficult one. On the one hand, the Regulator wants to see that applicants have enough cash to say they will do what their plan says they will do. On the other hand, people putting up the cash have no guarantee that they will receive a return on that cash, as they have no guarantee that a bank licence will be granted. This was the whole rationale for the 'licence with restrictions' or 'mobilisation application process'.

A dear friend of mine, who has now sadly passed, spent millions of pounds on a bank application, much of it on the instruction of the Regulator, only to be denied the licence. His application and a couple of other high-profile applications, where millions of pounds were spent only to result in failed applications, led the Regulator to change the bank licence application rules to enable applicants to only invest cash when they were certain a bank licence would be awarded. Unfortunately, it appears that the

Regulator has now returned us to the days when investors have no certainty when supporting bank applications. This will no doubt reduce the number of new bank applications over time.

The simple question of what available cash is, is not really simple at all. The Regulator has wonderful definitions of available cash, which we will explore in more detail in our review of the ICAAP.

In summary, the Prudential Regulatory Authority (PRA) will want to ensure that there is enough cash in the business to ensure that any credit losses on any assets created by the business can be absorbed by the cash put in by investors, and that the bank can meet any liquidity calls by its investors.

2.4.1 Enough Cash to Cover Losses

The safest model for the Regulator is if all cash is put in by investors to fund all the assets created by the bank. The key assets of a bank are usually cash and loans to customers. In this scenario, if anything goes wrong with the assets, the only parties that will suffer are the investors.

In reality of course the whole point of a bank is that assets will be funded by simple and innocent bank depositors like you and me. The Regulator will therefore want to ensure that where a bank has taken your or my cash into its accounts it is safe. Again, the safest way for a bank to look after our cash is to actually just hold our cash. In a deep and distant past, banks could actually make money from doing this, but not today. Today a bank will have to invest that cash in assets. If anything goes wrong with those assets, the Regulator will want to ensure that depositors are not harmed in anyway. The simple reason for this is that if depositors are harmed in any way the Regulator (or more accurately the government) will have to pay those depositors back.

Let's put it even more simply.

Mr. Greedy investor makes a £2million capital investment into a bank. The bank lends £2m. All of the loans that the bank makes default and the bank recovers nothing of the £2m lent. The bank loses £2m and Mr. Greedy investor loses £2m. It's sad for Mr. Greedy investor, but no depositors have lost any money. So not a real problem for the Regulator. (As an aside, there may still be a problem for the Regulator as unstable banks aren't good for the banking sector as a whole. We don't need to focus on that in this section.)

In another scenario Mr. Greedy investor makes a £1m capital investment into a bank. The bank then gets £9m of deposits from you and me. The bank lends £10m. All of the loans that the bank makes do not pay back and the bank recovers only £8m of the £10m lent. In this scenario, Mr. Greedy investor loses £1m and you and I lose £1m. Very bad from the Regulator perspective as they will have to pay us back the £1m of our money lost by the bank.

I hope you can see that in the second scenario, if Mr. Greedy investor has invested £2m, you and I would not lose any money. This is why the Regulator is fixated on the amount of investment by Mr. Greedy. The more he puts in the safer you and I are and the safer the Regulator is from having to pay us our money lost by the bank.

I hope you can also see the tension here. Mr. Greedy wants to minimise the amount of his investment, so that he can maximise his return. I will run you through the maths of that later, but in summary, the smaller the amount of cash Mr. Greedy puts in, the greater his chances of very high returns from his investment. In the heady days before the global financial crisis, where Mr. Greedy had invested in some banks like Lehman Brothers, his £2m investment could support lending of billions of pounds. His returns could, in theory, be astronomical.

As we have established, the Regulator is keen to see Mr. Greedy investor invest an adequate amount to support the assets of the bank in case something goes wrong with those assets.

The document governing the management of the bank's capital resources is called the Internal Capital Adequacy Assessment Plan (ICAAP). The benchmark is that the Regulator will require a bank to hold a minimum amount of 8% capital in respect of its assets. You would be wise in assuming that 8% of £100m of assets would be £8m, so a bank with £100m of assets would need to have £8m of capital. A wise assumption, but not a factually correct one. The Regulator has a complex set of rules that apply different risk weights to different assets. For example, if the bank's £100m of assets are all cash, the bank will only need to hold £1.6m capital. If the bank's £100m assets are all loans to small businesses, it will be required to hold £8m of capital.

The Regulator adds further capital requirements for other risks that it associates with banks so that the 8% capital requirement can easily be increased to 16% depending on the size and complexity of the bank. This is a reason why new banks find it so hard to compete with the existing and large incumbents. In the main, the older larger banks are required to hold less capital, as a percentage of their assets, than new banks and this immediately puts those newer banks at a disadvantage. This is also coupled with the fact that newer banks probably have to pay a little more for their deposits from you and me than the older, larger and more established banks.

2.4.2 Liquidity

The other key item that the Regulator is concerned about regarding financial resources is liquidity. There is an old saying in business, you can have an abundance of capital but still die of starvation if you do not have cash or more simply put cash is King. Same with a bank. The key role of a bank is liquidity conversion, i.e., a bank is able to transform short-term cash that you or I deposit into long-term debt for its customers. The best example of this is that we can put £1m in the bank that we can demand back on short notice, and a bank can take that £1m and lend it to Mrs. Smith for 25 years with a mortgage.

You can see the potential problem. In this dark art of liquidity conversion that banks are so expert in there is a slight flaw. What if we ask for our £1m back? If the bank has lent our £1m to Mrs Smith for 25 years the bank will not have the cash to pay us back. You could say this is completely obvious and you are correct; it is obvious that there may be a little problem in this scenario. Surely with all the wonderful bank regulations and years of banking that have taken place this isn't a real problem is it? Not in normal situations. However, if you look back at every banking crisis since the 18th century this little problem has nearly destroyed the banking industry and the whole economy on more than one occasion. Surely this couldn't happen today with all our clever and complex regulations, sophisticated computer technology and data tracking, and all the lessons we have learned over hundreds of years of banking business? Well it did happen as recently as 2008 and we are on schedule for another liquidity crisis in 2025 or are we already in one as I write this page in October 2022. As per historic crises, no one will really know the source of the crisis until it hits us, but as sure as eggs are eggs it will hit us.

So, Regulators are continually chasing their tail and trying to fix future problems by creating regulations that have been caused by past failures. The regulations will not prevent future failures and may not have even prevented past failures. Failure has great methods for avoiding prior detection.

A new bank applicant that has never taken deposits from the public before will need to demonstrate that, if there is a call on those deposits, the bank will be able to return deposits to depositors. There are a number of techniques for this and they form the whole dark art of treasury departments in banks. In its simplest form, banks are required to hold a cash pool ready to meet liquidity calls from depositors. As this money is effectively sitting on a bank's balance sheet doing nothing and not earning a return, investors are very sensitive to how much emergency liquidity they have to have to hand. The document governing a bank's liquidity strategy is called the Internal Liquidity Adequacy Assessment Plan (ILAAP) and will be discussed in detail in a separate chapter. Further documents called the Recovery Plan and Resolution Plan examine liquidity requirements in disaster scenarios and they, too, will form separate chapters of this book.

2.5 Non-Financial Resources

There is a natural tendency in business to believe that if you have the money you should be able to start the business.

This is not the Regulator's attitude to banks. Money is, of course, essential but just as essential is to demonstrate that the bank has the appropriate non-financial resources to operate its business. This broadly falls into two sections, people and IT.

2.5.1 People

The first non-financial resource, and one that is completely key to the Regulator, is the people who make up the Board and senior management of the bank who are going to operate the bank. The Regulator has a whole set of rules and guidelines on this topic encapsulated in the Senior Manager's Regime.

The Regulator will want to see as a minimum the following senior management team appointed and working on a bank application:

- A CEO, whose key role is to lead the Executive Directors and staff of the bank, to run the bank in accordance with the Board-approved Culture, Strategy and Business Plan;
- A CFO, whose key role is to take responsibility for the management of capital and liquidity of the bank, as set out in the ICAAP and ILAAP documents;
- A CRO, whose key role is to ensure that the bank is operating within its Risk Management Framework. We have not mentioned Risk Management yet and will deal with this in more detail in the ICAAP section.
- Potentially a CTO, whose key role will be to manage the IT operations and risk for the bank.
- An independent Chairman, who will lead the Board and ensure that there is effective challenge to the Executive and that the Board is provided with detailed and regular information on the operation of the business by the Executive in accordance with the Board approved Culture, Strategy and Business Plan of the bank.
- An independent non-executive director who will Chair the Audit Committee, to ensure that the financials of the bank are independently audited and that the systems and controls of the bank are independently audited. In essence this means a separate audit is carried out to ensure that the bank is complying with its policies and procedures.
- An independent non-executive director who will chair the Risk Committee, to ensure that the bank is operating in accordance with the Board-approved Risk Management Framework and Risk Appetite Statements.
- An independent non-executive director who will chair the Remuneration & Nominations Committee to ensure that there is an audit of Executive pay and that the bank has an adequate succession plan for key members of senior management.

The Regulator will want to see a detailed application from each member of the Board in a document called Form A. The Regulator will also want to see the process through which the Board Member was appointed, the references that were taken and the third-party checks, including criminal record checks, that were undertaken for each member of the Board. The Regulator will also want to see an analysis of the skills of the Board member (set out in a Skills-Gap analysis) and a training programme for the Board member. Finally, the Regulator will want to interview the Board member to determine his suitability. Believe me, the interviews are not mere formalities. They are tough. I have known former bank CEOs to fail on this part of the application.

2.5.2 IT

The second critical non-financial resource is IT. The key document that the Regulator requires each applicant to complete is called the Complex IT Controls Form, which covers the following areas:
- How is IT risk managed and what is the governance and risk management framework around IT risk?
- How is IT service delivery managed and how are IT service issues resolved?
- How are IT security and data security managed? Has IT security been tested? This has become a huge issue for the Regulator due to system failures at some high-profile banks over the last few years. The Regulator will be keen to understand how a bank's system might be broken into. A huge industry of advisors has been created as a result of this risk management and they are employed to try and break into a bank's system. As anyone in the IT industry knows, in reality it is near to impossible to block every method of penetrating a bank's system. A 'Pen Test' is therefore not conclusive one way or another that a bank's system will not be vulnerable. The Regulator has to show it is doing something and so regular Pen Testing is required for all bank IT systems.
- How are changes to IT managed?
- If IT is outsourced, as this is an outsourcing of a major part of the bank's business, how is the outsourcing arrangement managed?
- If the IT fails, what are the business continuity and disaster recovery plans of the bank to manage the impact of such failure?

2.6 Governance

The next section of the RBP should provide a detailed breakdown of how the bank will be governed and how risk will be managed at the bank.

The Regulator appears to be very concerned that strong governance is demonstrated in the structure of the Board, the Board and Executive Committees, and the composition of the Board. The Financial Conduct Authority (FCA) as usual is far more prescriptive and has introduced a Senior Managers Regime, which requires the careful and detailed completion of a number of application documents for each person that intends to be on the Board or have a significant role at the bank.

The Regulator is keen to understand and agree the composition of the Board and to understand the assessments carried out to determine that each Board member has the required skills and experience to perform their role at the bank.

On a strict reading of the guidelines for new bank applicants wishing to apply for the Mobilisation licence, it would appear that an applicant needs to have only a Chairman and CEO. No Mobilisation application has in fact gone through with just these two appointments to the Applicant's board.

In reality at least the following Board Members will need to be appointed before an application is submitted: a Chairman, a CEO, a CFO and at least one or two independent directors. A CFO will be required as well as a CEO as detailed capital and liquidity documentation will need to be submitted and in practice those documents will need to be led and presented by a CFO who will be responsible for the documents as the bank proceeds through its application process. The Chairman will demonstrate Board challenge and rigour but will not be able to also chair important committees such as Audit or Risk. A further independent director will therefore be required to demonstrate that there will be sufficient control and oversight of these significant functions at a new bank. In practice it appears that these appointments will need to be in place before the application is submitted.

From an FCA perspective, each senior manager will be required to complete an application form, which will have to be supported by regulatory references taken from former or current employers, and a criminal record check. The applicant will need to demonstrate that a Skills Gap Analysis was conducted in respect of each individual senior manager applicant and, where training is required (as it inevitably will be for any applicant), a training plan has been created and agreed. We will look at the detailed requirement of the SMR regime in a later chapter in this book.

The applicant will also need to demonstrate it has the correct Board and Executive Committee structure. Although this appears rather academic in an applicant that is not yet conducting any business, the Regulator will want to see that the Applicant is ready for business in as many areas as possible before the Mobilisation licence is granted. A great deal of time and effort will be expended in checking Board and Executive Committee Structures, reviewing Terms of Reference (ToRs) for each of the Committees and, where Board or Executive Committees are in place, reviewing their Agendas and in many case actual Minutes of each of the Committees. Prior to any Application being submitted, Applicants should ensure that their Minutes are up to date and that the Meetings are conducted in accordance with their ToRs.

2.7 Risk

The RBP will require a detailed analysis of how the applicant will manage risk in its institution. The ICAAP also has a detailed section on Risk Management, which is a further deep dive into how the applicant will manage all risks in its business.

There are some key documents and terms relating to risk, which need to be addressed in the documentation, and these are described below.

2.7.1 Risk Appetite Statements

These are a list of statements that set out the bank's approach to risk. You will see that the Risk Appetite Statements (RAS) of most banks are very similar and exactly what the Regulators would expect to see. Advisors are therefore simply able to advise each bank to ensure that certain wording is included within each bank's RAS.

Some example Risk Appetite Statements are set out below:

- We will maintain stakeholder confidence
- We will maintain adequate capital and resources
- We will protect our reputation
- We will limit the potential for credit losses
- We will effectively manage our operational risks and ensure operational resilience
- We will demonstrate high standards of conduct and compliance

2.7.2 Risk Appetite Metrics

A number of Risk Appetite Metrics (RAM) will be created to provide a point-in-time position and an indication of direction relating to the bank's Risk Appetite. The RAMs will usually cover a number of matters relating to the business of the bank specifically and the wider economy:

- The financial performance of the bank
- General economic conditions
- Capital held by the bank
- The liquidity position of the bank
- The impact of changes in liquidity costs for the bank
- The impact of poor performance of its assets on the bank
- The impact of occurrence of operational risks
- The impact of failures in conduct and compliance

The RAMs will set out the amount of risk the bank can operate at and also the levels of risk where remediation action is required, such remediation action ranging from simple actions by the Board to rectify the consequences of the risk to the drastic remediation of actually closing the bank down. The RASs and risk levels therefore feed into other core banking documentation such as the Recovery Plan, which sets out the path the bank will take to recover from a breach of its risk appetite levels, to a Resolution Plan, which sets out the path to closing down the bank where it is unable to recover from a breach of its risk appetite levels.

As with all matters relating to risk, example numbers and tables are far easier to follow than written explanations. We will provide these when we explore RAMs when we discuss the ICAAP in more detail in Chapter 3.

2.7.3 Risk and Compliance Management Framework

The Risk and Compliance Management Framework (RCMF) simply sets out the structure of how risk is managed within a bank. The RCMF's aim is to ensure that all types of risk are identified and managed in a consistent and compliant manner across the business. The RCMF sets the standard approach for the management of each principal risk and will generally comprise the following components, which again appear to be quite standardised across the banking community:

- Risk and Compliance Culture;
- Risk and Compliance Governance and Control;
- Risk and Compliance Strategy and Appetite;
- Risk and Compliance Measurement and Reporting; and
- Stress Testing and Contingency Planning.

2.7.4 Lines of Defence

To manage its risk, each bank will operate what are termed Lines of Defence. These are segregated into three distinct categories and so banks will have a Three Lines of Defence Risk Management Framework. How the lines are separated is different from institution to institution, but they will broadly follow the outline structures set out below.

The First Line of Defence – as you would expect the first line of defence is always the poor foot soldiers who operate the day-to-day business of the bank. The First Line of Defence will be required to follow Systems and Controls, which in lay terms just translates into broad Policies (Systems), which provide an outline of how risk is to be managed, to detailed Procedures (Controls), which provide more of a step-by-step check list of how the Policies are to be applied.

The Second Line of Defence – again no surprise, are the internal staff of the bank who check that the Systems and Controls are being complied with. The Second Line will usually be the bank's Risk and Compliance department, who review compliance with the bank's Systems and Controls. The Second Line of Defence will report to the bank's audit committee on the adherence of the business to its Systems and Controls. The Second Line of Defence will also be responsible for training and reporting on financial crime and provide the Risk Committee with a direct line of reporting on all risk matters and concerns.

The Third Line of Defence – this is actually a number of different lines which are all in effect ensuring that the operations of the business comply with the bank's defined Systems and Controls, and independently reviews the effectiveness of risk management at the bank.

The Board Risk Committee is chaired by an independent non-executive director and constituted of independent non-executive directors, and the Chief Risk Officer's core responsibility is to the Board Risk Committee and not to the CEO. The key reason for this is that the CRO should independently report on risk at the bank, independently of the CEO and other Executive Directors.

Risk and Compliance will report to the Risk Committee on compliance with Systems and Controls. The Risk Committee will also require an independent audit to be conducted in respect of operational Systems and Controls. This can be done by an independent internal audit function at a bank, but for most new banks is conducted by a third-party accountancy firm with a specialist internal audit function.

The Board Audit Committee is chaired by an independent non-executive director, who should have an accountancy background, and is constituted of non-executive directors and the CFO. The Audit Committee conducts an independent assessment of whether financial systems and controls as well as financial reporting are conducted in a satisfactory manner. To assist in this process the Audit Committee will appoint an independent firm of Auditors to conduct the financial audit of the bank.

2.7.5 Risk Register

For Operational Risk, the CRO will maintain a list of each Risk that the bank is subject to. Risks will generally be broken down into a number of levels. Level 1 Risks will be the key risk areas of the business. In a bank, these will broadly be broken down into Credit Risk, Financial Risk, Conduct Risk, Strategic Risk and Operational Risk. Level 2 Risks will be a subset of Level 1 Risks. For Example, Level 2 Risks for the Level 1 Credit Risk, may be Underwriting Risk or Collection Risk. The Risk Register will contain each level 1 Risk, each level 2 Risk associated to the Level 1 Risk and a summary of the risk.

Each risk on the Risk Register will be assessed for its 'inherent' (uncontrolled) probability and impact to create an inherent risk score. Controls are applied to the risk and the effectiveness of the controls determines not only the residual (controlled) probability and impact, but also whether further activity to improve the control environment is required.

The probability of a risk crystallising is assessed against a five-point scale, ranging from remote to certain.

The impact measurement could be direct, such as monetary loss or cost, or in terms of damage to the bank's reputation, the impact on customers or the management involvement away from 'business as usual' (BAU). Each impact is mapped to one of five degrees of severity with the monetary value mid-point being used in the calculation of consequences against the probability.

Risk probabilities are usually divided into the following categories:

- Remote
- Unlikely
- Possible
- Probable
- Certain

Simply put, the likelihood of the bank being subject to a risk can be certain, e.g., a bank will certainly be subject to credit risk in its day-to-day operations.

Risk impacts are usually divided into the following examples:

- Nominal
- Minor
- Significant
- Material
- Extreme

Again, simply put, the occurrence of the risk may present little or no risk to the bank and therefore be of nominal impact.

Impact is usually given as a cash value which is based on an estimate of the total cost of a highly probable event having an extreme impact on the bank.

Table 1 puts the above into numbers which are easier to translate.

Table 1: Example of Risk Impact & Likelihood Table.

Consequences				Likelihood				
Impact	Scoring Values	Range		Remote	Unlikely	Possible	Probable	Certain
		From	To	0.4%	1.5%	8.0%	40.0%	100.0%
Nominal	£1,000	£0	£2,000	£4	£15	£80	£400	£1,000
Minor	£6,000	£2,000	£10,000	£24	£90	£480	£2,400	£6,000
Significant	£30,000	£10,000	£50,000	£120	£450	£2,400	£12,000	£30,000
Material	£150,000	£50,000	£250,000	£600	£2,250	£12,000	£60,000	£150,000
Extreme	£1,250,000	£250,000	(Unlimited)	£5,000	£18,750	£100,000	£500,000	£1,250,000

Let's take an example of a risk that is Possible, which will have a Likelihood score of 3 on the Risk Register according to Table 1. For that Risk, we take an example Impact of Extreme, which will have an Impact score of 5 on the Risk Register. The inherent risk will produce a number based on the 3 and 5 numbers respectively, which in this case will be £60,000. This means that £60,000 of capital is required to be set aside to manage the cost of this risk, unless management action is taken to mitigate the risk. The Risk Register will then highlight the mitigation action taken by management and the resulting Likelihood and Impact scores.

The £60,000 is based on the percentage allocated to the Likelihood of the 3 risk being 8% multiplied by the mid-point of the estimated cost of an Extreme Risk of £250k to 5x£250k (i.e., £1.25m) – the maths is therefore 8% x (£250,000+£1,250,000 divided by 2) = £60,000.

Management actions could, for example, bring the Likelihood score down to 2 and the Impact score down to 4, which would mean a mere £450 in capital would have to be set aside for the risk.

A Risk Register will contain any number of risks, as you will see in the example Risk Register in the Template ICAAP in Chapter 3.7. This example has, say, 50 risks set out in detail across all the Level 1 and Level 2 risks impacting the business. The aggregate of the capital for each risk will be required to be set aside by the bank to manage such risks; if those risks occur, the bank will have the cash to pay for the consequences of the risk occurring and depositors will be safe.

It should be obvious how arbitrary this exercise is before a bank is operational and before the bank actually suffers any loss. I am sure that TSB Bank had system failure on its Risk Register, but I do not believe there is any way they would have held capital in reserve for the millions of pounds of costs that they suffered as a result of that IT failure.

2.8 Implementation Plan

Banks that are applying for Mobilisation permission will next need to demonstrate how they will be ready to fully function as a bank within the 12-month period that the Regulator permits for a bank to be open for business following obtaining its Mobilisation licence.

The Implementation Plan will be broken down into a number of areas that move the applicant to a fully operational level. The key areas of implementation will be around operations and capital.

2.8.1 Operations

Operations falls into a number of categories – Facilities, Staff, IT, Marketing, Deposits, Treasury, Risk and Compliance, Board and Committees, Finance, and Internal and External Audit.

Facilities – to meet Threshold Conditions, the applicant will have to demonstrate that it has a place of business in the UK. Most applicants will already have an office with a number of staff already in place.

Staff – the plan will need to demonstrate how the balance of staff required to operate the bank will be recruited. The key areas of operation of a bank – deposit administration, underwriting, collections, compliance, risk, sales, senior management and board – will need to be accounted for and reflected in the Implementation plan.

IT – the plan will need to identify the key areas of IT, which will be implemented in the Mobilisation Period. Most applicants will have engaged with a third-party software house for deposit software, loan administration software and regulatory reporting software prior to submitting their application. As these matters are key to the business, the Regulator will be keen to understand how the IT outsourcing arrangements will be managed and controlled by the Applicant. If the Applicant has developed its

own software, it will be required to complete a Complex IT Controls Form, which will explain how the applicant:
- manages and monitors its IT risks
- deals with service issues in its software and rectifies those issues
- ensures that its software and the data held through its software is secure
- manages changes to the software
- has and will manage disasters and what is its disaster recovery policy
- has and will manage any IT that is outsourced from third parties

The IT Controls Form could take up a book in its own right and will not be set out in detail in this book.

Marketing – the Implementation Plan will need to demonstrate how the bank will be marketed, which will include matters such as:
- appointment of PR agency
- website implementation
- communications strategy and plan

Deposits – as the bank will not have taken deposits historically, the Implementation Plan will need to set out details of the documentation, final deposit products and policies and procedures around the acceptance of bank deposits. The RBP will include details of how the bank intends to actually raise those deposits.

Treasury – as new banks will not usually be clearing banks, they will need to enter into an Agency banking relationship with one of the clearing bank institutions. Again, as the bank will not have taken deposits before, it will need a raft of new policies and procedures around the management of deposits and operation of the Treasury function within the bank and the management of the Reserve account with the Bank of England. The bank will also need to set up a facility to buy short-term UK government gilts, which is an important part of treasury and liquidity management for banks.

Risk and Compliance – the bank will have provided a Risk Management Framework as part of its application documents, but this will need to be finalised for the bank during Mobilisation. There will also need to be a detailed Staff Training Plan for all Risk and Compliance matters relating to the bank.

Board and Committees – the full corporate governance structure will have to be operational and effective during the Mobilisation period. All board committees and executive committees will have to be constituted and conducting business during the Mobilisation period.

Finance – the full regulatory reporting obligations of the bank will have to be finalised and fully tested during Mobilisation. A number of banks will outsource this function to a third-party provider. Third -party providers have failed on a number of key reporting matters historically and the Regulator is therefore keen to ensure that Regulatory Reporting, which is a key control for the Regulator, is accurate and effective.

External and Internal Audit – although Internal Audit can be conducted through bank staff, most new banks appear to prefer using a third-party accountancy firm to perform this function. A financial audit will be conducted by an external firm of accountants. The number of accountancy firms in the UK that are prepared to take on audit of a bank is very small and only includes the largest (read most expensive) firms in the UK.

2.8.2 Capital

This covers how the Applicant will demonstrate that it has sufficient capital for the completion of Mobilisation and for the operation of its business in the first few years of operation.

Although this sounds simple, it is not. In fact, there has been a change in the Regulators' approach to this matter. In earlier applications, the applicant was permitted to define how much capital it would require to complete its Mobilisation Plan, but not have to demonstrate that it actually had the capital. This makes sound business sense. There is no point for a business to raise a lot of capital and just put it in a bank account when it has zero comfort that the Regulator will grant it a bank licence. This was one of the key reasons for introducing the Mobilisation Process, so that investors could have the comfort that invested funds would be used to mobilise the bank after it had received its licences.

The problem with the original approach was that clever applicants could get all Application documentation drafted by very clever advisors for seven-figure sums, have key management in place and get a bank licence. Their standard approach was that, after getting the licence, they could convince early-stage investors to invest in them on the basis that the bank would be a phenomenal success in the future. Roll on Covid-19, where the investment market dried up for applicants with bank licences that needed capital to complete the mobilisation process. The Regulator then was in the rather embarrassing position of having approved banks which had no capital to complete Mobilisation – and there have been a number of them. The net result of this is that the Regulator had to withdraw those licences. Something it really did not want to do.

A new rule was therefore introduced of 'show me the money'. Simply put, if an applicant cannot show the Regulator that it has the money to complete the Mobilisation process, the Regulator will not grant the mobilisation licence. Although this sounds entirely reasonable, it isn't. The whole purpose of the Mobilisation process was that applicants did not have to commit significant investors capital before they had the confidence that the Regulator would grant them a bank licence. This purpose is now defeated. A number of the Challenger Banks currently gracing the UK market with their presence would not be trading today if this rule had existed when they applied.

The line is now blurring between an applicant that is fully ready to become a bank and an applicant that needs up to 12 months to become a bank. The Regulator has recognised that 12 months is a mere blink of an eye and therefore will require complete comfort that the applicant not only has a crystal clear and detailed plan on how it will be fully ready to be a bank, but also has the capital in the bank account to spend on executing that plan.

2.9 Conclusion

So that's the RBP in summary. From the above, it can be seen that the RBP is really a summary document of a number of more detailed documents relating to:

- how the bank will move from its current non-bank status to becoming a bank that can accept deposits from the public – the Mobilisation Plan
- the actual capital that will be required to operate the bank – the ICAAP
- how liquidity will be managed at the bank – the ILAAP
- how risk will be managed at the bank – the Risk Management Framework and the detailed Systems and Controls, i.e., Policies and Procedures, to operate the bank
- the senior management and governance regime of the bank, which will be encapsulated in an SMCR Policy and Corporate Governance Policy
- how the bank will correct itself if things go wrong – Recovery Plan
- how the bank will unwind if things go really wrong – Resolution Plan and
- how the bank will manage its IT – Complex IT Controls Form and supporting Policies and Procedures

Frustratingly for applicants, different people at the Regulator read different documents relating to the application and in many instances never appear to speak to each other. Therefore, applicants are often required to answer the same question put by the party reading one of the application documents, which they have already answered on a number of occasions to readers of other application documents.

This frustration follows through to the drafting of the documents. Each document will contain a lot of information and detail which has already been set out in one or more of the other core application documents and is just duplicated. Applicants should not try to cut corners by referring to the other documents in the application pack. Each document must be treated as stand-alone and should not require the reader to reference another document. Frustrating, but this is a fundamental requirement of the Regulator.

2.10 Template RBP

Contents

1 Executive Summary

1.1 Financial Backers and Controllers

Orchard Funding Group PLC (Orchard, UK registration no. 09618919) is an AIM listed finance company. Orchard specialises in providing finance to small and medium size enterprises (SMEs) and consumers in the insurance premium finance market and the professions finance market.

Orchard intends to seek approval ("Approval") to become a bank (to be called Orchard Bank Plc) in order to broaden its funding base by accessing retail deposits. The controlling shareholder will continue to be Mr. Ravi Takhar with a holding of 53.66%. The current Tier 1 capital base of Orchard (£14.04m as of 31 July 2018) will comprise the initial capital of the bank. The majority of Orchard's funding currently comes from a warehouse facility with Barclays of £15m, secured on the loan assets.

The Bank will appoint a Board of Directors ('Board'), which will be comprised of executive and independent non-executive directors. The executive management will be supported by a senior management team, which has a strong track record in banking and specialist lending. In the rest of this document Orchard should be read as Orchard Funding Group PLC or the new Orchard Bank PLC as the context requires.

1.2 Market Landscape and Opportunity

Based on the accounts of the largest lenders in the market, published statistics by ABI and management's experience, the general insurance market's gross written premiums are £35bn per annum, of which 38% (£13.3bn) are financed.

The fee finance segment of the professions finance market is estimated to be worth over £300m p.a. and the working capital segment of the professions finance market is estimated to be worth over £3bn p.a.

The current major players in the insurance premium finance market and the professions finance market are Premium Credit Limited (Premium Credit) and Close Brothers Bank PLC (Close Brothers). Premium Credit and Close Brothers lent circa £6.3bn into these markets in 2018. Orchard is well recognised as the third brand in the insurance premium finance market and professions finance market. Orchard's lending was £69m in the same markets in the 12 months ending July 2018, and aims to grow its book to £93m in the five years of the plan; this is less than 1% of the target financing market providing ample opportunity for conservative and achievable growth.

1.3 Viable and Sustainable Profitability

Gross yields on Orchard's loans are currently c. 15%-18% p.a. and its bank borrowing costs are c. 5% p.a. Post mobilisation Orchard will be able to attract deposit liabilities at a lower cost which, even after making provision for any rise in interest rates, margin compression to gain market share and changes in business cycles, will allow for a healthy net interest margin (NIM) of 14% to 15% and will enable profit after tax to grow from £1.0m in Year 1 to c. £6.0m in year 5 in its business plan.

1.4 Risk and Governance

Orchard recognises the concerns that the PRA has over 'dominant individuals' on bank boards and has put together a committee structure and recruited suitable INED's to mitigate this risk. The Board of the Bank will be five directors of which two will be executives and three will be independent non-executives. The Board reflects a blend of different experience and backgrounds. The Bank will operate within a risk management framework introduced and operated by the Chief Risk Officer.

1.5 Credit Risk Mitigation

Orchard provides finance for essential purchases such as insurance or professional services. Borrowers are therefore highly motivated to pay. Repayment of all finance provided by Orchard is guaranteed by the introducing insurance broker or professional services firm. Orchard's lending has, as a result, multiple layers of credit protection, which have resulted in low arrears and insignificant losses in the lending book. Orchard performs credit and affordability checks on consumers and SMEs and the related insurance brokers and professional firms.

1.6 Financial Resources and Market Access

Orchard has a significant capital buffer of 3–4 times greater than its estimated Total Capital Requirement ("TCR") throughout its 5 year plan and plans to maintain at least £5.5m surplus capital per the risk appetite statement. The deposits book during this time will comprise of 1 year and 2 year fixed term deposits, all of which will be within the FSCS limits. Attractive rates and tailored retention schemes will be offered to provide a low risk liability strategy. Liquidity will be maintained at a minimum of 16% of deposits by year 5 and will be held in cash in Orchard's nostro account, up to a balance of £1m and thereafter in its reserve account at the Bank of England. In addition, Orchard will make an application, in conjunction with the Bank of England Reserve account application, to enter into a repurchase agreement with the Bank of England in respect of its assets, subject to the rules of the Sterling Monetary Framework.

Orchard's receivables are currently encumbered against bank borrowings but this encumbrance will be eliminated within 12 months as the current portfolio is replaced by lending funded by deposits.

1.7 IT Strategy and Operational Capability

Orchard has been using a bespoke IT solution called LendXP since 2006 for its lending business. The system is capable of supporting the recording of transactions; cash flow modelling; portfolio monitoring; accounting/risk/regulatory reporting; and settlements through the payment systems. On the new deposit side of its business, Orchard will implement the systems of a proven software house to manage its deposit business through Mutual Vision Limited. Orchard also benefits from an experienced operations team that currently manages underwriting, compliance, disbursement, administration, monitoring and collections for its lending relationships within a proportionate control framework. Orchard intends to build its capabilities for deposits and treasury operations through the hiring of experienced professionals.

1.8 Recoverability and Resolvability

Orchard intends to maintain significant capital buffers and a conservative leverage ratio that will allow it to absorb losses resulting from stresses on its business (e.g., slower asset growth, loan losses, operational losses, deposit outflow etc.) and avert any cashflow crisis. The short average maturity of the loan book and the level of liquidity maintained, will reduce the risk of liquidity stress and ease resolvability. Further details on recovery and resolution strategy is documented in the Recovery Plan and Resolution Plan.

1.9 Conclusion

Orchard is a profitable organisation, already listed on AIM and operating in a sizeable lending market. It has the opportunity to further service its core lending markets and customers by becoming a bank. In order to achieve this, it has strengthened its Board and senior management team and is adopting enhanced risk management and governance policies and procedures to build a sustainable banking business.

2 Ownership & Business Model

2.1 Controllers

Orchard raised £10.0m (before expenses) by the issue of 10,416,667 shares on the London Stock Exchange in July 2015. The share capital, after expenses, of £9.8m along with Orchard's retained earnings (£4.2m as of July 2018) will be used as capital for the bank. The firm is and will continue to be listed on AIM. The principal shareholders are set out in Table 1 below:

Table 1: Principal Shareholders as at 30 April 2019.

Shareholders	Number of Shares	Share Capital %
Ravi Takhar	11,458,333	53.66%
Gresham House	2,280,166	10.68%
BMO Global Asset Management (UK)	2,045,169	9.58%
Garraway Capital Management	1,811,591	8.48%
Polar Capital	1,247,500	5.84%
Chelverton Asset Management	750,000	3.51%
Mrs Jasbir K Takhar	635,418	2.98%
Liontrust Asset Management	381,274	1.79%
Other (all below 1%)	744,716	3.49%
Totals	**21,354,167**	**100.00%**

The Board of Orchard as a bank will consist of five directors of which two are executive and three are non-executives as detailed below.

Table 2: Board Members.

Name	Board membership	Executive designation
	Independent Non-Executive Chairman	–
	Executive Director	Chief Executive Officer
	Executive Director	Chief Financial Officer (designate)
	Independent Non-Executive Director	–
	Independent Non-Executive Director	–

The Board is composed of individuals with diverse skills and experience, including banking, lending and deposit taking.

The senior management team of Orchard has been built up over a number of years and has considerable experience in the specialist credit market both within the group and, previously, with its competitors. The directors believe that this experience has helped to facilitate the continued profitable growth of the business of the group.

2.2 Related Group Entities

Currently, primarily for historic reasons, the group operates through two wholly owned subsidiaries Orchard Funding Limited (OFL) and Bexhill UK Limited (Bexhill). The current structure of the group is set out in Figure 1 below.

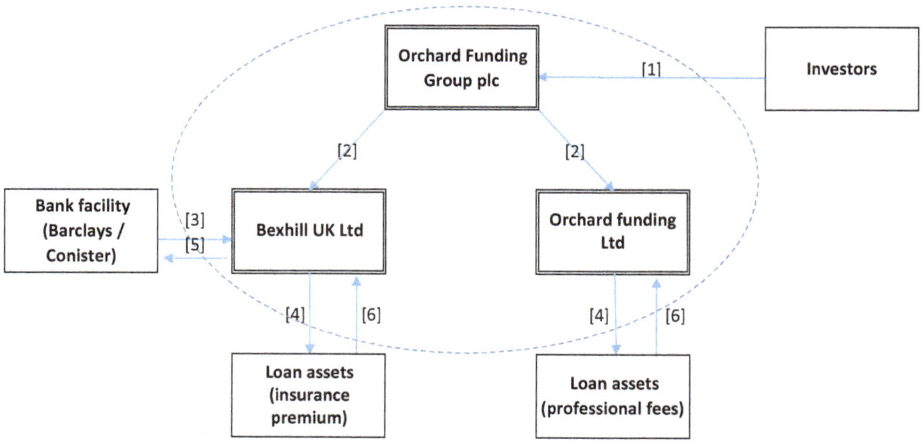

[1] Capital
[2] Intercompany loans from Group plc
[3] £17 million Barclays warehouse facility secured on loan assets
[4] Customer loans
[5] Charge over the loan agreements
[6] Monthly instalments

Figure 1: Orchard Funding Group – current structure chart.

Subject to tax and legal considerations the intention is that the 3 legal entities (within the dotted line) will be merged into one with all operational activities transferred into Orchard Funding Group PLC (Orchard) as reflected in Figure 2. Orchard Funding Group PLC will seek authorisation as a bank. The existing businesses carried on through OFL and Bexhill will continue to operate as profit centres within the merged legal entity.

These changes are intended to reduce the administrative burden of having multiple legal entities and allow resources to be shared across the company's divisions thus reducing risk and increasing efficiency. Bexhill and Orchard are currently authorised by the FCA as consumer credit lenders and credit brokers. Application will be made to pass on these authorisations to the new bank. Reducing the number of regulated entities from 2 to 1, which will streamline the FCA and PRA's regulatory processes.

The move from the current structure to the new banking structure will be planned in detail during mobilisation. It will include procedures to ring fence the encumbered assets against the bank borrowing as the loan assets are repaid and the bank facility is

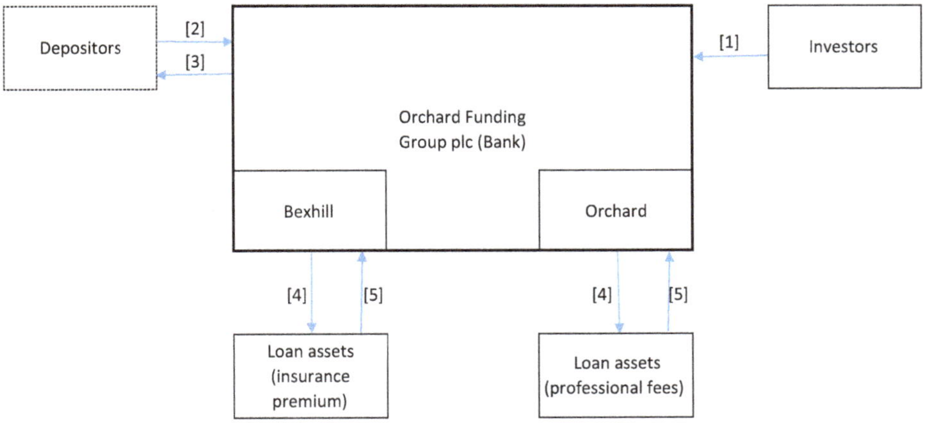

[1] Capital
[2] Proposed new fixed term deposits - 1 and 2 years
[3] Repay deposit with interest
[4] Customer loans
[5] Monthly instalments

Figure 2: Orchard Funding Group – target structure chart.

reduced. All new lending with related deposits will be recorded in the bank, separate from the historic asset.

Orchard also has some minority investments in a number of corporates which are not material and which will be retained post authorisation. These include a 20% stake in Accolade Education Finance Limited, a 30% stake in Open B Gateway Limited (a software development firm) and a 35% stake in Zebra Finance Limited. These are currently valued at zero and will be disposed of prior to mobilisation.

2.3 Historic Financial Performance

Orchard specialises in the insurance premium finance and the professions finance market. The group lent £68m in the 12 months to 31 July 2018, generated revenue of £5.2m and generated a profit before tax of £1.9m. The group's lending book was c. £31.0m as of the end of July 2018. The published key financials of the group, income statement and balance sheet, over the last three years to July 2018 are presented below.

The accounts to 31 July 2019, which are pending final shareholder approval, show lending book growing to £32.1m at the end of the financial year, revenue of £5.5m and profit before tax of £2.0m.

Table 3: Orchard Historic Financials – year ended July.

			£'000
Income Statement	**Actual 2016**	**Actual 2017**	**Actual 2018**
Revenue	3,469	4,560	5,174
Finance costs	(238)	(329)	(452)
Other operating costs	(76)	(78)	(83)
Gross Profit	**3,155**	**4,153**	**4,639**
Administration expenses	(1,884)	(2,512)	(2,746)
Operating profit before tax	**1,271**	**1,641**	**1,893**
Corporation tax	(267)	(303)	(381)
Profit after tax	**1,004**	**1,338**	**1,512**

Balance Sheet	**Actual 2016**	**Actual 2017**	**Actual 2018**
Assets			
Loans and advances	22,004	28,523	31,084
Cash at bank	1,390	1,728	1,286
Fixed assets	95	77	59
Other assets	44	98	60
Total assets	**23,533**	**30,426**	**32,489**
Liabilities			
Bank borrowing	9,208	13,734	16,008
Trade creditors	1,657	3,181	2,051
Tax liabilities	289	279	339
Non-current liabilities	37	65	54
Total liabilities	**11,191**	**17,259**	**18,452**
Equity			
Share capital	214	214	214
Share premium	8,692	8,692	8,692
Merger reserves	891	891	891
Retained earnings	2,545	3,370	4,240
Total equity	**12,342**	**13,167**	**14,037**
Total equity and liabilities	**23,533**	**30,426**	**32,489**

2.3.1 Key Objectives

Key objectives of Orchard over the next five years are:

- to create a bank focused on providing consistent, reliable and cost-effective liquidity to borrowers deserving of such liquidity in the insurance premium finance market and the professions finance market;
- to conduct its business with integrity and ensure that customers are always treated fairly;
- to offer fair rates to depositors and provide transparency and clarity to all stakeholders in respect of the business of the bank;

- to protect depositors by writing prudent and conservative business in its chosen markets;
- to establish a board and executive management team, with strong, complementary non-executive directors and executive directors having a strong track record in specialist lending, deposit taking and risk management;
- to implement a risk management framework, supported by an operational platform with strong systems and controls, to enable effective operations, oversight, regulatory compliance and excellent service to the bank's depositors and borrowers;
- to grow Orchard's share of its chosen markets by continuing to build long term partnerships with key industry players in insurance and professional services. Orchard will utilise the unparalleled expertise of its management team and experienced sales team to achieve its business plan projections;
- to achieve targeted/projected pre- and post-tax profit and return on capital employed (RoCE)
- to deliver good customer outcomes to all stakeholders – depositors, borrowers, staff and shareholders.

2.3.2 Business Proposition

Orchard provides finance in the insurance premium finance market and the professions finance market in the UK. Finance is provided to SMEs and consumers typically over a 10-month term on a fully amortising basis. All finance provided by Orchard is guaranteed by the introducing professional firm or insurance broker. The directors believe that the lending undertaken by the group is very low risk, demonstrated by the fact that Orchard has suffered minimal arrears and loan losses over the last seven years. A banking licence will allow Orchard to tap into the UK deposits market and obtain access to a more stable, reliable, cost-effective and scalable source of funding, enabling it to support SMEs and consumers with better access to financing.

Orchard has been trading since 2002 and operates an efficient and profitable lending model. Orchard has developed its own bespoke software, LendXP, to allow it to conduct day-to-day lending operations. The software has been used by the group for over eight years and has proven to be reliable and with appropriate levels of control. The group was shortlisted as finalist for "Outsourced Partner of the Year 2016" by British Insurance Awards and "Service Provider of the Year 2016" by The Insurance Times. Orchard has been awarded "Intermediary of the Year" by Commercial Broker Awards 2017.

2.4 Lending Target Market

Insurance Premium Financing

The insurance premium finance market is a large and active market, which is driven by the general insurance market. The general insurance market is estimated to be currently worth over £35bn p.a. (measured in terms of gross written premium). Based on historic growth rates in the market from the Association of British Insurers (ABI), management have estimated that the annual growth rate has averaged c. 20% over the last ten years. The proportion that is financed is c. 38%. Management expect this growth to continue over the next 5 years.

The market is dominated by Premium Credit and Close Brothers, who lent a combined £6.3bn in 2018, representing approximately 47% of the £13.3bn insurance premium finance market in the United Kingdom. There are over 3,800 insurance broker firms in the UK regulated by the Financial Conduct Authority (FCA). Premium Credit and Close Brothers focus on larger volume-driven insurance brokers. Despite its historic funding constraints, Orchard has lent successfully into the market and has contractual relationships with over 100 insurance brokers for direct facilities and for in house premium finance facilities. Through these contracts Orchard lent c. £58m into the premium financing market in 2018 and plans to grow annual lending to c. £201m at the end of its five year plan, still less than 1% of the entire market.

Professions Financing

There are over 6,600 accountancy firms in the UK according to data published by the Annual Survey of the Office of National Statistics with over 335,000[3] individual members registered with the seven UK accountancy bodies according to the Financial Reporting Council. At the smaller end of the market 52% of accountancy firms are sole practitioners, and another 44% have between 2 and 6 principals. The accountancy fee finance market is currently estimated to be worth £300m per year and the professions finance working capital market is estimated by the directors to be worth over £3bn p.a.

The group currently has contractual relationships with over 400 accountancy firms. Through these contracts Orchard provided c. £10m of financing in 2018, and looks to grow annual lending to c. £59m at the end of five years.

2.5 Lending Products

2.5.1 Existing Lending Product Lines

The Bank proposes to have the following business lines. All of the business lines are currently being originated and administered by Orchard:

1. Orchard provides finance to limited companies ("Broker Finance Companies"), which are owned and operated by insurance brokers. Broker Finance Companies provide finance to the clients of the related insurance broker to finance the insurance premiums of those clients. Orchard provides its finance to Broker Finance Companies, based upon and secured by the credit agreements between each Broker

3 Key facts and trends in the Accountancy Profession, June 2015, Financial Reporting Council

Finance Company and its client. Orchard takes a debenture from the Broker Finance Company and also a guarantee from the related insurance broker for all the obligations of the Broker Finance Company. Orchard's lending is for a maximum term of 12 months and is repaid on a fully amortising basis. Broker Finance Companies assign the benefit of all their credit agreements to Orchard and Orchard undertakes the collection and administration of the credit agreements;

2. Orchard provides finance to the clients of insurance brokers. The clients of insurance brokers are introduced to Orchard by the insurance broker. The clients can be consumers and non-consumers. A guarantee of the obligations of the clients is obtained from the introducing insurance broker;
3. Orchard provides finance to the clients of professional services firms, which are mainly accountancy practices. The clients of professional services firms are introduced to Orchard by the firms. The clients can be consumers and non-consumers. Orchard's lending is for a term of 12 months or less and is repaid on a fully amortising basis. A guarantee of the obligations of the clients is obtained from the introducing professional firm;
4. Orchard provides finance to professional services firms directly. This is all non-consumer business. The lending is for a term of 12 months or less and is repaid on a fully amortising basis. Guarantees are also provided by the partners of the professional firm;
5. Orchard provides a nominal amount of finance in adjacent markets to its core markets, such as golf fees, school fees and football season ticket fees. This is a relatively embryonic market and the current lending is very small. Orchard's core focus as a bank will continue to be the insurance premium finance market and professions finance market.

2.5.2 Lending product features

Structure

Bexhill – Insurance Premium Financing

Bexhill is currently a wholly owned subsidiary of Orchard. The Bexhill business will be folded into the new bank. Bexhill was established in 2002 and has achieved consistent revenue growth between 2002 and 2018. However, due to the global financial crisis, Bexhill's funding became significantly restricted in 2008. Bexhill continued to trade through the difficult period and supported its client base despite scarcity of available funding. Currently Bexhill has over 100 insurance broker clients.

Bexhill typically lends through a finance company owned and operated by an insurance broker (corporate insurance) for the purpose of providing finance to the clients of the insurance broker. All Bexhill's lending is guaranteed by the insurance broker and all credit agreements entered into by the finance company are assigned to Bexhill and Bexhill undertakes the collection and administration of those credit agreements.

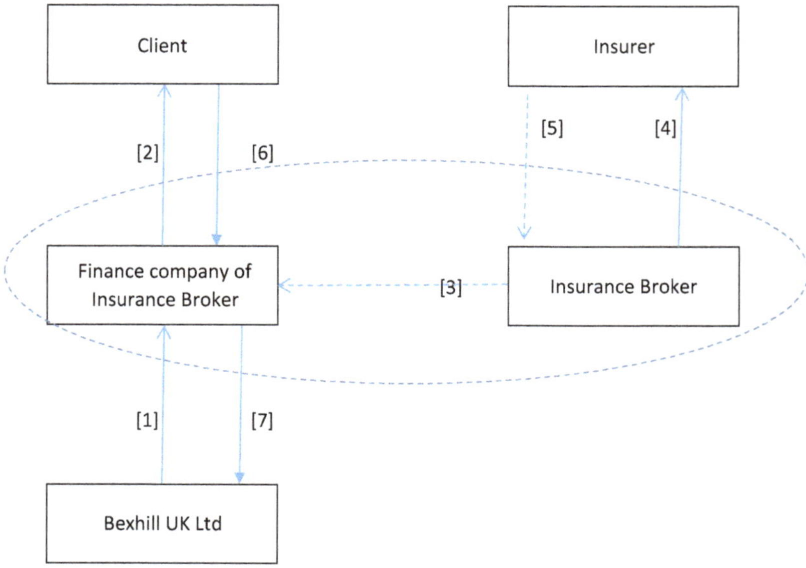

[1] Funding to financing company
[2] White-labeled finance agreement
[3] Guarantee from insurance broker
[4] Premium paid to the insurer
[5] Unearned premium on cancellation
[6] Monthly instalments
[7] Loan repayment

Figure 3: Corporate insurance structure.

Orchard – Professions Financing and Direct Insurance Lending

Orchard Funding Limited (OFL) is currently a wholly owned subsidiary of Orchard. The OFL business will be merged into the new bank. OFL was established in 2010 in order to take advantage of the withdrawal of one of the largest funders in the market for smaller professional practices. OFL's lending book has grown since its launch, despite its funding being relatively expensive and constrained. OFL has over 400 professional firm clients as at July 2018, most of which are accountancy firms. OFL's professional firm clients introduce their clients to OFL to finance their professional fees. OFL also provides facilities to a number of professional firms directly. OFL's insurance broker clients introduce their clients to OFL to finance their insurance premiums. OFL's client list has grown consistently year-on-year.

OFL typically lends directly to the client of the insurance broker (direct insurance), client of the professional firm; or the professional firm directly.

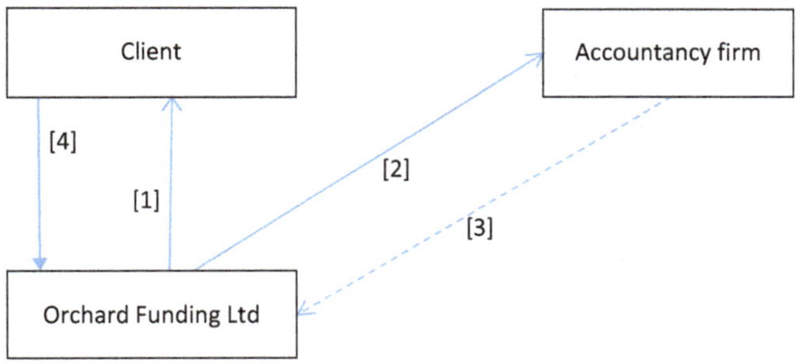

[1] Funding agreement
[2] Fees paid to the accountancy firm
[3] Guarantee from accountancy firm
[4] Monthly instalments

Figure 4: Accountancy fee funding structure.

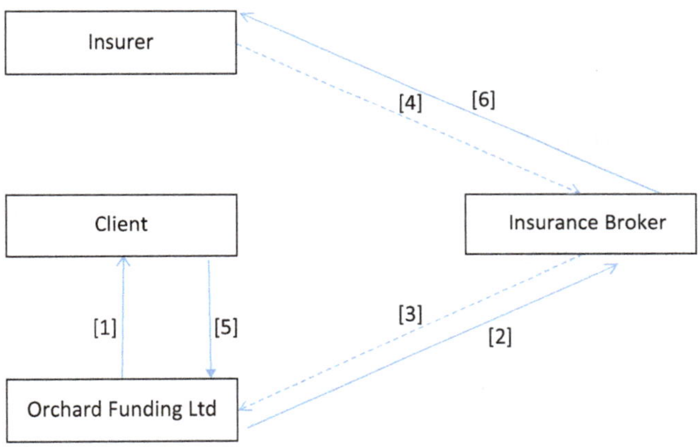

[1] Funding agreement
[2] Premium paid to the broker
[3] Guarantee from insurance broker
[4] Unearned premium
[5] Monthly instalments
[6] Premium paid to insurer

Figure 5: Direct insurance structure.

Product Terms

Orchard's lending products will have the following terms, which replicate the terms of the products currently originated and administered by the group:
- APR – target 15–18%;
- Maximum term – 12 months;
- Fully amortising over the term of the credit;
- Full agreement to pay from the introducing insurance broker or professional firm.

Although in isolation an APR of 15–18% appears relatively high, there are a number of factors, which suggest the rate is sustainable and fair to the borrower, including inter-alia:
- There are very limited sub-12 month amortising credit products available in the market. The larger financial institutions, including the banking market find the short-term nature and relatively small ticket size of this type of credit product unattractive;
- Unsecured overdrafts from banks can be over 20% APR and often over 30% APR;
- Credit card rates for borrowing are generally over 20% APR;
- Non-bank short-term credit terms can be punitively expensive;
- The rate paid by the Customer is often less than 10% APR, but Orchard is able to increase its IRR to over 15% by managing its settlement dates to the Introducer.

Financing through Orchard enables a borrower to still have the option of using its other credit providers for alternative spending.

Delivery Channels

Orchard currently uses a relationship-based model for lending origination which it plans to continue after authorisation.

Origination

Orchard has over 17 years of experience in its lending markets. The senior members of the sales team have decades of experience in the short-term financing market working with Orchard and previously with the leading competitors in the market. They have long-standing relationships with key players in the insurance brokerage sector and accountancy/law firms. The in-house solution offered by Bexhill allows insurance brokers to white-label the financing of insurance premiums to their clients, which is particularly attractive to a number of larger insurance brokers and may potentially lead to opportunities to scale up the lending business further in the future. Ongoing communication with the borrowers about loan administration is carried out over phone/email. An outline of a loan customer's journey with Orchard is set out in Appendix 1.

2.5.3 Lending Products – Conduct Risk

All new products are assessed for conduct risks, to ensure fair customer outcomes, and are signed off in accordance with the product approval policy. This includes:

- Product Characteristics
- Incentives/Income
- Pricing Structure
- Barriers to Exit
- Product Complexity
- Target Market
- Customer risk (performance metrics)
- Staff Competency
- Soft launch
- Monitoring
- Financial Promotions

All financial promotions require sign off from senior management and Compliance prior to publication.

2.5.4 Future Lending Products

Orchard has, in line with its key competitors, conducted test marketing in adjacent markets to its core insurance premium finance and accountancy fee funding market. The test marketing is currently less than 5% of Orchard's lending book and is not considered material. The adjacent markets are in service fee markets with similar characteristics, documentation and system requirements to its core markets, i.e., short-term credit where there is recourse to the introducer or a there are compelling reasons for the customer to ensure that its payments are made. Currently adjacent markets that are being tested are school fees, club fees and site fees. Orchard will continue to focus on the insurance premium market and accountancy fee funding market and consider adjacent markets where it can use its existing documentation, systems and expertise to ensure effective, profitable and controlled lending.

2.6 Deposit Target Market

Deposits Market

The total deposit base in the UK is over £2.9trn[4] of which the share of notice accounts is 12% (£350bn) and the share of fixed rate deposits is 7% (£200bn). The rate-sensitive share of the deposit market that is prone to switching is about 10% or £35bn and £20bn respectively for notice and fixed rate deposits according to market estimates of

4 Cash Savings – An International Comparison, A Study for the FCA, PwC, Sep 2014

PBF Solutions (an outsourced deposit management provider). Assuming the average behavioural maturity of fixed term deposits is 2 years (realistic as most of the fixed term deposits are of 1 year maturity), £10bn of fixed rate deposits migrate looking for attractive rates in the market. By all measures, the market is vast and Orchard's share (projected to be c. £76m even after five years of operation) will be a very small fraction of the total available market.

Orchard intends to raise liabilities in the retail deposits market and understands it is difficult to offer a deposit proposition which is significantly differentiated from that of the competition. However, Orchard will offer a simple set of deposit products with attractive interest rates and a simple postal application process, through conventional best-buy tables.

Details in respect of the projected deposits to be raised by Orchard are set out in the base financial operating plan. Our deposit raising numbers (amounts and customers) are extremely conservative. We are confident that such deposit levels will be capable of being raised through a prominent exposure on best buy tables.

In the context of Orchard's conservative deposit raising aspirations, we believe the following research we have undertaken is sufficient to determine whether there is a market for our deposit taking plans. We have reviewed a number of publicly available research documents on the subject, including the FCA's Cash Savings Market Study of the UK deposit market and believe that such research enables us to conclude that there is a deep enough deposit market for the numbers set out in our Plan.

The current rates offered in the market place have been studied through the best buy tables to assess the margins above the bank base rates for the top ten providers. The base plan has assumed similar margins above the base rate, which is presented below. The time period in the chart is the period post mobilisation and authorisation as a bank.

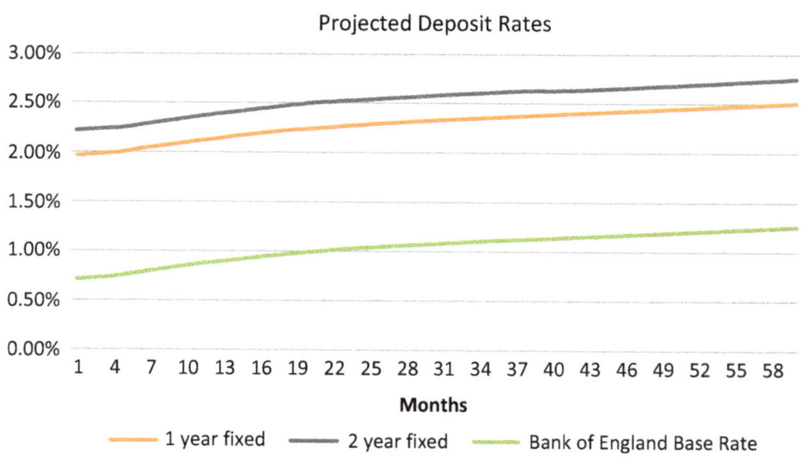

Figure 6: Deposit Rates.

2.7 Deposit Products

2.7.1 New Deposit Products

Orchard will initially have 2 deposit products:
1. 1 year fixed rate deposit
2. 2 year fixed rate deposit.

The proposed new bank will operate nationally across the UK from its base in Luton. Staff with relevant experience will be recruited to run the new retail deposits operation. As noted above, the markets in which the group currently lends are very large and provide ample opportunities for growth over the time horizon envisaged in this plan. The group's proposed new deposit taking activities will similarly form an even smaller share of the target market.

Orchard plans to have a low-risk liability strategy focusing on a limited product set (1 year and 2 year fixed rate deposit accounts) initially offered in tranches to retail customers, combined with a simple postal application process, attractive and consistently fair rates and targeted customer retention schemes. There are no plans to offer instant access or current accounts, but other term deposit products may be considered. Initially the Bank will develop brand awareness through prominence on the best-buy tables. Given the modest deposit raising plans in the projection (Orchard plans to have just over £76m in its deposit book at the end of year 5) these marketing efforts are considered to be adequate and proportionate.

Orchard will utilise the savings module of a proven software house, Mutual Vision Limited, for its deposit business. This software is used by a number of small building societies and banks.

2.7.2 Deposit Product Features

Structure

The fixed rate, fixed term deposits will have a minimum of £1K to cover operational costs and a maximum set to stay within the FSCS guarantee limit. Money will only be returned to the UK bank account where the deposit was credited from, with the option to roll over. Fixed term deposits will not be withdrawable before contractual maturity except in hardship conditions.

Product Terms

1-year fixed rate deposit

We have assumed a margin above base rate of 1.25% and average deposit size of £24,000. In year 1 we will therefore have approximately 525 depositors and this will increase to 1,900 over the 5-year life of the plan.

2-year fixed rate deposit

We have assumed a margin above base rate of 1.5% and average deposit size of £24,000. In year 1 we will therefore have approximately 336 depositors and this will increase to 1,216 over the 5-year life of the plan.

Deposit Delivery – Channels, Origination and Retention

Orchard initially intends to raise deposits through postal applications. It plans to offer simple deposit products with market-leading rates and a simple postal application process. Orchard will be a new entrant into the deposits market and intends to market its products through the best-buy tables. This will help build brand recognition among the target market of depositors (high net worth, cash-rich individuals such as pensioners) and will result in lower costs of customer acquisition, higher retention and lower deposit rates over time given the modest deposit requirements planned in the projections.

Monthly tranche limits will be set by ALCO in order to avoid peaks in funds inflows and, therefore, funds outflows at maturity. Deposit applications will be made by filling out a form downloaded from the Orchard website. The number of downloads will be monitored automatically in order to estimate the expected inflow of funds and flag where run-rates exceed or fall short of preset parameters. This will prompt adjustment to pricing or temporary withdrawal of products where necessary. Orchard recognises that the appearance of deposit products in the best buy tables could lead to increases in inflows of deposits in excess of the levels required leading to excess liquidity and thereby creating a negative carry cost and spikes in outgoing funds at maturity. Orchard will carefully manage this risk by closely monitoring the application activity by number of downloads of the application forms from the website to project expected volume and amend the interest rates on the deposit products to reduce new business levels if required.

Orchard recognises that the cost of acquiring new deposits is significantly higher than the cost of retaining existing deposits, and will design tailored retention schemes (depositors contacted 4–6 weeks prior to deposit maturity, offered market leading rates that are the same as what is offered to new customers) to preserve them.

In the event that customers are met with financial difficulties leading them to want to withdraw their deposit, Orchard will review each application to withdraw deposits prior to the contractual maturity date. As Orchard's assets are amortising and the liquidity buffers are extremely conservative throughout the term of the plan, Orchard will act in the manner of a reasonably prudent financial institution to determine whether a contractual deposit term can be broken. Our Deposit Hardship Policy sets out the basis on which each case will be determined, ensuring a fair and equitable outcome for the customer. It is anticipated that less than 1% (by value) of depositors will request a withdrawal of deposits prior to the contractual term date. An outline customer journey for Deposit customers with Orchard is attached in the Appendix.

All new products will be reviewed by EXCO, with oversight from Compliance, and taken to the Board for sign-off where appropriate.

Redemption Profile of Deposits

The majority of deposit stock will be below the FSCS limit lowering the risk of large-scale outflow in a stress scenario. Liability origination will be spread across the year by flexing the rate relative to competition to ensure no more than 12% of the existing liability stock contractually matures in a given month. Daily applications and new business will be tracked to manage the future maturity profile. At maturity, tailored retention schemes focused on a simple experience and consistently fair rates will help retain deposits and result in lower behavioural outflows. The terms of the deposit will clearly state that upon redemption a deposit will be rolled over for the same term at a rate that will be communicated to the depositor 4–6 weeks before the maturity of the deposit, and the depositor will be given an option to either switch to another deposit product or withdraw the proceeds altogether.

2.8 Competitive Advantages

The directors believe Orchard has the following key differentiators vis-à-vis its competitors:

- Orchard has been operating in the insurance premium finance market and professions finance market since 2002. In that time its senior management team has remained in place and developed strong and trusted relationships with its existing clients and with other key parties in its markets. The length of time that Orchard has operated in the market provides confidence to insurance brokers and professional firms that Orchard is a constant and reliable player in the market. This is very important as a number of companies have entered and exited the market since Orchard commenced its business.
- Orchard's senior management team has unparalleled experience in the premium finance and professions finance market. Unlike the management teams in the other leading competitors in the market, the management team has been exclusively focused on its markets since 2002 and in the case of some of the team since the late 1990s. Again, this depth of expertise provides a high level of confidence to insurance brokers and professional firms seeking a funding partner.
- The group understands the needs and requirements of insurance broker firms and professional firms and offers a fully tailored solution to the target market. The larger dominant market players are less focused on the smaller end of the lending market creating an opportunity for the group.
- Orchard is in regular contact with all its clients and strives to ensure that a high-quality service is consistently delivered. The larger players in both the insurance premium finance and professions finance market have in the past provided limited services to certain parts of the market allowing the group to build up a loyal customer base.

- The group's in-house premium finance product is unique and enables insurance brokers to take greater control and provide unparalleled service in the provision of premium finance to their clients. This product is very attractive to well capitalised insurance brokers who wish to ensure the highest levels of service are provided to their clients. No other company offers this product to insurance brokers and the product is attractive to some of the largest insurance brokers in the UK.
- The group does not impose any fees or require minimum levels of business for the availability of its facility to insurance brokers or professional firms.
- The group's online platform has the functionality to support white-label and direct financing and is simple to navigate and use. The system enables quick and efficient data entry for its insurance broker and professional firm clients, effective credit and affordability assessment and efficient production of compliant legal documentation for a client to sign either by hand or electronically.
- Senior management of the group is involved in all aspects of the business and in particular maintain close and strong relationships with the group's clients. The personal involvement of senior management in the needs and concerns of the group's client base is very important to the clients of the group. The group has always regarded itself as an SME and is therefore sympathetic to the needs and aspirations of insurance brokers and professional firms, many of which are themselves SMEs.
- The ability, given the pricing of its lending, to offer consistently attractive rates on a simple and transparent deposit range to raise and retain the requisite deposit base to develop its business.

Due to the simplicity of its lending products Orchard will provide transparency and openness to depositors and all other stakeholders on all aspects of its business.

3 Business viability

The Bank intends to provide unsecured short-term credit to limited companies, partnerships and consumers in the insurance premium finance market and the professions finance market, funding itself with a strong capital base and a stable stock of retail deposits. The loan book is projected to grow at a steady pace (from c. £33m at the end of year 1 to c. £93m at the end of year 5) and provide a commercially viable net interest margin (c. 14%-15%). Robust underwriting and guarantees from introducing insurance brokers and professional firms are expected to keep the loan loss rate low (assumed at 1% compared to the historic experience of very low levels of losses in the past eight years). Operating overheads in salaries and investments in better systems and controls are projected to grow from c. £2.8m in year 1 to £4.8m in year 5, allowing the capital resources to grow from c. £14.8m at the end of year 1 to c. £26.2m at the end of the fifth year of the business plan. Consequently, no plan for additional capital raising has been included in the projections.

3.1 Projections

The base financial operating plan is based on a fully operative bank and the first year equates to the first twelve months as a deposit taking bank. Hence, the plan is not presented in calendar years but presented from the time of bank inception.

As Orchard currently runs a profitable financing business, even after absorbing the additional investments and expenditure during the Bank building phase it is expected that the Bank will be profitable in its first year of operation. The high-level assumptions behind the projections are as follows:

- The direct insurance business will start from a small base of £5.4m in year 1 and will grow during the five years of projection horizon to £45.4m at the end of the period. Average rate will be 14% and average term will be 9 months.
- The corporate insurance business where Orchard has a more established presence in the market will start at £19.5m in year 1 and will grow to £28.5m at the end of the period. Average rate will be 14.99% and average term will be 9 months.
- The professional fee financing business will grow from a base of £8.1m in year 1 to £19.9m at the end of the period. Average rate will be 14% and average term will be 9 months.
- Deposit issuance will start at £1.7m per month (c.71 accounts per month) and will continue for a year to replace existing bank facilities and total £21m at the end of Year 1 of the Plan. Net new deposits will total £10m in each of Years 2 and 3 of the Plan and then rise to £13m in Year 4 and £22m in year 5 of the Plan.
- Only 1 year and 2 year fixed rate deposits will be offered at 60:40 split, respectively. Average rates will commence at circa 2% and increase to 2.6% over the term of the plan.
- At the end of the projection horizon the balance sheet will have £93m of loans and £12m of liquid assets and £1m of fixed and other assets that will be funded by £76m of deposits, £4m of other trade creditors and £26m of shareholder capital.

Orchard's Board reviewed the base operating plan on the 30th May 2019 and provided feedback. The final plan was approved by the Board on 16 July, 2019.

3.1.1 Loan Book Growth

Based on the origination experience of Orchard's management team it is expected that the Bank will grow the direct insurance business at the fastest pace as this is the largest segment of the insurance premium financing market. This is followed by moderate projected growth in the accountancy business and the corporate insurance business. Lending interest rates are expected to remain steady.

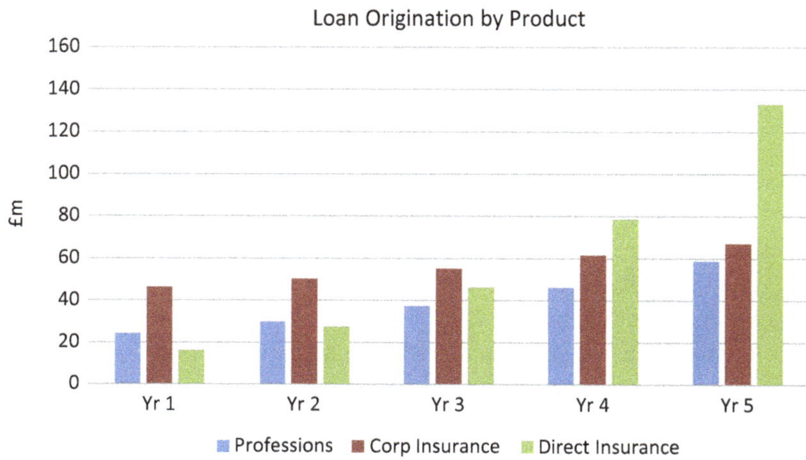

Figure 7: Loan origination volume (by loan type).

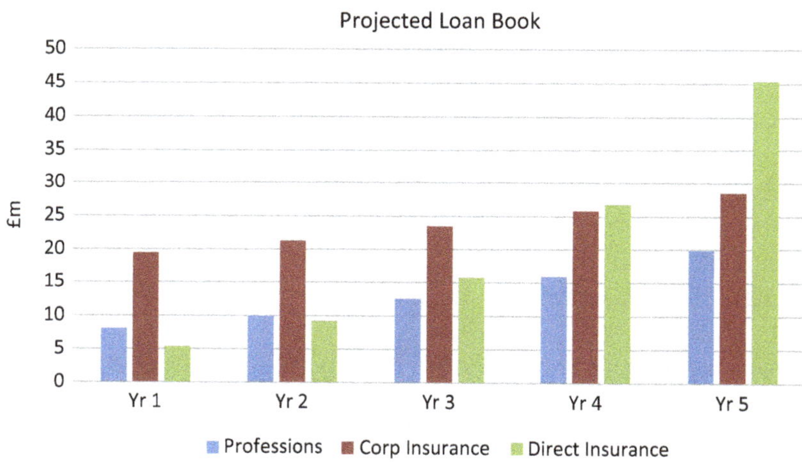

Figure 8: Projected loan book on balance sheet (by loan type).

3.1.2 Deposit Book Growth

The deposit book is projected to grow from £21m at the end of year 1 to c. £76m at the end of year 5. The liquidity strategy is maintained at low risk by offering only 1 year and 2 year fixed rate deposits that are contractually not withdrawable before maturity. The deposit rates are projected to go up in line with Bank of England base rate projections.

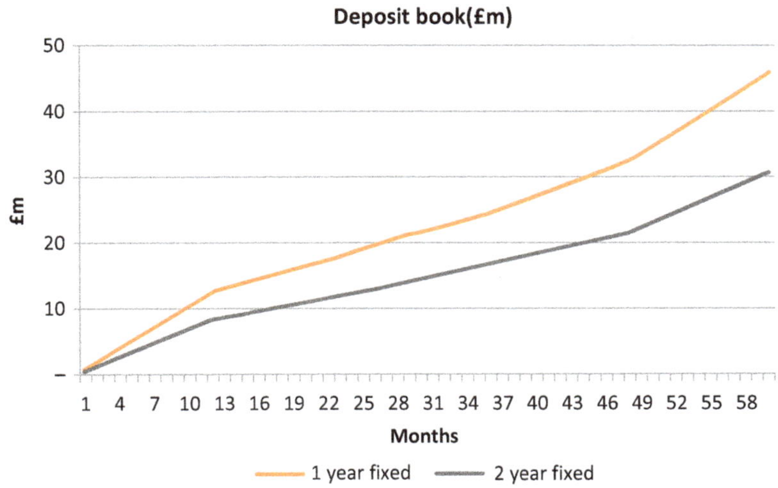

Figure 9: Projected deposit book on balance sheet (by deposit type).

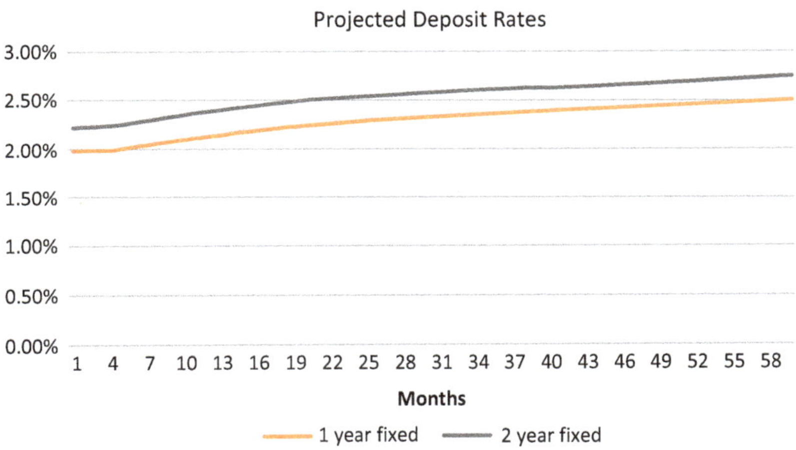

Figure 10: Projected deposit rates (by deposit type).

3.1.3 Income Statement, Balance Sheet & KPIs

The base financial operating plan that was reviewed by the Board on the 30 May 2019 and approved on the 16 July 2019 is presented below.

The financial operating plan is based on a fully operative bank and the first year equates to the first twelve months as a bank. Hence, the plan is not presented in calendar years but presented from the time of the Bank being able to take deposits.

Table 4: Orchard Projected Financials.

£'000

Income Statement	Actual 2018	Plan Year 1	Plan Year 2	Plan Year 3	Plan Year 4	Plan Year 5	CAGR
Interest Receivable	5,174	4,887	6,370	8,175	10,817	14,856	23.5%
Interest payable	(535)	(396)	(591)	(870)	(1,198)	(1,702)	26.0%
Net interest income	4,639	4,491	5,779	7,305	9,619	13,154	23.2%
Administration expenses	(2,746)	(2,870)	(3,267)	(3,651)	(4,184)	(4,820)	11.9%
Impairment charges	0	(312)	(393)	(498)	(653)	(888)	
Operating profit before tax	**1,893**	**1,308**	**2,119**	**3,156**	**4,782**	**7,446**	**31.5%**
Corporation tax	(381)	(257)	(403)	(600)	(909)	(1,415)	
Profit after tax	**1,512**	**1,051**	**1,716**	**2,556**	**3,874**	**6,031**	**31.9%**
Dividends	(642)	(210)	(343)	(511)	(775)	(1,206)	
Retained earnings	**870**	**841**	**1,373**	**2,045**	**3,099**	**4,825**	

£'000

Balance Sheet	2018	Year 1	Year 2	Year 3	Year 4	Year 5
Assets						
Loans and advances	31,084	32,762	40,475	51,531	67,917	92,953
Cash at bank	1,286	1,000	1,000	1,000	1,000	1,000
Liquid asset buffer	0	3,867	7,612	8,740	8,717	10,972
Fixed assets	59	483	556	621	681	737
Other assets	60	158	158	158	158	158
Total assets	**32,489**	**38,270**	**49,801**	**62,049**	**78,472**	**105,819**
Liabilities						
Customer deposits		21,000	31,000	41,000	54,000	76,000
Bank funding	16,008					
Trade creditors	2,051	2,051	2,051	2,051	2,051	2,051
Tax liabilities	339	257	403	600	909	1,415
Non-current liabilities	54	84	96	103	118	134
Total liabilities	**18,452**	**23,393**	**33,550**	**43,754**	**57,078**	**79,600**
Equity						
Share capital	214	214	214	214	214	214
Share premium	8,692	8,692	8,692	8,692	8,692	8,692
Merger reserves	891	891	891	891	891	891
Retained earnings	3,370	4,240	5,081	6,454	8,498	11,597
Current year retained earnings	870	841	1,373	2,045	3,099	4,825
Total equity	**14,037**	**14,878**	**16,251**	**18,295**	**21,394**	**26,219**
Total equity and liabilities	**32,489**	**38,270**	**49,801**	**62,049**	**78,472**	**105,819**

Table 5: Orchard Projected KPIs.

Key Ratios	unit	Year 1	Year 2	Year 3	Year 4	Year 5
Average interest earning assets (monthly weighted)	£'000	31,230	38,805	49,091	64,238	87,249
Gross interest margin	%	15.6%	16.4%	17%	16.8%	17.0%
Average cost of funds	%	2.1%	2.3%	2.4%	2.5%	2.6%
NIM	%	14.4%	14.9%	14.9%	15.0%	15.1%
Cost:Income ratio	%	64%	57%	50%	44%	37%
PAT growth YoY	%	-30%	63%	49%	52%	56%
Dividend per share (pence per share)	pence	1.0	1.6	2.4	3.6	5.6
ROE (PAT)	%	7.1%	10.6%	14.0%	18.1%	23.0%

The underlying business drivers, with volume assumptions and key financial assumptions are tabled below:

Table 6: Orchard Projected Volumes.

Base	Actual 2018	Plan Year 1	Plan Year 2	Plan Year 3	Plan Year 4	Plan Year 5
New Lending (£'000)	68,730	86,000	107,800	139,400	186,709	259,576
Lending growth %		25%	25%	29%	34%	39%
Lending stock (£'000)	31,084	32,762	40,475	51,531	67,917	92,953
Lending interest rate (wt. average)		14.53%	14.46%	14.40%	14.32%	14.26%
Corporate Insurance Loan stock (£'000)		19,484	21,432	23,575	25,933	28,526
Average loan size (£'000)		172	172	172	172	172
Number accounts (vols)		113	125	137	151	166
Direct Insurance loan stock (£'000)		5,124	8,849	15,213	26,057	44,517
Average loan size (£'000)		0.48	0.48	0.48	0.48	0.48
Number accounts (vols)		10,675	18,436	31,695	54,285	92,745
Accountancy Loan stock (£'000)		8,155	10,193	12,742	15,927	19,909
Average loan size (£'000)		5.10	5.10	5.10	5.10	5.10
Number accounts (vols)		1,599	1,999	2,498	3,123	3,904
New Deposits (inc rollovers) (£'000)		21,000	22,600	37,000	41,600	66,800
Deposit stock (£'000)		21,000	31,000	41,000	54,000	76,000
Deposit interest rate (wt. average)*		2.15%	2.32%	2.43%	2.51%	2.58%
Average deposit (£'000)		24	24	24	24	24
Number of deposit accounts stock (vol)		875	1,292	1,708	2,250	3,167
Number of new deposits		875	942	1,542	1,733	2,783
Number of new deposits per day		3	4	6	7	11

*Based on the Bank of England inflation report, February 2019

Table 7: Key Financial Assumptions.

Base	Plan Year 1	Plan Year 2	Plan Year 3	Plan Year 4	Plan Year 5
Annual losses % receivables (IFRS 9)	1.0%	1.0%	1.0%	1.0%	1.0%
Base rate (end of year)	0.9%	1.0%	1.1%	1.2%	1.3%
Corporation tax rate	19.7%	19.0%	19.0%	19.0%	19.0%

*Based on the Bank of England inflation report, February 2019

3.2 Stress Scenarios

3.2.1 Capital Stresses

Orchard has considered a range of stresses on its capital and liquidity, covering scenarios of systemic market-wide events, idiosyncratic events and combinations thereof. In addition, a reverse stress has also been considered. The PRA's ACS 2019, published in March 2019, has been considered for the economic variables for the market-wide stress and the combined stress. Orchard has endeavoured to build a bank with strong capital and liquidity ratios that will be able to withstand most stress scenarios with a high degree of confidence. It has identified key risk indicators and thresholds that would signify the occurrence of stress scenarios and will adopt invocation protocols documented with identified accountable individuals who would oversee the execution of pre-agreed management actions to alleviate the stress on the Bank and achieve recovery. In the event of extreme stress, a clearly delineated path to resolution is charted out and high capital ratios make an orderly resolution possible.

Systemic Market-Wide Stresses

Management has considered the impact on Orchard's business drivers during the last global financial crisis ("GFC") in 2008. The key adverse impact experienced by Orchard was an impact on available liquidity to fund its business. Orchard experienced limited impact on its lending volumes and the margins achieved on its lending business. Notwithstanding the limited impact on Orchard's business in the GFC, we have applied the following stresses to Orchard's business resulting from market-wide stresses:

- Base rates increase to 4%, with unemployment rising to a peak of 9.2% and consumer credit shrinking.
- Consumer credit shrinkage has been assumed to result in lower aggregate demand for lending.
- To attract new lending, rates are reduced.
- Higher unemployment drives higher loss rates.

- With high unemployment and less growth in household income, the level of savings reduces and hence, the level of new deposits.
- To be more competitive in the deposit market, rates are increased.

Idiosyncratic Stresses

Five scenarios, all around the idiosyncratic risk to Orchard were modelled for the idiosyncratic stresses. These scenarios relate to

1. Key person risk
2. Senior management conduct failure (ACS 2019 focuses on conduct risk)
3. Cyber risk, given recent market incidents
4. Third party and processing failure, again from recent market failures
5. Failure of fraud prevention

The highest impact of the idiosyncratic stresses resulted in a cost impact of £675k to Orchard.

Combined Stress

The combined stress takes account of the idiosyncratic stress as well as more severe market-wide stress variables, in part due to idiosyncratic stress driving a bigger impact on the business volumes. The combined stress is much more severe and results in breach of the Risk Appetite Target, triggering the requirement for management action.

Reverse Stress

The reverse stress is driven by a massive market shock, with high unemployment that severely impacts the customer's ability to repay the loan. At the same time, some brokers go into insolvency and hence, the guarantee no longer provides a safeguard against the losses. The escalating losses result in loss of confidence by depositors, resulting in little or no new deposits and very high attrition at maturity. Deposit rates are increased to manage both attrition and new business. However, this action does not close the funding gap and hence, bank borrowing is incepted. Given the weak trading position and the inability to charge assets, the margins charged above base rate on the borrowing are extremely high.

Stress Scenario Results

Table 8: Stress Scenario Results.
Capital stresses – impact on business drivers

	Base		Market wide		Idiosyncratic		Combined		Reverse	
	Year 2	Year 3	Year 2	Year 3	Year 2	Year 3	Year 2	Year 3	Year 2	Year 3
	£'000	£'000	%	%	%	%	%	%	%	%
Lending reduction relative to base	107,800	139,400	20.0%	10.0%	5.0%	5.0%	30.0%	15.0%	40.0%	40.0%
Lending rate reduction, absolute vs base	14.5%	14.4%	2.0%	2.0%	1.5%	1.5%	3.0%	2.0%	7.0%	7.0%
Deposit reduction relative to base	10,000	10,000	20.0%	5.0%	5.0%	5.0%	35.0%	20.0%	90.0%	100.0%
Deposit margin increase, absolute vs base	2.3%	2.4%	1.5%	1.0%	1.0%	1.0%	3.0%	3.0%	5.0%	5.0%
Bank funding margin increase, absolute vs base	3.5%	3.5%	0.0%	0.0%	0.0%	0.0%	0.0%	0.0%	7.0%	7.0%
Bad debts charge as % of asset	1.0%	1.0%	0.5%	0.2%	0.0%	0.0%	2.0%	2.0%	11.0%	9.0%
Expenses increase year-on-year	15.0%	5.0%	2.5%	0.0%	15.0%	0.0%	25.0%	15.0%	10.0%	15.0%
Idiosyncratic impact (£'000)			–	–	675	–	675	–	675	–

the base case drivers highlighted in blue are the underlying absolute values used to project the base financial plan

The impact of the stress on the capital resources and regulatory required capital ratios are as follows:

	Base		Market wide		Idiosyncratic		Combined		Reverse	
	Year 2 £'000	Year 3 £'000	Year 2 £'000	Year 3 £'000	Year 2 £'000	Year 3 £'000	Year 2 £'000	Year 3 £'000	Year 2 £'000	Year 3 £'000
Risk weighted assets	38,039	47,413	31,370	41,379	36,104	44,127	28,070	38,473	24,574	26,895
Reg. CET 1	15,761	17,744	14,602	15,062	14,529	15,271	12,274	10,132	9,191	2,748
Pillar 1	3,043	3,793	2,510	3,310	2,888	3,530	2,246	3,078	1,966	2,152
Pillar 2A	644	857	657	1,005	672	956	656	1,054	614	1,031
TCR	3,687	4,650	3,166	4,316	3,561	4,486	2,902	4,132	2,580	3,183

(continued)

	Base		Market wide		Idiosyncratic		Combined		Reverse	
	Year 2 £'000	Year 3 £'000	Year 2 £'000	Year 3 £'000	Year 2 £'000	Year 3 £'000	Year 2 £'000	Year 3 £'000	Year 2 £'000	Year 3 £'000
TCT plus Pillar 2B	4,789	5,808	4,269	5,473	4,663	5,644	4,004	5,289	3,682	4,341
Surplus / (deficit) regulatory capital	10,971	11,936	10,333	9,589	9,866	9,628	8,270	4,843	5,509	(1,593)
	%	%	%	%	%	%	%	%	%	%
Total Capital requirement % of RWAs	9.7%	9.8%	10.1%	10.4%	9.9%	10.2%	10.3%	10.7%	10.5%	11.8%
Reg. CET1 % of RWAs	41.4%	37.4%	46.5%	36.4%	40.2%	34.6%	43.7%	26.3%	37.4%	10.2%
Surplus / (Deficit)	31.7%	27.6%	36.5%	26.0%	30.4%	24.4%	33.4%	15.6%	26.9%	-1.6%

- Under market-wide stress the surplus capital increases in year 2 with lower RWA's but is slightly lower in year 3 as the drag from the net interest margin starts to impact the retained earnings.
- Idiosyncratic stress reduces the CET1 ratio by 2.8% (from 37.4% to 34.6%) in year 3
- The capital position under combined stress is still £4.8m above the total capital required (TCR) plus the Pillar 2B capital requirements. Since the risk appetite target is £5m above the TCR plus Pillar 2B, the stress will hit an amber trigger that will prompt management action.
- Reverse stress arises from multiple events and results in breaching the required CET 1 ratio.

3.3 Liquidity Stresses

Orchard has modelled a market-wide, an idiosyncratic and a combined stress scenario to determine the impact on the liquidity position of Orchard under each stress scenario. The stress is undertaken after month 12 and the stress period ranges from 2 weeks to 12 weeks.

For each of the stresses, the base plan drivers were flexed and daily cashflow modelled to assess the impact. The business driver under the base plan and the stresses are presented below:

Table 9: Liquidity Stresses Parameters.

	Base	Market wide	Idiosyncratic	Combined
Deposit retention rate at maturity	80%	75%	50%	25%
New deposits as a percentage of plan	100%	25%	20%	5%
Liquid assets buffer haircut	0%	5%	5%	5%
New loans as a percentage of plan	100%	80%	60%	65%
Loan default rates	0%	5%	3%	5%
Period of stress (weeks)	-	12	2	12

1. Systemic market-wide stresses

Orchard modelled the impact of a severe recession over the course of six months with negative growth. We used as the baseline Balance Sheet the position at the end of year 1.

- Deposit rollover rates would fall to 75%, i.e., 25% of deposits would be withdrawn at maturity and the accounts closed. This reflects the assumption that (a) in times of severe recession whilst there are no adverse credit events specifically impacting Orchard, it may nevertheless be the case that some depositors move their funds to highly capitalised banks such as HSBC; and (b) with consumers stressed by recession and unemployment we could anticipate that some of the savings on our balance sheet may be drawn down at rollover.
- The recession is assumed to reduce all economic activity and combined with a flight to quality which we anticipate would disproportionately impact new entrant banks, we have assumed that new deposits will be obtained at only 25% of the original planned rate
- Loan default rates spike from planned levels to 5%, reflecting the increased level of insolvencies during a recession.
- New lending declines from 100% to 80% of the planned levels. The level of 80% is consistent with retaining an adequate level of surplus cash (3 days outflows) in accordance with the banks risk appetite statement. Lending has been reduced to 80% and not to a lower level in order (i) to preserve the banks franchise and protect long term customer relationships, and (ii) to recognise that a reduction in economic activity will also lead to an increase in demand for credit from our customers.

2. Idiosyncratic stresses

Orchard has modelled a scenario in which there are widespread reports in the media that the Bank has experienced severe credit losses on loans, which although as yet uncrystallised are believed to have eliminated a significant portion of the bank's regulatory capital. The Bank is perceived to be a new and relatively inexperienced institution and as a result the press comment leads to significant deposit outflows.

- New deposit business runs at only 20% of the previously planned level and maturing deposits have a 50% attrition rate. These assumptions are relatively severe as a name specific stress on a new entrant to the deposit market, risk aversion from depositors will be high notwithstanding the availability of FSCS insurance.
- 40% of new loan business will cease, making new loans only in exceptional cases for existing relationships, and should therefore benefit from a steady net inflow of funds from maturing loans. As the stress scenario is bank specific there is no expectation that our customers would experience increased rates of insolvency. Nevertheless, it is likely that we would not receive all the funds due in for a variety of reasons such as (i) realising that the bank/customer relationship has likely terminated, borrowers may delay repayment (ii) some borrowers may seek to exploit the bank's difficulties and offer to repay on time, but only if they are given a financial incentive. (iii) some borrowers may be unable to repay as they had been budgeting to rollover the loans on maturity. To account for these factors, we have modelled a collection rate of 97% of the sums due.

3. Combined stress
Orchard has modelled the impact of a recession coupled with press speculation that Orchard Bank had suffered large losses on its loan portfolio, which had significantly reduced its regulatory capital.
- The deposit attrition at maturity has increased considerably to 75% and very little new deposits expected.
- The default rates have increased significantly and the level of new business has reduced to 65% of the plan lending.

4. Reverse stress
No reverse stress test has been undertaken given the short-term nature of the Orchard's lending book which drives considerable cash inflows as demonstrated in the stresses above and the significantly higher Pillar 1 ratios maintained, with high level of liquidity.

5. Stress scenario results
The impact on the liquidity position under each scenario relative to base is as follows:

4 Financial Resources

The Board intends to establish a bank with a conservative strategy. The group has over seventeen years of experience originating in the insurance and fee financing market, and looks to build on it further to acquire a larger share of the market.

Table 10: Liquidity Stresses Summary.

Period of stress (weeks)	Base Plan	Market wide	Idiosyncratic	Combined
	Year 1 £'000	Post 12 weeks £'000	Post 2 weeks £'000	Post 12 weeks £'000
Funding Source				
Deposits		625	83	125
Loan Repayment		20,947	3,565	20,947
Total Funding		**21,572**	**3,648**	**21,072**
Funding Consumption				
Loans		(20,753)	(2,638)	(16,862)
Deposit attrition		(1,575)	(525)	(4,725)
Total funding consumption		**(22,328)**	**(3,163)**	**(21,587)**
Net funding surplus / (consumption)		**(756)**	**485**	**(515)**
Liquid assets				
Cash at bank	1,000	1,000	1,000	1,000
Liquid asset buffer	3,867	3,111	4,352	3,352
Total liquid assets	**4,867**	**4,111**	**5,352**	**4,352**
Loan asset	**32,762**	**30,924**	**30,871**	**27,227**
Deposits	**21,000**	**20,050**	**20,558**	**16,400**
Ratios				
% Liquid Assets to Loans	15%	13%	17%	16%
% Liquid Assets to Deposits	23%	21%	26%	27%
% HQLA to Deposits	18%	16%	21%	20%
LCR %	3069%	2586%	3528%	3407%
NSFR %	154%	158%	164%	160%

Base equates to the start position before the stress and is as at the end of year 1.

From a capital perspective, the initial and projected capital base is sufficient to absorb losses under the severe stress scenarios applied to the business as detailed in the firm's ICAAP.

From a liquidity perspective, the deposit book will be built in the initial years with fixed term deposits, typically below the FSCS limits to lower the risk of large-scale withdrawals. This combined with a Liquid Asset Buffer (LAB) that is maintained at a minimum of 14% of the deposit book and held in the Bank of England reserve account results in limited liquidity risk in the business and the ability to withstand severe stress scenarios as detailed in the firm's ILAAP.

4.1 Capital Resources

4.1.1 Capital Requirement

The credit risk weight of the loan assets is calculated assuming lending is split between retail and SME on a 65% and 35% basis throughout the projection period as forecast from the firm's current actual experience. Although the loss experience over a number of years is very small, a higher than historic 1% impairment charge has been assumed for the financial plan. The financial model assumes a maximum cash balance of £1m is maintained in the nostro account, with all remaining surplus cash being held in the reserve account with the Bank of England. The Pillar I capital requirement is calculated as the sum of capital required in respect of credit risk on the loan assets, bank balances, fixed assets and operational risk where the operational risk charge is the average of the net income over the past three years. Orchard does not have any trading book and FX exposures and therefore does not have any Pillar 1 market risk. Detailed calculations, with risk weight percentages, are presented in the ICAAP.

Table 11: Pillar 1 Capital Requirements.

					£'000
Base	**Plan Year 1**	**Plan Year 2**	**Plan Year 3**	**Plan Year 4**	**Plan Year 5**
Pillar 1					
Credit risk on loan assets	1,839	2,272	2,893	3,812	5,218
Credit risk on bank balances	16	16	16	16	16
Fixed assets	5	5	6	6	6
Credit risk on HQLA	0	0	0	0	0
Total credit risk	**1,860**	**2,294**	**2,914**	**3,834**	**5,240**
Operational risk basic indicator	672	750	879	1,135	1,504
Pillar 1 capital requirements	**2,532**	**3,043**	**3,793**	**4,969**	**6,743**

For Pillar 2A the Bank intends to hold capital against:

1. Residual operational risk arising from the risk register after deducting the amount of capital provided under Pillar 1 for operational risk;
2. Credit concentration risk for single-name, sector and geographic concentration risk; and
3. Interest rate risk in the banking book (IRRBB) with a 200bps shift in the interest rate.

In the July 2014 the FCA and PRA publication 'A review of requirements for firms entering into or firms expanding in the banking sector: one year on', the approach for setting the Capital Planning Buffer (CPB) for new entrants was set out and has been used by Orchard to determine its capital requirements. The publication states that where new

Table 12: Pillar 2A Capital Requirements.

					£'000
Base	**Plan Year 1**	**Plan Year 2**	**Plan Year 3**	**Plan Year 4**	**Plan Year 5**
Pillar 2A capital requirements					
Operational risk	147	111	25	0	0
Business risk	0	0	0	0	0
Reputational risk	0	0	0	0	0
Credit concentration risk	319	391	494	647	881
Interest rate risk in the banking book (IRRBB)	165	142	338	325	325
Residual operational risk from risk register	0	0	0	0	0
Pillar 2A capital requirements	**631**	**644**	**857**	**972**	**1,206**

entrant banks are assessed as resolvable with no systemic impact, the CPB will be set at a level equal to the wind down costs of the new entrant bank.

Hence, the Pillar 2B capital requirement is based on the wind-down costs of the bank. The wind-down cost has been modelled through scenario analysis where the loan book and deposits are reduced to zero. Given the loan book term is 12 months, the wind-down period has been assumed to be 12 months. The annualised operating costs are reduced for those costs that can be mitigated such as marketing and sales staff and costs have been increased for one off costs such as redundancy. These costs are pro-rated over a 12 month period.

The wind-down scenario results in a loss of £1.05m, which has been considered appropriate for the Pillar 2B add on.

Table 13: Pillar 2B Capital Requirements.

		£'000
Income Statement	**WINDDOWN Year 2**	**Base Case Year 2**
Interest Receivable	1,627	*6,370*
Interest payable	(204)	*(591)*
Net interest income	**1,422**	***5,779***
Administration expenses	(2,648)	*(3,267)*
Impairment charges	(71)	*(393)*
Operating profit before tax	**(1,296)**	***2,119***
Corporation tax	246	*(403)*
Profit after tax	**(1,050)**	***1,716***
Dividends	0	*(343)*
Retained earnings	**(1,050)**	***1,373***

Table 14: Wind-down operating expenses analysis.

	Year 1	£'000 Year 2
Total opex (base)	**2,870**	**3,267**
Cost not incurred in wind-down		
Sales force		430
IT development		115
Underwriting		132
Reducing ops headcount		101
Advertising		58
Entertainment		35
Travel		40
Deposit raising expenses		30
Bank charges		86
Bonus		294
Total costs not incurred on wind-down		**1,320**
One off costs in wind-down		
Redundancy/retention (25% of annual salaries)		468
Legal and professional costs		184
3rd party contracts – early termination costs		50
Total additional costs		**702**
Total annual opex on wind-down		**2,649**

Table 15: Wind-down scenario balance sheet.

		£'000
Balance Sheet	**WINDDOWN Year 2**	***Base Case Year 2***
Assets		
Loans and advances	(2)	*40,475*
Cash at bank	1,000	*1,000*
Liquid asset buffer	13,998	*7,612*
Fixed assets	556	*556*
Other assets	158	*158*
Total assets	**15,710**	***49,801***
Liabilities		
Customer deposits	0	*31,000*
Trade creditors	2,051	*2,051*
Tax liabilities	(246)	*403*
Non-current liabilities	78	*96*
Total liabilities	**1,882**	***33,550***

Table 15: (continued)

Balance Sheet	**WINDDOWN Year 2**	***Base Case Year 2***
Equity		
Share capital	214	*214*
Share premium	8,692	*8,692*
Merger reserves	891	*891*
Retained earnings	5,081	*5,081*
Current year retained earnings	(1,050)	*1,373*
Total equity	**13,828**	***16,251***
Total equity and liabilities	**15,710**	***49,801***

Table 16: Summary Capital Requirements.

Base	**Plan Year 1**	**Plan Year 2**	**Plan Year 3**	**Plan Year 4**	**Plan Year 5**
					£'000
Pillar 1 capital requirements	2,532	3,043	3,793	4,969	6,743
Pillar 2A capital requirements	631	644	857	972	1,206
Total capital requirement (Pillar 1 + Pillar 2A)	**3,163**	**3,687**	**4,650**	**5,942**	**7,949**
Pillar 2B	1,050	1,102	1,158	1,215	1,276
TCR plus P2B	**4,213**	**4,789**	**5,808**	**7,157**	**9,226**
Total Capital resources	**14,457**	**15,761**	**17,744**	**20,786**	**25,558**
Risk weighted assets	31,652	38,039	47,413	62,117	84,294
Total Capital requirement % of RWAs	10.0%	9.7%	9.8%	9.6%	9.4%
TCR + Pillar 2B % of RWAs	13.3%	12.6%	12.2%	11.5%	10.9%
CET1 % of RWAs	47.0%	42.7%	38.6%	34.4%	31.1%
Surplus / (deficit) capital	10,244	10,971	11,936	13,629	16,332

The group intends to grow the balance sheet of the Bank by leveraging on internally generated capital resources rather than introducing any additional capital over the plan period and in the three years projects to increase capital by £4.2m, a 30% increase.

4.1.2 Capital Related Risk Appetite

The Bank intends to have a number of explicit capital risk metrics:
- CET 1 ratio;
- Surplus capital over TCR plus Pillar 2B; and
- Leverage ratio

The capital risk metrics will be monitored regularly and presented to the Executive Committee and Board by the CFO at least monthly as part of the monthly management information. While the Bank anticipates adequate capital throughout its plan period, it is confident of raising further capital from institutional shareholders to supplement the current capital resources if the asset origination growth significantly exceeds expectation.

If the forecast earnings fall well short of plan the bank will have a number of options available to it including to:
1. Revise planned lending numbers and re-forecast the plan;
2. Consider carrying out a rights issue, even at a discounted price, taking advantage of Orchard's AIM listing and the quality of its' shareholder base;
3. Consider revision to the dividend policy;
4. Reduce operational costs, without compromising customer service or risk management.

Orchard considers that it has sufficient capital for its 5 year plan and therefore has not approached shareholders for further capital. Orchard shareholders include some substantial institutions, which have the capacity to introduce further capital to Orchard but have not, at this stage, been tested to determine whether they have the appetite for such investment.

4.2 Liquidity Resources

4.2.1 Liquidity Requirement

The Bank has designed its liability strategy to maintain a low and conservative level of liquidity risk. It plans to issue 1 year and 2 year fixed rate bonds to grow its deposit book. The loans to be originated by Orchard will have a maximum maturity of 12 months and average maturity of 5–6 months, ensuring low liquidity gap risks on the balance sheet. The HQLA will be maintained at a minimum of 14% of deposits by year 5 and will be held in cash with the Bank of England.

The bank's conservative stance towards liquidity management is demonstrated in its projection of key liquidity ratios – Liquidity Coverage Ratio (LCR) and Net Stable Funding Ratio (NSFR) and its percentage of liquid assets against loans and deposits.–

Table 17: Liquidity adequacy.

					£'000
	Plan Year 1	**Plan Year 2**	**Plan Year 3**	**Plan Year 4**	**Plan Year 5**
Funding Source	21,000	31,000	41,000	54,000	76,000
Deposits					
Equity	14,878	16,251	18,295	21,394	26,219
Bank Loans	-	-	-	-	-
Total Funding	**35,878**	**47,251**	**59,295**	**75,394**	**102,219**
Funding Consumption					
Loans	**32,762**	**40,475**	**51,531**	**67,917**	**92,953**
Liquid assets					
Cash at bank	1,000	1,000	1,000	1,000	1,000
Liquid asset buffer	3,867	7,612	8,740	8,717	10,972
Other Corp. bonds	-	-	-	-	-
Total liquid assets	**4,867**	**8,612**	**9,740**	**9,717**	**11,972**
Ratios					
% Liquid Assets to Loans	15%	21%	19%	14%	13%
% Liquid Assets to Deposits	23%	28%	24%	18%	16%
% HQLA to Deposits	18%	25%	21%	16%	14%
NSFR	154%	160%	160%	154%	154%
LCR	3069%	4093%	3553%	2690%	2406%

4.2.2 Liquidity Related Risk Appetite

The Bank intends to establish reporting and monitoring of a number of liquidity related risk metrics:

- LCR (with a buffer over the minimum regulatory requirement)
- NSFR (with a buffer over the minimum regulatory requirement)
- HQLA as percentage of deposits
- Maximum deposit redemption in one month as a percentage of the deposit book
- Deposit retention rate
- LAB composition (initially, short term UK government treasury bills and, when available, cash held in the Bank of England reserve account)

The liquidity risk metrics will be monitored regularly and presented to the Executive Committee and Board by the CFO at least monthly within the monthly management information. While the Bank anticipates adequate liquidity throughout its plan period, it has a number of strategies available to it to address any liquidity shortfall, including:

- increasing deposit intake (using a mix of higher rates and greater marketing efforts);
- increasing deposit retention (through targeted preferential rates); and
- reducing loan origination (slowing down or stopping new net lending, etc.).

5 Non-Financial Resources

5.1 Human Resources

Orchard currently operates an efficient lending operation with a proven track record of promoting an appropriate culture and expertise in strategy formulation, product design and execution in its specialist lending market. The directors on the board have decades of experience in financial markets, specialist lending, the SME market and listed company administration. The board is supported by a highly experienced executive team who over the years have built strong relationships within the insurance brokerage and professional services industry. The company has a proven IT platform and strong controls, risk management procedures and operational processes to support its lending book while maintaining regulatory compliance. Table 19 below contains brief biographies of the current board of directors of Orchard and the proposed board of the bank, subject to regulatory approval.

Figure 11 shows an organisation chart of the Bank in mobilisation. Over time headcount is expected to increase as business volumes increase, in particular with regard to customer-facing staff. Opportunities for automation will be looked for including underwriting using open banking software. There are also plans to bring in outsourced company secretarial services to deal with the increased governance workload in the form of minute-taking and tracking actions from the Board and management committees.

5.2 IT Resources

The group's software system, LendXP, is a proven loan administration system. LendXP has been specially developed for the Group's business model and was installed and launched in 2006. The system is secure and web-based with an off-site backup.

5.2.1 Description of LendXP

A full description of LendXP and its functionality is set out in the draft IT Plan, which will be finalised during mobilisation.

5.2.2 Suitability of LendXP

The directors believe that LendXP provides a number of competitive advantages to the group. The LendXP system:

- covers all aspects of the group's interaction with insurance brokers, professional firms and customers
- enables the input of on-line applications for finance and the on-line credit and affordability assessment of these applications;

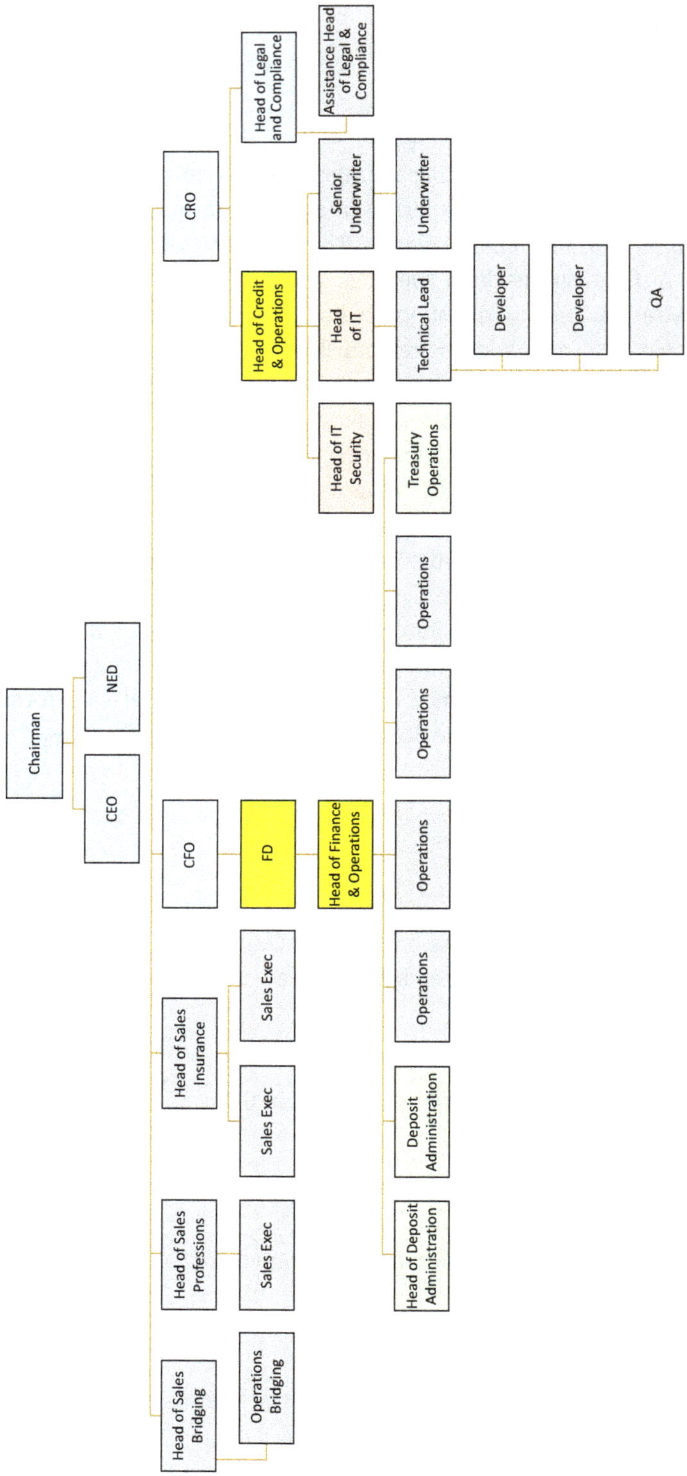

Figure 11: Organisation Chart.

- enables the status of proposals and deals to be viewed quickly and easily as well as changed
- records all interactions with insurance brokers or professional firms and creates standard documentation automatically
- enables staff to monitor the finance information and payment status on each transaction
- manages all direct debits to be collected by the group
- has an integrated general ledger
- creates all management accounts for the business
- streamlines the decision-making process and acts as a management information tool to assist the directors.

5.2.3 Future developments

Orchard will implement a proven software system to manage its deposit taking business. Orchard intends to utilise the deposit software system of Mutual Vision Limited. Apart from Direct Debit access Orchard has CHAPS/Faster payments access through its clearing bank. Orchard will also gain access to other payment systems (e.g., SWIFT) via Bottomline. For customer relationship management (CRM) with borrowers Orchard currently uses Zoho CRM. The scope of the CRM will be extended to enable tracking of deposit and loan workflows and provide improved integration with the LendXP core banking platform.

Orchard will bolster its staff resources accordingly to manage and administer its new deposit taking business. Given its relatively modest deposit-raising ambitions it is envisaged only a limited number of dedicated deposit administration staff will be required.

5.3 Access to Payment and Financial Messaging Systems

Orchard will set up an agency banking relationship to support deposit taking and get access to additional payment mechanisms to provide back-up. Application will be made to the Bank of England during the mobilisation phase to get membership of the Sterling Monetary Framework (SMF) to enable the deposit of excess cash in the reserve account, with accompanying access to BoE EnquiryLink either directly through SWIFT or via Bottomline. Whilst Orchard awaits the approval of the BoE reserve account, the liquidity requirements will be managed by investing in very short term (less than 3 months maturity) UK government treasury bills.

5.4 Access to Payment Services

Orchard has access to BACS through its Direct Debit facility, and CHAPS/Faster payments through its relationship with its clearing bank. It has been utilising the payment services for loan payment and redemption settlements since 2002. Orchard will establish an agency banking relationship with one of the UK GBP clearing banks to get back-up access to payment systems. Orchard will also set up access to SWIFT either directly or via Bottomline to be able to use the Bank of England's Real Time Gross Settlement (RTGS) system for Reserve account administration.

5.5 Outsourced Functions

The following table describes Orchard's current key outsourcing relationships to be retained as a bank. These cover the IT infrastructure as well as bespoke IT platforms.

Table 18: Outsourced Functions.

Function	Company	Description	Control/Mitigants
Servers + Infrastructure	Assign-IT	Assign IT manage OFG's general IT infrastructure, such as file storage and system security. All the data is stored on servers maintained in the office.	Service Level Agreements are in place with Assign IT. The relationship is regularly reviewed by the Head of Operations and the Audit Committee.
Bexhill Email	Assign-IT	Hosted on Microsoft Exchange, maintained by Assign IT.	See above.
Orchard Funding Email	Assign-IT	Hosted on Microsoft Exchange, maintained by Assign IT.	See above.

In addition to the existing vendor relationships Orchard will establish the following outsourcing arrangements to deliver end-to-end banking services to its depositors and borrowers:

- Agency banking relationship with Orchard's existing GBP clearing bank, Barclays, to enable deposit account creation and administration;
- An outsourced provider to provide deposit taking software after full due diligence assessment;
- An outsourced provider to assist Orchard in the preparation of its regulatory reports, subject to due diligence and approval by CFO;
- Bottomline for payment mechanisms (SWIFT for RTGS, and deposit integration); and

- Professional accounting firms for internal audit and external audit through formal tender process, with appointment approved by Audit Committee
- Company secretarial services to deal with the increased governance workload in the form of minute-taking and tracking actions from the Board and management committees.

All material outsourcing arrangements will comply with Orchard's Outsourcing Policy, which will be consistent with the FCA/PRA rules on Outsourcing and finalised during Mobilisation.

6 Governance & Risk

6.1 Board Composition

The directors recognise the importance of sound corporate governance and comply with the QCA Corporate Governance Code (as devised by the QCA in consultation with a number of significant institutional small company investors). In addition, the PRA and FCA set standards for Board Governance in Banks, which Orchard will comply with.

Orchard recognises the concerns that the PRA has over 'dominant individuals' on bank boards and has put together a committee structure and recruited suitable INED's to help mitigate this risk. The Board of the Bank will comprise five directors of which two will be executives and three will be independent non-executives. The Board reflects a blend of different experience and backgrounds.

The objective of the Board will be to enhance the long-term success of the Bank by developing a sustainable business model. This will be supported by approving and setting strategy, risk appetite and culture in line with the business model and in light of changing business opportunities, environment and risk.

The Board will delegate the day to day implementation of the strategy, business plans, policies, procedures and risk appetite within the approved policy statements to the Executive Committee and it will be the responsibility of the Board to monitor the overall performance of the business. In addition, the risk management framework and control environment will enable the Board (through the oversight of the Audit and Risk Committees) to gain assurance that it is operating as designed and within the tolerances set by its risk appetite.

Orchard has a full and detailed Corporate Governance Policy, which will be finalised during Mobilisation.

Brief biographies of the directors are shown in Table 19 below. Board roles and responsibilities are detailed in the Table 21 below.

Table 19: Brief biography of the directors.

Name	Board Membership	Brief Biography
	Independent Non-Executive Chairman	
Ravi Takhar	Chief Executive Officer	Mr Ravi Takhar has over 25 years' experience in the acquisition, growth, financing and disposal of financial businesses. Mr Takhar founded the business in 2002 and has led the growth of the UK business to its current size. Prior to creating the group, Ravi was an investment banker and Head of Financial Services investment at Nikko, the Japanese investment bank, from 1998 to 2002 as well as Chairman of Mortgages PLC, the mortgage lender. Mr Takhar was also Head of Mortgage Principal Finance at Investec Bank PLC from 2005 to 2008. He qualified as a banking solicitor at Clifford Chance, a leading international law firm, and has an MA from the University of Oxford.
	Chief Financial Officer	
	Non-Executive Director	
	Non-Executive Director	

Table 20: Brief biography of the CRO.

Name	Senior Management Role	Brief Biography
	Chief Risk Officer	

Table 21: Orchard Funding Group PLC – Board Roles & Responsibilities.

Role	Key Reponsibilities	Appointment
Chief Executive and Board Director SMF1 SMF 3 SMF 24	The CEO is responsible for: – effective day to day management of the business – operating the business in accordance with board approved strategies, plans and policies – ensuring an effective systems and control environment – managing overall enterprise risk and returns – setting the corporate culture – primarily responsible for the relationship with the relevant regulatory bodies and for all other stakeholders in the business – compliance with Board Risk Appetite Statement	Ravi Takhar

Table 21 (continued)

Role	Key Reponsibilities	Appointment
	The CEO is Chairman of the Executive Committee and member of ALCO and Credit Committee. The CEO is also responsible for ensuring that the board members are: – able to sufficiently challenge the executive and understand the business model – provided with a full understanding of higher risk activities and products – in receipt of appropriate management information to be able to carry out their oversight role The CEO will have oversight responsibility for HR and marketing. The CEO also has oversight responsibility for: – the effective development of the bank's retail savings business in terms of its administration functions, ensuring that high standards of performance and service are achieved at all times and that it operates at all times within the policies and parameters set by the board – ensuring that all staff members within the retail savings business act at all times in compliance with the letter and the spirit of all laws and regulations applying to the business The CEO also holds primary responsibility for: – management, stability, security and effectiveness of the systems and communications used in the bank – operating within parameters and budgets set by the Board and the Executive Committee – ensuring the Bank remains appropriately positioned to address its business needs, provide operational resilience, security risks and to respond to identified opportunities and threats relevant to IT and Communications – managing the secure delivery of the bank's website and email communications. – Business Continuity and Disaster Recovery Plan, maintaining it up to date at all times and ensuring it is subject to appropriate and regular testing – Bank-wide project management – Outsourcing arrangements – Facilities management	
Chief Financial Officer and Board Director SMF2, SMF3	The CFO has overall responsibility for: – overseeing the Finance and Treasury functions of the Bank and ensuring that each operates within the parameters and policies set by the Board and Executive Committee – primary accountability for the quality of the business-wide financial and management information – all statutory and regulatory reporting – oversight of the principal financial systems and controls of the business	

Table 21 (continued)

Role	Key Reponsibilities	Appointment
	– the preparation of the ILAAP, ICAAP, Recovery Plan and Resolution Plan – the financial and treasury related risks of the Bank on a day to day basis including capital management, liquidity management and compliance with IFRS. – managing the production of and present the medium term financial plan for approval to the Board – compliance with Board Risk Appetite Statement As a member of the Executive Committee the CFO is responsible for contributing to overall direction of the business in terms of its strategies, performance, systems and controls. The CFO is a member of the Executive Committee and Credit Committee and Chair of ALCO. Working with the CEO, the CFO will take primary responsibility for the delivery of the bank's deposit strategy, ensuring that the Bank achieves the right mix of funding across its target customer segments and at an acceptable cost of funds. The CFO is also responsible for: – the production of all financially related statutory and regulatory returns in accordance with prescribed timetables – production of timely management information, pulling this together from across all areas of the bank – operation of the payments and reconciliations of the Bank which is a key area of control – ensuring that finance operations function within Board and Executive Committee approved parameters and policies	
CRO SMF4, SMF 16 & 17	The CRO has primary responsibility to the Board on the quality of the Bank's overall risk management framework. He is a key link between the Board and the business with the ability to translate what is at times highly technical and often detailed reporting of risk into high level information for the Board to understand and interpret at a strategic level. The CRO attends all the executive committees of the Bank providing internal challenge and is a Member of ALCO and Credit Committee. As a member of the Executive Committee the CRO is responsible for contributing to the overall direction of the business in terms of its strategies, performance, systems and controls. In addition to enterprise-wide risk management, the CRO has primary oversight responsibility for: – legal and compliance (including conduct risk) – financial crime prevention	

Table 21 (continued)

Role	Key Reponsibilities	Appointment
	– fraud management – Credit risk and credit systems – Operational risk – compliance with Board Risk Appetite Statement The CRO will be responsible for: – ensuring the Bank meets all its statutory and regulatory requirements relating to the operation of the Bank other than the financial ones undertaken by the Finance Director and CFO – ensuring compliant procedures are in place to enable the business operations to comply with current legislation and regulations – taking responsibility for the effective management, measurement and monitoring of exposure to Conduct Risk – monitoring compliance with Complaints Handling and Treating Customers Fairly – documenting and reporting results of legal and compliance monitoring to the Board, Audit& Risk and Executive Committees as appropriate – compliance with Board Risk Appetite Statement He also acts as Money Laundering Reporting Officer (MLRO). As MLRO he has responsibility for: – ensuring all statutory and regulatory responsibilities are discharged on behalf of the bank – the implementation of and compliance with anti-money laundering procedures and policies – receiving and reviewing suspicious transaction reports and advising SOCA as necessary He is responsible for developing and delivering all compliance training requirements. His legal responsibilities relate to taking primary responsibility for: – reviewing all terms and conditions of products, third party contracts for services and business relationships – and ensuring that they are appropriate within the context of the board approved policies and parameters and applicable laws and regulations.	
Chairman (Board) & Chairman of Noms and Rems INED SMF 9 SMF 12 SMF 13	Responsible for leading the Board and ensuring effective direction and challenge for management Setting Board Agenda (in consultation with Management) Chair of Noms and Rems Committee Setting tone from the top in terms of the Culture of the Organisation Board training agenda Board Evaluation (annual) Appraisal of performance of Board members and CEO Ensuring appropriate balance of skills and diversity of Board	

Table 21 (continued)

Role	Key Reponsibilities	Appointment
Chair of Audit INED SMF 10	Responsible for ensuring an effective Audit Committee operating in the interests of all stakeholders Ensuring regulatory and listing responsibilities are discharged effectively Audit Committee Agenda (in consultation with Management) Oversight of head of Internal Audit (including assessing performance in conjunction with CEO) Liaising with External Auditors Audit Committee Evaluation (annual)	
Chair of Risk INED SMF 11	Responsible for ensuring an effective Risk Committee in accordance with its terms of reference Setting Risk Committee Agenda Oversight of CRO (including assessing performance in conjunction with CEO) Risk Committee Evaluation (Annual) Responsible for the maintenance of an appropriate Whistleblowing process for customers, staff and other stakeholders of the business.	

6.2 Improvement of Governance Structure

The corporate governance structure has been enhanced to prepare for Orchard becoming a bank as follows:

1. The appointment of an independent non-executive Chairman and independent non-executive directors with many years of recent and current banking experience in SMF designated roles;
2. The independent non-executive directors comprising a majority of the Board and supported by an appropriate quorum voting structure;
3. A new Board Risk Committee and continuance of the Board Audit Committee and the Board Nominations & Remuneration Committee comprised only of independent non-executive directors.
4. The appointment of a new CFO and new CRO with recent bank experience, who will provide an executive balance to the CEO.
5. The Board will appoint an external party to carry out its internal audit function.
6. The enhancement of the governance structure with more detailed and regular board and committee meetings, supplemented with enhanced regular management information, to ensure effective corporate governance.

The Board is satisfied that the profile and experience of the independent NEDs and the new executive appointments, together with the enhanced corporate governance structure will be provide effective and controlled governance of Orchard as a bank.

6.3 Assessment of Board Skills and Experience

Orchard has been operating in its core market for 17 years and the Board and senior management have a strong understanding of (i) the risks associated with Orchard's regulated activities and (ii) the regulatory requirements which govern the way in which Orchard conducts its regulated activities.

The Board and senior management recognise that, as a Bank, Orchard will be subject to additional regulatory requirements and are confident that they have the experience and skills to ensure compliance with these new obligations. We have undertaken an assessment for the Board and senior management to identify areas where skills and knowledge can be further enhanced.

Orchard's board is now comprised of senior individuals with many years of recent experience in the banking industry. Gaps in the skills and experience of individual directors and senior managers will continue to be addressed through an ongoing training program. The Skills and Experience Matrix in the table below summarises the current assessment of the Board.

6.3.1 Skills and Experience Matrix

Table 22: Orchard Funding Group PLC – Board Skills Matrix.

Code: 1-Specialist experience (e.g executive function holder within past 5 years CRO, CFO, CIO etc) 2- Good Experience (but not specialist function holder in past 5 years) 3- Knowledgeable but no direct experience (capable of development with support/training) 4- Not considered essential as sufficiently covered by others	Ravi Takhar CEO	CFO	CRO	INED Chairman	INED Chairman of Audit Committee	INED Chairman of Risk Committee
Risk Management and setting risk appetite	1	3	1	2	2	1
Technology including Business continuity, resilience and security	2	2	2	2	1	2
Treasury management including asset and liability management	1	2	2	2	1	2
Operations and project management	1	2	2	2	2	1
Financial statements and reporting, including regulatory	2	1	4	1	1	2

Table 22 (continued)

Prudential and Conduct regulation, including conduct, SYSC, threshold conditions (PRA and FCA), SMCR	1	2	1	1	1	1
Business strategy, including for Orchard's chosen markets	1	2	2	1	2	2
Retail deposits marketing and operations	3	2	2	1	1	2

Table 23: Orchard Funding Group PLC – Board Behaviours Matrix for Performance Evaluation.

Code: 1-Strong requirement 2- Requirement 3- Not required	Ravi Takhar CEO	CFO	CRO	INED Chairman	INED Chairman of Audit Committee	INED Chairman of Risk Committee<
Customer Focus	1	1	1	1	1	1
Challenges Executives	NA	NA	NA	1	1	1
Actively participates in debates	1	1	1	1	1	1
Prepares properly for meeting and reads papers	1	1	1	1	1	1
Up to date in own area of expertise	1	1	1	1	1	1
Board Committees Chairman – Leadership qualities/effectiveness/ potential	1	1	2	1	1	1

6.4 Board Structure

The Orchard Board at launch of the Bank and during mobilisation will have the following composition:

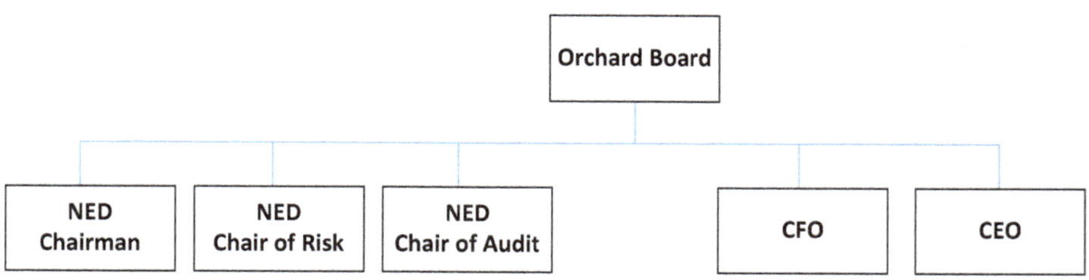

Figure 12: Orchard Board Composition.

6.5 Committee and Management Structure Charts

The following section describes the relationships and functions of the key governance committees proposed for Orchard.

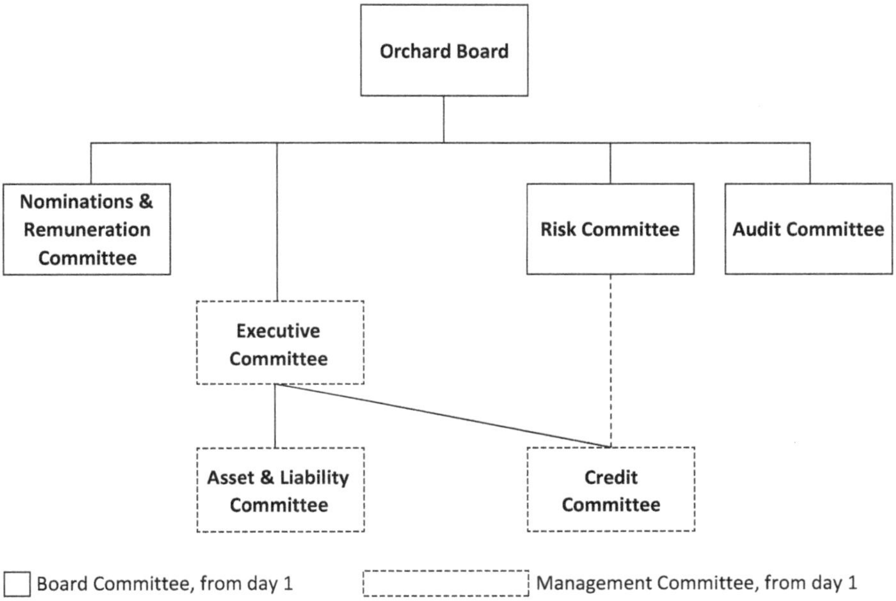

Figure 13: Orchard Governance Committees.

6.6 Governance Framework – Board and Board Sub-Committees

A summary table of the Board and Board Sub-Committees is presented below:

Table 24: Orchard Board and Board Sub-Committees.

Committee	Quorum	Members	Frequency
Board	3 (at least 2 INEDs)	Chairman CEO CFO INEDs	Ten times a year, or more frequent if required by the Chairman
Risk Committee	2	Chair of Risk, INEDs (inc Board Chairman) [CEO, CFO and CRO standing invitees]	Four times a year, or more frequent if required by the committee chair

Table 24 (continued)

Committee	Quorum	Members	Frequency
Audit Committee	2	Chair of Audit, INED [Internal Audit, External Audit, Chairman of the Board, CEO, CFO and CRO standing invitees]	Four times a year, or more frequent if required by the committee chair
Nominations & Remuneration Committee	3	Chairman CEO (non-voting) INEDs	At least twice a year, or more frequent if required by committee chair

6.6.1 Board

The Board's primary role is to provide leadership, ensure that the Bank is appropriately managed and deliver long term shareholder value. It sets the strategic objectives and provides direction.

The Board is responsible for managing the Bank on behalf of its shareholders and each Director must act in a manner that he/she considers promotes effective working of the Board and the long term success of the Bank for the benefit of those shareholders, its employees and all of its customers. The Board will meet as necessary, but typically on a monthly basis, with the exception of August and December months (to allow for holidays).

The Board will ensure there are appropriate controls in place and that there is a healthy balance between promoting long term growth and delivering short term performance, but it will place the emphasis on the longer-term health and sustainability of the Bank.

The Board delegates responsibility for the day-to-day management of the Bank to the executive management team, led by the Chief Executive and through the Executive Committee. However, certain matters are specifically reserved for the Board and these include the approval, monitoring and review of:

- Setting business strategy, plans and budgets from time to time
- Monitoring business performance and effectiveness
- Oversight of regulatory compliance and internal controls
- Financial statements and significant changes to accounting policies and practices
- Board terms of reference, membership and powers including the appointment and removal of board members
- Principal policies of the Bank, committee terms of reference and the overall governance framework, systems and controls
- Risk appetite, risk management, insurance and mitigation
- Corporate initiatives such as mergers and acquisitions or significant business partnerships.

- Culture, values and attitudes of the management and staff of the Bank towards both its customers and the risks that are taken
- Remuneration, benefits and incentive policy and appointment of senior management
- Regulatory and statutory compliance
- Prudential and regulatory matters including but not limited to ICAAP, ILAAP and RRP.

Board performance will be reviewed at least annually. The Chairman will meet annually with the non-executive directors. The non-executive directors will meet annually to appraise the Chairman's performance.

At each regular scheduled meeting the board will receive reports from the Chief Executive and Chief Financial Officer on the performance, results, strategic developments and initiatives, operating functions, legal, compliance, human resources and corporate development matters.

There will be an annual schedule of rolling agenda items to ensure that all matters are given due consideration and are reviewed at the appropriate point in the financial and regulatory cycle.

Meetings are structured to ensure that there is sufficient time for consideration and debate of all matters.

6.6.2 Risk Committee

The Committee is responsible for the identification, management and mitigation of risk as a fundamental requirement for the success of the Bank. The Committee plays an important role in setting the tone and culture that promotes effective risk management across Orchard. The Risk Committee will typically meet quarterly.

6.6.3 Audit Committee

The Committee is responsible for oversight of the systems of internal control in operation in the Bank, the integrity of its financial statements and regulatory reports and the oversight of both external and internal audit. The Audit Committee will meet quarterly.

6.6.4 Nominations and Remuneration Committee

The Committee is responsible for ensuring the recruitment and selection of appropriately qualified experienced and skilled individuals into senior positions within the organisation and the setting of remuneration, rewards and benefits at levels which attract, retain and motivate employees, whilst being affordable and appropriate. The Committee will meet as required, but a minimum of once per year.

The Committee must ensure that the Bank conforms in all respects with the recruitment policies set out in the staff handbook particularly with regard to the avoidance of unfair discrimination in the recruitment of employees and Board members, and also ensuring that it conforms to the CRD IV proposals regarding diversity in board composition.

6.7 Governance Framework –Management Committees

A summary table of the Management Committees is set out below:

Table 25: Orchard Management Committees.

Committee	Quorum	Members	Frequency
Executive Committee	3	CEO CFO CRO Head of Finance & Operations Head of Credit & Operations	Once a fortnight, or more frequent if required by committee chair
Asset & Liability Committee (ALCO)	3 with CFO	CEO CFO CRO Head of Finance & Operations Head of Credit & Operations	Once a month, or more frequent if required by committee chair
Credit Committee	3 with CRO	CEO CFO CRO Head of Finance & Operations Head of Credit & Operations	Twice a month, or more frequent if required by the committee chair

6.7.1 Executive Committee

The Executive Committee has its authority delegated to it by the Board of Directors. It represents the principal forum for conducting the business of the Bank and takes day to day responsibility for the efficient running of the business. In addition the Executive Committee is responsible for the formulation and implementation of Board approved strategies and plans. It is responsible for ensuring the performance of the business in accordance with plans. It will review prudential and regulatory matters including but not limited to ICAAP, ILAAP and other reviews.

6.7.2 Asset and Liability Committee

The Asset and Liability Committee's (ALCO's) purpose is to manage the assets and liabilities of the Bank in respect of duration, interest rate and liquidity risk. It is responsible for determining the Bank's strategy in respect to its balance sheet assets, capital, funding and liquidity profiles, seeking to understand and anticipate future market and economic developments affecting the Bank and considering these in the context of the Bank's ILAAP.

6.7.3 Credit Committee

The Credit Committee is the body charged with the transactional credit responsibility for the Bank. It operates within policy parameters approved by the Board in carrying out the approval and monitoring of the credit business of the Bank.

6.8 Board and Committee Membership

Orchard's Board and committee membership is summarised in the table below:

Table 26: Orchard SMR Responsibilities Map.

6.9 SMR Responsibilities

The allocation of Senior Management Regime responsibilities is summarised in the table below:

Table 27: Orchard SMR Responsibilities Map.

6.10 Management of Conflict of Interest of Ravi Takhar as CEO and Majority Shareholder of Orchard.

Ravi Takhar has been CEO and majority shareholder of Orchard since its flotation in 2015. In that time, the potential conflict between his actions as CEO and his actions as a shareholder has been managed and controlled by Orchard's governance being comprised of: a Board with 2 independent non-executive directors; a Board Committee structure of Audit & Risk Committee and Remuneration and Nominations Committee, comprising only NEDs.

The management and control of the potential conflicts of interest will be enhanced when Orchard becomes a bank as follows:

1. The appointment of an independent non-executive Chairman and independent non-executive directors with recent and current banking experience;
2. The independent non-executive directors comprising a majority quorum of the Board;
3. A new Board Risk Committee and continuance of the Board Audit Committee and Board Remuneration Committee comprised only of independent non-executive directors.

4. The appointment of a new CFO and new CRO with recent bank experience, who will provide executive balance to the CEO.
5. The enhancement of the governance structure with more detailed and regular board and committee meetings to ensure that potential conflicts are managed in a timely manner.
6. The introduction of a clear and transparent approach to Conflicts of Interest with a register of interests maintained for the Board and Board and Committee procedures which call out any actual or potential conflicts which may arise.

The Board is satisfied that the profile and experience of the independent NEDs and the new executive appointments, together with the enhanced corporate governance structure will be able to manage any potential conflicts of interest between the CEO's position as an executive and majority shareholder of Orchard.

Orchard also recognizes that Ravi Takhar has not held a CEO position at a deposit taking institution, and hence, the composition of the Board, both executive as well as non-executive, has been strengthened to include individuals with strong banking experience.

6.11 Risk Appetite

The level of risk that Orchard is prepared to accept and the tolerance limits around the acceptable risk is set out in the risk appetite. The risk appetite is both qualitative and quantitative and covers the risks identified in the business. These are categorised as level 1 risks, with more granularity under level 2. The identified risks are set out in the table below:

Table 28: Orchard Level 1 and Level 2 Risks.

Level 1	Credit Risk	Financial Risk	Conduct Risk	Strategic Risk	Operational Risk
Level 2	Credit	Financial Reporting and tax Model	Conduct Legal Regulatory Compliance	Strategic	Business continuity Data management Financial crime Fraud Information security (incl.Cyber) People Physical security and safety Third party Transaction processing

The Board is responsible for setting Orchard's risk appetite and delegates the responsibility for the setting of limits and policies and monitoring of processes, systems and reporting to the Risk Committee. Orchard's risk appetite sets out the level of risk that it is willing to accept in pursuit of its business objectives.

Risk appetite statements have been created for each Level 1 and Level 2 Risk category and provide an articulation of Orchard's tolerance for risk in both quantitative measures and qualitative terms. They have been created following discussions among Orchard's executive management and with members of the Risk Committee and the Board. They are used in mapping key risks and assessing their materiality and ultimately underpin Orchard's overall risk management framework.

The risk appetite statements are reviewed formally on an annual basis by the Board as part of budget setting and the review of Orchard's medium-term strategy. They combine a top-down view of Orchard's overall risk capacity with a bottom-up view of the risk profile requested and recommended by the business area (which will be previously discussed and reviewed by the Risk Committee).

Throughout the year all aspects of the risk appetite statement (which will be monitored by the CRO) will be reported to the Risk Committee and Board. In particular, the CRO will be responsible for assessing the impact on Orchard's risk appetite of any changes in circumstances (internal or external) that may warrant a change to the risk appetite statements and recommending any consequent changes to the Risk Committee and the Board ahead of the scheduled annual review.

6.11.1 Overarching Risk Appetite Statements

A set of overarching principles has been established, which govern the articulation of the lower-level risk appetite statements. These principles are that Orchard's risk appetite should:

- Reflect the bank's strategy and its culture;
- Focus on manageable, forward looking measures of risk, rather than on backward looking measures of loss;
- Include qualitative description, quantitative measures and prescribed behaviours;
- Facilitate understanding of why limits have been set at the level determined;

These will be communicated, throughout the organisation, in a way that enables each individual to see how risk appetite influences the way they carry out their job responsibilities.

The qualitative Board Risk Appetite statements:

- Cover each Level 1 and Level 2 risk category;
- Are approved by the Board and reviewed at least annually in consultation with all key stakeholders taking into account business changes and reported at least quarterly.

Overarching statements as detailed below express Orchard's broad risk appetite at a whole business level, whilst underlying limits cover specific aspects of Orchard's operations.

We will maintain stakeholder confidence – by operating the business in such a way that we deliver against key objectives, both financial and non-financial and remain within our risk appetite;

We will maintain adequate capital and liquid resources – we will maintain a sufficient level of capital and liquidity to effectively support the lending activity of the business and ensure that all liabilities will be met as they fall due under both normal conditions and under a range of stress scenarios and regulatory guidance;

We will protect our reputation – we will be a safe haven for retail depositors and can be seen as an organisation that treats all our customers and employees fairly. We have no appetite for material negative or adverse reputational events;

We will limit the potential for credit losses – by being aware of and managing key concentrations, lending in markets where we can demonstrate expertise to credit worthy borrowers where affordability can be demonstrated and consistent with risk adjusted returns;

We will effectively manage our operational risks and operational resilience – we have a low tolerance of operational risk failures (including IT systems failures and cyber-crime) and will ensure that all our people are properly trained, procedures are thoroughly documented and supervisory controls and reporting methodologies are in place and minimize the impact of adverse operational risk events that disrupt customer service;

We will demonstrate high standards of conduct and compliance – we have a low tolerance for material conduct and compliance related adverse events, or breaches of a regulatory or legal nature and will operate the business in such a way as to minimise the potential for such adverse events to occur.

6.12 Risk Management Framework

6.12.1 Overview of Three Lines of Defence

Orchard is working to establish a Risk Management Framework (RMF) that provides guidance for cohesive and consistent risk management activity across the whole business. The aim of the RMF is to ensure that all types of risk are identified and managed in a consistent manner across Orchard. The RMF sets the standard approach for the management of each Principal Risk and comprises the following components:

- Risk Culture;
- Risk Governance and Control;
- Risk Strategy and Appetite;
- Risk Measurement and Reporting; and
- Stress Testing and Contingency Planning

The RMF will be enacted through a series of policies and processes, setting out our risk management approach and appetite in respect of each of the major risks identified. The adherence to each policy and risk appetite limit will be monitored by management through the establishment of a formal governance process. Performance is measured for, and reported to, ExCo and the Risk Committee, with material risk issues explicitly highlighted as they arise and formally reported on a monthly basis.

The RMF will be submitted to the Risk Committee for challenge and debate, following which it will be submitted to the Board for formal approval and adoption. It will be reviewed at least annually by the Risk Committee.

6.12.2 Three Lines of Defence Model

To manage its risks, Orchard will operate a Three Lines of Defence model which segregates risk management by each of the three distinct categories.

6.12.3 First Line of Defence

Operationally, Management have primary responsibility for the identification, measurement and management of all risks. Clear ownership of each specific risk is set out in the Board approved RMF policy documents which establish the limit structures within which Orchard operates. In addition to the day to day risk management processes of Orchard, risk management is overseen through a number of management committees.

The table below provides a more detailed responsibility map against each activity.

Table 29: 1st Line (Ownership and Control) Business Units.

Role	Responsibility
Provision of risk management and control	– Implementation of risk policies – Ensuring compliance with policy across the business – Identification and escalation of incidents, in line with policy – Operations of controls
Development of the understanding of risk	– Development and management of risk mitigation plans – Undertaking scenario analysis
Engagement with the business and customers	– Understanding of, and provision of input to, risk policies – Highlighting specific risk-related issues – Educating staff in the need for risk awareness
Definition and defence of risk strategy	– Input to risk appetite definition through Credit Committee – Implementation of policies, framework and methodology in line with defined appetite and strategy
Taking responsibility for regulatory compliance	– Ensuring that Orchard remains compliant with all relevant laws and regulations – Implementation of changes and enhancements to risk management methodology

6.12.4 Second Line of Defence

The Risk function has responsibility for owning Orchard's RMF, developing the usability of the RMF and for the oversight and challenge of the day to day management, control and reporting of risks. In addition, the function is responsible for providing advisory support to the business on risk related matters.

Risk is responsible for collating and aggregating risk reporting to support the function with regards to forming an independent view of Orchard's overarching risk profile.

The Risk Committee, supported by the Risk function:
- assists the Board in the formulation of Orchard's desired risk culture, risk appetite, risk management strategies, policies and limit structures;
- leads the overall design, implementation and ongoing maintenance of Orchard's RMF; and
- oversees and objectively challenges the management, control and reporting of risks.

The Risk function is responsible for the timely identification of key regulatory changes impacting Orchard, and the development of the Risk & Governance Culture as well as Legal and Regulatory Compliance.

The CRO has a reporting line to the Chairman of the Risk Committee. The table below provides more detailed responsibility map against each activity.

Table 30: 2nd Line (Risk and Compliance).

Role	Responsibility
Policies	Update and challenge of risk policies, which provides the principles and minimum standards for effective risk management
Methodology and Tools	Ownership, development and maintenance of the risk management framework
Training and Communications	Delivery of regular communication to the business on risk- related topics Provision of risk-related training to the Business Units
Oversight	Oversight and challenge of the Business Units on the adequacy and effectiveness of the use of the risk management and methodology in the business The provision of expert support and advice to the business on risk management, including how to interpret and comply with the Risk Policies and to meet the requirements of the respective frameworks
Governance	Communication of concerns to the appropriate manager and of unresolved concerns to Board

6.12.5 Third Line of Defence

Internal Audit is responsible for independent review of the effectiveness of risk management and the control environment at Orchard. Internal Audit report directly to the Chairman of the Audit Committee and have a dotted line to the CEO for day to day operational purposes.

Orchard intends to outsource this work to third party specialists in Internal Audit on an on-going basis. By bringing in an outsourced facility, the following benefits will be realised:
- Suitably qualified and experienced resources from a reputable firm;
- Depth of resources from an outsourced provider available when required and with a greater potential for specific experience in Orchard's specialist business activities;

- Access to external benchmarking and experience through the outsource provider into practices in other banks in the industry as well as expertise in advising on trends and regulatory developments; and
- Appropriate balance of cost against benefit.

The Internal Auditor is required to undertake a program of audit work on a planned and ad hoc basis under the direction of the Audit Committee. They act independently, but will meet with the senior management of Orchard prior to the commencement of any particular audit to discuss their specific audit plans and to ensure that they also address areas of particular concern to management.

Internal audit will further investigate any actual or suspected frauds and any serious control failures under the direction of the CEO and/or the Audit Committee as a third line after Risk. Internal Audit will attend each Audit Committee meeting.

The outsourcing arrangements will remain under review as the business evolves and grows in the future to ensure that it remains the best option. A future solution may be co-sourcing between in-house resources and third parties for specialist capabilities such as IT and cyber risk.

6.12.6 Primary Board Risk Appetite Metrics and Reporting

Periodically the Board and management will review the corporate plan, performance against the plan and the key underpinning assumptions. Reviews can take place more frequently if circumstances change although typically the formal annual review of the Corporate Plan alongside Risk Appetite provides the foundation for review of the key annual regulatory submissions, specifically the ICAAP, ILAAP, Recovery Plan and Resolution Plan.

The detailed risk appetite limits and Early Warning Indicators (EWI) thresholds based on the current business plan are reflected in the ICAAP.

The risk profile will be reported monthly to the ExCo, the Audit Committee, the Risk Committee and the Board supported by commentary on an exception basis (Amber and Red indicators) where they are subject to review and challenge.

The metrics will provide both a point in time position (current month RAG) and an indication of direction of travel versus short and medium term plans. As a consequence, the Board and Executive management are better equipped to decide, at an early stage, whether changes to the plan or to levels of appetite require further consideration.

Full details of the Board Risk Appetite metrics are set out in the ICAAP and ILAAP.

7 Implementation Plan

Orchard will submit its application and has opted to take the mobilisation route to further build teams, products, systems and processes to launch the Bank in 2020.

7.1 Systems plan

The technology development in respect of Orchard's banking business will be in three stages:

1. During mobilisation the core functionalities will be built or enhanced and the Mutual Vision Limited software implemented as well as the API integration into a 3rd party regulatory reporting provider;
2. Up to six months after launch to provide improved customer experience, control and efficiency;
3. During the next 2 years when new products and functionalities will be added.

7.2 Deposits Plan

Orchard will utilise the savings module of a proven software house, Mutual Vision Limited for its deposit business. This software is used by a number of small building societies and banks.

7.3 Lending and Treasury Plan

LendXP will be enhanced to further develop loan underwriting and decision functionality. This will be augmented by Treasury functionality and deposits accounting information to be specified, designed and implemented in mobilisation.
Orchard's options for IT are set out in its IT Plan, which will be finalised during mobilisation.

7.4 Governance

Orchard's Implementation Plan provides for resource and time to create all the processes and the controls that ensure reliability and lower operational risk. The plan also takes into account the task of building the policies and procedures required within the governance framework.

7.5 Generic Implementation Plan

Table 31 below sets out the key work streams during the Mobilisation period. Orchard has produced a detailed Gantt chart, Table 32 (below), which sets out each step to be taken to complete the work streams in the mobilisation period.

Figure 14: Technology build plan.

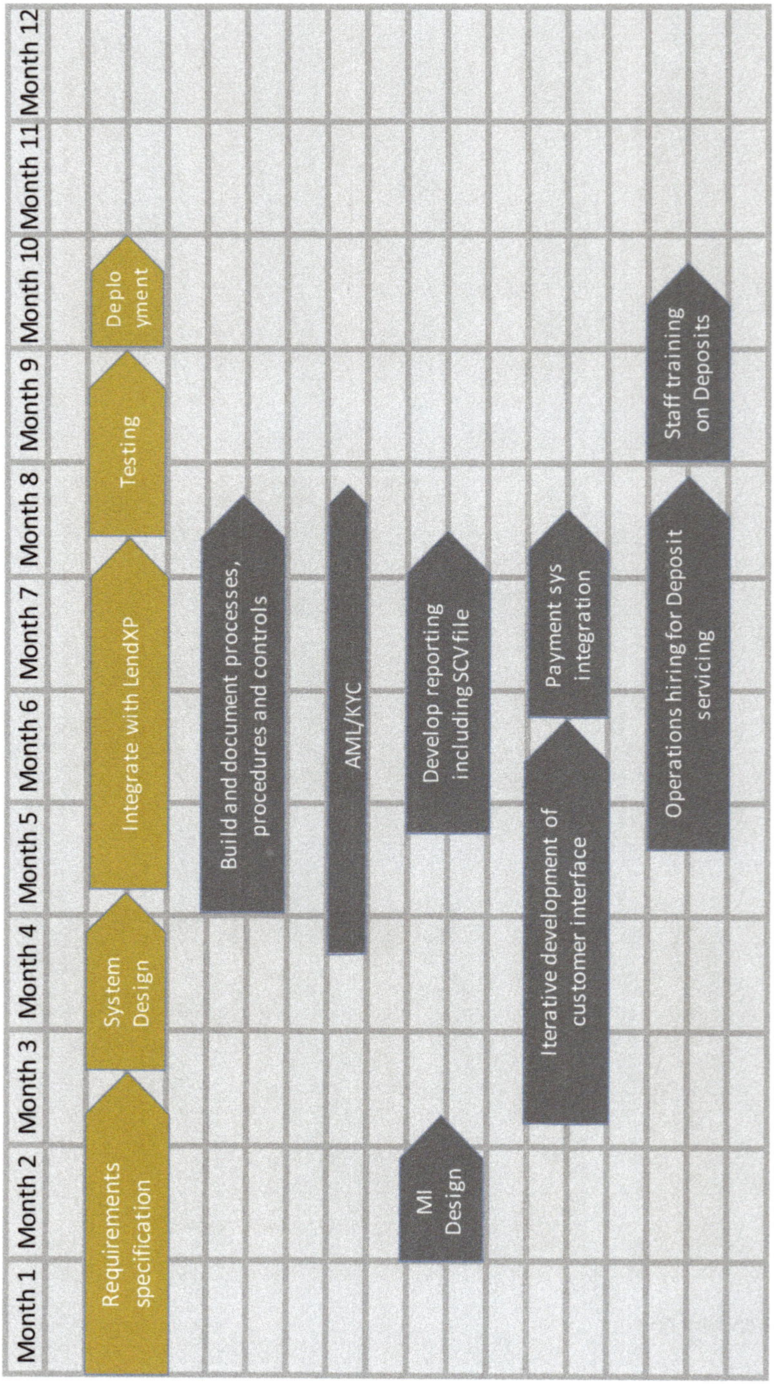

Figure 15: Deposit Software Implementation plan.

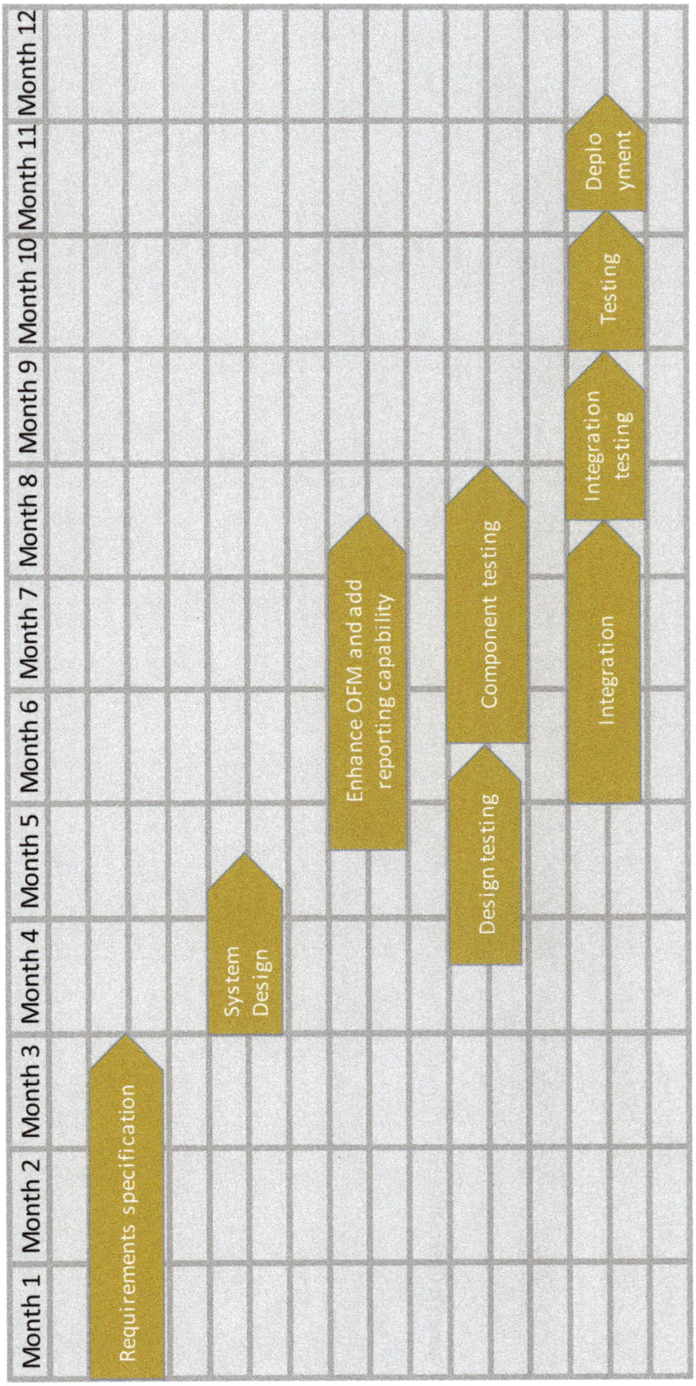

Figure 16: Lending and Treasury plan.

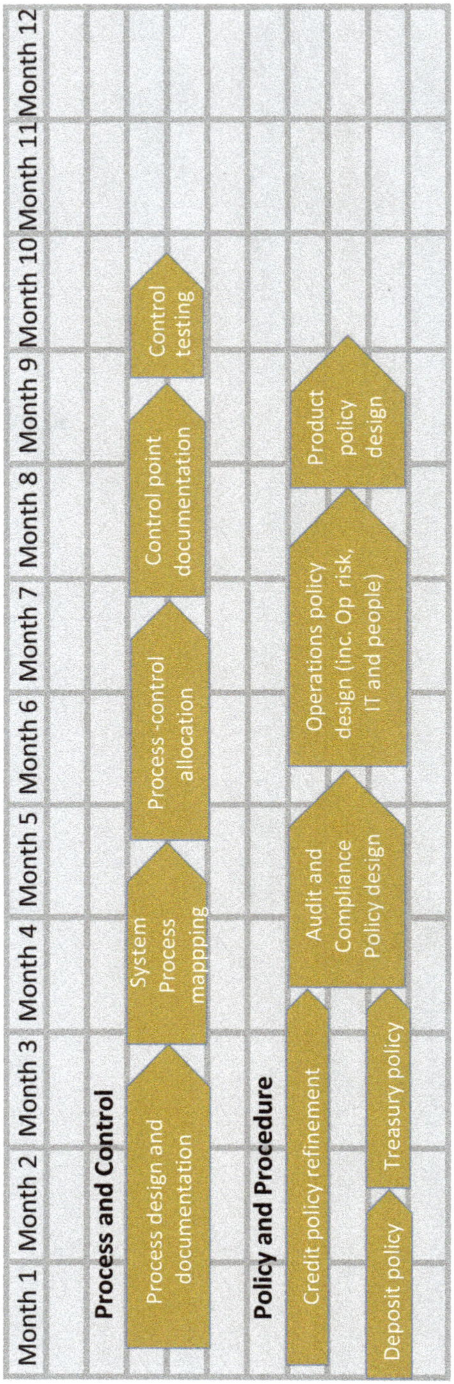

Figure 17: Governance.

Table 31: Generic Implementation Plan.

Group Structure Reorganisation	IT & Infrastructure	People	Marketing	Deposits	Treasury	Risk & Compliance	Board & Committees	Finance	External & Internal Audit
Merging of subsidiaries into PLC	Reporting Changes –New Reports –Analytics & MI –Liquidity Management –SCV Report	Appointment of CFO Appointment of NED	Confirm Name & Brand Appoint Partners (PR, Advertising) Logo, Stationary	Legal documentation	Policies & Procedures	Finalise RMF Finalise Policies & Manuals for all Level 1 & Level 2 Risks	Approve TORs Board Training Program	Due diligence of outsourced provider for regulatory reporting – Test and Finalised Regulatory Reporting Requirements	Appoint External & Internal Auditor
	Documentation –Policies & Procedures –Training Docs –Complex IT Form Completion	Recruitment -CRO -Deposit Administration -IT Assistant -Treasury Assistant	Web-site implementation	Final Product Approval Update Procedures AML Checking Procedures	Complete Agency banking relationship	Compliance –Manual –Processes & Procedures -Training -Plan		Assess system requirements for management reporting, including monitoring of regulatory ratios and requirement.	
	Central Systems –Additional Security Protocols	Documentation –Update SMF and HR Policies	Communications Strategy & Plan		Reporting –Regulatory -ALCO –Deposits –Treasury -Reserve account with BoE			Legal, tax and regulatory implications of reorganisation of the group structure	

Table 31 (continued)

Group Structure Reorganisation	IT & Infrastructure	People	Marketing	Deposits	Treasury	Risk & Compliance	Board & Committees	Finance	External & Internal Audit
	Testing –Penetration Testing –Load Testing –DR Testing –End to End Testing	Assess organisation structure to ensure appropriateness to manage all the activities as a bank and at the same time drive synergies within teams.			Set up the ability to buy short term UK government gilts			Assess control framework and documentation	
	Audit							In conjunction with IT, understand the system architecture, reporting capabilities (current and enhencements)	
	Go Live Outsourcing –Provider Selection –Controls and oversight								

Table 32: Gantt chart.

	Category	Item	Start Date	Time Estimate (Days)
		Mobilisation Start Date	01/07/2020	
IT Systems and Infrastructure	Loan Management	Document Changes	01/07/2020	5
	Loan Management	Testing	01/07/2020	7
	Deposit Management	Agreement of Implementation Timetable	01/07/2020	7
	Deposit Management	Product Design	08/07/2020	7
	Deposit Management	Build Functionality	15/07/2020	14
	Deposit Management	Testing	29/07/2020	90
	Deposit Management	Training	08/07/2020	30
	Deposit Management	UAT	07/08/2020	30
	Deposit Management	Single Customer View	06/09/2020	4
	General Ledger	Deposit Mapping	10/09/2020	5
	General Ledger	Testing	15/09/2020	5
	Integration	Regulatory Reporting	15/07/2020	90
	Reporting Changes	New Reports	13/10/2020	7
	Reporting Changes	Analytics + MI	20/10/2020	14
	Reporting Changes	Liquidity Management	03/11/2020	14
	Reporting Changes	SCV Report	17/11/2020	2
	Documentation	Policies and Procedures	01/07/2020	30
	Documentation	Training Documentation	06/09/2020	7
	Documentation	Complex IT Controls Form	01/07/2020	120
	Central Systems	Data Centre set-up	01/07/2020	14
	Central Systems	Additional Security Protocols	15/07/2020	14
	Testing	Penetration Testing	06/09/2020	3
	Testing	Load Testing	09/09/2020	3
	Testing	DR Test	12/09/2020	1
	Testing	End-to-End Testing	13/09/2020	25
	Audit	External Audit + Sign-Off	08/10/2020	25
	Go-Live	Deployment	02/11/2020	5
	Outsourcing	SLAs with Outsourcing Providers	15/07/2020	14
	Outsourcing	Outsourcing provider selection	01/07/2020	7
	Outsourcing	Outsourcing Controls and oversight arrangements	08/07/2020	7
People	Recruitment	Commence recruitment of Deposit Administration Personnel	01/07/2020	30
	Recruitment	Commence recruitment of Financial Analyst	31/07/2020	30
	Recruitment	Commence recruitment of IT Assistant	30/08/2020	30
	Documentation	Update SMF and HR Policies	30/08/2020	20
Group Structure	Reorganisation	Instruct RSM to consider Corporate re-organisation	01/07/2020	10
	Reorganisation	Instruct RSM to consider Corporate re-organisation	11/07/2020	14
	Reorganisation	Commence discussions with Barclays on warehouse into PLC	25/07/2020	30
	Reorganisation	Effect merging of group entities into PLC	24/08/2020	60
	Reorganisation	Enter into new documentation with Barclays on warehouse into Pl	23/10/2020	30
	Reorganisation	Effect assignment of benefit of all Orchard Funding and Bexhill co	22/11/2020	5
	Reorganisation	Maintain brand names and web-sites for Orchard Funding and Bex	00/01/1900	0
Marketing	Branding	Confirm name and brand	27/11/2020	5
	PR	Select and appoint partners (PR, Advertising, design, creative etc)	27/11/2020	5
	Branding	Logos for headed stationery	02/12/2020	15
	PR	Communications strategy and plan	02/12/2020	30
	PR	Product literature and brochureware, Business cards	17/12/2020	30
	Branding	Website implementation	17/12/2020	30
	PR	Regulatory statements	16/01/2021	30
	PR	Correspondence style and tone	01/01/2021	30
	PR	Press campaign and management	31/01/2021	20
	PR	Advertising	20/02/2021	30
	PR	Customer communications	20/02/2021	30
	PR	Meetings with aggregators (Moneysupermarket, Moneyfacts etc)	16/01/2021	21

(continued)

Table 31 (continued)

	Category	Item (Mobilisation Start Date: 01/07/2020)	Start Date	Time Estimate (Days)
Savings	Recruitment	Commence recruitment of deposit administration personnel	01/07/2020	30
	Training	Train deposit administration personnel	31/07/2020	30
	Legal	Legal documentation	01/07/2020	14
	Legal	Draft customer letters for LendXP	01/07/2020	14
	Operations	Evaluate overflow telephone back up procedures	01/07/2020	7
	Operations	Product development and approval	01/07/2020	7
	Operations	Define procedures and workflow processes	01/07/2020	30
	Operations	AML Checking procedures	01/07/2020	7
	Operations	Key controls - static data, payments processing, cheque processing	01/07/2020	14
	Operations	PEP Sweep processes	01/07/2020	14
	Risk Management	Regulatory risk assessment	01/07/2020	30
	Operations	Define internal hand-offs - marketing, finance, treasury	01/07/2020	7
	Product	Develop SME/commercial deposit product procedures	01/07/2020	7
	Operations	Define key control reports	15/07/2020	14
Treasury	Treasury policy and proc	Document and agree treasury procedures	01/07/2020	5
	Treasury policy and proc	Define and develop spreadsheets for Treasury management	06/07/2020	7
	Treasury policy and proc	Define key controls and mechanisms	13/07/2020	7
	Treasury policy and proc	Establish counterparty limits and facilities	20/07/2020	7
	Treasury policy and proc	Develop asset and liability management techniques, facilities, rep	20/07/2020	14
	Treasury policy and proc	Establish ILAA and ICAAP operating framework	20/07/2020	14
	Treasury policy and proc	Establish Contingency Funding Plan procedures	03/08/2020	7
	Banking counterparties	Approach Barclays for Agency Banking	01/07/2020	7
	Banking counterparties	Develop relationships with banking counterparties	08/07/2020	4
	Banking counterparties	Open Crest Account	01/07/2020	5
	Banking counterparties	Establish basis for day 1 liquid assets buffer	03/08/2020	30
	Reporting	Define regulatory reports	01/07/2020	2
	Reporting	ALCO reporting	03/07/2020	30
	Reporting	Deposits reporting	03/07/2020	5
	Reporting	Treasury Holdings	03/07/2020	70
	Reserve Ac	Open reserve account facilities with Bank of England	02/09/2020	14
Risk & Compliance	Risk Management	Finalise risk management framework	01/07/2020	7
	Risk Management	Define key controls	08/07/2020	7
	Risk Management	Define risk management monitoring and reporting requirements	15/07/2020	7
	Risk Management	Define risk appetite for Board approval and on-going monitoring	08/07/2020	14
	Risk Management	Define credit control procedures	15/07/2020	14
	Risk Management	Training and development of staff	29/07/2020	7
	Risk Management	Update AML procedures and policy	15/07/2020	7
	Compliance	Update Compliance Manual	03/08/2020	4
	Compliance	Update Compliance processes and procedures	29/07/2020	5
	Compliance	Update Compliance risk assessment framework	03/08/2020	5
	Compliance	Update Compliance training programmes for all staff	03/08/2020	30
	Risk Management	Concentration Risk Policy	29/07/2020	7
	Risk Management	Provisioning Policy	29/07/2020	7
	Risk Management	Financial Risk Management Policy	22/07/2020	7
	Compliance	Initial 12 month compliance plan	15/07/2020	7
Board	Board & Committee	Approve terms of reference	06/07/2020	5
	Board & Committee	Draw up timetable and agendas for Committees	11/07/2020	7
	Board & Committee	Board training programme	11/07/2020	7
Internal Audit	Internal Audit	Business requirements specification	01/07/2020	7
	Internal Audit	Tender process	08/07/2020	21
	Internal Audit	Selection Committee	29/07/2020	7
	Internal Audit	Evaluation, interview, selection and appointment	05/08/2020	14
	Internal Audit	Structure and Resources	19/08/2020	7
	Internal Audit	Methodology	26/08/2020	14
	Internal Audit	Plan for 12 months from Authorisation	09/09/2020	14
Finance	Regulatory Reporting	Define regulatory and statutory reporting procedures, formats and	01/07/2020	7
	Regulatory Reporting	Define COREP/FINREP requirements	08/07/2020	14
	Regulatory Reporting	Evaluate CRD IV requirements and timetable	08/07/2020	14
	Agency Banking	Consider bank account for deposits	08/07/2020	14
	Audit	Open dialogue with auditors	01/07/2020	7

8 Appendix 1: Customer Journey

Orchard Direct Business Customer Journey

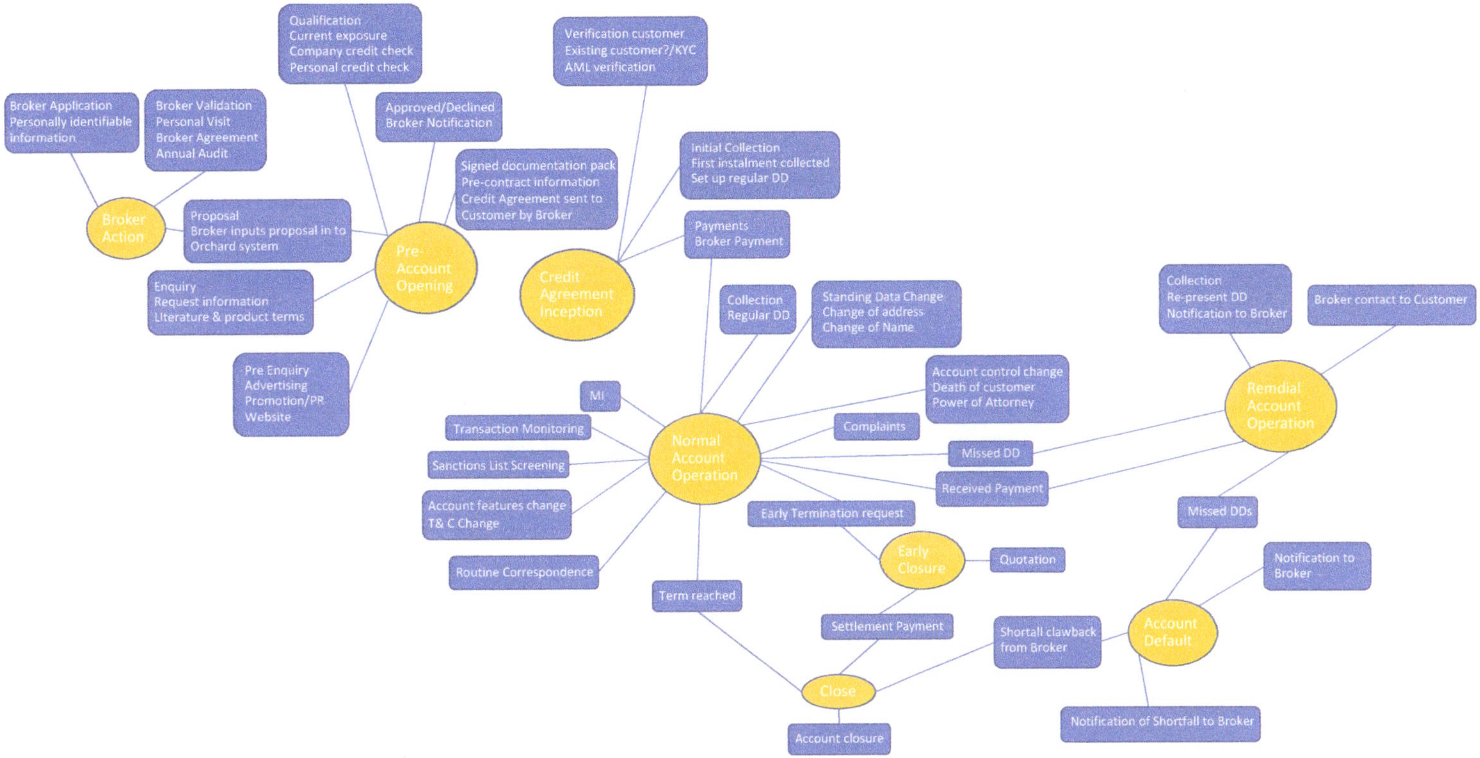

During mobilisation the areas of greatest risk in the customer journeys will be identified and a control framework will be put around them using the 3 lines of defence.

Orchard Customer Journey for Depositors

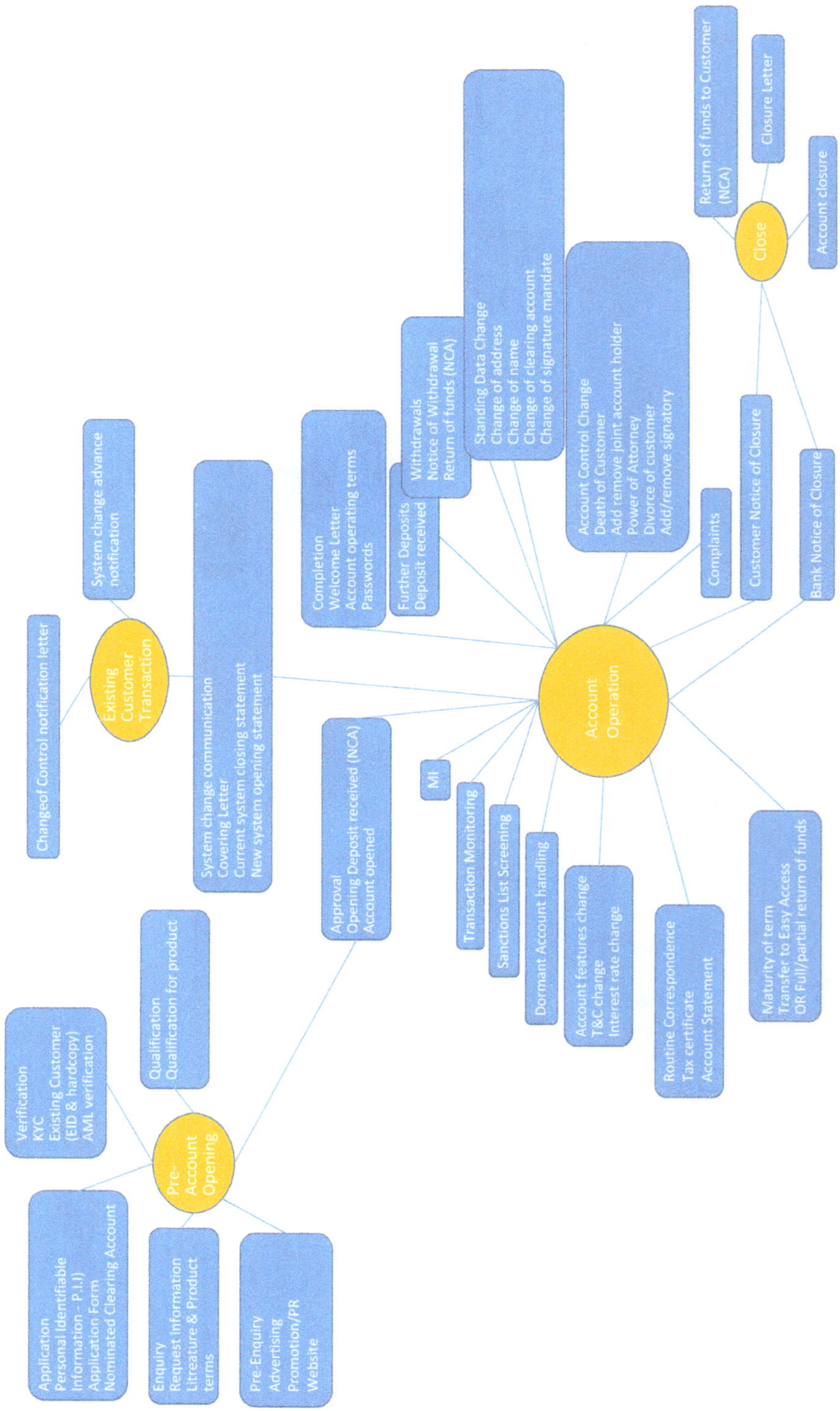

3 The Internal Capital Adequacy Assessment Plan (the "ICAAP")

3.1 What is Capital and Why is It so Important?

In simple terms capital is that cash amount that is due to the shareholders of a company. It is made up of the amount invested in the company and the profits that have been retained (i.e., not paid out) by the company.

Let's put some numbers around this. The shareholders of a new company put £10,000,000 cash into the company. The company makes £1,000,000 profit each year for 5 years after it has paid all its expenses including tax. At the end of year 5, the company has capital of £15m.

Let's now assume the Company is a bank. The bank has £15m capital. If the bank lends £15m and loses it all, the shareholders have lost all their money. This is sad for the shareholders but doesn't really impact anybody else, so in this situation there is no real adverse impact to society or the financial system.

What a bank can do, which is quite unique to a bank, is leverage its capital with the benefit of that leverage being guaranteed by the UK government. So the parties providing that leverage will always get their leverage back.

Let's explain this in a little more detail. A CFO of a listed company once asked me what leverage is – so it's a very fair question and very often completely misunderstood.

Again let's put some numbers around this. Our little bank has £15m of capital. With its bank licence it can ask the public to deposit £100 million cash with it. The public are very happy to do this as they know that the repayment of their deposit is guaranteed by the government. The public want a return of course but due to the UK government guarantee of repayment, the public are very happy with a very modest return.

So look what's happened to our little bank. It started with £15m capital, which let's say is £15m cash. Now with the benefit of the deposits from the public it has £115m cash. The cash it started with is now miraculously levered by over 6 times and it currently only holds 15% capital, i.e., £15m on its deposits of £100m.

So let's assume it now makes £115m of loans with its cash and £115m of loans go bad. Now not only have our poor shareholders lost their investment, but it looks like all of the public's cash has been lost as well. As stated the public will ask the government to pay them back and the government will have to do this. Now our problems really start.

First, the government has had to pay out depositors. As money doesn't grow on trees, the public will end up paying for this either in increased taxes or reduced services.

That's bad enough, but second and more dangerous is the impact to the financial system.

https://doi.org/10.1515/9783111101545-003

Seeing one bank failing may cause depositors in other banks to ask for their money back from the bank, so they can safely put it under their mattress. This shouldn't be a problem, should it? You put your money into the bank and therefore as the bank has big safes and puts all our money into those safes, surely when we ask for it back, they just open the safe and give it back to us. Again, not so simple. When we deposit our money into the bank, the bank in our example uses that money to make loans. These loans may be perfectly safe. The problem is that depositors may have put their money into the bank for a short term, but a loan will generally be for a longer term. This is what banks do, they turn our short-term deposits into longer-term loans for their other customers, who are borrowers. Depositors are of course also very important customers. The term of art for this is maturity transformation and is a key function of the banks.

In summary, therefore, a depositor asks for its money back, but the bank says 'Sorry I have lent that money and haven't got cash at the moment. Do you mind waiting a bit?' This of course leads to panic. Again, the government gets called up and must make the payment to the depositors.

You can see the problem if depositors keep asking for their money back, and banks have to rely on the government to pay their depositors: more and more depositors ask their bank for their cash back; the government has to make more and more pay-outs; and eventually the banks have no cash to make new loans to their customers or to make profit from those loans, and so the economy slowly but surely grinds to a complete halt. This is exactly what happened in the Depression of the 1930s. It was worse then, as all depositors did not have the benefit of the government guarantee, but the principle is the same as even in the Global Financial Crisis of 2008, where there were government guarantees, depositors queuing outside Northern Rock Bank PLC for the return of their deposits nearly brought down the financial system.

How does this all relate to the question we started with? What is capital and, more importantly, how does it protect depositors and the financial system.

Going back to our first example where the bank only had £15m capital and made £15m of bad loans, only the shareholders of the bank lost out.

In the second scenario we still have £15m capital, but now we had £115m of cash and in this case when the bank made £115m bad loans, it put the financial system in crisis.

How can we then protect the financial system?

In the extreme the bank could be told that it was only allowed to keep the cash raised from the public in the bank. This would be great from a security perspective, but not very good for the bank as it would have to pay interest on that cash and not be earning any money on it and not very good for the economy as borrowers could not borrow that money to buy things with.

So, we need a compromise. That compromise and balance and the rules around that compromise and balance can easily fill huge buildings with complex financial and legal documentation. As always, it can still be kept relatively simple so that bank CEOs can actually understand what they are supposed to do. They can of course get this horribly, horribly wrong even under the keen eyes of a Regulator. The latest example being the financial crisis of 2008. Therefore, at times keeping things as simple and clear as possible enables everyone to at least understand and hopefully apply the rules that maintain the balance.

Let's use numbers again.

Currently bank regulators believe a prudent starting point is to look all of the assets of the bank and then determine the minimum level of capital that is required to protect depositors, if the assets default.

Let's say the assets are the £115m of loans referred to above. Table 2 provides a breakdown of the Assets.

Table 2: Breakdown of Funding of Assets.

Assets (Loans)	£115m
Cash	£0 (it's all been lent out!)
Depositors Money	£100m
Shareholders' Investment	£15m

In this scenario (Table 2), £15m of the Loans would have to not pay, before Depositors could lose any money.

In simple terms you could say the Shareholders Investment of £15m is protecting the Depositors as their £15m (13%) will be lost first if the Loans don't pay.

Just for the record, 13% loss would be considered a very high and unprecedented number for a normal bank.

For example, mortgages require 2.8% minimum capital to be held by the bank. Therefore, if our bank wrote £115m of mortgage loan assets, it would only be required to hold £3.2m of capital. It has £15m of capital, so in this case the bank is considered to be very well-capitalised.

Unsecured loans however require 8% minimum capital to be held by the bank. Therefore, if our bank wrote £115m of unsecured loans, it would be required to hold £9.2m of capital. As it has £15m of capital, the bank is again considered to be very well-capitalised.

In order of priority, the ICAAP must be regarded as the second key document that forms part of the bank licence application. As its name clearly suggests the ICAAP will contain a very thorough review of the bank's capital and the adequacy of that capital to deal with a variety of bad things (stresses) happening to the bank.

Exasperating for Applicants, different people at the Regulator read different documents relating to the Application and in many instances never appear to speak to each other. Therefore, Applicants are often frustrated by having to answer the same question put by the party reading one application document, which has already been answered to a party reading another application document.

This frustration follows through to the drafting of each of the documents. Each document will contain a lot of information and detail, which has already been set out in the other documents and is just duplicated in each of the core application documents. Applicants should not try to cut corners by referring to the other documents in the application pack. Each document must be treated as stand-alone and not require the reader to reference another application document. Frustrating, but at least you know up front that this is a fundamental requirement of the Regulator.

Now let's walk through the document, which has been known to strike fear and panic into the strongest of Chief Financial Officers.

3.2 Background to Business Activities of the Applicant

This section is a verbatim copy of the RBP, which sets out the following matters from the RBP.

1. Historic financial performance of the applicant;
   a. Lending Target market;
   b. Lending products;
   c. Deposit Target market;
   d. Deposit products;

3.3 Business Viability

This section will again be taken verbatim from the RBP and will set out the business projections of the bank and why they are viable. This section will highlight the trajectory of loan book and deposit book growth of the bank.

3.4 Financial and Operating Statistics

Without wanting to labour the point, this section is also a verbatim copy of the RBP and sets out the 5-year plan financial statements including:

a. Income statement
b. KPIs
c. Lending volumes
d. Deposit volumes
e. Balance Sheet
f. A summary of the Capital Requirements of the bank as a result of the financials set out above and a summary of the key liquidity ratios.
g. After Capital Requirements, this section of the ICAAP will include a summary of capital resources and other funding resources of the bank.

3.5 Governance

You will not be surprised to know that again, this section is a verbatim copy from the RBP of the Governance Framework of the bank. The ICAAP will set out again:

a. A description of each member of the board and their role, with a detailed summary CV of each member of the Board.
b. A detailed description of each board members roles and responsibilities;
c. A detailed assessment of each board members skills and experience, including a Skills & Experience Matrix which sets out in tabular format the scoring of each board members skill set and marks them from 1–4 from expert, to 4, where the relevant skill is managed by another board member.
d. A detailed description of each of the board and executive committees, their composition and a summary of their Terms of Reference.
e. An SMR Responsibilities Map, which sets out each senior management function and the relevant member of the board who will be responsible for that function.

So, the first 100-odd pages of an ICAAP are usually exactly the same as the RBP. The reasons for this are as stated.

3.6 Risk & Compliance Management Framework

The next section of the ICAAP, is the commencement of the more rigourous review of the Risk Management Framework of the bank and the detailed analysis of the capital requirements of the bank in its normal day-to-day business and when it suffers financial distress caused by its own actions or caused by the market in general or by a combination of internal and market causes. One of the key drivers of the ICAAP is to determine what will break the bank, the infamous Reverse Stress Test and what impact that will have on the capital resources of the bank.

The ICAAP considers each risk that may affect the bank in detail. We will review each of these risks below.

1. Credit risk. Credit risk is defined as the risk of a borrower failing to pay interest or fees or to repay the principal on a loan on time. Interestingly a bank has 2 key types of credit risk. The obvious one from lending its money to borrowers and a less obvious credit risk which arises from the fact that it has to deposit the cash given to it in a financial institution (either itself or another institution)

The money can be put into the Bank of England or into other financial institutions. Financial institutions can go bust so banks have limits on the credit quality of the institutions that cash can be deposited with and the amount of cash placed with one financial institution.

2. Capital Risk
This is the risk that the bank will have insufficient capital to cover unexpected losses, meet regulatory requirements or support the growth plans of the Bank.

A bank will take the Pillar 1 capital formula calculations, which provide a standardised approach for credit, market and operational risk. This will then be required to show that it has fully considered whether the standardised approach provides sufficient capital to adequately absorb potential losses arising from the anticipated risks that may impact the bank. The PRA also are very interested in the nature of the capital that will support the bank's business. For new banks the Regulator will want to see all or most of the capital comprised as Core Tier 1. This effectively means that the capital has bas been invested into the bank as equity and is only returnable to investor through an effective wind-down of the banks operation and is subordinate to the claims of all third parties to which the bank has a liability. Most importantly for the bank capital can never be repaid to investors before all claims to depositors have been repaid in full.

Due to the mathematics of risk weighting and the alchemy of financial engineers the capital for the bank can still be a tiny percentage of all the assets on the balance sheet of the bank. Pre-global financial crisis a number of banks had managed to engineer their assets so that the banks' capital actually formed less than 1% of the total assets owned by the bank. If most of those assets are for example sub-prime mortgage loans it can be seen how a small change in the quality and performance of the assets can quickly drain the capital that is supposed to be supporting those assets.

The Regulator has therefore introduced a further ratio called the Leverage Ratio. This ratio stated that regardless of the capital requirement produced by applying risk-based models to the assets of a bank, the bank will be required to hold a minimum of 3.5% of capital against all its assets. The Leverage Ratio therefore limits the total leverage that can be obtained on the assets of the bank to a maximum of 96.5% of the value of those assets. Still quite high, but not as high at the 1000s of percent, that some institutions achieved pre the Global Financial Crisis.

The Regulator requires banks to maintain additional capital to its Pillar 1 capital requirements in the form of Pillar 2A capital. Pillar 2A capital is related to further capital to manage potential losses arising from operational failure at the ban.

Finally, the Regulator may require further capital buffers under Pillar 2B. These further buffers will be based on an assessment of the bank's risk management and governance framework. Further capital buffers for capital conservation, market cycles (counter cyclical buffers) and for systematically important banks may also be imposed on a bank. The additional buffers will be applied if they exceed the PRA buffer, i.e., those buffers will not simply all be applied on top of the PRA buffer but only to the extent that they exceed such buffers.

3. Liquidity Risk
This risk is the risk that the bank is unable to meet its financial obligations as they fall due.

Banks are required to comply with a number of liquidity ratios. The key ratios are set out and will be discussed in more detail in the ILAAP chapter.

Liquidity Coverage Ratio.
The LCR calculates the cash flows expected to come into the bank and the expected cash outflows from the bank. (Cash inflows are usually related to the cash that will be collected in from the assets of the bank and outflows on the expected withdrawal of deposits and maturity of deposits.)

A bank must demonstrate in flows will meet outflows. The Regulator has a minimum 100% requirements on this ratio.

Net Stable Funding Ratio
The NSFR examines the stable funding available to the bank in the form of capital and deposits and the employment of that funding in-to the assets of the bank. Again, the Regulator will need to be satisfied that the NSFR is at least 100%.

4. Interest Rate Risk in the Banking Book
This is the risk arising from unhedged or mismatched assets and liability positions, which are sensitive to interest rate movements.

Interest rate risk arises in the following circumstances:

Re-pricing risk	Timing differences between maturities of fixed-rate assets and liabilities and re-pricing of variable-rate assets and liabilities (including off-balance sheet). This can expose Orchard to changes in the shape of the yield curve
Basis risk	Asset and liabilities re-price at the same time but in line with a different interest rate basis, e.g., assets re-price with reference to Bank of England base rate but liabilities re-price with reference to LIBOR.
Pipeline risk	The uncertainties arising where actual movements do not match those that were expected.
Optionality risk	Where early terminations of assets and liabilities compared to the original term can worsen mismatch positions.

Banks are required to set a sensitivity level in terms of impact on CET1 capital arising from interest rate risk.

5. Operational Risk
Operational risk is the risk of loss resulting from inadequate or failed processes or controls, weak or failed governance, adverse people-related issues, system failures, or from external adverse events (including those arising from financial crime incidents, conduct issues, cyber risks and failings in the management of legal or regulatory issues). Such events, were they to materialise, would adversely affect the ability of the bank to achieve its corporate objectives or adversely impact the reputation of the bank.

Banks are expected to have a low operational risk appetite, with the understanding that a zero-tolerance level is not realistic.

Banks will set a maximum appetite for operational risk in an amount of pounds sterling over the course of a year, with a maximum amount for individual incidents.

There are a number of components of operational risk which are set out below:
1. Infrastructure and Operational Resilience
2. Conduct Risk, including Treating Customers Fairly
3. Data Management
4. Financial Crime & Sanctions
5. Financial Reporting Tax & Audit
6. Fraud
7. Security & Cyber risk
8. Legal & Regulatory
9. Model Risk
10. People Risk
11. Physical Security & Safety
12. Regulatory Compliance
13. Strategy and Governance
14. Third Party Management
15. Transaction Processing

Risk Register

As a core component of its RCMF, a bank will be required to create a Risk Register. The Risk Register is also utilised to determine whether sufficient capital has been allocated to Operational and other risks by comparing the total residual score to the minimum capital requirement for operational risk under CRD IV.

An example of a Risk Register and the detail of the risks captured are set out in the ICAAP chapter 3.7.

Risk Scoring

Each risk on the Risk Register is assessed for its "inherent" (uncontrolled) probability and impact to create an inherent risk score. Controls applied to this risk, and the effectiveness of the controls determines not only the "residual" (controlled) probability and impact, but also whether further activity to improve the control environment is required.

Probability (Likelihood) of a Risk Materialising into an Event

The probability of a risk crystallising is assessed against a 5-point scale, ranging from remote to certain. The exact interpretation of the points on the scale is guided by reference to the frequency of the activity in the Table 3, which also includes the values used for scoring the probability in calculating consequences.

Table 3: Probability of Risk Materialising into an Event.

Term	Frequency of Activity/Operation			Value
	Daily operations	**Weekly and monthly operations**	**Quarterly, bi-annual or annual operations**	
Remote	Once per year	Once every 5 years	Once in a century	0.40%
Unlikely	Every two months	Once per year	Once in 25 years	1.50%
Possible	Every month	Twice per year	Once in a decade	8.00%
Frequent	Every week	Once per quarter	Once a year	40.00%
Certain	Every day	Every week	Every occasion	100.00%

Impact Measurement

As well as a direct monetary loss or cost, it is possible for impact to be measured in terms of damage to the Bank's reputation, the impact on customers, or the management involvement away from business as usual ('BAU'). Each of these is mapped to one of five aligned degrees of severity, with the monetary value mid-point being used in the calculation of consequences against the probability. Thus, it is possible to consider each impact, for example disruption to the bank's customers, in terms of other impacts, such as the management time and cost of rectification. Each level of severity is also mapped to the management of the risk (when applied to the residual consequence) and the timescale and management oversight and reporting for events.

The threshold for an extreme monetary loss is set with reference to the maximum aggregate operational losses during a year, as expressed in the Statement of Risk Appetite. Any risk with a residual score above this criticality threshold requires the active management of the Risk Committee as it is outside of the bank's risk appetite and therefore has the potential to cause extreme disruption, although this does not mean *ipso facto* that the management team have failed to manage the risk. Criticality thresholds for other levels were determined by dividing the extreme threshold by 5. Let us assume the extreme threshold is £250k, this would therefore be £50k and £10k. For 'Extreme' events this is set at 5 times the threshold value and would in our example therefore produce a result of £1.25m to the threshold of £250k. This represents a consistent step change in the monetary value used for calculating the consequence of a risk. The monetary value of the mid-point is the average of the ranges specified for the degree of severity.

Table 4 sets out the criticality of Risk Impacts from Nominal to Extreme.

Risk Scoring

The product of the likelihood and the (monetary) impact produces a consequence. As the table of risk impacts (Table 4) provides insight into the criticality of an impact, the table of consequences (Table 5) can be shaded to guide the management of risks, including the appropriate level of ownership and oversight. This empowers the relevant levels

Table 4: Risk Impacts.

	Category				
	Nominal	**Minor**	**Significant**	**Material**	**Extreme**
Escalation timescales for loss events	One working day	End of working day	Within 1 hour	Immediate	
Information escalation	Manager	Senior Manager/ Head of Function	Executive	Executive (& Board for information)	Board
Management of Risks	Control Operators	Manager	Senior Manager/ Head of Function	Executive Committee	Risk Committee
Ownership of Risks	Manager	Senior Manager/ Head of Function	Executive Committee	Risk Committee	Board
Monetary	£0 – £2,000	£2,000 – £10,000	£10,000 – £50,000	£50,000 – £250,000	Over £250,000
Reputational – Potential Regulatory impact – Potential media or social media interest	Potential for media interest but unlikely	Local media interest	Need to inform Regulator Local media coverage Industry coverage	High level of Regulator interest National Media Coverage Some wider public interest	Formal disclosure to Regulator Potential s166 action High level of national media interest
	Notify Executive Manager **immediately** Executive Manager will inform Board	Notify Executive Manager **immediately** Executive Manager will inform Board	Notify Executive Manager **immediately** Executive Manager will inform Board	Notify Executive Manager **immediately** Executive Manager will inform Board	Notify Executive Manager **immediately** Executive Manager will inform Board
Customer – Impact on customers	Limited customer impact (fewer than 20)	Small Number of customers (20 – 100 customers)	Some customers (100 to 5% of customer base)	Major customer impacts (5% to 10% of customer base)	Customer impacts across Bank (>10% of customer base)

Table 4 (continued)

	Category				
	Nominal	**Minor**	**Significant**	**Material**	**Extreme**
Management - Potential impact on colleagues/ management - Potential impact on achievement of business objectives	Small incident that is managed as part of BAU	Response has limited impact on management or colleagues Temporary impact on Business objectives	Some impact on business objectives and/or Income	Formal response invoked (e.g., BCP) 10% of colleagues affected. Income reduced by <10%	Significant Exec involvement, over 25% of colleagues affected Severe impact on Business Objectives and Income

of the business to actively manage their own risks, and to consider whether the assessed level of residual risk is acceptable, as (for example) an improvement in controls could cost more than the anticipated reduction in the residual risk score, indicating that this particular risk control would not be cost effective.

Table 5: Risk Impacts of Table of Consequences.

Consequences			Likelihood				
Impact	**Range**		**Remote**	**Unlikely**	**Possible**	**Probable**	**Certain**
	From	**To**	**0.4%**	**1.5%**	**8.0%**	**40.0%**	**100.0%**
Nominal	**£0**	**£2,000**	£4	£15	£80	£400	£1,000
Minor	**£2,000**	**£10,000**	£24	£90	£480	£2,400	£6,000
Significant	**£10,000**	**£50,000**	£120	£450	£2,400	£12,000	£30,000
Material	**£50,000**	**£250,000**	£600	£2,250	£12,000	£60,000	£150,000
Extreme	**£250,000**	**(Unlimited)**	£5,000	£18,750	£100,000	£500,000	£1,250,000

Criticality of risks is determined by comparison of the residual risk score against the criteria used to assess the impact ratings. Thus, any risk is assigned a level of management and oversight appropriate to the criticality of its risk exposure after the application of controls. Any risks with a residual score greater than the threshold value for 'Extreme' will be managed under the control of Risk Committee, and ownership (ultimate accountability) and oversight rests with the Board, who would need to determine how the activity giving rise to the residual score should be mitigated: tolerated (accepted, at least for now, with regular reviews); terminated (the activity should cease within a specified timescale); transferred (for example, an insurance policy would be taken out against the risk materialising); or treated (controls improved to an agreed plan and timescale). Risks with a 'nominal' residual score (that is, less than £2,000) would be managed by those who operate the controls with oversight from their line manager. This allows the bank's Executive to exercise oversight of nominal, minor and significant risks and to manage any risks with a material residual consequence, keeping the material and extreme risks in sight of the Board and the Risk Committee.

3.7 Pillar 1

Now at last we come to the Pillar 1 capital requirements. Here starts the journey on determining the amount of capital a bank will require for the operation of its business.

As its name suggests, Pillar 1 capital is the first and minimum level of capital required by a bank to conduct its business.

Pillar 1 Credit Risk
Credit risk is the risk of suffering financial loss, should any of a bank's customers or counterparties fail to fulfil their contractual obligations to the bank.

Pillar 1 Credit Risk Calculation
Pillar 1 Credit Risk Weighted Assets (RWAs) are calculated by what is known as the standardised approach (CRD IV CRR Part 3, Title II, Chapter 2), which effectively uses the asset exposure multiplied by predefined percentages that vary with the exposure type to give a risk-weighted asset (RWA). The predefined percentages are termed standardised risk weights and examples of these are provided below:

- Exposures to the Bank of England. A bank will be exposed to the Bank of England if it deposits cash with the Bank:
  - 0% Risk Weight (RW) per article 114(4)

Therefore, if a bank deposits £1m with the Bank, the 0% RW confirms that there is no risk to the bank getting that money back and therefore no capital has to be set aside to manage that risk.

- Exposures to financial institutions:
  - RW between 20%-100% driven by the credit rating of the institution and the term of the exposure.

Therefore, if a bank deposits its cash with another bank, there is a risk that that bank may not be able to pay back that cash. If the cash is deposited with one of the High Street banks for a short-term, will generally lead to a 20% risk weighting.

- Loans to individuals and SME clients:
  - 75% for live loans <€1m and where the customer meets the 'Retail' definition (as per CRR Article 123).

  - 150% on all non-performing loans
  - A scalar of 0.7619 applied to SME's in line with CRR Article 501

RWs in this section move between 75% to 150% depending on the risk associated with the asset. As can be seen, a non-performing asset is given a 150% RW due to the obvious risk to the bank of getting paid back.

- Loans to Corporates
  - 100% for exposures to unrated corporates (Article 122)

As corporate borrowing is generally limited in liability to the assets of the corporate, a 100% RW is applied to lending to corporates who do not have a credit rating from a recognised credit rating agency.

- All other assets (e.g., fixed):
  - 100% per Article 134. Intangible assets are deducted from capital per article 36.

Pillar 1 capital requirement for credit risk is then calculated at 8% of credit RWAs.

For example, if a bank has or plans to have £10m of corporate loans to unrated corporates on its balance sheet, the Pillar 1 Credit Risk calculation will be:

£10m X 8% = £800k. The bank will therefore need to demonstrate that it has £800k equity capital to support its £10m loan book. In other words, if 8% of the £10m is not repaid to the bank, the £800k capital will be able to absorb that loss.

Pillar 1 Operational Risk

Operational Risk is the risk of loss as a result of inadequate or failed internal processes, people, systems, and/or external events.

Pillar 1 Operational Risk Calculation

The capital allocation is based on the Basic Indicator Approach (BIA), Title III, Chapter 2 of CRD IV, which is 15% of a three-year average of the sum of the bank's net interest income and net non-interest income. For existing banks, this is a calculation based on historic net income numbers. For new banks, this is based on a projection of future net income.

Pillar 1 Market Risk Calculation

Market risk is the risk that the bank's earnings or capital, or its ability to meet business objectives will be adversely affected by changes in the level or volatility of market rates or prices such as interest rates and equity prices

Most new banks will not plan to have a trading book of bonds, for example, whose value is directly impacted by changes in interest rates. New banks will therefore generally not need to hold capital under this part of the Pillar 1 calculation. Capital for interest rate risk in the bank's assets may still need to be held aside under Pillar 2A, which will be discussed in more detail below.

3.8 Pillar 2A

Pillar 2A risks are risks that are either not considered under Pillar 1, or are risks that are considered under Pillar 1 but where the bank believes that the Pillar 1 capital amount is insufficient to address the risks.

We will review each Pillar 2A Risk in detail below.

Pillar 2A Credit Risk

Capital is set aside under the Pillar 1 calculations set out above. Under Pillar 2A the bank will need to consider and assess whether the capital set aside under Pillar 1 for credit risk is adequate. If the capital for credit risk under Pillar 1 is determined to be insufficient, additional capital will require to be allocated under Pillar 2A for credit risk. One method for determining whether Pillar 1 credit risk capital is adequate is to look at historic losses for the bank. Where the bank does not have a track record of credit performance the bank should point to credit loss information in respect of the asset class from other bank lenders in the market.

Pillar 2A Operational Risk

Pillar 2A Operational Risk assessment reviews the risk register, governance process and risk appetite of a bank to determine whether additional capital is required other than the Pillar 1 Operational Risk calculation.

We will review each part of the Pillar 2A operational risk calculation.

– Risk Register

Each identified risk is included separately in the Risk Register in a specified category as set out in the Risk & Compliance Management Framework with a full description of the risk and a *probability x impact* inherent score and the residual score after mitigating factors. The risks are then assessed for potential capital eroding factors over and above that captured by the Pillar 1 operational risk capital resource requirement.

– Pillar 2A Operational Risk Add-on

Pillar 1 states the minimum capital requirements for operational risk under the Basic Indicator Approach (BIA). In testing the capital adequacy of this amount, the Pillar 1 requirement is compared to the outcome from idiosyncratic stress used in evaluating the impact of stress testing (see below) and also to the residual risk score from the risk register. If either the idiosyncratic scenario or the risk register is found to be greater than the minimum requirement, then the difference is additional Pillar 2A operational risk capital requirement. If both are greater than the minimum, then the higher value of the two is used to estimate the Pillar 2A operational risk requirement.

Pillar 2A Credit Concentration Risk

Credit concentration risk is the risk of losses to a bank arising from concentrations of exposures due to imperfect diversification. This imperfect diversification can arise from the small size of a portfolio or a large number of exposures to specific obligors (single name concentration) or from imperfect diversification with respect to economic sectors or geographical regions.

Following publication of updated PRA's Statement of Policy 'The PRA's methodologies for setting Pillar 2 Capital' in April 2018, the PRA now requires firms to submit data to enable them to calculate a credit concentration risk measure, the Herfindahl-Hirschman Index ('HHI') for single name, sectoral and geographical credit concentration risk. The HHI index is based on risk-weighted assets ('RWAs') to reflect a degree of risk sensitivity and is mapped into a capital add-on range for the purposes of calculating the Pillar 2A concentration risk component.

The key drivers of concentration risk and the portfolios in scope under the new Pillar 2 approach are as follows:

- Single name concentration risk: top 20 wholesale credit (non-retail) portfolio exposures excluding intragroup exposures and defaulted assets. This might include 'cash at bank' as the loan book is all non-wholesale (either SME or Retail SME).
- Sector concentration risk: wholesale credit (non-retail) portfolio exposures excluding intragroup exposure and defaulted assets. This may include exposure arising from 'cash at bank'.
- Geographic (international) concentration risk: wholesale and retail credit portfolio. For a UK bank only, this includes all credit risk exposures in the UK.

In the updated Statement of Policy, the PRA noted that in order to promote consistency of judgement, there will be a default presumption that, unless there are compelling reasons to deviate from it, the credit concentration risk add-on will fall to the mid-point of the capital range for each credit concentration risk bucket.

Although the explanation of the concentration risk capital calculation is complex, the actual calculation itself is relatively simple.

The credit exposure to each of the buckets is calculated, from that calculation, the RWAs are calculated and then a percentage add-on is applied for each category.

For example, in numeric terms Table 6 sets out an example of the additional Capital required for each concentration risk:

Table 6: Pillar 2A Credit Concentration Risk Calculation.

	Credit Exposure	RWAs	Capital add-on %	Pillar 2A Concentration Capital
Single Name Concentration	1,000,000	200,000	3.5%	7,000
Sector Concentration	1,000,000	200,000	1.75%	3,500
Geographic Concentration (eg all UK)	34.075m	23.113m	1.33%	307

Pillar 2A – Interest Rate Risk in the Banking Business
Pillar 1 Interest Rate Risk deals with interest rate risk arising from Market Risk. New banks will almost invariably not be trading instruments such as bonds and therefore Pillar 1 is less relevant. Under Pillar 2B, Interest Rate Risk is the risk from changes in market interest rates that adversely impact the Net Interest Income (NII) arising from a bank's assets and liabilities. This is far more relevant to new banks, whose business plan will predominantly focus on the creation of assets in the form of a loan book and the creation of new liabilities in the form of customer deposits. Therefore, the adverse impact on NII can mainly arise from three different risk types.

1. Duration risk
   This risk arises from maturity mismatch of fixed rate assets and liabilities. A shift in market interest rate becomes effective with re-pricing when the assets and liabilities mature and hence, a mismatch will result in some assets/ liabilities re-pricing earlier and others later, which will therefore impact the Net Interest Income.
2. Basis risk
   This risk arises from the different market rate basis used as the anchor point to determine the product pricing. Since the different available market rates, e.g., Bank base rate, or other reference rate, do change on a different basis as there is no perfect correlation between the pricing of assets on one market benchmark and the pricing on another. This will therefore give rise to a risk on NII.
3. Optionality
   This risk arises from the flexibility built into contractual terms, i.e., the flexibility to repay a fixed rate loan earlier or withdraw a fixed rate deposit. In certain instances, the cost of optionality risk is factored into the contractual terms, which will penalise early settlement.

Other interest rate risk is the pipeline risk, which arises from the variation in the expected verses actual business written.

Each bank is expected to complete form FSA017 to indicate the economic value at risk arising from a 2% parallel shift in Year 1, i.e., what impact does a 2% shift in the bank base rate have on the NII of the bank and as a consequence how much capital a bank should set aside to manage this risk. A bank's risk-appetite for IRRBB will be determined by this assessment. For example, a target impact on CET1 may be set at, say 2%, with an Amber Trigger at 2.7% and a Red Trigger at 3%.

Business Risk

Business risk is defined as the potential loss (or inability to realise planned revenues) arising from the inability to properly implement strategic plans.
As this risk is covered by so many other capital requirements, and most banks will argue that the risk will be heavily mitigated, most banks will not allocate further capital under this Pillar 2A capital calculation.

Reputational Risk

Reputational risk is the risk of a loss of reputation of the bank, for example, as a consequence of a failure to manage principal risks or from inappropriate conduct by any member of staff – particularly senior management given their relatively higher visibility in the market.

Each bank will state that it has considered all potential risks in the risk register, some of which could impact the reputation of the firm. Each bank will also state that the costs for these risks have all been considered, including the associated reputation risk that would arise as a result and therefore no further capital allocation is required beyond that already included in the operational risk add-on.

Money Laundering Risk

Money laundering is the risk of accepting deposits from illegal activities.

Again, any bank worth its salt will demonstrate that it has a control environment in place to prevent money laundering risk, so additional capital under this heading is not generally applied by new bank applicants.

Insurance Risk

Again, for new bank applications the allocation of any capital for this risk will not be applicable. Generally, new bank applicants will have very general insurance cover for standard business risks, including buildings and contents, a banker's blanket bond policy, computer crime, PI, if applicable, and D&O cover.

Pension Obligation Risk

Again, new bank applicants will not generally be exposed to risk relating to pensions liabilities and no Pillar 2A capital calculation will therefore be applicable.

Securitisation Risk

Again, new bank applications will generally not have been involved in the securitisation of assets and no Pillar 2A capital calculation will therefore be applicable.

Key Person Risk

Key Person risk is the risk that a key person is no longer able to work for the bank or that a key person leaves the business.

Most new bank applications will provide for a period of recruitment costs and interim management if a key board member is no longer available to work for the bank. The additional capital cost is therefore mitigated and should not add a material amount to the capital calculation.

Residual Risk

Residual risk covers the inadequacy of credit risk mitigation techniques including the residual value of loan collateral and any other unknown risk (including loss of business, internal fraud, external fraud and/or emergency recruiting costs) that might arise in the course of business.

New bank applicants will state that the controls employed by their business to control their operational and other risks are included within the risk register. The 'residual risk score' will be the estimated exposure to bank after the application of these controls. This will be compared to the Pillar 1 operational risk capital requirement, and if the total residual risk score is higher than the requirement, the additional amount is included in the Pillar 2A operational risk charge.

In general, all new bank applicants will state that all residual risks will be covered by the Pillar 2A operational risk charge and further capital is not required to be allocated under the Pillar 2A Residual Risk calculation.

Therefore, we have dealt with Pillar 1 and Pillar 2A capital requirements. As described above, the requirements are largely prescriptive, and many are completely irrelevant for new bank applications.

However, our story on Capital is very far from over.

As well as Pillar 1 and Pillar 2A capital requirements, there is a further set of capital requirements called the Pillar 2B Capital Requirements or the PRA Buffer.

3.9 Pillar 2B Capital Requirements – the PRA Buffer

The Pillar 2B Capital Requirements provide a further layer of capital over the Pillar 1 and Pillar 2A capital requirements. Pillar 2B calculations are broken down into 2 parts:

1. A simple calculation of capital based on a percentage of RWA for each of the 3 capital buffers set out in CRD IV:
   a. Capital conservation buffer – for example 2.5% of RWAs;

b. Countercyclical buffer – for example this could be set at 1% of RWAs; and
c. Systemic buffer – a capital buffer to address the systemic importance of the bank to the financial system. As this will obviously not apply to a new bank applicant it is not considered relevant for this discussion.

Therefore, as can be seen from the above the PRA capital buffers could add a significant uplift to the 8% standardised capital requirement.

2. A calculation of the additional capital that will be required to cover losses that may arise under a severe stress scenario that may impact the bank. The stresses that are applied to the bank are called Market-wide, Idiosyncratic and Combined. Each of these stresses will be considered in more detail below.

The Pillar 2B capital calculation therefore starts with the PRA Capital Buffers and then compares them to the additional capital that would be required by the bank to cover losses under the sever stress scenarios. If calculation 2) is less than calculation 1), no further capital will be required. If 2) is greater than 1) then the incremental capital representing the difference will be added to the bank's total capital requirement.

There is an additional Pillar 2B requirement for risk management and governance weaknesses that is determined by the PRA based on their assessment of a firm's risk management and governance. Under the guidelines in the publication 'A review of requirements for firms entering into or firms expanding in the banking sector: one year on', this is less likely to be applied for new bank applicants. In essence, this is due to the fact that the PRA will not grant a licence to a new applicant unless they are entirely satisfied with the applicant's ability to manage risk and entirely satisfied with its senior management and governance arrangements.

One further point to note for new bank applications. As new banks will not be able apply stresses to a long-standing historic business, the PRA has stated that the Pillar 2B capital requirement will be simply calculated by applying an additional capital requirement equal to the projected wind-down costs of the new bank. This in effect ensures that in addition to the Pillar 1 and 2 capital requirements a new bank will have sufficient capital to wind itself down in an orderly manner.

3.10 Stress Testing

Stress testing is designed to determine capital levels that will be required by a bank to withstand bad things happening to the bank. Bad things are put into three buckets, with a fourth added for completeness and I am sure for some entertainment:

1. Market-wide – this is also known as the 'Anchor' scenario. As the name suggests a number of market-wide stresses are applied to the business of the bank to determine the impact of those stresses on the bank's capital. The scenarios are created

by the Bank of England. The key elements of these scenarios are deep simultaneous recessions in the UK and global economies.

2. Idiosyncratic stress – As the name suggests a number of stresses relating to the business of the bank specifically are applied to determine the impact of those stresses on the bank's capital.
3. Combined stress – This stress is a combination of market-wide and idiosyncratic stress. Due to the idiosyncratic stress, the impacts from the market-wide stress will be exacerbated.
4. The reverse stress is driven by a massive market shock and its intention is to determine what would cause the bank to effectively reduce the capital of the bank to below the minimum requirements of the PRA.

Market-Wide Stress

Each bank will review the Bank of England Anchor Scenario and select the economic variables that are the most relevant to the bank's business.

The bank will then design a simple relationship of the selected macroeconomic variables to the business drivers by associating the relative change between its base and stressed economic variables to the business drivers. The economic variables applied to the business drivers of the bank may therefore be as follows:

- Unemployment rate, which may for example be assumed to drive the level of impairment losses
- Household income, which may for example be assumed to drive the level of savings
- Base rate, which may for example be assumed to drive both the cost of funds as well as the lending rate
- Consumer credit, which may, for example be assumed to drive the lending originated by the bank

Based on the above assumptions, the impact on the business drivers is presented below.

The Anchor stress may also include an independent stress of misconduct costs.

Table 7 below shows an example of the derivation of the impact on key business drivers from forecast macro-economic statistics in a market-wide stress.

Table 7 sets out a base case scenario that a bank may utilise in its forecasts of key macro-economic variables:

Table 7: Base Case Scenarios.

Base Case	**Year 1**	**Year 2**	**Year 3**	**Year 4**	**Year 5**
Unemployment (%)[1]	4.1	4.1	3.9	3.8	3.8
Household income (£bn)[2]	382.8	394.3	411.0	428.0	445.4
Base rate (quarterly average – %)[3]	0.90%	1.01%	1.11%	1.18%	1.23%
Consumer credit (%)[4]	6.10%	6.00%	6.10%	6.10%	6.30%

Table 8 sets out an example of the Anchor scenario for each of the key macro-economic variables set out above.

Table 8: Market-Wide Stress Scenarios.

	Plan	**Plan**	**Plan**	**Plan**	**Plan**
Market -Wide	**Year 1**	**Year 2**	**Year 3**	**Year 4**	**Year 5**
Unemployment (%)[1]	8.3	9.2	8.6	7.9	7.3
Household income (£bn)[2]	361.4	374.1	394.8	412.2	428.5
Base rate (quarterly average – %)[3]	4.00%	4.00%	4.00%	3.75%	3.25%
Consumer credit (%)[4]	(0.60%)	(4.70%)	(0.10%)	2.50%	4.80%

A simple comparison of the 2 tables demonstrates that in the base case employed by the bank there is for example an assumption that unemployment will be 4.1%. This materially increased in the Anchor scenario to 8.3%. Equally, household income materially falls within the same period, the base rate is increased materially from 0.9% to 4% and the level of the growth rate of consumer credit falls substantially in the same period.

demonstrates an example of how the Anchor Stresses are assumed to impact the business of the bank pre any management action being taken to manage the impacts.

Table 9: Anchor Stress Impacts pre- Management-Actions.

Anchor pre mgt action	**Year 1**	**Year 2**	**Year 3**	**Plan**	**Plan**
Impact on business drivers					
New lending	(6.7%)	(10.7%)	(6.2%)	(3.6%)	(1.5%)
Loan Rate	+3.1%	+3.0%	+2.9%	+2.6%	+2.0%
Net new Deposits volumes	(5.6%)	(5.1%)	(3.9%)	(3.7%)	(3.8%)
Deposit rate	+3.1%	+3.0%	+2.9%	+2.6%	+2.0%
Impairment charge % of asset	+1.0%	+1.2%	+1.2%	+1.1%	+0.9%
Expenses increase from prior period	+0.0%	+0.0%	+0.0%	+0.0%	+0.0%
Bank funding margin increase vs plan	+3.1%	+3.0%	+2.9%	+2.6%	+2.0%

The bank will then need to set out the management actions that it will take in response to the stress.

The following list includes examples of actions that could be taken by management:

- Drop lending rates to maintain volume. For example, it could be assumed that a 25 bps reduction in lending rates would mitigate the adverse impact on volumes of lending by half.
- Raise deposit rates to maintain funding. For example, it could be assumed that a 25 bps increase in deposit rates would mitigate the adverse impact on volumes of new deposits by half.
- Reduce the dividend paid to investors to retain capital.

Further actions could also be considered by management, for example:

- The introduction of new lending products to enable the maintenance of margins
- A review of the deposits strategy, for example to consider whether 3 and 6 month products could be introduced

Table 10 sets out the effect of management actions on the business drivers set out in the table above.

Table 10: Stress Impacts post Management Actions.

Stress input parameters – impact of mgt action	Year 1	Year 2	Year 3	Year 4	Year 5
Lending volumes increase	+3.4%	+5.4%	+3.1%	+1.8%	+0.8%
Loan rates reduction (bps)	25	25	25	25	25
Deposit volumes increase	+2.8%	+2.6%	+2.0%	+1.8%	+1.9%
Deposit rates increase (bps)	25	25	25	25	25
Dividend payout	(20.0%)	0%	0%	0%	0%

Idiosyncratic Stress

For the idiosyncratic stress a bank will generally look at operational risks and credit risk, which are relevant to its business. Therefore, for credit risk, losses could be inflated from the base case assumptions to higher levels, for example where base case is 1% losses, credit losses could be increased to 3%.

Operational risks relevant to the bank and set out in the Risk Register will be considered and the impact of stresses on those risks can also be calculated. As well as the direct impact of the operational shortcomings, the indirect impact on business drivers should also be considered as part of this stress test.

Operational Risk
A bank will consider the increased capital required due to stresses being applied to a number of key operational areas of the bank.

For example, stresses may be applied in respect of the business areas listed below:

1. Key persons – the bank will consider the impact of sudden and unforeseen resignations of one or more key members of staff and the capital that will be required to remedy this for the business;
2. Senior Management Conduct failure – the bank will consider the impact of the business of the bank being conducted in a manner which is detrimental to customer interests;
3. Cyber-attack – the bank will determine the impact of a cyber-attack that stops staff or customers from accessing the bank's IT systems;
4. Third-Party & Processing Failure – the bank will determine the impact of a main IT supplier's system failure;
5. Failure of Fraud Prevention – the bank may consider the fraudulent re-direction of depositors' money to fraudster's accounts.

The bank will assess each operational risk quantitatively and calculate the additional capital that will be required to absorb the losses from those stresses.

As a result of an idiosyncratic operational risk stress, a bank will also need to consider the knock -on impact that such a stress will have on business drivers.

A bank may, for example, determine that the idiosyncratic operational risk will reduce its lending by 20% or reduce the volume of deposits that it is able to attract by 20%.

A bank will demonstrate that it will take a number of actions in response to an idiosyncratic stress, for example:

- Management will initiate the Recovery Plan immediately.
- There will be pro-active communication with customers, introducers of business and depositors to provide assurance and updates on the status of the business.
- As lending volumes suffer, the lending rate is reduced to generate more business. An assumption could be made that a 25 bps reduction will mitigate the adverse impact on volumes by half.
- Deposits rates are increased to attract and retain deposits. Again an assumption can be made that a 25 bps increase will mitigate the adverse impact on volumes by half.
- Expenses are increased over Years 2 and 3 to resolve the underlying operational issues.
- Dividends paid by the bank could be reduced or not paid for a period so that capital can be preserved and utilised to manage the idiosyncratic stresses.

As well as operational idiosyncratic stresses impacting capital requirement, a bank will also run idiosyncratic stresses relating to its own business, for example in the form of a stress which increases the loss rate on its loan book.

The idiosyncratic operational stress impact will be compared against the idiosyncratic credit stress impact and the higher of the capital impacts will be taken as the additional Pillar 2B idiosyncratic capital requirement.

Combined Stress

A bank will be expected to combine the market-wide stress with the idiosyncratic stress and should also assume that its business drivers will be further impacted *cumulatively* by the combination of the stress scenarios. Table 11 provides an example of the impacts that could be modelled on the key business drivers in the Combined Stress Scenario. The references to Idiosyncratic scenarios 2 and 4 are to the idiosyncratic operational stress scenarios referred to above.

Table 11: Combined Stress Impacts Pre-Management-Actions.

Combined pre mgt actions input parameters	Year 1	Year 2	Year 3	Year 4	Year 5
Lending volumes reduction	26.7%	30.7%	21.2%	13.6%	6.5%
Loan rates increase (bps)	310	299	289	257	202
Deposit volumes reduction	15.6%	15.1%	11.4%	8.7%	6.3%
Deposit rates increase (bps)	335	324	314	282	227
Bad debts % of lending	2.02%	2.24%	2.21%	2.08%	1.92%
Bank funding margin increase	+310	+299	+289	+257	+202
Idiosyncratic scenarios 2 and 4	1,265,000	0	0	0	0
Dividend payout (% PBT)	40%	40%	40%	40%	40%

After a Combined Stress Management could respond in a number of ways to manage the stresses. Examples of potential management actions are set out below:

The following actions will be taken by management and are modelled below:

- Drop lending rates to maintain volume. For example, it could be assumed that a 25 bps reduction will mitigate the adverse impact on volumes by half.

- Raise deposit rates to maintain funding. For example, it could be assumed that a 25 bps increase will mitigate the adverse impact on volumes by half.
- Incur expenditure to resolve the underlying issues
- Cut the dividend to zero for all 5 years

Other actions that could be considered by management:
- Reduce lending to lower margin customers.
- Decrease deposit rates at the cost of lower deposits. At the same time, make a concerted effort through pro-active customer contact to retain maturing deposits.

Stop non-essential operating expenses such as marketing, given the objective of not attracting new business. Expenses and staff recruitment would be deferred where possible.

Reverse Stress

The final series of stresses to be applied to the bank's business is termed the Reverse Stress Test. The Reverse Stress test is viewed separately since it is specifically designed to model circumstances that render the bank's business model unviable.

The Reverse Stress can for example be driven by a massive market shock that impacts the customers' loan repayment ability severely.

The escalating losses could result in depositors losing confidence in the bank, resulting in a dramatic decrease of deposits available for the bank. In order to manage retention of existing deposits, interest rates may have to be increased. This action still does not close the funding gap and hence, the lending plan is revised downwards. The remaining funding gap is closed by bank facilities. Given the overall deteriorating position of the business the bank facilities are offered at much higher rates.

Table 12 sets out an example of the Reverse Stress test impacts on key drivers of the bank.

Table 12: Reverse Stress Impacts.

	Year 1	Year 2	Year 3
Lending volumes reduction	40.0%	40.0%	40.0%
Loan rates reduction	7.0%	7.0%	7.0%
Deposit volumes reduction	90.0%	100.0%	100.0%
Deposit rates increase	5.0%	5.0%	5.0%
Bad debts	12.0%	12.0%	10.0%
Expenses increase YoY	25.0%	25.0%	20.0%
Bank funding margin increase	7.0%	7.0%	7.0%

The Reverse Stress Test scenario is designed to create several unprecedented and very severe stresses to the business of the bank in order to determine the level of stress that would effectively make the business insolvent.

In a Reverse Stress scenario example management actions that could be taken are as follows:

- Initiate wind-down of the bank's business to ensure depositors are repaid
- A shut down of all non-essential activities to manage down the costs and preserve as much of the capital as possible
- Reduction of new lending
- Although unlikely to materialise, assess the possibility of further capital injections from investors to maintain the business of the bank

Therefore, as summarised above, the bank will need to determine the extra capital required to manage and maintain the capital of the bank in the stress scenarios referred to above. The extra capital required will form the Pillar 2B capital requirement of the bank.

Mobilisation

Where a new bank plans on undertaking a Mobilisation of its business prior to obtaining its full licence to obtain deposits, the ICAAP will set out full detail of the Mobilisation Plan.

3.11 Template ICAAP

Contents

Tables

Figures

1 Introduction

1.1 Scope of the ICAAP

This is the first Internal Capital Adequacy Assessment Process ("ICAAP") prepared by Orchard Funding Group PLC ("Orchard") in support of its banking licence application.

Orchard is an AIM listed finance company specialising in providing finance to SMEs and consumers in the insurance premium finance market and the professions finance market.

The Orchard group lent £68.7m in the year to 31 July 2018 and generated revenue of £5.2m and profit before tax of £1.9m. The group's lending book was £31m at 31 July 2018. The accounts to 31 July 2019, which are subject to approval at Orchard's AGM, show lending book growing to £32.1m at the end of the financial year, revenue of £5.5m and profit before tax of £2.0m.

Orchard raised £10.0m (before expenses) of capital through the issuance of 10.4m shares on AIM in July 2015. The current capital base of Orchard is £14.0m at 31 July 2018 and subject to shareholder approval £14.97m at 31 July 2019. This will comprise the initial capital (subject to deduction of intangible assets) of the proposed new bank, which will be called Orchard Bank PLC.

For the purposes of this document Orchard should be read as Orchard Funding Group PLC or the newly licensed Orchard Bank PLC, as the context so requires.

This ICAAP is underpinned by and will demonstrate a number of matters:

1. Due to Orchard's short-term amortising credit products with an average life of less than 6 months, Orchard's lending book can be converted to cash in a very short period of time.
2. The purpose of the credit products to finance essential items such as insurance or professional fees means that there is a very high propensity to ensure payments

are met. This is demonstrated by Orchard's minimal losses on its credit products throughout its 16-year history of lending.

3. Unlike other lending business, Orchard's credit products are fully guaranteed by the introducing broker or professional firm.
4. In summary, Orchard therefore has a very high degree of confidence based on its historic experience that loans written by Orchard will repay fully over a short period of time.
5. The historic experience of Orchard's performance over a 17-year period, coupled with Orchard's current capital base, provides comfort that Orchard's capital base will always exceed its regulatory capital requirements throughout the base financial operating plan.
6. This ICAAP will provide a detailed breakdown of the regulatory capital that Orchard has calculated that is required to be held in respect of its business in accordance with regulatory requirements.
7. The ICAAP will also demonstrate that the actual capital that Orchard will hold will always materially exceed the required capital to be held by Orchard by over 300% during the entire 5-year plan.

The ICAAP is the process under which the management and Board of Orchard oversees and regularly assesses:
- Orchard's processes, strategies and systems;
- the major sources of risk to Orchard's ability to meet its liabilities as they fall due;
- the results of internal stress testing of these risks to assess capital adequacy under stress conditions; and
- the amounts and types of its financial and capital resources, and whether or not these are adequate to meet regulatory requirements.

This document sets out the framework for Orchard's internal governance, and the operation of the risk and capital management arrangements. In particular the document sets out:
- the internal governance structure;
- the key risk areas that are relevant to Orchard;
- the risk management framework;
- the adequacy of capital resources in relation to the overall risk profile and hence, Orchard's overall ability to meet its liabilities as they fall due; and
- how the ICAAP is used in the business.

The ICAAP is proportionate to Orchard's business model, scale, complexity and risk appetite, and takes into account all sources of capital. Its key purpose is to document and demonstrate the level of capital which the Board and management of Orchard believe is necessary for its prudent operation and management under both, normal business conditions and stress conditions.

For the purposes of this ICAAP, the business plan assumes no material change in Orchard's business strategy which alters or increases its risk profile over the business plan period.

The ICAAP process will be carried out annually or more frequently if there are changes in Orchard's business strategy, balance sheet, the nature or scale of its activities, or its operational environment suggest that the level of capital resources is no longer appropriate.

Monitoring and maintenance of capital adequacy will take place on a regular basis.

The assessment set out in this document is undertaken on a forward-looking basis from the first year of deposit taking activity post approval under the base case and from the second year under the stresses.

1.2 Process and Methodology

The ICAAP process in Orchard is interactive and involves all relevant parts of the Orchard business. Whilst carrying out the ICAAP, the Board of Orchard has considered and assessed the universe of risks that are being run in Orchard. The financial risks (Credit Risk, Market Risk, Capital & Liquidity Risk) were assessed looking at maximum possible capital requirements in extreme stress scenarios.

For non-financial risks, conduct, operational and the other risks which are sub-sets of operational risk, a top-down risk assessment of the business has been performed by the Board. For each risk, all Orchard's controls and other mitigants which are or will be in place were considered, and the risk scores recalibrated to produce a residual risk. The impact and probability have been multiplied to produce a potential capital cost for that risk as detailed in section 8.3, Operational Risk.

1.3 Challenge and Approval by the Board

Review, challenge, agreement and approval has formally been provided by the Board at various stages of the ICAAP process, including but not limited to, the approval of the base business plan that was reviewed on 30 May 2019 and approved on 16 July 2019, review and challenge to the stress scenarios on 30 May 2019 resulting in changes to the stress scenarios and review of the stress output to assess the implications for the business and the approval of this document. After the implementation of amendments required and a further review by the Board, the ICAAP was formally reviewed and challenged by the Board on 17 October 2019 and 14 November 2019.

The ICAAP will be updated at least annually and more frequent reviews will be undertaken, if appropriate, in the light of changes in market or circumstances specific to Orchard.

The Board has ultimate responsibility for the ICAAP and submission to the PRA. The Board will ensure that the ICAAP is fully integrated into the day-to-day risk management processes of Orchard as set out under section 1.4 below. Capital adequacy will be a standing agenda item at the Board.

The ICAAP will be updated annually for submission to the PRA on request, but the risk identification process that supports the ICAAP is embedded in the work of Orchard's Board Committees and, in particular, the Risk Committee. The Board, which has ultimate accountability for setting risk appetite (which is formulated and recommended by the Risk Committee), challenges risks identified and ensures that the appropriate mitigants are put in place to assure these are managed appropriately.

Orchard has devised and run a number of stress scenarios against its Base Financial Operating Plan and has identified the key risks to the business and the mitigants that can be employed by management to manage these risks.

The processes for the governance, challenge and adoption of the ICAAP are set out in sections 5 and 6 of this document.

1.4 Use of the ICAAP

At the highest-level Orchard uses the ICAAP as a mechanism for keeping capital requirements under ongoing review both to ensure compliance with PRA requirements but also to understand the risks and capital implications of any changes to the business strategy (e.g., the introduction of new products, customer segments and regulatory changes) and market conditions. Specifically, it uses the ICAAP for three primary purposes:

- Stress testing to identify key vulnerabilities to certain stress scenarios. These also help to provide feedback to the Board in relation to certain aspects of the agreed risk appetite.
- Capital planning – The approaches and methodologies given in the ICAAP document are incorporated into the forward business plans in order to provide a forward view of capital adequacy, and therefore to determine whether there is sufficient capital available to support planned business growth. Also, assessing the impact on capital where there is a significant change to the strategic business plan.
- To identify, monitor, and report material risks inherent within the business model and to assist in the management of those risks on an ongoing basis.

The outputs of the ICAAP process have been incorporated in the Key Risk Indicators, with set targets, early warning indicators and triggers to actively manage, monitor and if necessary, take management action.

1.5 Executive Summary

Orchard has been trading as a finance business since 2002. As a result, it will commence its deposit taking activities as a bank with core tier 1 equity of more than £14m.

The table below shows capital projections over a 5 year period.

Table 1: Orchard 5 Year Capital Forecast.

Base	**Plan Year 1**	**Plan Year 2**	**Plan Year 3**	**Plan Year 4**	**Plan Year 5**
Pillar 1					
Credit risk on loan assets	1,839	2,272	2,893	3,812	5,218
Credit risk on bank balances	16	16	16	16	16
Fixed assets	5	5	6	6	6
Credit risk on HQLA	0	0	0	0	0
Total credit risk	**1,860**	**2,294**	**2,914**	**3,834**	**5,240**
Operational risk basic indicator	672	750	879	1,135	1,504
Pillar 1 capital requirements	**2,532**	**3,043**	**3,793**	**4,969**	**6,743**
Pillar 2A capital requirements					
Operational risk	147	111	25	0	0
Business risk	0	0	0	0	0
Reputational risk	0	0	0	0	0
Credit concentration risk	319	391	494	647	881
Interest rate risk in the banking book (IRRBB)	165	142	338	325	325
Residual operational risk from risk register	0	0	0	0	0
Pillar 2A capital requirements	**631**	**644**	**857**	**972**	**1,206**
Total capital requirement (Pillar 1 + Pillar 2A)	**3,163**	**3,687**	**4,650**	**5,942**	**7,949**
Share capital	9,797	9,797	9,797	9,797	9,797
Audited retained earnings	5,081	6,454	8,498	11,597	16,422
DTA on operating losses (Deduction)	0	0	0	0	0
Intangible Assets (Deduction)	(421)	(490)	(552)	(608)	(661)
Total Capital resources	**14,457**	**15,761**	**17,744**	**20,786**	**25,558**
Risk weighted assets (Credit + Ops)	**31,652**	**38,039**	**47,413**	**62,117**	**84,294**
Total Capital requirement % of RWAs	**10.0%**	**9.7%**	**9.8%**	**9.6%**	**9.4%**
Pillar 2B	**1,050**	**1,102**	**1,158**	**1,215**	**1,276**
TCR + Pillar 2B % of RWAs	**13.3%**	**12.6%**	**12.2%**	**11.5%**	**10.9%**
CET1 % of RWAs	**47.0%**	**42.7%**	**38.6%**	**34.4%**	**31.1%**
Surplus / (deficit) capital	**10,244**	**10,971**	**11,936**	**13,629**	**16,332**

Orchard has completed a number of stress tests, over a three year period, in respect of its future business projections to assess the impact of such stresses on the capital position of the business.

The 4 key stress tests conducted by Orchard are as follows:

1. Market-wide (anchor) stress
2. The stress has been designed to test the impact of a number of combined stresses on the business. The stresses are designed to be extreme and severe to determine the impact on capital requirements, liquidity and Orchard's financial position.
3. Idiosyncratic stress
4. Management has assessed the operational risk quantitatively via five idiosyncratic scenarios and with due consideration, taken the "Third Party and Operational Failure" scenario. The direct impact of this scenario is £675k of costs in respect of an alternative IT supplier and fines. In addition, there are adverse impacts on business drivers, including additional operating costs.
5. Combined stress
6. This stress takes account of a more severe market-wide stress scenario, in combination with the idiosyncratic stress scenario.
7. The reverse stress
8. This stress is driven by a massive market shock that impacts the loan book impairment charges and in turn, results in depositors losing confidence and hence, initiating other expensive funding options. This drives the business model to become unviable with the capital resources being eroded to below minimum requirements.

The economic variables from the most recent PRA ACS 2019 used for the base and stress scenarios are as follows:

Table 2: Economic assumptions.

Base Case	Actual 2018 Q4	Plan Year 1	Plan Year 2	Plan Year 3	Plan Year 4	Plan Year 5
Unemployment (%)[1]	4.0	4.1	4.1	3.9	3.8	3.8
Household income (£bn)[2]	372.0	382.8	394.3	411.0	428.0	445.4
Base rate (quarterly average – %)[3]	0.75%	0.90%	1.01%	1.11%	1.18%	1.23%
Consumer credit (%)[4]	6.60%	6.10%	6.00%	6.10%	6.10%	6.30%

Table 2 (continued)

Market -Wide	Actual 2018 Q4	Plan Year 1	Plan Year 2	Plan Year 3	Plan Year 4	Plan Year 5
Unemployment (%)[1]		8.3	9.2	8.6	7.9	7.3
Household income (£bn)[2]		361.4	374.1	394.8	412.2	428.5
Base rate (quarterly average – %)[3]		4.00%	4.00%	4.00%	3.75%	3.25%
Consumer credit (%)[4]		(0.60%)	(4.70%)	(0.10%)	2.50%	4.80%

[1]UK unemployment rate (LFS definition, all, aged 16 and over, seasonally adjusted, %). ONS code: MGSX.
[2]UK household nominal income (nominal disposable income, adjusted for pensions contributions, £bn). ONS code: RPQK
[3]Quarterly average of official Bank Rate (%)
[4]Quarterly 12 month growth rate of total (excluding the Student Loans Company) sterling net consumer credit to individuals (in percent) seasonally adjusted.

The market -wide economics are also used for the combined scenario. However, the adverse impact on the business drivers have been increased as the idiosyncratic stresses are assumed to exacerbate the market-wide stresses.

The resultant impacts on the business drivers are as follows:

Summarised impact on capital position under each of the scenarios is as follows:

- Under the market-wide stress the percentage surplus capital increases in year 2 as a result of lower RWA's from the lower asset base but is slightly lower in year 3 as the drag from the net interest margin starts to impact the retained earnings.
- Idiosyncratic stress reduces the CET1 ratio by 2.8% (from 37.4% to 34.6%) in year 3 driven by the lower retained earnings as a result of increased costs, fines and indirect impact on business drivers from year 2.
- The capital surplus position under the combined stress is still £4.8m above the total capital required (TCR) plus the Pillar 2B capital requirements. However, the risk appetite target approved by the Board of £5.5m above the TCR plus Pillar 2B will breach the early warning indicator and will require management action.
- Reverse stress arises from multiple events and results in breaching the required CET 1 ratio.
- Orchard's Pillar 2B capital is not impacted by the stress scenarios except the reverse stress.

Orchard's TCR comprised of Pillar 1 and Pillar 2A capital requirements is broadly calculated at 10% of RWAs for the term of Orchard's five-year plan under base case. Orchard's CET 1 percentage of RWAs will reduce from 47% to 31% over the plan period as the growth in lending exceeds the build-up of capital through retained earnings.

Orchard has a capital surplus to meet its regulatory capital requirements over the Base Financial Operating Plan period.

Table 3: Scenario business drivers relative to base.

	Base		Market wide		Idiosyncratic		Combined		Reverse	
	Year 2	Year 3	Year 2	Year 3	Year 2	Year 3	Year 2	Year 3	Year 2	Year 3
	£'000	£'000	%	%	%	w%	%	%	%	%
Lending reduction relative to base	107,800	139,400	20.0%	10.0%	5.0%	5.0%	30.0%	15.0%	40.0%	40.0%
Lending rate reduction, absolute vs base	14.5%	14.4%	2.0%	2.0%	1.5%	1.5%	3.0%	2.0%	7.0%	7.0%
Deposit reduction relative to base	10,000	10,000	20.0%	5.0%	5.0%	5.0%	35.0%	20.0%	90.0%	100.0%
Deposit margin increase, absolute vs base	2.3%	2.4%	1.5%	1.0%	1.0%	w1.0%	3.0%	3.0%	5.0%	5.0%
Bank funding margin increase, absolute vs base	3.5%	3.5%	0.0%	0.0%	0.0%	0.0%	0.0%	0.0%	7.0%	7.0%
Bad debts charge as % of asset	1.0%	1.0%	0.5%	0.2%	0.0%	0.0%	2.0%	2.0%	11.0%	9.0%
Expenses increase year-on-year	15.0%	5.0%	2.5%	0.0%	15.0%	0.0%	25.0%	15.0%	10.0%	15.0%
Idiosyncratic impact (£'000)			-	-	675	-	675	-	675	-

Table 4: Summary capital impacts under each scenario.

	Base		Market wide		Idiosyncratic		Combined		Reverse	
	Year 2 £'000	**Year 3 £'000**	**Year 2 £'000**	**Year 3 £'000**	**Year 2 £'000**	**Year 3 £'000**	**Year 2 £'000**	**Year 3 £'000**	**Year 2 £'000**	**Year 3 £'000**
Risk weighted assets	38,039	47,413	31,370	41,379	36,104	44,127	28,070	38,473	24,574	26,895
Reg. CET 1	15,761	17,744	14,602	15,062	14,529	15,271	12,274	10,132	9,191	2,748
Pillar 1	3,043	3,793	2,510	3,310	2,888	3,530	2,246	3,078	1,966	2,152
Pillar 2A	644	857	657	1,005	672	956	656	1,054	614	1,031
TCR	3,687	4,650	3,166	4,316	3,561	4,486	2,902	4,132	2,580	3,183
TCT plus Pillar 2B	4,789	5,808	4,269	5,473	4,663	5,644	4,004	5,289	3,682	4,341
Surplus / (deficit) regulatory capital	10,971	11,936	10,333	9,589	9,866	9,628	8,270	4,843	5,509	(1,593)
	%	**%**	**%**	**%**	**%**	**%**	**%**	**%**	**%**	**%**
Total Capital requirement % of RWAs	9.7%	9.8%	10.1%	10.4%	9.9%	10.2%	10.3%	10.7%	10.5%	11.8%
Reg. CET1 % of RWAs	41.4%	37.4%	46.5%	36.4%	40.2%	34.6%	43.7%	26.3%	37.4%	10.2%
Surplus / (Deficit)	31.7%	27.6%	36.5%	26.0%	30.4%	24.4%	33.4%	15.6%	26.9%	-1.6%

2 Background to Orchard Business Activities

2.1 Historic Financial Performance

Orchard specialises in the insurance premium finance and the professions finance market. The group lent £68m in the 12 months to 31 July 2018, generated revenue of £5.2m and generated a profit before tax of £1.9m. The group's lending book was c. £31.0m as of the end of July 2018. The published key financials of the group, income statement and balance sheet, over the last three years to July 2018 are presented below.

The accounts to 31 July 2019, which are subject to approval at Orchard's AGM, show lending book growing to £32.1m at the end of the financial year, revenue of £5.5m and profit before tax of £2.0m.

Table 5: Orchard Historic Financials – year ended July.

Income Statement	**Actual 2016**	**Actual 2017**	**Actual 2018**
Revenue	3,469	4,560	5,174
Finance costs	(238)	(329)	(452)
Other operating costs	(76)	(78)	(83)
Gross Profit	**3,155**	**4,153**	**4,639**
Administration expenses	(1,884)	(2,512)	(2,746)
Operating profit before tax	**1,271**	**1,641**	**1,893**
Corporation tax	(267)	(303)	(381)
Profit after tax	**1,004**	**1,338**	**1,512**

Balance Sheet	**Actual 2016**	**Actual 2017**	**Actual 2018**
Assets			
Loans and advances	22,004	28,523	31,084
Cash at bank	1,390	1,728	1,286
Fixed assets	95	77	59
Other assets	44	98	60
Total assets	**23,533**	**30,426**	**32,489**
Liabilities			
Bank borrowing	9,208	13,734	16,008
Trade creditors	1,657	3,181	2,051
Tax liabilities	289	279	339
Non-current liabilities	37	65	54
Total liabilities	**11,191**	**17,259**	**18,452**
Equity			
Share capital	214	214	214
Share premium	8,692	8,692	8,692
Merger reserves	891	891	891
Retained earnings	2,545	3,370	4,240

Table 5 (continued)

Balance Sheet	Actual 2016	Actual 2017	Actual 2018
Total equity	**12,342**	**13,167**	**14,037**
Total equity and liabilities	**23,533**	**30,426**	**32,489**

2.1.1 Key objectives

Key objectives of Orchard over the next five years are:

- to create a bank focused on providing consistent, reliable and cost-effective funding to borrowers deserving of such liquidity in the insurance premium finance market and the professions finance market;
- to conduct its business with integrity and ensure that customers are always treated fairly;
- to offer fair rates to depositors and provide transparency and clarity to all stakeholders in respect of the business of the bank;
- to protect depositors by writing prudent and conservative business in its chosen markets;
- to establish a board and executive management team, with strong, complementary non-executive directors and executive directors having a strong track record in specialist lending, deposit taking and risk management;
- to implement a risk management framework, supported by an operational platform with strong systems and controls, to enable effective operations, oversight, regulatory compliance and excellent service to the bank's depositors and borrowers;
- to grow Orchard's share of its chosen markets by continuing to build long term partnerships with key industry players in insurance and professional services. Orchard will utilise the unparalleled expertise of its management team and experienced sales team to achieve its business plan projections;
- to achieve targeted/projected pre- and post-tax profit and return on capital employed (RoCE)
- to deliver good customer outcomes to all stakeholders – depositors, borrowers, staff and shareholders.

2.1.2 Business Proposition

Orchard provides finance in the insurance premium finance market and the professions finance market in the UK. Finance is provided to SMEs and consumers typically over a 10-month term on a fully amortising basis. All finance provided by Orchard is guaranteed by the introducing professional firm or insurance broker. The directors believe that the lending undertaken by the group is very low risk, demonstrated by the fact that Orchard has suffered minimal arrears and loan losses over the last seven years. A banking licence will allow Orchard to tap into the UK deposits market and obtain access to a more stable, reliable, cost-effective and scalable source of funding, enabling it to support SMEs and consumers with better access to financing.

Orchard has been trading since 2002 and operates an efficient and profitable lending model. Orchard has developed its own bespoke software, LendXP, to allow it to conduct day-to-day lending operations. The software has been used by the group for over eight years and has proven to be reliable and with appropriate levels of control. The group was shortlisted as finalist for "Outsourced Partner of the Year 2016" by British Insurance Awards and "Service Provider of the Year 2016" by The Insurance Times. Orchard has been awarded "Intermediary of the Year" by Commercial Broker Awards 2017.

2.2 Lending Target Market

Insurance Premium Financing

The insurance premium finance market is a large and active market, which is driven by the general insurance market. The general insurance market is estimated to be currently worth over £35bn p.a. (measured in terms of gross written premium). Based on historic growth rates in the market from the Association of British Insurers (ABI), management have estimated that the annual growth rate has averaged c. 20% over the last ten years. The proportion that is financed is c. 38%. Management expect this growth to continue over the next 5 years.

The market is dominated by Premium Credit and Close Brothers, who lent a combined £6.3bn in 2018, representing approximately 47% of the £13.3bn insurance premium finance market in the United Kingdom. There are over 3,800 insurance broker firms in the UK regulated by the Financial Conduct Authority (FCA). Premium Credit and Close Brothers focus on larger volume-driven insurance brokers. Despite its historic funding constraints, Orchard has lent successfully into the market and has contractual relationships with over 100 insurance brokers for direct facilities and for in house premium finance facilities. Through these contracts Orchard lent c. £58m into the premium financing market in 2018 and plans to grow annual lending to c. £201m at the end of its five year plan, still less than 1% of the entire market.

Professions Financing

There are over 6,600 accountancy firms in the UK according to data published by the Annual Survey of the Office of National Statistics with over 335,000[5] individual members registered with the seven UK accountancy bodies according to the Financial Reporting Council. At the smaller end of the market 52% of accountancy firms are

5 Key facts and trends in the Accountancy Profession, June 2015, Financial Reporting Council

sole practitioners, and another 44% have between 2 and 6 principals. The accountancy fee finance market is currently estimated to be worth £300m per year and the professions finance working capital market is estimated by the directors to be worth over £3bn p.a.

The group currently has contractual relationships with over 400 accountancy firms. Through these contracts Orchard provided c. £10m of financing in 2018, and looks to grow annual lending to c. £59m at the end of five years.

2.3 Lending Products

2.3.1 Existing Lending Product Lines

The Bank proposes to have the following business lines. All of the business lines are currently being originated and administered by Orchard:

1. Orchard provides finance to limited companies ("Broker Finance Companies"), which are owned and operated by insurance brokers. Broker Finance Companies provide finance to the clients of the related insurance broker to finance the insurance premiums of those clients. Orchard provides its finance to Broker Finance Companies, based upon and secured by the credit agreements between each Broker Finance Company and its client. Orchard takes a debenture from the Broker Finance Company and also a guarantee from the related insurance broker for all the obligations of the Broker Finance Company. Orchard's lending is for a maximum term of 12 months and is repaid on a fully amortising basis. Broker Finance Companies assign the benefit of all their credit agreements to Orchard and Orchard undertakes the collection and administration of the credit agreements;
2. Orchard provides finance to the clients of insurance brokers. The clients of insurance brokers are introduced to Orchard by the insurance broker. The clients can be consumers and non-consumers. A guarantee of the obligations of the clients is obtained from the introducing insurance broker;
3. Orchard provides finance to the clients of professional services firms, which are mainly accountancy practices. The clients of professional services firms are introduced to Orchard by the firms. The clients can be consumers and non-consumers. Orchard's lending is for a term of 12 months or less and is repaid on a fully amortising basis. A guarantee of the obligations of the clients is obtained from the introducing professional firm;
4. Orchard provides finance to professional services firms directly. This is all non-consumer business. The lending is for a term of 12 months or less and is repaid on a fully amortising basis. Guarantees are also provided by the partners of the professional firm;
5. Orchard provides a nominal amount of finance in adjacent markets to its core markets, such as golf fees, school fees and football season ticket fees. This is a relatively embryonic market and the current lending is very small. Orchard's core

focus as a bank will continue to be the insurance premium finance market and professions finance market.

2.3.2 Lending Product Features

Structure

Bexhill – Insurance Premium Financing

Bexhill is currently a wholly owned subsidiary of Orchard. The Bexhill business will be folded into the new bank. Bexhill was established in 2002 and has achieved consistent revenue growth between 2002 and 2018. However, due to the global financial crisis, Bexhill's funding became significantly restricted in 2008. Bexhill continued to trade through the difficult period and supported its client base despite scarcity of available funding. Currently Bexhill has over 100 insurance broker clients.

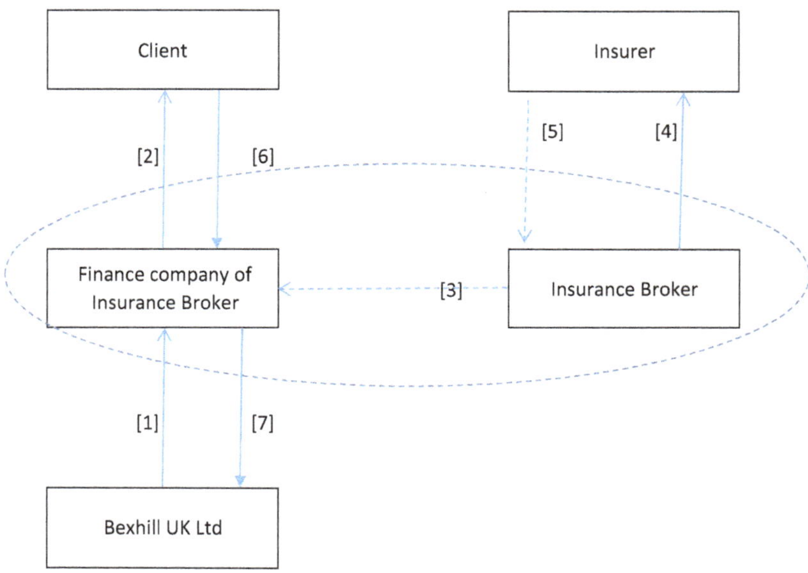

[1] Funding to financing company
[2] White-labeled finance agreement
[3] Guarantee from insurance broker
[4] Premium paid to the insurer
[5] Unearned premium on cancellation
[6] Monthly instalments
[7] Loan repayment

Figure 1: Corporate insurance structure.

Bexhill typically lends through a finance company owned and operated by an insurance broker (corporate insurance) for the purpose of providing finance to the clients of the insurance broker. All Bexhill's lending is guaranteed by the insurance broker and all credit agreements entered into by the finance company are assigned to Bexhill and Bexhill undertakes the collection and administration of those credit agreements.

Orchard – Professions Financing and Direct Insurance Lending

Orchard Funding Limited (OFL) is currently a wholly owned subsidiary of Orchard. The OFL business will be merged into the new bank. OFL was established in 2010 in order to take advantage of the withdrawal of one of the largest funders in the market for smaller professional practices. OFL's lending book has grown since its launch, despite its funding being relatively expensive and constrained. OFL has over 400 professional firm clients as at July 2018, most of which are accountancy firms. OFL's professional firm clients introduce their clients to OFL to finance their professional fees. OFL also provides facilities to a number of professional firms directly. OFL's insurance broker clients introduce their clients to OFL to finance their insurance premiums. OFL's client list has grown consistently year-on-year.

OFL typically lends directly to the client of the insurance broker (direct insurance), client of the professional firm; or the professional firm directly.

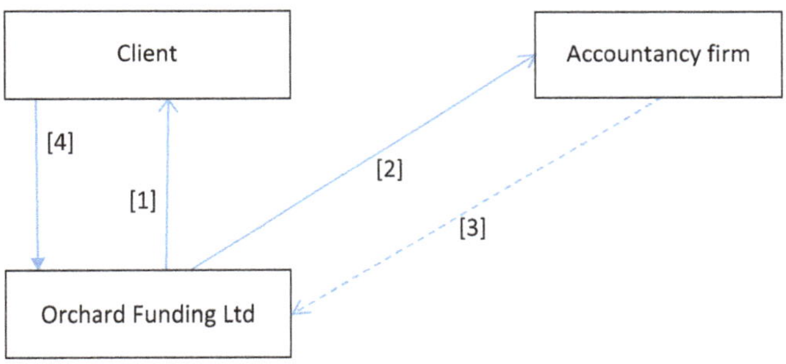

[1] Funding agreement
[2] Fees paid to the accountancy firm
[3] Guarantee from accountancy firm
[4] Monthly instalments

Figure 2: Accountancy fee funding structure.

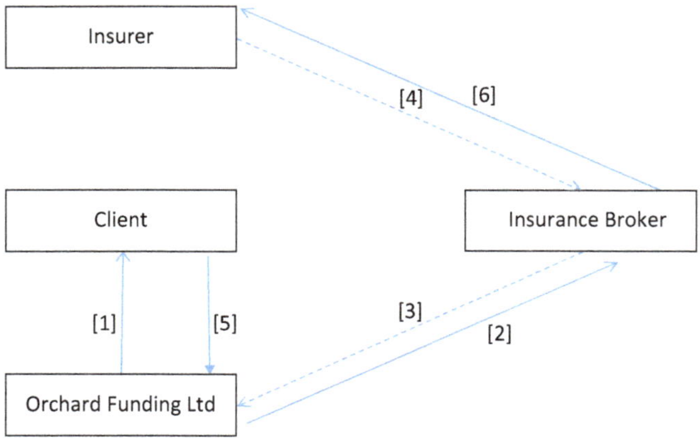

[1] Funding agreement
[2] Premium paid to the broker
[3] Guarantee from insurance broker
[4] Unearned premium
[5] Monthly instalments
[6] Premium paid to insurer

Figure 3: Direct insurance structure.

Product Terms

Orchard's lending products will have the following terms, which replicate the terms of the products currently originated and administered by the group:

- APR – target 15–18%;
- Maximum term – 12 months;
- Fully amortising over the term of the credit;
- Full agreement to pay from the introducing insurance broker or professional firm.
- Although in isolation an APR of 15–18% appears relatively high, there are a number of factors, which suggest the rate is sustainable and fair to the borrower, including inter-alia:
- There are very limited sub-12 month amortising credit products available in the market. The larger financial institutions, including the banking market find the short-term nature and relatively small ticket size of this type of credit product unattractive;
- Unsecured overdrafts from banks can be over 20% APR and often over 30% APR;
- Credit card rates for borrowing are generally over 20% APR;
- Non-bank short-term credit terms can be punitively expensive;
- The rate paid by the Customer is often less than 10% APR, but Orchard is able to increase its IRR to over 15% by managing its settlement dates to the Introducer.

Financing through Orchard enables a borrower to still have the option of using its other credit providers for alternative spending.

Delivery Channels
Orchard currently uses a relationship-based model for lending origination which it plans to continue after authorisation.

Origination
Orchard has over 17 years of experience in its lending markets. The senior members of the sales team have decades of experience in the short-term financing market working with Orchard and previously with the leading competitors in the market. They have long-standing relationships with key players in the insurance brokerage sector and accountancy/law firms. The in-house solution offered by Bexhill allows insurance brokers to white-label the financing of insurance premiums to their clients, which is particularly attractive to a number of larger insurance brokers and may potentially lead to opportunities to scale up the lending business further in the future. Ongoing communication with the borrowers about loan administration is carried out over phone/email.

2.3.3 Lending Products – Conduct Risk

All new products are assessed for conduct risks, to ensure fair customer outcomes, and are signed off in accordance with the product approval policy. This includes:
- Product Characteristics
- Incentives/Income
- Pricing Structure
- Barriers to Exit
- Product Complexity
- Target Market
- Customer risk (performance metrics)
- Staff Competency
- Soft launch
- Monitoring
- Financial Promotions

All financial promotions require sign off from senior management and Compliance prior to publication.

2.3.4 Future Lending Products

Orchard has, in line with its key competitors, conducted test marketing in adjacent markets to its core insurance premium finance and accountancy fee funding market. The test marketing is currently less than 5% of Orchard's lending book and is not considered material. The adjacent markets are in service fee markets with similar characteristics, documentation and system requirements to its core markets, i.e., short-term credit where there is recourse to the introducer or a there are compelling reasons for the customer to ensure that its payments are made. Currently adjacent markets that are being tested are school fees, club fees and site fees. Orchard will continue to focus on the insurance premium market and accountancy fee funding market and consider adjacent markets where it can use its existing documentation, systems and expertise to ensure effective, profitable and controlled lending.

2.4 Deposit Target Market

Deposits Market

The total deposit base in the UK is over £2.9trn[6] of which the share of notice accounts is 12% (£350bn) and the share of fixed rate deposits is 7% (£200bn). The rate-sensitive share of the deposit market that is prone to switching is about 10% or £35bn and £20bn respectively for notice and fixed rate deposits according to market estimates of PBF Solutions (an outsourced deposit management provider). Assuming the average behavioural maturity of fixed term deposits is 2 years (realistic as most of the fixed term deposits are of 1 year maturity), £10bn of fixed rate deposits migrate looking for attractive rates in the market. By all measures, the market is vast and Orchard's share (projected to be c. £76m even after five years of operation) will be a very small fraction of the total available market.

Orchard intends to raise liabilities in the retail deposits market and understands it is difficult to offer a deposit proposition which is significantly differentiated from that of the competition. However, Orchard will offer a simple set of deposit products with attractive interest rates and a simple postal application process, through conventional best-buy tables.

Details in respect of the projected deposits to be raised by Orchard are set out in the base financial operating plan. Our deposit raising numbers (amounts and customers) are extremely conservative. We are confident that such deposit levels will be capable of being raised through a prominent exposure on best buy tables.

In the context of Orchard's conservative deposit raising aspirations, we believe the following research we have undertaken is sufficient to determine whether there is a market for our deposit taking plans. We have reviewed a number of publicly available research documents on the subject, including the FCA's Cash Savings Market Study of the UK deposit market and believe that such research enables us to conclude that there is a deep enough deposit market for the numbers set out in our Plan.

The current rates offered in the market place have been studied through the best buy tables to assess the margins above the bank base rates for the top ten providers. The

6 Cash Savings – An International Comparison, A Study for the FCA, PwC, Sep 2014

base plan has assumed similar margins above the base rate, which is presented below. The time period in the chart is the period post mobilisation and authorisation as a bank.

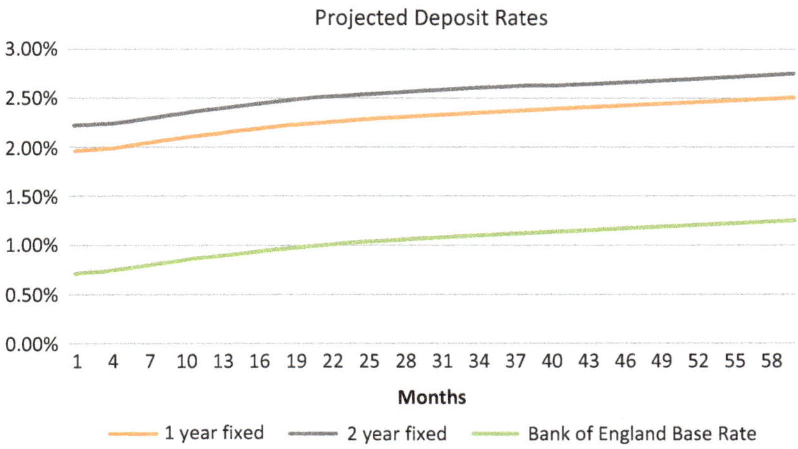

Figure 4: Deposit Rates.

2.5 Deposit Products

2.5.1 New Deposit Products

Orchard will initially have 2 deposit products:

1. 1 year fixed rate deposit
2. 2 year fixed rate deposit.

The proposed new bank will operate nationally across the UK from its base in Luton. Staff with relevant experience will be recruited to run the new retail deposits operation. As noted above, the markets in which the group currently lends are very large and provide ample opportunities for growth over the time horizon envisaged in this plan. The group's proposed new deposit taking activities will similarly form an even smaller share of the target market.

Orchard plans to have a low-risk liability strategy focusing on a limited product set (1 year and 2 year fixed rate deposit accounts) initially offered in tranches to retail customers, combined with a simple postal application process, attractive and consistently fair rates and targeted customer retention schemes. There are no plans to offer instant access or current accounts but other term deposit products may be considered. Initially the Bank will develop brand awareness through prominence on the best-buy tables. Given the modest deposit raising plans in the projection (Orchard plans to have just over £76m in its deposit book at the end of year 5) these marketing efforts are considered to be adequate and proportionate.

Orchard will utilise the savings module of a proven software house, Mutual Vision Limited, for its deposit business. This software is used by a number of small building societies and banks.

2.5.2 Deposit Product Features

Structure

The fixed rate, fixed term deposits will have a minimum of £1K to cover operational costs and a maximum set to stay within the FSCS guarantee limit. Money will only be returned to the UK bank account where the deposit was credited from, with the option to roll over. Fixed term deposits will not be withdrawable before contractual maturity except in hardship conditions.

Product Terms

1-year fixed rate deposit
We have assumed a margin above base rate of 1.25% and average deposit size of £24,000. In year 1 we will therefore have approximately 525 depositors and this will increase to 1,900 over the 5-year life of the plan.

2-year fixed rate deposit
We have assumed a margin above base rate of 1.5% and average deposit size of £24,000. In year 1 we will therefore have approximately 336 depositors and this will increase to 1,216 over the 5-year life of the plan.

Deposit Delivery – Channels, Origination and Retention

Orchard initially intends to raise deposits through postal applications. It plans to offer simple deposit products with market-leading rates and a simple postal application process. Orchard will be a new entrant into the deposits market and intends to market its products through the best-buy tables. This will help build brand recognition among the target market of depositors (high net worth, cash-rich individuals such as pensioners) and will result in lower costs of customer acquisition, higher retention and lower deposit rates over time given the modest deposit requirements planned in the projections.

Monthly tranche limits will be set by ALCO in order to avoid peaks in funds inflows and, therefore, funds outflows at maturity. Deposit applications will be made by filling out a form downloaded from the Orchard website. The number of downloads will be monitored automatically in order to estimate the expected inflow of funds and flag where run-rates exceed or fall short of preset parameters. This will prompt adjustment to pricing or temporary withdrawal of products where necessary. Orchard recognises that the appearance of deposit products in the best buy tables could lead to increases in inflows of deposits in excess of the levels required leading to excess liquidity and thereby creating a negative carry cost and spikes in outgoing funds at maturity. Orchard will carefully manage this risk by closely monitoring the application activity by number of downloads of the application forms from the website to project expected volume and amend the interest rates on the deposit products to reduce new business levels if required.

Orchard recognises that the cost of acquiring new deposits is significantly higher than the cost of retaining existing deposits, and will design tailored retention schemes (depositors contacted 4–6 weeks prior to deposit maturity, offered market leading rates that are the same as what is offered to new customers) to preserve them. Orchard will also work to build a brand that reflects partnership with the SME sector that over time will help it attract/retain deposits without paying market-leading interest rates.

In the event that customers are met with financial difficulties leading them to want to withdraw their deposit, Orchard will review each application to withdraw deposits prior to the contractual maturity date. As Orchard's assets are amortising and the liquidity buffers are extremely conservative throughout the term of the plan, Orchard will act in the manner of a reasonably prudent financial institution to determine whether a contractual deposit term can be broken. Our Deposit Hardship Policy sets out the basis on which each case will be determined, ensuring a fair and equitable outcome for the customer. It is anticipated that less than 1% (by value) of depositors will request a withdrawal of deposits prior to the contractual term date.

All new products will be reviewed by EXCO, with oversight from Compliance, and submitted to the Board for sign-off where appropriate.

Redemption Profile of Deposits

All deposit stock will be up to the FSCS limit lowering the risk of large-scale outflow in a stress scenario. Liability origination will be spread across the year by flexing the rate relative to competition to ensure no more than 12% of the existing liability stock contractually matures in a given month. Daily applications and new business will be tracked to manage the future maturity profile. At maturity, tailored retention schemes focused on a simple experience and consistently fair rates will help retain deposits and result in lower behavioural outflows. The terms of the deposit will clearly state that upon redemption a deposit will be rolled over for the same term at a rate that will be communicated to the depositor 4–6 weeks before the maturity of the deposit, and the depositor will be given an option to either switch to another deposit product or withdraw the proceeds altogether.

2.6 Competitive Advantages

The directors believe Orchard has the following key differentiators vis-à-vis its competitors:

- Orchard has been operating in the insurance premium finance market and professions finance market since 2002. In that time its senior management team has remained in place and developed strong and trusted relationships with its existing clients and with other key parties in its markets. The length of time that Orchard has operated in the market provides confidence to insurance brokers and professional firms that Orchard is a constant and reliable player in the market. This is very important as a number of companies have entered and exited the market since Orchard commenced its business.
- Orchard's senior management team has unparalleled experience in the premium finance and professions finance market. Unlike the management teams in the other leading competitors in the market, the management team has been exclusively focused on its markets since 2002 and in the case of some of the team since the late 1990s. Again, this depth of expertise provides a high level of confidence to insurance brokers and professional firms seeking a funding partner.
- The group understands the needs and requirements of insurance broker firms and professional firms and offers a fully tailored solution to the target market. The larger dominant market players are less focused on the smaller end of the lending market creating an opportunity for the group.
- Orchard is in regular contact with all its clients and strives to ensure that a high-quality service is consistently delivered. The larger players in both the insurance premium finance and professions finance market have in the past provided limited services to certain parts of the market allowing the group to build up a loyal customer base.
- The group's in-house premium finance product is unique and enables insurance brokers to take greater control and provide unparalleled service in the provision of premium finance to their clients. This product is very attractive to well capitalised insurance brokers who wish to ensure the highest levels of service are provided to their clients. No other company offers this product to insurance brokers and the product is attractive to some of the largest insurance brokers in the UK.
- The group does not impose any fees or require minimum levels of business for the availability of its facility to insurance brokers or professional firms.
- The group's online platform has the functionality to support white-label and direct financing and is simple to navigate and use. The system enables quick and efficient data entry for its insurance broker and professional firm clients, effective credit and affordability assessment and efficient production of compliant legal documentation for a client to sign either by hand or electronically.
- Senior management of the group is involved in all aspects of the business and in particular maintain close and strong relationships with the group's clients. The per-

sonal involvement of senior management in the needs and concerns of the group's client base is very important to the clients of the group. The group has always regarded itself as an SME and is therefore sympathetic to the needs and aspirations of insurance brokers and professional firms, many of which are themselves SMEs.
- The ability, given the pricing of its lending, to offer consistently attractive rates on a simple and transparent deposit range to raise and retain the requisite deposit base to develop its business.
- Due to the simplicity of its lending products Orchard will provide transparency and openness to depositors and all other stakeholders on all aspects of its business.

3 Business Viability

The Bank intends to provide unsecured short-term credit to limited companies, partnerships and consumers in the insurance premium finance market and the professions finance market, funding itself with a strong capital base and a stable stock of retail deposits. The loan book is projected to grow at a steady pace (from c. £33m at the end of year 1 to c. £93m at the end of year 5) and provide a commercially viable net interest margin (c. 14%-15%). Robust underwriting and guarantees from introducing insurance brokers and professional firms are expected to keep the loan loss rate low (assumed at 1% compared to the historic experience of very low levels of losses in the past eight years). Operating overheads in salaries and investments in better systems and controls are projected to grow from c. £2.8m in year 1 to £4.8m in year 5, allowing the capital resources to grow from c. £14.8m at the end of year 1 to c. £26.2m at the end of the fifth year of the business plan. Consequently, no plan for additional capital raising has been included in the projections.

3.1 Projections

The base financial operating plan is based on a fully operative bank and the first year equates to the first twelve months as a deposit taking bank. Hence, the plan is not presented in calendar years but presented from the time of bank inception.

As Orchard currently runs a profitable financing business, even after absorbing the additional investments and expenditure during the bank building phase it is expected that the Bank will be profitable in its first year of operation. The high-level assumptions behind the projections are as follows:
- The direct insurance business will start from a small base of £5.4m in year 1 and will grow during the five years of projection horizon to £45.4m at the end of the period.

- The corporate insurance business where Orchard has a more established presence in the market will start at £19.5m in year 1 and will grow to £28.5m at the end of the period.
- The professional fee financing business will grow from a base of £8.1m in year 1 to £19.9m at the end of the period.
- Deposit issuance will start at £1.7m per month (c.71 accounts per month) and will continue for a year to replace existing bank facilities and total £21m at the end of Year 1 of the Plan. Net new deposits will total £10m in each of Years 2 and 3 of the Plan and then rise to £13m in Year 4 and £22m in year 5 of the Plan.
- Only 1 year and 2 year fixed rate deposits will be offered at 60:40 split, respectively.
- At the end of the projection horizon the balance sheet will have £93m of loans and £12m of liquid assets and £1m of fixed and other assets that will be funded by £76m of deposits, £4m of other trade creditors and £26m of shareholder capital.

Orchard's Board reviewed the base operating plan on the 30th May 2019 and provided feedback. The final plan was approved by the Board on 16 July, 2019.

3.1.1 Loan Book Growth

Based on the origination experience of Orchard's management team it is expected that the Bank will grow the direct insurance business at the fastest pace as this is the largest segment of the insurance premium financing market. This is followed by moderate projected growth in the accountancy business and the corporate insurance business. Lending interest rates are expected to remain steady.

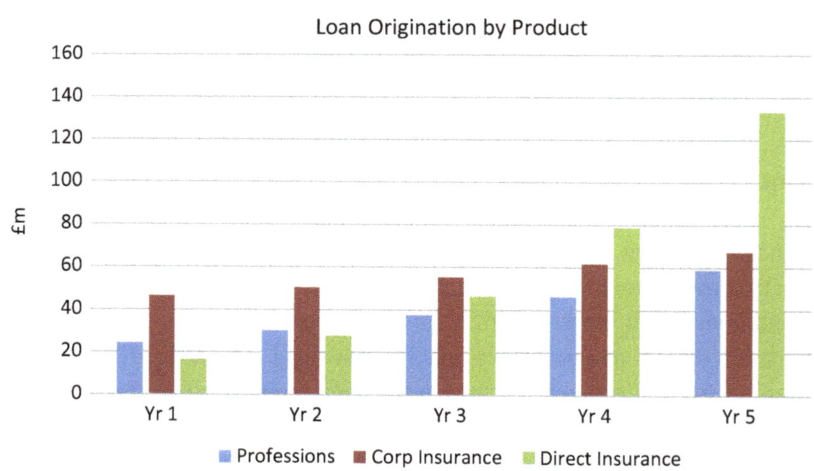

Figure 5: Loan origination volume (by loan type).

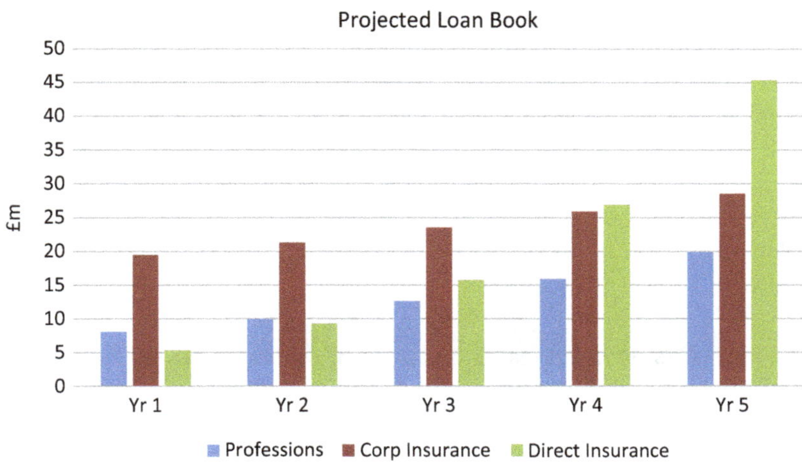

Figure 6: Projected loan book on balance sheet (by loan type).

3.1.2 Deposit Book Growth

The deposit book is projected to grow from £21m at the end of year 1 to c. £76m at the end of year 5. The liquidity strategy is maintained at low risk by offering only 1 year and 2 year fixed rate deposits that are contractually not withdrawable before maturity. The deposit rates are projected to go up in line with Bank of England base rate projections.

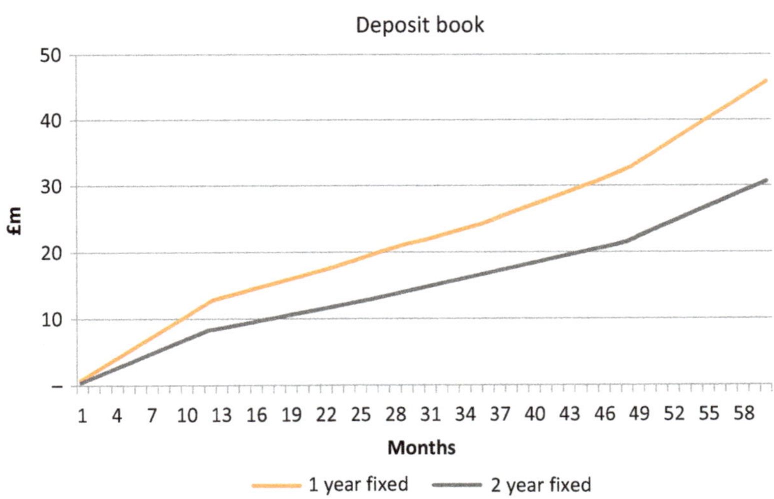

Figure 7: Projected deposit book on balance sheet (by deposit type).

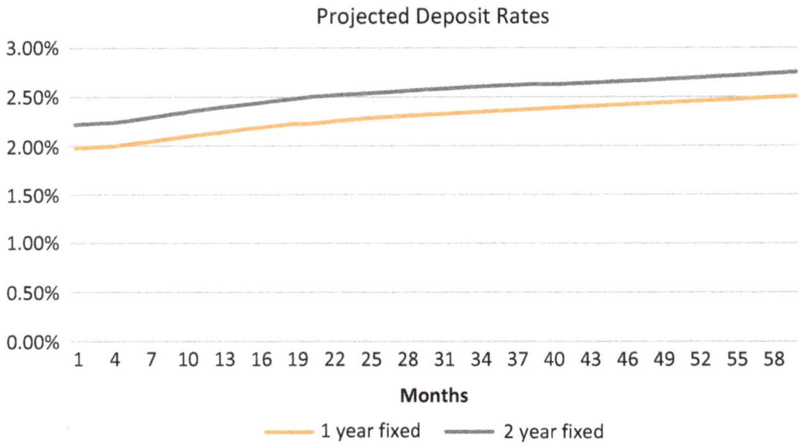

Figure 8: Projected deposit rates (by deposit type).

4 Financial and Operating Statistics

4.1 Income Statement

The first year of the Base Financial Operating Plan equates to the first year of fully operational bank. The income statement over the plan period under base case is presented below:

Table 6: Orchard Projected Income Statement.

Income Statement	**Actual 2018**	**Plan Year 1**	**Plan Year 2**	**Plan Year 3**	**Plan Year 4**	**Plan Year 5**	**CAGR**
Interest Receivable	5,174	4,887	6,370	8,175	10,817	14,856	23.5%
Interest payable	(535)	(396)	(591)	(870)	(1,198)	(1,702)	26.0%
Net interest income	4,639	4,491	5,779	7,305	9,619	13,154	23.2%
Administration expenses	(2,746)	(2,870)	(3,267)	(3,651)	(4,184)	(4,820)	11.9%
Impairment charges	0	(312)	(393)	(498)	(653)	(888)	
Operating profit before tax	**1,893**	**1,308**	**2,119**	**3,156**	**4,782**	**7,446**	**31.5%**
Corporation tax	(381)	(257)	(403)	(600)	(909)	(1,415)	
Profit after tax	**1,512**	**1,051**	**1,716**	**2,556**	**3,874**	**6,031**	**31.9%**
Dividends	(642)	(210)	(343)	(511)	(775)	(1,206)	
Retained earnings	**870**	**841**	**1,373**	**2,045**	**3,099**	**4,825**	

Table 7: Key income statement ratios.

Key Ratios	unit	Year 1	Year 2	Year 3	Year 4	Year 5
Average interest earning assets (monthly weighted)	£'000	31,230	38,805	49,091	64,238	87,249
Gross interest margin	%	15.6%	16.4%	17%	16.8%	17.0%
Average cost of funds	%	2.1%	2.3%	2.4%	2.5%	2.6%
NIM	%	14.4%	14.9%	14.9%	15.0%	15.1%
Cost:Income ratio	%	64%	57%	50%	44%	37%
PAT growth YoY	%	-30%	63%	49%	52%	56%
Dividend per share (pence per share)	pence	1.0	1.6	2.4	3.6	5.6
ROE (PAT)	%	7.1%	10.6%	14.0%	18.1%	23.0%

The underlying business drivers, with volume assumptions and key financial assumptions are tabled below:

Table 8: Orchard Projected Volumes.

Base	Actual 2018	Plan Year 1	Plan Year 2	Plan Year 3	Plan Year 4	Plan Year 5
New Lending (£'000)	68,730	86,000	107,800	139,400	186,709	259,576
Lending growth %		25%	25%	29%	34%	39%
Lending stock (£'000)	31,084	32,762	40,475	51,531	67,917	92,953
Lending interest rate (wt. average)		14.53%	14.46%	14.40%	14.32%	14.26%
Corporate Insurance Loan stock (£'000)		19,484	21,432	23,575	25,933	28,526
Average loan size (£'000)		172	172	172	172	172
Number accounts (vols)		113	125	137	151	166
Direct Insurance loan stock (£'000)		5,124	8,849	15,213	26,057	44,517
Average loan size (£'000)		0.48	0.48	0.48	0.48	0.48
Number accounts (vols)		10,675	18,436	31,695	54,285	92,745
Accountancy Loan stock (£'000)		8,155	10,193	12,742	15,927	19,909
Average loan size (£'000)		5.10	5.10	5.10	5.10	5.10
Number accounts (vols)		1,599	1,999	2,498	3,123	3,904
New Deposits (inc rollovers) (£'000)		21,000	22,600	37,000	41,600	66,800
Deposit stock (£'000)		21,000	31,000	41,000	54,000	76,000
Deposit interest rate (wt. average)*		2.15%	2.32%	2.43%	2.51%	2.58%
Average deposit (£'000)		24	24	24	24	24
Number of deposit accounts stock (vol)		875	1,292	1,708	2,250	3,167
Number of new deposits		875	942	1,542	1,733	2,783
Number of new deposits per day		3	4	6	7	11

*Based on the Bank of England inflation report, February 2019

Table 9: Key Financial Assumptions.

Base	Plan Year 1	Plan Year 2	Plan Year 3	Plan Year 4	Plan Year 5
Annual losses % receivables (IFRS 9)	1.0%	1.0%	1.0%	1.0%	1.0%
Base rate (end of year)	0.9%	1.0%	1.1%	1.2%	1.3%
Corporation tax rate	19.7%	19.0%	19.0%	19.0%	19.0%

*Based on the Bank of England inflation report, February 2019

- Gross interest income in Year 1 of the Plan is slightly lower than actual experience in 2018 as a result of the mix of business, but thereafter, continues to rise as the mix of the business weights towards slightly higher margin product.
- Interest payable benefits from the lower funding rate as a result of initiating deposit taking activities.
- Administration expenses rises in the first year at 5% and in the subsequent years, by c. 12% to 15% as a result of additional cost associated with banking operations (technology, staffing and regulation) and increased sales activities.
- Although the current experience on impairment charges is extremely low, the plan assumes impairment charges of 1% of asset.
- Dividend distribution is assumed at 20% of distributable profits for the year.
- Profit after tax rise from £1m to £6.0m in year 5.
- Orchard considers its return on equity (RoE) as being one of the best measures of its financial well-being. From 7% per annum in year 1, it rises to 23% in year 5

4.2 Balance Sheet

The projected balance sheet over the plan period is presented below:

Table 10: Orchard Projected Balance Sheet.

Balance Sheet	2018	Year 1	Year 2	Year 3	Year 4	Year 5
Assets						
Loans and advances	31,084	32,762	40,475	51,531	67,917	92,953
Cash at bank	1,286	1,000	1,000	1,000	1,000	1,000
Liquid asset buffer	0	3,867	7,612	8,740	8,717	10,972
Fixed assets	59	483	556	621	681	737
Other assets	60	158	158	158	158	158
Total assets	**32,489**	**38,270**	**49,801**	**62,049**	**78,472**	**105,819**
Liabilities						
Customer deposits	16,008	21,000	31,000	41,000	54,000	76,000
Bank funding						
Trade creditors	2,051	2,051	2,051	2,051	2,051	2,051

Table 10 (continued)

Balance Sheet	2018	Year 1	Year 2	Year 3	Year 4	Year 5
Tax liabilities	339	257	403	600	909	1,415
Non-current liabilities	54	84	96	103	118	134
Total liabilities	**18,452**	**23,393**	**33,550**	**43,754**	**57,078**	**79,600**
Equity						
Share capital	214	214	214	214	214	214
Share premium	8,692	8,692	8,692	8,692	8,692	8,692
Merger reserves	891	891	891	891	891	891
Retained earnings	3,370	4,240	5,081	6,454	8,498	11,597
Current year retained earnings	870	841	1,373	2,045	3,099	4,825
Total equity	**14,037**	**14,878**	**16,251**	**18,295**	**21,394**	**26,219**
Total equity and liabilities	**32,489**	**38,270**	**49,801**	**62,049**	**78,472**	**105,819**

- Asset growth is assumed at c. 19% in the first year and accelerates from 25% in second year to 39% in year 5.
- Bank funding is repaid in the first year of the plan and replaced by retail deposits. At the same time, Liquid asset buffer is built up to cover the liquidity requirements.
- Deposits stock increases from £21m in Year 1 to £76m in Year 5. The net new deposits in year 1 are £21m to manage down the bank borrowing and thereafter, reduces to £10m p.a. for year 2 and 3 before accelerating in years 4 and 5.
- Total equity increases by 30% over the 5 year period to £26m as earnings after payment of dividends are retained in accordance with Orchard's intended dividend policy when it becomes a bank.

Table 11: Key balance sheet ratios.

Key Ratios	unit	Year 1	Year 2	Year 3	Year 4	Year 5
Risk weighted assets	£'000	31,652	38,039	47,413	62,117	84,294
CET 1 % of RWA	%	47.0%	42.7%	38.6%	34.4%	31.1%
Leverage	%	43.2%	38.5%	34.3%	30.7%	27.6%
HQLAs to Deposits	%	18.4%	24.6%	21.3%	16.1%	14.4%

4.3 Capital Requirements.

The capital requirements under base case are summarised below:

Table 12: Orchard Capital Requirements.

£'000

Base	Plan Year 1	Plan Year 2	Plan Year 3	Plan Year 4	Plan Year 5
Pillar 1 capital requirements	2,532	3,043	3,793	4,969	6,743
Pillar 2A capital requirements	631	644	857	972	1,206
Total capital requirement (Pillar 1 + Pillar 2A)	**3,163**	**3,687**	**4,650**	**5,942**	**7,949**
Pillar 2B	1,050	1,102	1,158	1,215	1,276
TCR plus P2B	**4,213**	**4,789**	**5,808**	**7,157**	**9,226**
Total Capital resources	**14,457**	**15,761**	**17,744**	**20,786**	**25,558**
Risk weighted assets	31,652	38,039	47,413	62,117	84,294
Total Capital requirement % of RWAs	10.0%	9.7%	9.8%	9.6%	9.4%
TCR + Pillar 2B % of RWAs	13.3%	12.6%	12.2%	11.5%	10.9%
CET1 % of RWAs	47.0%	42.7%	38.6%	34.4%	31.1%
Surplus / (deficit) capital	10,244	10,971	11,936	13,629	16, 332

Further breakdowns of individual buffers, detailed calculations and basis for each of the components are presented in sections 7 to 10.

4.4 Liquidity

The LCR is a requirement under Basel III for a bank to hold high-quality liquid assets (HQLAs) sufficient to cover 100% of its stressed net cash requirements over 30 days. Orchard's Liquidity Coverage Ratio under the base case is significantly higher than the regulatory requirement of 100% as set out in the firms ILAAP document.

The Net Stable Funding ratio seeks to calculate the proportion of Available Stable Funding ("ASF") through the balance sheet liabilities over Required Stable Funding ("RSF") through the assets, with weightings applied based on the type of liability or asset. Orchard's Net Stable Funding Ratio (NSFR) is also materially above the regulatory requirement of 100% as set out in the firm's ILAAP document.

The table below presents the key liquidity ratios with risk appetite target under the base financial operating plan.

Detailed calculations to support the key liquidity ratios are presented in the ILAAP document.

Table 13: Key liquidity ratios.

	Target	Year 1	Year 2	Year 3	Year 4	Year 5
LCR	150%	3069%	4093%	3553%	2690%	2406%
NSFR	125%	154.3%	160.3%	160.3%	153.9%	154.2%
% Liquid Assets to Loans		15%	21%	19%	14%	13%
% HQLA to Deposits	14%	18%	25%	21%	16%	14 %

4.5 Capital Resources and Funding Sources

The capital resources available to Orchard are the issued share capital (after issuance expenses) of £9.8m and the retained earnings that increase through the plan period to £16.4m, resulting in core equity of £26.2m by the end of year 5 of the Base Financial Operating Plan.

The funding sources are the core equity and the net new retail deposits raised over the plan period of £76m.

5 Governance Framework

5.1 Board composition

The directors recognise the importance of sound corporate governance and comply with the QCA Corporate Governance Code (as devised by the QCA in consultation with a number of significant institutional small company investors). In addition, the PRA and FCA set standards for Board Governance in Banks, which Orchard will comply with.

Orchard recognises the concerns that the PRA has over 'dominant individuals' on bank boards and has put together a committee structure and recruited suitable INED's to mitigate this risk. The Board of the Bank will comprise of five directors of which two will be executives and three will be independent non-executives. The Board reflects a blend of different experience and backgrounds.

The objective of the Board will be to enhance the long-term success of the Bank by developing a sustainable business model. This will be supported by approving and setting strategy, risk appetite and culture in line with the business model and in light of changing business opportunities, environment and risk.

The Board will delegate the day to day implementation of the strategy, business plan, policies, procedures and risk appetite within the approved policy statements to the Executive Committee and it will be the responsibility of the Board to monitor the overall performance of the business. In addition, the Risk & Compliance Management Framework and control environment will enable the Board (through the oversight of the Audit and Risk Committees) to gain assurance that it is operating as designed and within the tolerances set by its risk appetite.

Orchard has a full and detailed Corporate Governance Policy, which will be finalised during Mobilisation.

Brief biographies of the directors are shown in Table 14 below.

Board roles and responsibilities are detailed in the Table 16 below.

Table 14: Brief biography of the directors.

Name	Board Membership	Brief Biography
	Independent Non-Executive Chairman	
Ravi Takhar	Chief Executive Officer	Mr Ravi Takhar has over 25 years' experience in the acquisition, growth, financing and disposal of financial businesses. Mr Takhar founded the business in 2002 and has led the growth of the UK business to its current size. Prior to creating the group, Ravi was an investment banker and Head of Financial Services investment at Nikko, the Japanese investment bank, from 1998 to 2002 as well as Chairman of Mortgages PLC, the mortgage lender. Mr Takhar was also Head of Mortgage Principal Finance at Investec Bank PLC from 2005 to 2008. He qualified as a banking solicitor at Clifford Chance, a leading international law firm, and has an MA from the University of Oxford.
	Chief Financial Officer	
	Non-Executive Director	
	Non-Executive Director	

Table 15: Brief biography of the CRO.

Name	Senior Management Role	Brief Biography
	Chief Risk Officer	

Table 16: Orchard Funding Group PLC – Board Roles & Responsibilities.

Role	Key Reponsibilities	Appointment
Chief Executive and Board Director SMF1 SMF 3 SMF 24	The CEO is responsible for: – effective day to day management of the business – operating the business in accordance with board approved strategies, plans and policies – ensuring an effective systems and control environment – managing overall enterprise risk and returns – setting the corporate culture	Ravi Takhar

Table 16 (continued)

Role	Key Reponsibilities	Appointment
	– primarily responsible for the relationship with the relevant regulatory bodies and for all other stakeholders in the business – compliance with Board Risk Appetite Statement The CEO is Chairman of the Executive Committee and member of ALCO and Credit Committee. The CEO is also responsible for ensuring that the board members are: – able to sufficiently challenge the executive and understand the business model – provided with a full understanding of higher risk activities and products – in receipt of appropriate management information to be able to carry out their oversight role The CEO will have oversight responsibility for HR and marketing. The CEO also has oversight responsibility for: – the effective development of the bank's retail savings business in terms of its administration functions, ensuring that high standards of performance and service are achieved at all times and that it operates at all times within the policies and parameters set by the board – ensuring that all staff members within the retail savings business act at all times in compliance with the letter and the spirit of all laws and regulations applying to the business The CEO also holds primary responsibility for: – management, stability, security and effectiveness of the systems and communications used in the bank – operating within parameters and budgets set by the Board and the Executive Committee – ensuring the Bank remains appropriately positioned to address its business needs, provide operational resilience, security risks and to respond to identified opportunities and threats relevant to IT and Communications – managing the secure delivery of the bank's website and email communications. – Business Continuity and Disaster Recovery Plan, maintaining it up to date at all times and ensuring it is subject to appropriate and regular testing – Bank-wide project management – Outsourcing arrangements – Facilities management	

Table 16 (continued)

Role	Key Reponsibilities	Appointment
Chief Financial Officer and Board Director SMF2, SMF3	The CFO has overall responsibility for: – overseeing the Finance and Treasury functions of the Bank and ensuring that each operates within the parameters and policies set by the Board and Executive Committee – primary accountability for the quality of the business-wide financial and management information – all statutory and regulatory reporting – oversight of the principal financial systems and controls of the business – the preparation of the ILAAP, ICAAP, Recovery Plan and Resolution Plan – the financial and treasury related risks of the Bank on a day to day basis including capital management, liquidity management and compliance with IFRS. – managing the production of and present the medium term financial plan for approval to the Board – compliance with Board Risk Appetite Statement As a member of the Executive Committee the CFO is responsible for contributing to overall direction of the business in terms of its strategies, performance, systems and controls. The CFO is a member of the Executive Committee and Credit Committee and Chair of ALCO. Working with the CEO, the CFO will take primary responsibility for the delivery of the bank's deposit strategy, ensuring that the Bank achieves the right mix of funding across its target customer segments and at an acceptable cost of funds. The CFO is also responsible for: – the production of all financially related statutory and regulatory returns in accordance with prescribed timetables – production of timely management information, pulling this together from across all areas of the bank – operation of the payments and reconciliations of the Bank which is a key area of control – ensuring that finance operations function within Board and Executive Committee approved parameters and policies	
CRO SMF4, SMF 16 & 17	The CRO has primary responsibility to the Board on the quality of the Bank's overall risk management framework. He is a key link between the Board and the business with the ability to translate what is at times highly technical and often detailed reporting of risk into high level information for the Board to understand and interpret at a strategic level.	

Table 16 (continued)

Role	Key Reponsibilities	Appointment
	The CRO attends all the executive committees of the Bank providing internal challenge and is a Member of ALCO and Credit Committee. As a member of the Executive Committee the CRO is responsible for contributing to the overall direction of the business in terms of its strategies, performance, systems and controls. In addition to enterprise-wide risk management, the CRO has primary oversight responsibility for: – legal and compliance (including conduct risk) – financial crime prevention – fraud management – Credit risk and credit systems – Operational risk – compliance with Board Risk Appetite Statement The CRO will be responsible for: – ensuring the Bank meets all its statutory and regulatory requirements relating to the operation of the Bank other than the financial ones undertaken by the Finance Director and CFO – ensuring compliant procedures are in place to enable the business operations to comply with current legislation and regulations – taking responsibility for the effective management, measurement and monitoring of exposure to Conduct Risk – monitoring compliance with Complaints Handling and Treating Customers Fairly – documenting and reporting results of legal and compliance monitoring to the Board, Audit& Risk and Executive Committees as appropriate – compliance with Board Risk Appetite Statement He also acts as Money Laundering Reporting Officer (MLRO). As MLRO he has responsibility for: – ensuring all statutory and regulatory responsibilities are discharged on behalf of the bank – the implementation of and compliance with anti-money laundering procedures and policies – receiving and reviewing suspicious transaction reports and advising SOCA as necessary He is responsible for developing and delivering all compliance training requirements. His legal responsibilities relate to taking primary responsibility for: – reviewing all terms and conditions of products, third party contracts for services and business relationships	

Table 16 (continued)

Role	Key Reponsibilities	Appointment
	– and ensuring that they are appropriate within the context of the board approved policies and parameters and applicable laws and regulations.	
Chairman (Board) & Chairman of Noms and Rems INED SMF 9 SMF 12 SMF 13	Responsible for leading the Board and ensuring effective direction and challenge for Management Setting Board Agenda (in consultation with Management) Chair of Noms and Rems Committee Setting tone from the top in terms of the Culture of the Organisation Board training agenda Board evaluation (annual) Appraisal of performance of Board members and CEO Ensuring appropriate balance of skills and diversity of Board	
Chair of Audit INED SMF 10	Responsible for ensuring an effective Audit Committee operating in the interests of all stakeholders Ensuring regulatory and listing responsibilities are discharged effectively Audit Committee Agenda (in consultation with Management) Oversight of Internal Audit (including assessing performance in conjunction with CEO) Liaising with External Auditors Audit Committee Evaluation (annual)	
Chair of Risk INED SMF 11	Responsible for ensuring an effective Risk Committee in accordance with its terms of reference Setting Risk Committee agenda Oversight of CRO (including assessing performance in conjunction with CEO) Risk Committee evaluation (Annual) Responsible for the maintenance of an appropriate Whistleblowing process for customers, staff and other stakeholders of the business.	

5.2 Improvement of Governance Structure

The corporate governance structure has been enhanced to prepare for Orchard becoming a bank as follows:

1. The appointment of an independent non-executive Chairman and independent non-executive directors with many years of recent and current banking experience in SMF designated roles;
2. The independent non-executive directors comprising a majority of the Board;

3. A new Board Risk Committee and continuance of the Board Audit Committee and the Board Nominations & Remuneration Committee comprised only of independent non-executive directors.
4. The appointment of a new CFO and new CRO with recent bank experience, who will provide an executive balance to the CEO.
5. The Board will appoint an external party to carry out its internal audit function.
6. The enhancement of the governance structure with more detailed and regular board and committee meetings, supplemented with enhanced regular management information, to ensure effective corporate governance.

The Board is satisfied that the profile and experience of the independent NEDs and the new executive appointments, together with the enhanced corporate governance structure will be provide effective and controlled governance of Orchard as a bank.

5.3 Assessment of Board Skills and Experience

Orchard has been operating in its core market for 17 years and the Board and senior management have a strong understanding of (i) the risks associated with Orchard's regulated activities and (ii) the regulatory requirements which govern the way in which Orchard conducts its regulated activities.

The Board and senior management recognise that, as a Bank, Orchard will be subject to additional regulatory requirements and are confident that they have the experience and skills to ensure compliance with these new obligations. We have undertaken an assessment for the Board and senior management to identify areas where skills and knowledge can be further enhanced.

Orchard's board is now comprised of senior individuals with many years of recent experience in the banking industry. Gaps in the skills and experience of individual directors and senior managers will continue to be addressed through an ongoing training program. The Skills and Experience Matrix in the table below summarises the current assessment of the Board.

5.3.1 Skills and Experience Matrix

Table 17: Orchard Funding Group PLC – Board Skills Matrix.

Code: 1- Specialist experience (eg executive function holder within past 5 years CRO, CFO, CIO etc) 2- Good Experience (but not specialist function holder in past 5 years) 3- Knowledgeable but no direct experience (capable of development with support/training) 4- Not considered essential as sufficiently covered by others	Ravi Takhar CEO	CFO	CRO	INED Chairman	INED Chairman of Audit Committee	INED Chairman of Risk Committee
Risk Management and setting risk appetite	1	3	1	2	2	1
Technology including Business continuity, resilience and security	2	2	2	2	1	2
Treasury management including asset and liability management	1	2	2	2	1	2
Operations and project management	1	2	2	2	2	1
Financial statements and reporting, including regulatory	2	1	4	1	1	2
Prudential and Conduct regulation, including conduct, Sysc, threshold conditions (PRA and FCA), SMCR	1	2	1	1	1	1
Business strategy, including for Orchard's chosen markets	1	2	2	1	2	2
Retail deposits marketing and operations	3	2	2	1	1	2

Table 18: Orchard Funding Group PLC – Board Behaviours Matrix for Performance Evaluation.

Code: 1- Strong requirement 2- Requirement 3- Not required	Ravi Takhar CEO	CFO	CRO	INED Chairman	INED Chairman of Audit Committee	INED Chairman of Risk Committee
Customer Focus	1	1	1	1	1	1
Challenges Executives	NA	NA	NA	1	1	1
Actively participates in debates	1	1	1	1	1	1
Prepares properly for meeting and reads papers	1	1	1	1	1	1
Up to date in own area of expertise	1	1	1	1	1	1
Board Committees Chairman – Leadership qualities/effectiveness/potential	1	1	2	1	1	1

5.4 Board Structure

The Orchard Board at launch of the Bank and during mobilisation will have the following composition:

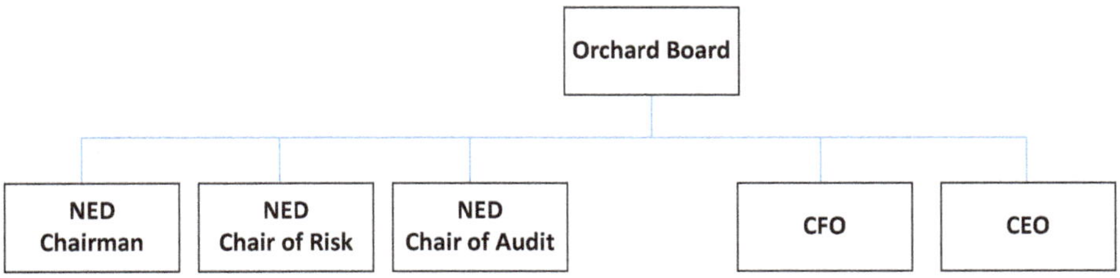

Figure 9: Orchard Board Composition.

5.5 Committee and Management Structure Charts

The following section describes the relationships and functions of the key governance committees proposed for Orchard.

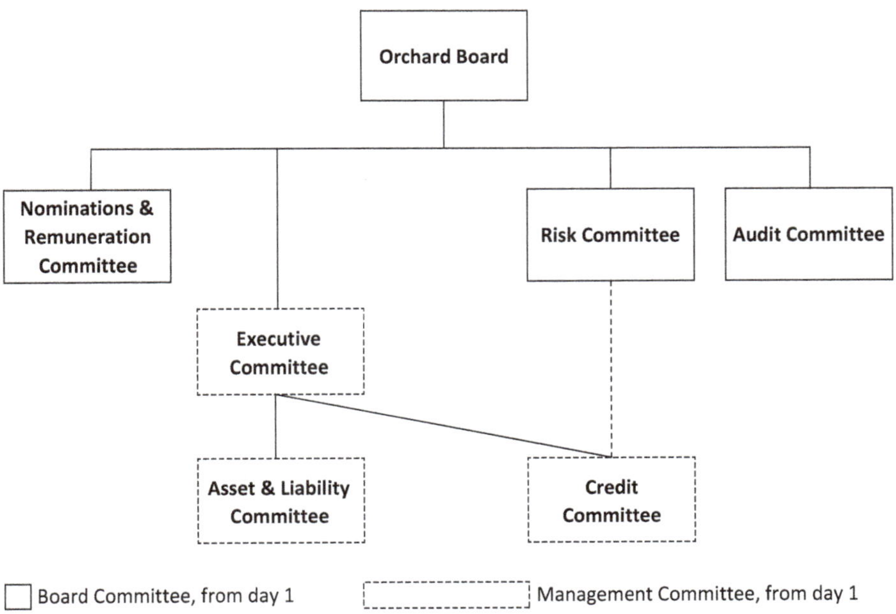

Figure 10: Orchard Governance Committees.

5.6 Governance framework – Board and Board Sub-Committees

A summary table of the Board and Board Sub-Committees is presented below:

Table 19: Orchard Board and Board Sub-Committees.

Committee	Quorum	Members	Frequency
Board	3 (at least 2 INEDs)	Chairman CEO CFO INEDs	Ten times a year, or more frequent if required by the Chairman
Risk Committee	2	Chair of Risk, INEDs (inc Board Chairman) [CEO, CFO and CRO standing invitees]	Four times a year, or more frequent if required by the committee chair
Audit Committee	2	Chair of Audit, INED [Internal Audit, External Audit, Chairman of the Board, CEO, CFO and CRO standing invitees]	Four times a year, or more frequent if required by the committee chair
Nominations & Remuneration Committee	3	Chairman CEO (non-voting) INEDs	At least twice a year, or more frequent if required by committee chair

5.6.1 Board

The Board's primary role is to provide leadership, ensure that the Bank is appropriately managed and deliver long term shareholder value. It sets the strategic objectives and provides direction.

The Board is responsible for managing the Bank on behalf of its shareholders and each Director must act in a manner that he/she considers promotes effective working of the Board and the long term success of the Bank for the benefit of those shareholders, its employees and all of its customers. The Board will meet as necessary, but typically on a monthly basis, with the exception of August and December months (to allow for holidays).

The Board will ensure there are appropriate controls in place and that there is a healthy balance between promoting long term growth and delivering short term performance, but it will place the emphasis on the longer term health and sustainability of the Bank.

The Board delegates responsibility for the day-to-day management of the Bank to the executive management team, led by the Chief Executive and through the Executive Committee. However, certain matters are specifically reserved for the Board and these include the approval, monitoring and review of:

- Setting business strategy, plans and budgets from time to time
- Monitoring business performance and effectiveness

- Oversight of regulatory compliance and internal controls
- Financial statements and significant changes to accounting policies and practices
- Board terms of reference, membership and powers including the appointment and removal of board members
- Principal policies of the Bank, committee terms of reference and the overall governance framework, systems and controls
- Risk appetite, risk management, insurance and mitigation
- Corporate initiatives such as mergers and acquisitions or significant business partnerships.
- Culture, values and attitudes of the management and staff of the Bank towards both its customers and the risks that are taken
- Remuneration, benefits and incentive policy and appointment of senior management
- Regulatory and statutory compliance
- Prudential and regulatory matters including but not limited to ICAAP, ILAAP and RRP.

Board performance will be reviewed at least annually. The Chairman will meet annually with the non-executive directors. The non-executive directors will meet annually to appraise the Chairman's performance.

At each regular scheduled meeting the board will receive reports from the Chief Executive and Chief Financial Officer on the performance, results, strategic developments and initiatives, operating functions, legal, compliance, human resources and corporate development matters.

There will be an annual schedule of rolling agenda items to ensure that all matters are given due consideration and are reviewed at the appropriate point in the financial and regulatory cycle.

Meetings will be structured to ensure that there is sufficient time for consideration and debate of all matters.

5.6.2 Risk Committee

The Committee will assist the Board to manage the risks faced by the Bank and is responsible for the identification, management and mitigation of risk and will review the effectiveness of the risk management and the compliance frameworks of the Bank. The Committee plays an important role in setting the tone and culture that promotes effective risk management across Orchard. The Risk Committee will typically meet quarterly.

5.6.3 Audit Committee

The Committee is responsible for oversight of the systems of internal control in operation in the Bank, the integrity of its financial statements and regulatory reports and the oversight of both external and internal audit. The Audit Committee will meet quarterly.

5.6.4 Nominations and Remuneration Committee

The Committee is responsible for ensuring the recruitment and selection of appropriately qualified experienced and skilled individuals into senior positions within the organisation and the setting of remuneration, rewards and benefits at levels which attract, retain and motivate employees, whilst being affordable and appropriate. The Committee will meet as required, but a minimum of once per year.

The Committee must ensure that the Bank conforms in all respects with the recruitment policies set out in the staff handbook particularly with regard to the avoidance of unfair discrimination in the recruitment of employees and Board members, and also ensuring that it conforms to the CRD IV proposals regarding diversity in board composition.

5.7 Governance Framework –Management Committees

Summary tables of the Management Committees are presented below:

Table 20: Orchard Management Committees.

Committee	Quorum	Members	Frequency
Executive Committee	3	CEO CFO CRO Head of Finance & Operations Head of Credit & Operations	Once a fortnight, or more frequent if required by committee chair
Asset & Liability Committee (ALCO)	3 with CFO	CEO CFO CRO Head of Finance & Operations Head of Credit & Operations	Once a month, or more frequent if required by committee chair
Credit Committee	3 with CRO	CEO CFO CRO Head of Finance & Operations Head of Credit & Operations	Twice a month, or more frequent if required by the committee chair

5.7.1 Executive Committee

The Executive Committee has its authority delegated to it by the Board of Directors. It represents the principal forum for conducting the business of the Bank and takes day to day responsibility for the efficient running of the business. In addition, the Executive Committee is responsible for the formulation and implementation of Board approved strategies and plans. It is responsible for ensuring the performance of the business in accordance with plans. It will review prudential and regulatory matters including but not limited to ICAAP, ILAAP and other reviews.

5.7.2 Asset and Liability Committee

The Asset and Liability Committee's (ALCO's) purpose is to manage the assets and liabilities of the Bank in respect of duration, interest rate and liquidity risk. It is responsible for determining the Bank's strategy in respect to its balance sheet assets, capital, funding and liquidity profiles, seeking to understand and anticipate future market and economic developments affecting the Bank and considering these in the context of the Bank's ILAAP.

5.7.3 Credit Committee

The Credit Committee is the body charged with the transactional credit responsibility for the Bank. It operates within policy parameters approved by the Board in carrying out the approval and monitoring of the credit business of the Bank.

5.8 Board and Committee Membership

Orchard's Board and committee membership is summarised in the table below:

Table 21: Orchard SMR Responsibilities Map.

5.9 SMR Responsibilities

The allocation of Senior Management Regime responsibilities is summarised in the table below:

Table 22: Orchard SMR Responsibilities Map.

5.10 Management of Conflict of Interest of Ravi Takhar as CEO and Majority Shareholder of Orchard.

Ravi Takhar has been CEO and majority shareholder of Orchard since its flotation in 2015. In that time, the potential conflict between his actions as CEO and his actions as a shareholder has been managed and controlled by Orchard's governance being comprised of: a Board with 2 independent non-executive directors; a Board Committee structure of Audit & Risk Committee and Remuneration and Nominations Committee, comprising only NEDs.

The management and control of the potential conflicts of interest will be enhanced when Orchard becomes a bank as follows:

1. The appointment of an independent non-executive Chairman and independent non-executive directors with recent and current banking experience;
2. The independent non-executive directors comprising a majority quorum of the Board;
3. A new Board Risk Committee and continuance of the Board Audit Committee and Board Remuneration Committee comprised only of independent non-executive directors.
4. The appointment of a new CFO and new CRO with recent bank experience, who will provide executive balance to the CEO.
5. The enhancement of the governance structure with more detailed and regular board and committee meetings to ensure that potential conflicts are managed in a timely manner.

The Board is satisfied that the profile and experience of the independent NEDs and the new executive appointments, together with the enhanced corporate governance structure will be able to manage any potential conflicts of interest between the CEO's position as an executive and majority shareholder of Orchard.

Orchard also recognizes that Ravi Takhar has not held a CEO position at a deposit taking institution, and hence, the composition of the Board, both executive as well as non-executive, has been strengthened to include individuals with strong banking experience.

5.11 Risk Appetite

The level of risk that Orchard is prepared to accept and the tolerance limits around the acceptable risk is set out in the risk appetite. The risk appetite is both, qualitative and quantitative and covers the risks identified in the business. These are categorised as level 1 risks, with more granularity under level 2. The identified risks are set out in the table below:

Table 23: Orchard Level 1 and Level 2 Risks.

Level 1	**Credit Risk**	**Financial Risk**	**Conduct Risk**	**Strategic Risk**	**Operational Risk**
Level 2	Credit	Financial Reporting and tax Model	Conduct Legal Regulatory Compliance	Strategic	Business continuity Data management Financial crime Fraud Information security (incl. Cyber) People Physical security and safety Third party Transaction processing

The Board is responsible for setting Orchard's risk appetite and delegates the responsibility for the setting of limits and policies and monitoring of processes, systems and reporting to the Risk Committee. Orchard's risk appetite sets out the level of risk that it is willing to accept in pursuit of its business objectives.

Risk appetite statements have been created for each Level 1 and Level 2 Risk category and provide an articulation of Orchard's tolerance for risk in both quantitative measures and qualitative terms. They have been created following discussions among Orchard's executive management and with members of the Risk Committee and the Board. They are used in mapping key risks and assessing their materiality and ultimately underpin Orchard's overall risk management framework.

The risk appetite statements are reviewed formally on an annual basis by the Board as part of budget setting and the review of Orchard's medium-term strategy. They combine a top-down view of Orchard's overall risk capacity with a bottom-up view of the risk profile requested and recommended by the business area (which will be previously discussed and reviewed by the Risk Committee).

Throughout the year all aspects of the risk appetite statement (which will be monitored by the CRO) will be reported to the Risk Committee and Board. In particular, the CRO will be responsible for assessing the impact on Orchard's risk appetite of any changes in circumstances (internal or external) that may warrant a change to the risk appetite statements and recommending any consequent changes to the Risk Committee and the Board ahead of the scheduled annual review.

5.11.1 Overarching Risk Appetite Statements

A set of overarching principles has been established, which govern the articulation of the lower-level risk appetite statements. These principles are that Orchard's risk appetite should:

- Reflect its strategy and culture;
- Focus on manageable, forward looking measures of risk, rather than on backward looking measures of loss;
- Include qualitative description, quantitative measures and prescribed behaviours;
- Facilitate understanding of why limits have been set at the level determined.

These will be communicated, throughout the organisation, in a way that enables each individual to see how risk appetite influences the way they carry out their job responsibilities.

The qualitative Board Risk Appetite statements:

- Cover each level 1 and level 2 risk category;
- Are approved by the Board and reviewed at least annually in consultation with all key stakeholders, taking into account business changes, and reported at least quarterly.

Overarching statements, as detailed below, express Orchard's broad risk appetite at a whole business level, whilst underlying limits cover specific aspects of Orchard's operations.

We will maintain stakeholder confidence – by operating the business in such a way that we deliver against key objectives, both financial and non-financial and remain within our risk appetite;

We will maintain adequate capital and liquid resources – we will maintain a sufficient level of capital and liquidity to effectively support the lending activity of the business and ensure that all liabilities will be met as they fall due under both normal conditions and under a range of stress scenarios;

We will protect our reputation – we will be a safe haven for retail and SME depositors and can be seen as an organisation that treats all our customers and employees fairly. We have no appetite for material negative or adverse reputational events;

We will limit the potential for credit losses – by being aware of and managing key concentrations, lending in markets where we can demonstrate expertise, lending to credit worthy borrowers where affordability can be demonstrated and ensuring budgeted risk adjusted returns are achieved;

We will effectively manage our operational risks and operational resilience – we have a low tolerance of operational risk failures (including IT systems failures and cyber-crime). We will ensure that all our people are properly trained, procedures are thoroughly documented and supervisory controls and reporting methodologies are in place to minimise the impact of adverse operational risk events that disrupt customer service;

We will demonstrate high standards of conduct and compliance – we have a low tolerance for material conduct and compliance related adverse events, or breaches of a regulatory or legal nature and will operate the business in such a way as to minimise the potential for such adverse events to occur.

The Risk & Compliance Management Framework sets out the quantitative measures to manage the key risks with target, early warning indicators and trigger points. The Risk Metrics will be the mechanism through which the quantitative risk measures will be monitored and where necessary, corrective action taken.

6 Risk & Compliance Management Framework

6.1 Overview of Three Lines of Defence

Orchard is working to establish a Risk & Compliance Management Framework (RCMF) that provides guidance for cohesive and consistent risk management activity across the whole business. The aim of the RCMF is to ensure that all types of risk are identified and managed in a consistent and compliant manner across Orchard. The RCMF sets the standard approach for the management of each Principal Risk and comprises the following components:

- Risk & Compliance Culture;
- Risk & Compliance Governance and Control;
- Risk & Compliance Strategy and Appetite;
- Risk & Compliance Measurement and Reporting; and
- Stress Testing and Contingency Planning

The RCMF will be enacted through a series of policies and processes, setting out our risk and compliance management approach and appetite in respect of each of the major risks identified. The adherence to each policy and risk appetite limits will be monitored by management through the establishment of a formal governance process. Performance is measured for, and reported to, ExCo and the Risk Committee, with material risk issues explicitly highlighted as they arise and formally reported on a monthly basis.

The RCMF will be submitted to the Risk Committee for challenge and debate, following which it will be submitted to the Board for formal approval and adoption. It will be reviewed at least annually by the Risk Committee.

6.2 Three Lines of Defence Model

To manage its risks, Orchard will operate a Three Lines of Defence model which segregates risk management by each of the three distinct categories.

6.2.1 First Line of Defence

Operationally, Management have primary responsibility for the identification, measurement and management of all risks and issues, and for compliance regulatory, legal and internal policies and limits. Clear ownership of each specific risk is set out in the Board approved RCMF policy documents which establish the limit structures within which Orchard operates. In addition to the day to day risk management processes of Orchard, risk management is overseen through the management committees.

The table below provides more detailed responsibility map against each activity.

Table 24: 1st Line (Ownership and Control) Business Units.

Role	Responsibility
Provision of risk management and control	Implementation of risk policies Ensuring compliance with policy across the business Identification and escalation of incidents, in line with policy Operation of controls
Development of the understanding of risk	Development and management of risk mitigation plans Undertaking scenario analysis

Table 24 (continued)

Role	Responsibility
Engagement with the business and customers	Understanding of, and provision of input to, risk policies Educating staff in the need for risk awareness
Definition and defence of a risk strategy	Input to risk appetite definition through Credit Committee Implementation of policies, framework and methodology in line with defined appetite and strategy
Taking responsibility for regulatory compliance	Ensuring that Orchard remains compliant with all relevant laws and regulations Implementation of changes and enhancements to risk management methodology

6.2.2 Second Line of Defence

The Risk and Compliance function has responsibility for owning Orchard's RCMF, developing the usability of the RCMF and for the oversight and challenge of the day to day management, control and reporting of risks. In addition, the function is responsible for providing advisory support to the business on risk- and compliance- related matters, and for supporting the Governance Oversight of the Bank.

The Risk and Compliance function is responsible for collating and aggregating risk reporting to support the function with regards to forming an independent view of Orchard's overarching risk and compliance profile. The Risk and Compliance function is responsible for creating and managing the Compliance Monitoring Plan, and for reporting on the Bank's adherence to this at the Audit Committee. Oversight of the Bank's implementation of policies against financial crime, money laundering and terrorist financing is provided by the Risk and Compliance function.

The Risk Committee, supported by the Risk and Compliance function:

- assists the Board in the formulation of Orchard's desired risk culture, risk appetite, risk management strategies, policies and limit structures;
- ensures that Orchard has the processes and internal controls to meet the requirements imposed by governmental bodies, regulators, industry mandates or internal policies;
- leads the overall design, implementation and ongoing maintenance of Orchard's RCMF;
- monitors the performance and delivery of the Compliance Monitoring Plan; and
- oversees and objectively challenges the management, control and reporting of risks.

The Risk and Compliance function is responsible for the timely identification of key regulatory changes impacting Orchard, and the development of the Risk, Compliance & Governance Culture as well as Legal and Regulatory Compliance.

The CRO has a reporting line to the Chairman of the Risk Committee, with a dotted line to the CEO. The table below provides more detailed responsibility map against each activity.

Table 25: 2nd Line (Risk and Compliance).

Role	Responsibility
Policies	Update and challenge of risk and compliance policies Update and provision of financial crime, etc. policies
Methodology and Tools	Ownership, development and maintenance of the Risk and Compliance Framework
Training and Communications	Delivery of regular communication to the business on risk-, compliance- and crime- related topics Provision of risk and compliance training to the business
Oversight	Oversight and challenge of the business on the adequacy and effectiveness of the use of the risk and compliance management and methodology in the business The provision of expert support and advice to the business on risk management, including how to interpret and comply with the risk and compliance policies and to meet the requirements of the respective frameworks
Financial Crimes	Independent oversight and reporting on Money Laundering Provision of support and guidance on requirements for monitoring against financial crime, criminal activity, terrorist financing, bribery, corruption and identification of PEPs
Governance	Communication of concerns to the appropriate manager and of unresolved concerns to the Risk Committee

6.2.3 Third Line of Defence

Internal Audit is responsible for independent review of the effectiveness of risk management at Orchard. Internal Audit reports directly to the Chairman of the Audit Committee, with a "dotted line" to the CEO.

Orchard intends to outsource this work to Internal Auditors on an on-going basis. By bringing in an outsourced facility, the following benefits will be realised:

- Suitably qualified and experienced resources from a reputable firm;
- Depth of resources from an outsourced provider available when required and with a greater potential for specific experience in Orchard's specialist business activities;
- Access to external benchmarking and experience through the outsource provider into practices in other banks in the industry as well as expertise in advising on trends and regulatory developments; and
- Appropriate balance of cost against benefit.

The Internal Auditor is required to undertake a program of audit work on a planned and ad hoc basis under the direction of the Audit Committee, with management by the

CEO. They will act independently, but will meet with the senior management of Orchard prior to the commencement of any particular audit to discuss their specific audit plans and to ensure that they also address areas of particular concern to management.

Internal audit will further investigate any actual or suspected frauds and any serious control failures under the direction of the CEO and/or the Audit Committee as a third line after Risk. Internal Audit will attend each Audit Committee meeting.

6.3 Organisation Structure and Reporting Lines

Orchard's organisation chart is set out below. The team will be augmented further through mobilisation and during the early years of operation as a bank to bring in specific expertise and capacity to handle greater lending and deposit volumes. During mobilisation experienced deposit administration staff will be recruited to the Company. Towards the end of year 1 when the balance sheet grows in size and additional efforts are required to monitor and manage cash, liquidity and interest rate risk, the team will add a senior member of staff to provide treasury expertise to the Company. The sales team will be supplemented further in year 2 or 3 (depending on lending growth) by adding sales personnel for both insurance premium and professional fee financing. The Bank intends to use services of a professional accounting firm for its internal audit function.

6.4 Primary Board Risk Appetite Metrics and Reporting

Periodically the Board and management will review the corporate plan, performance against the plan and the key underpinning assumptions. Reviews can take place more frequently if circumstances change although typically the formal annual review of the Corporate Plan alongside Risk Appetite provides the foundation for review of the key annual regulatory submissions, specifically the ICAAP, ILAAP, the Recovery Plan and the Resolution Plan.

The detailed risk appetite limits and Early Warning Indicators (EWI) thresholds based on the current business plan are presented below.

The risk profile will be reported monthly to the ExCo, the Risk Committee and the Board supported by commentary on an exception basis (Amber and Red indicators) where they are subject to review and challenge.

The metrics will provide both a point in time position (current month RAG) and an indication of direction of travel against the base financial operating plan. As a consequence, the Board and Executive management are better equipped to decide, at an early stage, whether changes to the plan or to levels of appetite require further consideration. The Primary Board Risk Appetite metrics are presented below:

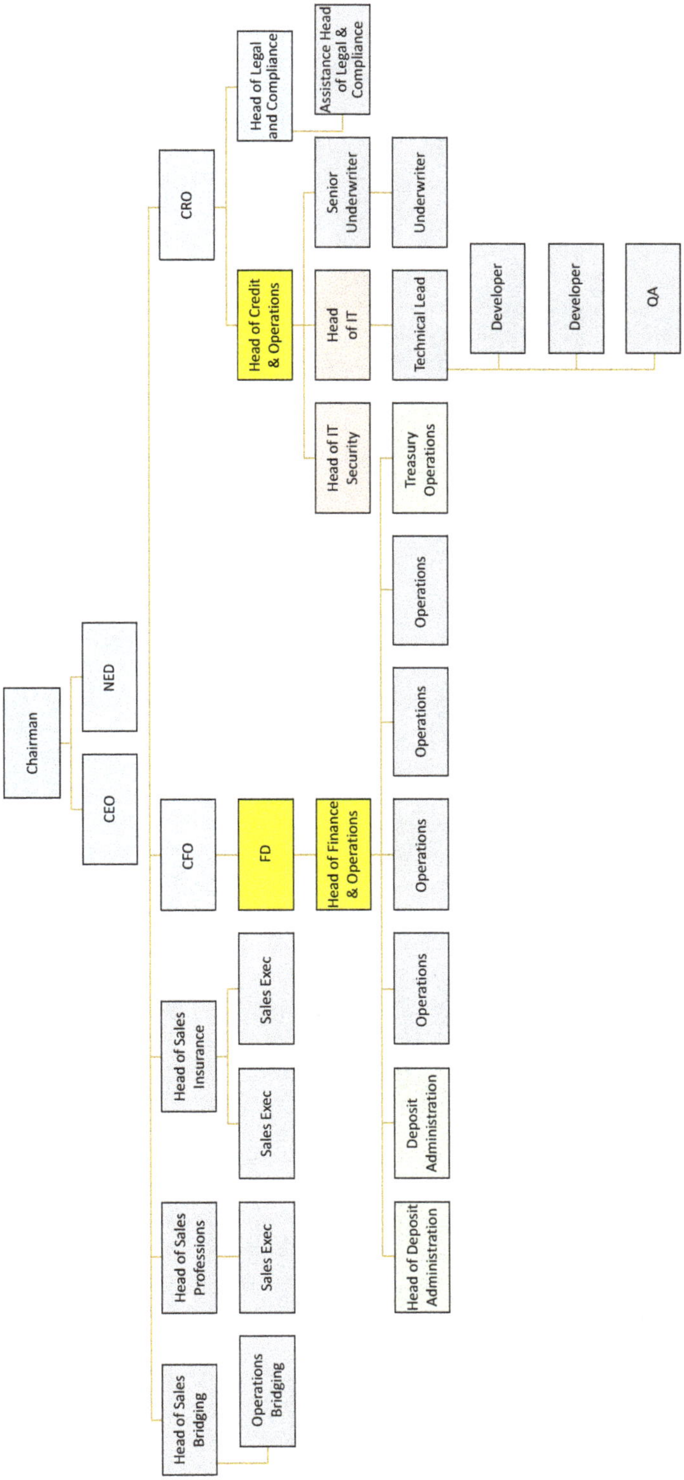

Figure 11: Organisation Chart.

Table 26: Risk Metrics Table.

Limit category		Target	Early warning indicator (Amber)	Trigger (Red)	Primary Responsibility
Credit	Loan losses as percentage of total loan portfolio	1%	Equal to or >1.5%	Equal to or >2%	Credit Team
	60 days arrears % of loan asset	<3%	Equal to or >3%	Equal to or >5%	Credit Team
Operations	Total Operational Losses (inc Fraud)	£0	>£200k <£250k	>£250k	Operations
	Operation Risk – Unavailability of Systems	0 days	1 day	2 days	IT/Operations
	Operational Risk – Loss of Key Personnel (Board Directors and direct reports) over six month rolling period	0 persons	2 persons	4 persons	Operations
	Operational Risk – Loss due to failure of Controls	£0 loss	Near miss or potential loss of any amount	An actual loss of >=£62,000	Operations
	1st LOD Control Assurance Plan Results	100–95%	94–85%	<85%	Operations
	2nd LOD Control Assurance Plan Results	100–95%	94–85%	<85%	CRO
	Third Party SLA violation	0	1 Minor	>1 minor	CRO
Conduct & Compliance	Current Complaints as %age customer base	0	0.50%	1%	Compliance
	Total Upheld FOS complaints as %age customer base	0	0.25%	0.50%	Compliance
	Reportable Compliance Breaches YTD	0	Minimal <2pa		Compliance
	Regulatory Permission – Sanction or Withdrawal of Permission	0	Major systems or controls breakdown. Going concern issue.	Notice from PRA	Compliance and CEO

Credit	**Loan losses as percentage of total loan portfolio**	1%	Equal to or >1.5%	Equal to or >2%	Credit Team
	60 days arrears % of loan asset	<3%	Equal to or >3%	Equal to or >5%	Credit Team
Operations	**Total Operational Losses (inc Fraud)**	£0	>100k <£150k	>£150k	Operations
	Operation Risk – Unavailability of Systems	0 days	1 day	2 days	IT/Operations
	Operational Risk – Loss of Key Personnel (Board Directors and direct reports) over six month rolling period	0 persons	2 persons	4 persons	Operations
	Operational Risk – Loss due to failure of Controls	£0 loss	Near miss or potential loss of any amount	An actual loss of >=£62,000	Operations
	1st LOD Control Assurance Plan Results	100–95%	94–85%	<85%	Operations
	2nd LOD Control Assurance Plan Results	100–95%	94–85%	<85%	CRO
	Third Party SLA violation	0	1 Minor	>1 minor	CRO
Conduct & Compliance	**Current Complaints as %age customer base**	0	0.50%	1%	Compliance
	Total Upheld FOS complaints as %age customer base	0	0.25%	0.50%	Compliance
	Reportable Compliance Breaches YTD	0	Minimal <2pa		Compliance
	Regulatory Permission – Sanction or Withdrawal of Permission	0	Major systems or controls breakdown. Going concern issue.	Notice from PRA	Compliance and CEO

6.5 Risk Categories – Detailed Underlying Metrics

6.5.1 Credit Risk

Credit risk is defined as the risk of a borrower or counterparty failing to pay the interest or to repay the principal on a loan on time. Credit Risk also encompasses Concentration Risk.

Risk appetite for the lending business is detailed within the Underwriting Policy.

Treasury Lending

Table 27: Treasury Lending Limits.

Limit	Metric
Total credit exposure to an institution or a group of connected institutions	£1m for all bank accounts, except Bank of England Reserve Account which is unlimited Initially, to cover the liquidity requirements with HQLA, investment in short term (<3 months remaining maturity) UK Government Gilts will be purchased.
Conditions	Must be: – With a UK incorporated institution – Have a short-term credit rating of at least A-2, P-2 and F-2 for S&P, Moody's and Fitch respectively. – Maximum maturity of 90 days

Counterparty Credit Risk

The risk that Orchard incurs losses in the event of default of a counterparty.

Cash placement exposes Orchard to credit risk, as, in the event of default, it will be treated as an unsecured creditor. Total credit exposure with any one institution or connected institutions will not exceed 25% of the eligible capital of Orchard as required by CRR Article 395 without the prior approval of the PRA (subject to institutional exemption as below).

All exposures in excess of 10% of eligible capital will be notified to the PRA on the common reporting template (COREP).

Exemptions

Any exposure to government or central Banks, which carry a 0% risk weighting as per the standardized credit risk approach, are exempt from the counterparty and exposure limits (CRR Article 395).

Institutional Exemption

Small institutions may have exposures to other institutions in excess of 25% of eligible capital subject to a cap of the lower of Euro 150m or 100% of eligible capital.

Cash Placements

Any institution with which deposits are placed must be UK registered and have a minimum short-term credit rating of at least credit quality step 2, as defined under Part Three, Title II, Chapter 2, of Capital Requirements Regulation (CRR), being A-2, P-2 and F-2 for S&P, Moody's and Fitch respectively.

The list of institutions with whom Orchard is authorised to place deposits, along with the maximum allowable exposure will be included in the overarching Treasury Policy. This will be updated on a periodic basis to take account of any changes in ratings. Any cash placement will be for a maximum maturity period of 90 days.

6.5.2 Capital Risk

This is the risk that Orchard will have insufficient capital to cover unexpected losses, meet regulatory requirements or support growth plans. It is captured within the ICAAP (this document), and reflects a failure to anticipate possible future losses, or a failure to grow the business in accordance with regulatory prudential requirements.

Qualitative

Orchard's Internal Capital Adequacy Assessment Process ('ICAAP') is predicated on the assumption that it is willing to take a balanced approach towards risk and return. The ICAAP is central to the capital management framework and is used to inform the Board of the ongoing assessment and quantification of Orchard's risks, how Orchard mitigates those risks and manages capital adequacy of Orchard.

The ICAAP is embedded in the Risk & Compliance Management Framework for Orchard and is subject to ongoing updates and revisions when necessary. However, at a minimum, the ICAAP is updated annually as part of the business planning process. The ICAAP is a process that brings together the management framework (i.e., the policies, procedures, strategies and systems that Orchard has implemented to identify, manage and mitigate its risks) and the financial disciplines of business planning and capital management.

The Board takes the Pillar 1 capital formula calculations (standardised approach for credit, market and operational risk) as a starting point, and then considers whether each of the calculations deliver sufficient capital to adequately cover management's anticipated risks. Where the Board considered that the Pillar 1 calculations does not adequately reflect the risk, an additional capital add-on in Pillar 2A is applied, as per the Total Capital Requirement (TCR) issued by the PRA.

At all times Orchard's capital position must be aligned with capital adequacy limits to maintain robust capital management under "normal" and "stressed" conditions. With regard to capital management this means:

- Maintaining a sufficient level of capital above the minimum that is set by the PRA in the Total Capital Requirement ("TCR").
- All capital comprises of Core Tier 1.

Quantitative

Table 28: Capital risk appetite.

Limit category		Target	Early warning indicator (Amber)	Trigger (Red)
Capital	CET1 Ratio (PRA min 8%)	30%	22.50%	20%
	Leverage Ratio (PRA min 3.25%)	28%	25%	22%
	Surplus Capital over TCR & Pillar 2B	£5.5m	>£5.5m	>£2.5m

Common Equity Tier 1 (CET1) Ratio Orchard has determined that its CET1 ratio should not fall below 30% under normal business conditions in year 1.

Given that deposit taking activity is new, a conservative target has been set, which is broadly, three times the regulatory minimum.

Leverage Ratio

The leverage ratio, introduced by "Basel III, CRD IV", is a non-risk-based measure that is designed to act as a supplement to risk-based capital requirements. The ratio measures the relationship between the capital resources of the organisation and its total assets. The purpose of monitoring and managing this metric is to enable regulators to constrain the build-up of excessive leverage.

Basel III's leverage ratio is defined as the "capital measure" (the numerator) divided by the "exposure measure" (the denominator) and is expressed as a percentage. The capital measure is currently defined as Tier 1 capital and the minimum leverage ratio is 3%. The Board has set Orchard's target leverage ratio at 28% for year 1.

The PRA has proposed that firms covered by the Leverage rules should include all PRA-regulated banks and building societies with total retail deposits equal to or greater than £50 billion, whether on an individual or a consolidated basis, on a firm's financial year end date.

The PRA considers that the proposed £50 billion retail deposit threshold will identify a group of firms whose size and provision of critical financial services to the UK economy means that their failure could pose material threats to domestic financial stability. This would be consistent with the PRA's objective of promoting the safety and soundness of firms primarily by seeking to ensure that their business is carried on in a way which avoids any adverse effect on the stability of the UK financial system.

Regulatory capital Requirement

Over and above the total capital requirement (TCR) that consists of Pillar 1 and Pillar 2A capital requirements, an additional PRA buffer capital under Pillar 2B may be required, subject to PRA assessment of Risk Management and Governance framework, over and above the CRD IV buffer requirements for the capital conservation buffer (CCoB), Counter Cyclical Buffer (CCyB) and the systemic buffer for systematically important firms.

The systemic buffer has not been included as Orchard is not considered to be a systemically important firm. The CCoB is expressed as a percentage of Risk Weighted Assets ('RWAs') and is set at 2.50% of RWAs. CCyB is expressed as a percentage of RWAs and is set at 1%.

As a new entrant, the Pillar 2B capital requirements for Orchard are less stringent and the Pillar 2B capital requirements have been based on the wind-down costs as presented in section 10.

6.5.3 Liquidity Risk

The risk that Orchard is unable to meet its financial obligations as they fall due, or can do so only at excessive cost.

Orchard will undertake an Individual Liquidity Adequacy Assessment Process (ILAAP) at least annually, which documents its approach to management of liquidity risk and compliance with the Overarching Liquidity Adequacy Rule (OLAR). As part of this process, Orchard has set both qualitative and quantitative limits to ensure liquidity risk is being managed appropriately.

Qualitative

Orchard will hold a sufficient quantity and quality of liquidity instruments or cash to ensure that all liabilities will be met as they fall due under normal market conditions and under a range of stress market conditions.

Quantitative

Orchard has set the following Primary metrics for managing liquidity risk:

Table 29: Liquidity Metrics.

Limit category		Target	Early warning indicator (Amber)	Trigger (Red)
Liquidity	Liquidity Coverage Ratio (LCR PRA min 100%)	150%	125%	110%
	Net Stable Funding Ratio (NSFR 100%)	125%	110%	105%
	Survival Horizon under stress (PRA min 30days)	90 days	75 days	60 days
	HQLAs to Deposits	14%	12%	8%

Table 29 (continued)

Limit category		Target	Early warning indicator (Amber)	Trigger (Red)
	Increase in cost of fundsfor deposits above the average of top ten providers on Money.co.uk website	Av. Of top ten providers for 1 year and 2 year fixed rate deposits	= or >100 basis points	= >200 basis points

Survival Time Horizon

Under the CRD IV liquidity requirements, firms are required to assess their cashflows over a 30 day time horizon under stressed conditions to determine whether these are able to stay within the minimum regulatory liquidity ratios or within the firms' own risk appetite, if higher. As a new entrant, the Board has approved a higher risk appetite target of 90 days, which is three times higher than the minimum regulatory requirement.

The PRA has stated that banks are allowed to use their liquidity buffers to meet outflows and holding a further buffer on top of the liquidity buffer is not required. Under this revised approach to liquidity management, Orchard could fall below its operational target of 90 days in the normal course of its business, with close monitoring if 75 days is breached and escalation, with proactive management action required once Orchard breaches, or is expected to breach, the 60 days threshold.

The trigger of 60 days limit is still twice the regulatory minimum requirement of 30 days, but given that Orchard has limited contingent funding options, Management has determined that the 60 day limit is appropriate.

Net Stable Funding Ratio

The 125% target for the NSFR is felt to be appropriate to allow for 25% headroom against the regulatory minimum given a new entrant and to ensure adequate available funding to avoid disruption in the lending activities. Also, the level of available stable funding, which is the key figure in the NSFR, is expected to be much higher than the value of HQLA, which is the key measure of the LCR. This makes the NSFR far less volatile, so a small headroom between the regulatory requirement and risk appetite is appropriate.

Orchard will also monitor the following secondary indicators:

Table 30: Secondary Liquidity Risk Indicators.

Metric	Trigger (Red)
Deposit Inflows as proportion of budgeted inflows	Min 70%, Max 130%
Retention rate of maturing fixed term deposits	Min 50%

Table 30 (continued)

Metric	Trigger (Red)
Proportion of deposits which are 'high risk'	Max 5%
Number of payment systems	Min 2
Savings Operational Trigger per month in Year 1 of the plan	Postal applications volume >75 (value – £1.8m) Web application form downloads >300

6.5.4 Interest Rate Risk in the Banking Book

This is the risk arising from unhedged or mismatched assets and liability positions, which are sensitive to interest rate movements.

Interest rate risk arises from the following:

Re-pricing risk	Timing differences between maturities of fixed-rate assets and liabilities and re-pricing of variable-rate assets and liabilities (including off-balance sheet). This can expose Orchard to changes in the shape of the yield curve
Basis risk	Asset and liabilities re-price at the same time but in line with a different interest rate basis, e.g., assets re-price with reference to Bank of England base rate but liabilities re-price with reference to LIBOR.
Pipeline risk	The uncertainties arising where actual movements do not match those that were expected.
Optionality risk	Where early terminations of assets and liabilities compared to the original term can worsen mismatch positions.

Orchard has set the following qualitative and quantitative measures to mitigate exposure to interest rate risk:

Qualitative

Orchard's assets and liabilities in the base plan are fixed term and fixed rate. Although there will be timing difference between maturities of assets and liabilities, the underlying risk will be managed by ALCO and monitored regularly against the Board approved risk appetite.

Quantitative

Table 31: Interest Rate Risk in the Banking Book.

Limit category		Target	Early warning indicator (Amber)	Trigger (Red)
Market	Interest Rate Risk Sensitivity – % of CET1	2.3%	2.70%	3%

6.5.5 Operational Risk (Incorporating Financial Crime Risk and Conduct Risk) Definition

Operational risk is the risk of loss resulting from inadequate or failed processes or controls, weak or failed governance, adverse people related issues, system failures or from external adverse events (including those arising from financial crime incidents, conduct issues, cyber risks and failings in the management of legal or regulatory issues). Such events, were they to materialise, would adversely affect the ability of Orchard to achieve its corporate objectives or adversely impact the reputation of Orchard.

As a core component of its RCMF, Orchard's risk taxonomy is built upon the ORX risk categorisations, which is being developed to monitor each risk to which the business believes it is exposed.

- Business Continuity
- Conduct
- Credit*
- Data management
- Financial Crime
- Financial Reporting & Tax
- Fraud
- Information Security (including Cyber)
- Legal
- Model
- People
- Physical Security and Safety
- Regulatory Compliance
- Strategic Risk**
- Third Party
- Transaction Processing

*Credit risk is assessed according to regulatory formulae, as detailed elsewhere in this document.
**Strategic risk is usually excluded from operational risk, but has been included within the broader category of "Enterprise Risks", as it has a high degree of correlation with operational risks in a new and small bank.

Overall Appetite Statement

The Board requires that the Operational Risk appetite of Orchard is low, acknowledging that a zero-tolerance level is not realistic with some level of accumulated operational loss possible and realistic.

- In financial terms however, the maximum appetite for operational risk is for aggregate losses of GBP 250,000 over the course of a year, and not exceeding £62,000 for individual incidents. This loss appetite will be reviewed and revised, as appropriate, as the scale of Orchard increases.

The individual components of operational risk are addressed below:

Infrastructure and Operational Resilience

The Bank intends to maintain high levels of customer service and customer accessibility to its systems will be of paramount importance.

- We have no appetite for material or recurring technology or operational failures and as such we will maintain the availability of IT systems with agreed Service Level Agreements to minimise disruption to business operations and customer service.
- We have no appetite for Orchard to operate without a detailed Business Recovery and Continuity Plan that has been tested at least once in the past 12 months.
- We have no appetite for material or recurring technology or operational failures and as such we will manage technology change, including the choice of IT services and solutions, in a manner that supports business strategy and minimises the likelihood of disruption to business operations and customer service.
- Note that 'material' variance in project tolerance terms is 10% over agreed cost budget / 10% over agreed delivery time.

Conduct Risk, including Treating Customers Fairly (TCF)

- We will adopt behaviours and judgements that result in fair outcomes for our customers, including vulnerable customers who will be proactively identified so they receive the necessary help and support.
  - Our risk appetite is to design products that meet our customers' needs and expectations and which are approved within a structured governance framework; and
  - We will use defined sales processes to promote our products. We will establish our customers' needs and circumstances so our products are suitable, and we will provide appropriate advice where required.
- In dealing with customer complaints, it is our policy to fulfil the expectations of the FCA and to:
  - take complaints from customers or potential customers seriously;
  - deal with complaints from customer or potential customers fairly and promptly;
  - identify the underlying root causes of complaints and learn any lessons for the future; and
  - ensure that all identification and reporting of complaints is robust and accurate.

Data Management

We recognise that, with vast amounts of data, mistakes will occur in processing data, but we have no appetite for these mistakes impacting the relationship with Orchard's customers.

Financial Crime and Sanctions

- Our overall appetite for financial crime, of any sort, is NIL. Any detected instance will be investigated immediately, and if necessary, reported to the appropriate authorities.
- Comply with EU and UK law and regulation on the prevention of money laundering and combating the financing of terrorism, and the laws and regulations on the prevention of money laundering and combating the financing of terrorism of all other countries, where applicable to our business or the currencies in which we do business; and
- Never knowingly allow ourselves to be used in connection with money laundering, financial crime or the financing of terrorist activities.
- The Bank will take a zero-tolerance approach to bribery and corruption and will conduct our business in an honest and ethical manner;
  - act professionally, fairly and with integrity in all our business dealings and relationships;
  - implement and enforce effective systems to counter bribery and corruption;
  - comply with EU and UK law and regulation on the prevention of fraud, bribery and corruption, and the laws and regulations on the prevention of fraud, bribery and corruption of all other countries, where applicable to our business or the currencies in which we do business; and
  - never knowingly allow ourselves to be used in connection with fraudulent, or bribery and corruption, activities.

Financial Reporting, Tax and Audit

- We have no appetite for external financial or regulatory returns being submitted with errors, incomplete information, or later than the due date or for any tax due to be paid late.

Fraud

- We will comply with EU and UK law and regulation on the prevention of fraud, bribery and corruption, and the laws and regulations on the prevention of fraud, bribery and corruption of all other countries, where applicable to our business or the currencies in which we do business; and
- We will never knowingly allow ourselves to be used in connection with fraudulent, or bribery and corruption, activities.

- Our policy is to comply with EC and UK competition law, and the competition laws of all other countries where we are construed or deemed to be doing business.

Security & 'Cyber' Risk

- Security includes the effective management and control / protection of key assets and resources.
- Such assets include:
- physical (primarily premises and equipment),
  - human resources (employees, customers and visitors/contractors) and
  - technological (primarily IT systems and data).
- We have no appetite for material or recurring control failures and as such we will take sufficient measures to manage, control and protect our key assets and resources from accidental, as well as deliberate or malicious events. This category specifically includes the development of a robust 'cyber risk' defensive / protective framework to minimise the impact of such threats alongside the development of effective recovery and disaster continuity plan.

Legal and Regulatory

- We have no appetite for Orchard failing to comply with the laws, regulations (including financial regulation) and statutes of the jurisdictions in which it operates or, should there be any reportable breach of these, failing to report this breach promptly and accurately.
- We will always ensure that independent legal advice, where required, is sought from suitably qualified firms with adequate professional indemnity cover.

Model Risk

- Our appetite for model risk is to have adequate and effective controls in place to build and test models that minimise the risk of errors arising in their use so that operational, tactical and strategic decisions are not made on false knowledge.

People

- It is our policy at Orchard to provide an encouraging, supportive and safe working environment for our staff, who represent such a key component of our business. This extends to us having in place a clear recruitment policy, terms and conditions of employment which conform to regulatory and legal requirements, having in place clearly defined role and responsibility profiles and a performance management and development framework founded upon behavioural and cultural expectations including a clear understanding of respective responsibilities for risk management.

- Orchard believes in developing people from within the organisation, but recognises that in a small bank, there will always be a limited number of people who form key person dependencies. As part of the training and development programme for staff, cross-training and cross-skilling will form a key activity.

Physical Security and Safety

- Our appetite is to operate in an environment safe from foreseeable accidents and to prevent our people from being exposed to risks from customers and third parties.

Regulatory Compliance

- Our risk appetite is to comply with all relevant regulatory requirements impacting the Bank. Records held by the Bank will be accurate, easily retrievable and destroyed in line with regulatory requirements.

Strategy and Governance

- Ensuring an adequate corporate governance structure exists and is appropriately managed
- We have no appetite for any of the governance bodies operating without agreed, documented Terms of References or with any meeting of any one of these bodies convening without an agreed agenda and minutes.

Third Party Management

- We have no appetite for Orchard engaging with any critical service provider (including but not exclusively IT related) without an appropriate level of due diligence being conducted that establishes the maintenance of confidentiality, integrity and availability of such services alongside appropriate contracts or acceptable service and/or license agreement

Transaction Processing

We have no appetite for:

- External payments not being made when due; or
- An incorrect amount being paid; or
- Any occurrence of a payment being made to the wrong payee.
- We require that all key operational processes and procedures are adequately documented with a minimal appetite for process errors or failures. Key process controls will be subject to regular review in terms of design and operational effectiveness via the Risk Committee.

6.6 Risk Register

As a core component of its RCMF, Orchard has created a Risk Register based upon the Operational Riskdata Exchange ("ORIX") risk categorisations, which is being developed to monitor each risk to which the business believes it is exposed. The Risk Register is also utilised to determine whether sufficient capital has been allocated to Operational or other risk in the Bank by comparing the total residual risk score to the minimum capital requirement for operational risk under CRD IV.

The risks captured in the Risk Register are set out in the table below table. The full risk register is appended to this document.

Table 32: Risk Register Level 1 and 2 Risks.

Nature of Risk	Enterprise Risk	Level 2	Risk (Level 2)	Risk Summary
Conduct	**Con1. Conduct**	Con1.1	Product Design	Failure to design products that meet our customers' needs and expectations. Products or services that do not meet customer needs or are targeted inappropriately.
		Con1.2	Distribution	The Bank's distribution processes result in the customer selecting a product or service which is inappropriate for their needs or circumstances.
		Con1.3	Governance, Culture	The Bank's governance processes fail to identify, manage, or reduce conduct risk. Also includes conduct risks stemming from an inappropriate strategy or culture which places insufficient emphasis on good customer outcomes.
		Con1.4	Governance Structures	Failure to practice good governance due to a weakness in the design or execution of the governance structures.
	Con2. Legal	Con2.1	Legal	Failure to comply with any legislative requirements which apply to the Bank such as breaches of OFT guidelines, Consumer Credit requirements and Environmental and Corporate Responsibility requirements. Breaches of the Data Protection Act should be captured under "Ops 4.1 Information Management".

Table 32 (continued)

Nature of Risk	Enterprise Risk	Level 2	Risk (Level 2)	Risk Summary
	Con3. Regulatory Compliance	Con3.1	Regulatory – Prudential	Failure to comply with EU or UK prudential, securities or markets (PSM) regulation issued or supervised by the PRA or FCA; or European authorities such as the EC, EBA and ESMA.
		Con3.2	Regulatory – Conduct	Failure to comply with any Financial Conduct Authority (FCA) regulatory requirement applicable to the Bank or its subsidiaries.
Credit	**Crd1. Credit**	Crd1.1	Wholesale Credit Risk	Failure to limit credit exposures associated with counterparty failure.
		Crd1.2	Credit Losses	Failure to control retail credit activities such that losses are outside of Risk Appetite.
Financial	**Fin1. Financial Reporting & Tax**	Fin1.1	Financial Accounting & Tax Errors	Failures in financial management. Failure to calculate, report or disclose the Bank's tax liabilities.
		Fin1.2	Internal / External Financial Reporting	Failures to produce timely and accurate and complete reporting both internally and externally.
	Fin2. Model	Fin2.1	Business Models	The risk that Models are applied to activities for which they are inappropriate or are implemented or operated incorrectly.
		Fin2.2	Capital Adequacy Risk	Failure to hold an adequate capital position to meet our regulatory requirements.
		Fin2.3	Liquidity and Funding	Failure to maintain sufficient liquidity and a stable funding profile of appropriate duration to meet adverse outflows.
		Fin2.4	Interest Rate Risk on the Banking Book	Failure to manage the potential impact on both Net Interest Income and Economic Value.
Operational	**Ops1. People**	Ops1.1	Employment diversity, discrimination and harassment	The Bank's governance processes fail to identify, manage, or reduce discrimination and harassment or fail to support promote employment diversity.

Table 32 (continued)

Nature of Risk	Enterprise Risk	Level 2	Risk (Level 2)	Risk Summary
		Ops1.2	Business Disruption – Employee Related	Risk of business disruption due to workforce unavailability.
	Ops2. Business Continuity	Ops2.1	IT Architecture Design and Development	Inappropriate architecture (e.g., systems integration through merger); strategic risk (platform / supplier / outsourcing); Inadequate systems capacity planning; obsolescence of hardware or software; lack of alignment with business strategy; business requirement inconsistent with strategic IT architecture.
		Ops2.2	IT Availability Network / Hardware / Software	Failures in the delivery of IT services; change control failures; failures in incident management; IT system failure and business disruption for all aspects of IT infrastructure and operating systems (including network, hardware and software failure).
		Ops2.3	Change	Risks associated with individual projects, programmes of change and the portfolio of change (i.e., all projects and programmes).
	Ops3. Data management	Ops3.1	Failure to maintain the accuracy of data	The risk that reports are delivered based on data which are inappropriate or inaccurate.
	Ops4. Information Security (including Cyber)	Ops4.1	Information Management	Failure to manage the confidentiality, integrity and availability of information or personal data in use within the Bank whether physical of electronic in format. This includes the failure to manage the storage and destruction of data and information.

Table 32 (continued)

Nature of Risk	Enterprise Risk	Level 2	Risk (Level 2)	Risk Summary
		Ops4.2	System Security	Failure to manage the confidentiality, integrity and availability of the systems that provide access to data and information. This includes the failure to manage against the threat of Internal and External attack against the Bank.
	Ops4. Information Security (including Cyber)	Ops4.3	End User Computing and Application Failure	Failure to manage the confidentiality, integrity and availability of the data and information on the Bank's systems deployed to third parties, e.g., intermediaries.
	Ops5. Physical Security and Safety	Ops5.1	Business Disruption – Workplace Related	Risk of disruption to the Bank due to issues affecting access to the Bank's premises or the premises impacting the staff within its building(s).
		Ops5.2	Malicious Damage / Physical Security	Malicious damage to the Bank's property or reputation. This includes malicious comment or publicity against the Bank
	Ops6. Third Party	Ops6.1	Procurement	The failure of third party supplier (external) to provide the service required by the Bank (either through their own organisational failure or substandard performance).
		Ops6.2	Supplier Management / Delivery	Failure to identify, select and set up appropriate contracts and agreements with suppliers of goods and services to the Bank.
	Ops7. Financial Crime	Ops7.1	Financial Crime	Non-compliance with legal and regulatory obligations (including Money Laundering Regulations, Proceeds of Crime Act and Terrorism Act) leading to failure to prevent and detect money laundering and other financial crimes not covered under bribery, competition or fraud.
		Ops7.2	Bribery & Corruption	The Bank fails to prevent bribery and corruption.

Table 32 (continued)

Nature of Risk	Enterprise Risk	Level 2	Risk (Level 2)	Risk Summary
	Ops8. Fraud	Ops8.1	Internal Fraud	Abuse of position committed by an employee(s) through the deliberate misuse or misapplication of the Bank's resources or assets, usually for personal gain.
		Ops8.2	External Fraud	Fraud perpetrated against the Bank and/or customers by an external party, usually for personal gain. Includes third party fraud (committed by a person with no obvious connection to the Bank) and first party fraud (committed by a customer), including benefit fraud.
	Ops9. Transaction Processing	Ops9.1	Post Sales Product Delivery and Operation	Customers are not treated fairly after the point of sale, service or transaction. Also covers failures in complaints handling process.
		Ops9.2	Financial Transaction Payment Processing	Mistakes, errors and/or process failures related to the management and execution of all customer financial transactions. This includes "Manual data entry errors".
		Ops9.3	Customer on-boarding and account management	Failures in non-payment administration processes. This includes delivery of the administration process and customer relationship management.
		Ops9.4	Lending Quality	Failure to lend in line with Policy objectives and to maintain sufficient quality to withstand macro-economic stresses.
Strategic	**Stg1. Strategic Risk**	Stg1.1	Concentration	Lack of sufficient product diversity. Business concentrated via a small number of intermediaries.
		Stg1.2	Changes in Business Conditions	Failure to plan for changes in business conditions e.g., impact of Brexit, new entrant, change in commission payments to intermediaries
		Stg1.3	Changes in Market Competition	Failure to plan for new competition

6.6.1 Risk Scoring

Each risk on the Risk Register is assessed for its "inherent" (uncontrolled) probability and impact to create an inherent risk score. Controls applied to this risk, and the effectiveness of the controls determines not only the "residual" (controlled) probability and impact, but also whether further activity to improve the control environment is required.

Probability (Likelihood) of a Risk Materialising into an Event

The probability of a risk crystallising is assessed against a 5 point scale, ranging from remote to certain. The exact interpretation of the points on the scale is guided by reference to the frequency of the activity in the table below, which also includes the values used for scoring the probability in calculating consequences.

Table 33: Risk Probability.

Term	Frequency of Activity/Operation			Value
	Daily operations	Weekly and monthly operations	Quarterly, bi-annual or annual operations	
Remote	Once per year	Once every 5 years	Once in a century	0.40%
Unlikely	Every two months	Once per year	Once in 25 years	1.50%
Possible	Every month	Twice per year	Once in a decade	8.00%
Frequent	Every week	Once per quarter	Once a year	40.00%
Certain	Every day	Every week	Every occasion	100.00%

Impact Measurement

As well as a direct monetary loss or cost, it is possible for impact to be measured in terms of damage to the Bank's reputation, the impact on customers, or the management involvement away from BAU. Each of these is mapped to one of five aligned degrees of severity, with the monetary value mid-point being used in the calculation of consequences against the probability. Thus, it is possible to consider each impact, for example disruption to Orchard's customers, in terms of other impacts, such as the management time and cost of rectification. Each level of severity is also mapped to the management of the risk (when applied to the residual consequence) and the timescale and management oversight and reporting for events.

The threshold for an extreme monetary loss is set with reference to the maximum aggregate operational losses during a year, as expressed in the Statement of Risk Appetite. Any risk with a residual score above this criticality threshold requires the active management of the Risk Committee as it is outside of Orchard's appetite and therefore has the potential to cause extreme disruption, although this does not mean *ipso facto* that the management team have failed to manage the risk. Criticality thresholds for other levels were determined by dividing the extreme threshold (£250k) by 5, hence

£50k and £10k. For "Extreme" events this is set at 5 times the threshold value, producing £1.25m if the threshold is £250k. This represents a consistent step change in the monetary value used for calculating the consequence of a risk. The monetary value of the mid-point is the average of the ranges specified for the degree of severity.

Table 34: Risk Impacts.

	Category				
	Nominal	**Minor**	**Significant**	**Material**	**Extreme**
Escalation timescales for loss events	One working day	End of working day	Within 1 hour	Immediate	
Information escalation	Manager	Senior Manager/ Head of Function	Executive	Executive (& Board for information)	Board
Management of Risks	Control Operators	Manager	Senior Manager/ Head of Function	Executive Committee	Risk Committee
Ownership of Risks	Manager	Senior Manager/ Head of Function	Executive Committee	Risk Committee	Board
Monetary	£0 – £2,000	£2,000 – £10,000	£10,000 – £50,000	£50,000 – £250,000	Over £250,000
Reputational – Potential Regulatory impact – Potential media or social media interest	Potential for media interest but unlikely	Local media interest	Need to inform Regulator Local media coverage Industry coverage	High level of Regulator interest National Media Coverage Some wider public interest	Formal disclosure to Regulator Potential s166 action High level of national media interest
	Notify Executive Manager **immediately** Executive Manager will inform Board	Notify Executive Manager **immediately** Executive Manager will inform Board	Notify Executive Manager **immediately** Executive Manager will inform Board	Notify Executive Manager **immediately** Executive Manager will inform Board	Notify Executive Manager **immediately** Executive Manager will inform Board

Table 34 (continued)

	Category				
	Nominal	**Minor**	**Significant**	**Material**	**Extreme**
Customer – Impact on customers	Limited customer impact (fewer than 20)	Small Number of customers (20 – 100 customers)	Some customers (100 to 5% of customer base)	Major customer impacts (5% to 10% of customer base)	Customer impacts across Bank (>10% of customer base)
Management – Potential impact on colleagues/ management – Potential impact on achievement of business objectives	Small incident that is managed as part of BAU	Response has limited impact on management or colleagues Temporary impact on Business objectives	Some impact on business objectives and/or Income	Formal response invoked (e.g., BCP) 10% of colleagues affected. Income reduced by <10%	Significant Exec involvement, over 25% of colleagues affected Severe impact on Business Objectives and Income

Risk Scoring

The product of the likelihood and the (monetary) impact produces a consequence. As the table of risk impacts provides insight into the criticality of an impact, the table of consequences can be shaded to guide the management of risks, including the appropriate level of ownership and oversight. This empowers the relevant levels of the business to actively manage their own risks, and to consider whether the assessed level of residual risk is acceptable, as (for example) an improvement in controls could cost more than the anticipated reduction in the residual risk score, indicating that this particular risk control would not be cost effective.

Table 35: Residual risk heat map.

Consequences			**Likelihood**				
Impact	**Range**		**Remote**	**Unlikely**	**Possible**	**Probable**	**Certain**
	From	**To**	**0.4%**	**1.5%**	**8.0%**	**40.0%**	**100.0%**
Nominal	**£0**	**£2,000**	£4	£15	£80	£400	£1,000
Minor	**£2,000**	**£10,000**	£24	£90	£480	£2,400	£6,000
Significant	**£10,000**	**£50,000**	£120	£450	£2,400	£12,000	£30,000
Material	**£50,000**	**£250,000**	£600	£2,250	£12,000	£60,000	£150,000
Extreme	**£250,000**	**(Unlimited)**	£5,000	£18,750	£100,000	£500,000	£1,250,000

Risk Criticality
Criticality of risks is determined by comparison of the residual risk score against the criteria used to assess the impact ratings. Thus, any risk is assigned a level of management and oversight appropriate to the criticality of its risk exposure after the application of controls. Any risks with a residual score greater than the threshold value for "Extreme" will be managed under the control of Risk Committee, and ownership (ultimate accountability) and oversight rests with the Board, who would need to determine how the activity giving rise to the residual score should be mitigated: tolerated (accepted, at least for now, with regular reviews); terminated (the activity should cease within a specified timescale); transferred (for example, an insurance policy would be taken out against the risk materialising); or treated (controls improved to an agreed plan and timescale). Risks with a "nominal" residual score (that is, less than £2,000) would be managed by those who operate the controls with oversight from their line manager (see the lines for management and ownership of risks in table 24, above). This allows the Bank's Executive to exercise oversight of nominal, minor and significant risks and to manage any risks with a material residual consequence, keeping the material and extreme risks in sight of the Board and the Risk Committee.

6.6.2 Internal Controls

Within each ORIX Risk Category there can be a number of risks, for example "People" is subdivided into "Employment diversity, discrimination and harassment" and "Business Disruption – Employee Related" (which is separate from Business Continuity). These risks may be further subdivided into risk event types, reflecting operational processes which can give rise to a risk materialising and which will be used in recording risk incidents. It is at the level of risks and risk event types that Orchard operates its controls.

The internal control framework of Orchard is owned by Risk Committee and comprises all the processes used for financial reporting and monitoring the safety of the assets of the Bank and its customers. Individual controls are provided by both the first and second lines of defence (e.g., compliance advice) and *operated* by the risk owners within the first line.

Fundamental principles of the control systems are
- the appointment of sufficiently qualified employees and their continuous further education;
- strict compliance with the four eyes principle; and
- a clear separation of tasks to avoid actual and perceived conflicts of interests.

Responsibility for meeting the firm's control framework is clearly allocated to managers and supervisors and responsible persons are made aware of failings through the use of an error log (whether there was an incident that materialised into a risk event or not) which is periodically reported to the ExCo and Risk Committee if appropriate, the level of detail reported (from summary information to an in-depth root-cause analysis) being determined according to the criticality of an event.

Regular reviews of errors will be undertaken by internal audit, whether or not these have led to losses, in addition to their reviews of the operation of other internal controls.

6.7 Structure, Resources and Reporting Lines for Compliance

Conduct risk is defined as the risk of the integrity of the institution or the financial system being affected by the improper, unethical conduct of the organisation, its staff or management in contravention of legislation and regulation or the standards set by the firm. Management of Conduct Risks is integrated into the RCMF and the CRO is responsible for their oversight and management, but specific attention is paid to the following areas.

6.7.1 Conduct Risk Areas

Staff Issues

- Monitoring potential conflicts of interest
- Competence and training
- Private investment transactions

Customer Issues

- Monitoring the duty of care to customers
- Customer due diligence and enhanced due diligence and PEP's
- Complaints' handling
- Treating Customers Fairly
- Vulnerable customers

Transactional Issues

- Sanctions monitoring
- Anti-money laundering
- Prevention of financial crime

Organisational Issues

- New product approvals
- Data protection

6.7.2 Independence of Compliance

The Bank's CRO will report to Orchard's Risk Committee (with a dotted line to the CEO), which will be responsible for his appointment or dismissal. The CRO will be the MLRO and Head of Compliance. As the need arises, the Bank will recruit additional resource for monitoring Compliance activities.

It is important to ensure the compliance function is independent of the functions which have primary responsibility for the implementation and maintenance of proper control measures – e.g., operations and credit. To ensure independence is established and maintained the Bank will constitute the compliance function following certain key principles:

- The CRO has a dotted reporting line to the Board;
- The CRO will issue regular reports on compliance matters to the ExCo and to the Board;
- The CRO will have access to any information or resources necessary to perform his duties and will have the right to attend Board or Board sub-committee meetings.

6.7.3 Compliance Responsibilities

The key responsibilities of the compliance function cover all the key compliance risk areas

Regulatory Rules and Legislation

- Identify compliance risk-related laws, regulations, rules, and establish good business standards
- Translate compliance risk-related laws, regulations and rules and good business standards, as well as expectations from regulators and other monitoring authorities into compliance requirements
- Monitor regulatory requirements and changes
- Report deficiencies to management and provide advice to improve the compliance environment and exercise control over remediation of reported deficiencies
- Provide advice to staff on the interpretation of the various rules and standards
- Maintain an open relationship with the PRA and FCA and other regulatory authorities
- Maintain contacts with industry associations.

Information and Training

- Embed compliance in the culture and behaviour of all Orchard staff
- Ensure the compliance function itself remains up-to-date with changing industry requirements

Compliance Risk Identification, Assessment and Monitoring

- Identify the relevant compliance risks, and assess priorities
- Advise, support and/or challenge the business on the mitigation of identified compliance risks, and on the design and implementation of proper control measures to mitigate such risks
- Monitor actions undertaken to mitigate compliance risks or other compliance issues
- Develop and deliver the annual Compliance Monitoring Plan (CMP)

Instructions and Investigations

- The Board may give the CRO the authority to give instructions to staff and to grant or withhold approval for actions by staff
- The compliance function has the authority to take the initiative to investigate supposed breaches of any law, regulations, internal rules or standards, seeking assistance from other support functions or external parties as necessary
- The compliance function has the authority to request a copy of any document from management, any other staff member, any customer or third party if such document is deemed necessary for effective compliance risk management at the sole discretion of the compliance function

Reporting

- Based on an annual review the CRO will produce a compliance report to the Risk Committee including proposals for compliance activity in the coming year
- In addition, the CRO will produce a compliance monitoring report for each Risk Committee meeting and other incidental reports as required

6.8 Internal Audit Function

Orchard intends to outsource its internal audit function in the initial years and will tender during mobilisation, with Audit Committee approving the appointment. Given the small balance sheet and modest scale of operations, engaging staff from a reputed accounting firm will allow Orchard to access their breadths and depths of expertise in a cost-effective manner. Rotation of auditors would be performed periodically to minimise the potential for or appearance of loss of objectivity. The scope of the audit will be clearly articulated in a comprehensive engagement letter, to be supplemented with frequent written and oral communication. The directors and senior managers are fully aware that they will continue to be accountable for maintaining an effective system of internal control and for overseeing the internal audit function.

6.8.1 Role and Mandate of Internal Audit

The primary role of Orchard's internal audit function is to help to protect the assets, reputation and sustainability of the business operations of the organisation. It does this by assessing whether all significant risks are identified and appropriately reported to the Board and executive management; assessing whether they are properly controlled; and by challenging executive management to improve the effectiveness of governance, risk management and internal controls. The role of internal audit will be set out in an internal audit terms of reference document.

6.8.2 Scope and Priorities of Internal Audit

In setting its scope, internal audit will determine independently the key risks facing the organisation, including emerging and systemic risks, and how effectively these risks are being managed. In particular it will take account of:

- The design and operating effectiveness of governance structures and processes
- The strategic and management information presented to the Board
- The processes and controls supporting strategic decision making
- The setting of, and adherence to, risk appetite
- The risk and control culture
- The risk of poor customer outcomes, giving rise to conduct or reputational risk
- Whether products, services and supporting processes are designed in line with conduct regulation, compliance with financial crime regulations and Orchard's customer strategy, values and standards
- Whether Orchard is acting with integrity in its dealings with all customers and in its interaction with relevant markets
- The management of risks relating to Orchard's capital and liquidity
- The controls and accuracy around financial reporting and regulatory reporting
- Business process changes, introduction of new products and services, outsourcing decisions and acquisitions/divestments
- The adequacy and effectiveness of the design, as well as the implementation, of policies and processes
- The IT infrastructure appropriate for the business, with sufficient controls around cyber risks.

6.8.3 Prioritisation of Internal Audit Work

- Internal audit will make a risk-based decision as to which areas within its scope should be included in the audit plan, and its proposals will be approved annually by the Audit Committee
- Internal audit will attend and deliver reports to the Audit Committee focusing on:
  - significant control breakdowns together with a robust root-cause analysis
  - thematic issues identified across the organisation
  - an independent view of management's reporting on risk management
  - assessment of the overall effectiveness of the governance, and risk and control framework of the organisation

6.8.4 Interaction With Other Control Functions

Internal audit will include within its scope an assessment of the adequacy and effectiveness of the risk management, compliance and finance functions ensuring it remains as a 3rd line of defence and does not become involved in line management or place undue reliance on the other control functions.

6.8.5 Independence and Authority

The outsourced internal auditor will report directly to the Chair of the Audit Committee, a non-executive director, and have the appropriate standing and authority to challenge executive directors. The chair of the Audit Committee will have the final say on the appointment of the outsourced internal auditor.

The outsourced Internal Auditor will have the right to attend all management committee meetings and will have access to key management information and the firm's records.

The internal auditor will have an open, constructive and co-operative relationship with regulators which supports sharing of information relevant to carrying out their respective responsibilities.

7 Capital Planning

7.1 Capital Management and Monitoring

Orchard will monitor and manage its capital levels via a regular management information report, which will be produced by the Finance team and distributed by the CFO to ExCo. The Board approved capital risk appetite will form the main basis for monitoring and reporting.

7.2 Identification of Capital Requirement

Orchard's overall objectives when managing capital are:
- To comply with the capital requirements set by the PRA;
- To safeguard Orchard's ability to continue as a going concern;
- To maintain a strong capital base to support the development of its business; and
- Safeguard the interest of the depositors.

Accordingly, the purpose of Orchard's capital management is essentially that of ensuring the efficient use of capital, taking into account Orchard's risk appetite and profile as well as its objectives for business development.

Orchard has calculated the required capital under the Regulatory Guidelines for the inherent risks in the business. This comprises of:
- Pillar 1 capital requirements for credit, market and operational risk
- Pillar 2A capital requirements for all other residual risks; and
- Pillar 2B capital requirements to provide for additional buffers.

The sum of the capital requirement calculated under Pillar 1 and the additional requirement identified under Pillar 2A represents the total capital required ("TCR") under the PRA guidelines.

The overall methodology and principles applied in calculating the capital requirement are based on the PRA's guidance. The Pillar 1 calculation has been calculated using the Basel III rules as outlined in Regulation (EU) No. 575/2013 of the European Parliament and of the Council dated 26th June 2013, also referred to as Capital Requirement Directive (CRD) IV. The CRD IV rules came into effect from 1st January 2014, and Orchard complies with these new rules. Pillar 2 calculations and buffers are based on the PRA's guidance outlined in PS17/15 (Assessing capital adequacy under Pillar 2).

These capital amounts will be calculated regularly to monitor and manage the capital requirements.

8 Pillar 1 Risks and Methodologies

8.1 Pillar 1 Overview

The Pillar 1 capital requirements are presented below in the table, with subsequent sections expanding on the basis of calculation.

Table 36: Pillar 1 Capital Requirements.

Base	Plan Year 1	Plan Year 2	Plan Year 3	Plan Year 4	Plan Year 5
Pillar 1					
Credit risk on loan assets	1,839	2,272	2,893	3,812	5,218
Credit risk on bank balances	16	16	16	16	16
Fixed assets	5	5	6	6	6
Credit risk on HQLA	0	0	0	0	0
Total credit risk	**1,860**	**2,294**	**2,914**	**3,834**	**5,240**
Operational risk basic indicator	672	750	879	1,135	1,504
Pillar 1 capital requirements	**2,532**	**3,043**	**3,793**	**4,969**	**6,743**

8.2 Pillar 1 Credit Risk

8.2.1 Pillar 1 Credit Risk Calculation

Pillar 1 Credit Risk Weighted Assets (RWAs) have been calculated using the standardised approach (CRD IV CRR Part 3, Title II, Chapter 2), which effectively uses the asset exposure multiplied by predefined percentages that vary with the exposure type to give a risk weighted asset (RWA). The RWAs have been calculated using the product level loan and asset balances from the financial model, with the following standardised risk weights applied (please see below for detailed interpretation of these defaults and their application to Orchard's exposures):

- Exposures to the Bank of England:
  - 0% Risk Weight (RW) per article 114(4)
- Exposures to financial institutions:
  - RW between 20%-100% driven by the credit rating of the institution. Orchard's exposures to financial institutions are risk weighted at 20% reflecting a credit quality step of CQS2 or better and a maturity of less than three months.
- Loans to individuals and SME clients:
  - 75% for live loans <€1m and where the customer meets the 'Retail' definition (as per CRR Article 123).
  - 150% on all non-performing loans
  - A scalar of 0.7619 applied to SME's in line with CRR Article 501
- Loans to Corporates
  - 100% for exposures to unrated corporates (Article 122)
- All other assets (e.g., fixed):
  - 100% per article 134. Intangible assets are deducted from capital per article 36.
- No uncommitted facilities are provided by Orchard.

Pillar 1 capital requirement for credit risk is then calculated at 8% of credit RWAs.

Based on the above requirements, Orchard's credit risk capital requirements under the base financial operating plan are calculated as presented in the table below.

Orchard's loans are to a mixture of individuals and SME's and meet the criteria set out in Article 123 to be classified as 'retail' i.e.

- Exposure is to individual persons or SME's
- There is a significant number of exposures with similar characteristics
- No exposure is greater than 1 million euros

The forecast value of exposures is split between individuals and SME's (which attract the 0.7619 scalar) based on an analysis of the current loan book.

8.2.2 Credit Risk

Definition and Nature of Risk

Credit risk is the risk of suffering financial loss, should any of Orchard's customers or counterparties fail to fulfil their contractual obligations to Orchard.

Mitigation

The loans are all subject to a rigorous underwriting process and are secured by a debenture in the case of lending to insurance broker finance companies. Where the loan is directly to the client of the broker or accountant, the broker or accountant guarantees

Table 37: Projected Pillar 1 Credit Risk Capital Requirements.

Assets	CRD IV Article Reference	Risk weight	Forecast Exposure Amount	Risk Weighted Exposure Amount	Forecast Exposure Amount	Risk Weighted Exposure Amount	Forecast Exposure Amount	Risk Weighted Exposure Amount	Forecast Exposure Amount	Risk Weighted Exposure Amount	Forecast Exposure Amount	Risk Weighted Exposure Amount
			Year 1		**Year 2**		**Year 3**		**Year 4**		**Year 5**	
Loan Book												
Retail	Article 123	**75%**	21,168	15,876	26,155	19,616	33,298	24,974	43,884	32,913	60,058	45,043
SME	Article 123	**75%x0.7619**	11,576	6,615	14,304	8,173	18,210	10,406	23,999	13,714	32,844	18,768
Non Performing Loans	Article 127	**150%**	331	496	409	613	520	780	686	1,029	938	1,408
Liquid asset buffer	Article 114	**0%**	3,867	0	7,612	0	8,740	0	8,717	0	10,972	0
Cash at bank	Article 120	**20%**	1,000	200	1,000	200	1,000	200	1,000	200	1,000	200
Fixed Assets (Tangible)	Article 134	**100%**	63	63	66	66	69	69	72	72	76	76
Fixed Assets (Intangible)	Article 36	**0%**	421	0	490	0	552	0	608	0	661	0
Total assets / RWA			**38,425**	**23,250**	**50,036**	**28,669**	**62,389**	**36,429**	**78,967**	**47,928**	**106,550**	**65,495**
Capital Required at 8%				**1,860**		**2,294**		**2,914**		**3,834**		**5,240**

repayment of the loan. Further where the loan is in respect of insurance premiums, the guaranteeing broker has the ability to claw back insurance premiums from the related insurance company.

The Credit Committee is responsible for assessing and monitoring the credit risk management of Orchard, for making recommendations for changes and improvements and for escalating issues to the Risk Committee as appropriate.

Orchard has established credit exposure limits in line with the risk appetite set by the Board and as described fully in Orchard's Credit Policy.

Exposures remain under close scrutiny at monthly Credit Committees and also as and when adverse information comes to light. This includes watch-listing where appropriate.

Capital Allocation

Orchard's capital allocation for Pillar 1 credit risk is set out in Table 37 above.

8.3 Pillar 1 Operational Risk

8.3.1 Pillar 1 Operational Risk Calculation

The capital allocation is based on the Basic Indicator Approach (BIA), Title III, Chapter 2 of CRD IV, which is 15% of a three-year average of the sum of Orchard's net interest income and net non-interest income. This is shown for each of the three-year projections in the table below. Separately, where the Risk Matrix presented in Appendix 1 indicates that the capital required for operational risk is higher than the amount set aside under the Pillar 1 calculation, additional capital will be allocated under Pillar 2A.

Table 38: Pillar 1 Operational Risk.

	2016 Actual	2017 Actual	2018 Actual	Year 1 Plan	Year 2 Plan	Year 3 Plan	Year 4 Plan	Year 5 Plan
Net interest income plus other income (net operating income)	3,231	4,231	4,722	4,491	5,779	7,305	9,619	13,154
3 Year Average			4,061	4,481	4,997	5,858	7,568	10,026
Ops Capital required at 15% of average income			**609**	**672**	**750**	**879**	**1,135**	**1,504**

8.3.2 Operational Risk

Definition and Nature of Risk
Operational Risk is the risk of loss as a result of inadequate or failed internal processes, people, systems, and/or external events.

Mitigation
The Audit and Risk Committees are responsible for ensuring that appropriate testing and challenge is conducted and recorded to confirm the adequacy of all controls, systems and risk management frameworks in place. An incident reporting process and Key Risk Indicators (KRI) provide additional tools for management for identifying any existing or potential issues that could indicate deterioration in risk profile. A KRI Index is calculated and this index is a trigger event in Orchard's Recovery Plan and Resolution Plan.

Key oversight for operational risk within Orchard resides with the CRO who reports directly to the Risk Committee with a dotted line to the CEO

8.4 Market Risk

8.4.1 Pillar 1 Market Risk Calculation
Orchard does not currently have and has no plans for a trading book and hence, no capital is allocated for market risk. The inherent interest rate risk in the banking book is provided under Pillar 2A.

8.4.2 Market Risk

Definition and Nature of Risk
Market risk is the risk that Orchard's earnings or capital, or its ability to meet business objectives will be adversely affected by changes in the level or volatility of market rates or prices such as interest rates and equity prices.

Orchard does not have a trading book and does not plan to have a trading book.

Mitigation
Orchard does not have a trading book. Orchard has no foreign exchange risk.

9 Pillar 2A Risk

9.1 Pillar 2A Risk Assessment

This section identifies the Pillar 2A risks that Orchard is exposed to and provides details of the measures that are taken to mitigate these risks. These are risks that are either not considered under Pillar 1, or are risks that are considered under Pillar 1 but where Orchard believes that the Pillar 1 capital amount is insufficient to address the risks.

The methodology is in line with the PRA's updated statement of policy PS9/18 'The PRA's methodologies for setting Pillar 2 capital'.

The table below summarises the Pillar 2A capital requirements with reference to the section that gives details of the basis for the capital requirements.

Table 39: Pillar 2A add-on requirements.

		Year 1 Plan	Year 2 Plan	Year 3 Plan	Year 4 Plan	Year 5 Plan
Section	**Risks**					
8.2	Credit	–	–	–	–	–
8.3	Operational	147	111	25	0	0
8.4	Credit concentration	319	391	494	647	881
8.5	Interest rate (IRRBB)	165	142	338	325	325
8.6	Business	–	–	–	–	–
8.7	Reputational	–	–	–	–	–
8.8	Money laundering	–	–	–	–	–
8.9	Insurance	–	–	–	–	–
8.10	Pension	–	–	–	–	–
8.11	Securitisation	–	–	–	–	–
8.12	Key persons	–	–	–	–	–
8.13	Residual	–	–	–	–	–
	Total Pillar 2A additional capital requirement	**631**	**644**	**857**	**972**	**1,206**
	Percentage of RWA's	**2.7%**	**2.2%**	**2.4%**	**2.0%**	**1.8%**

Where it is considered appropriate to hold additional capital in respect of a risk, this is set out net of the mitigation resulting from controls and management actions. The firm's Pillar 2A add-on amount is the sum of the additional capital held in respect of each risk. Even where a risk is considered material, this may not result in Orchard holding additional capital, as mitigation of such risk may be through another mechanism, for example a control or management action.

It is acknowledged that some risks cannot be mitigated by merely holding additional capital and management consider other approaches to mitigating those risks.

For each of the key risks, the following are considered.

- Risk characteristics and how the risk might affect Orchard;
- Likelihood of crystallisation of risk (net of controls);
- Whether the capital held under Pillar 1 in respect of that risk is sufficient;
- How the risk will be mitigated at Orchard.
  - **Control** – description of control and how it will mitigate the risk;
  - **Additional capital** – how much additional capital, above the Pillar 1 calculations, will be required and the methodology for calculating this;
  - **Management action** – description of the management action that would be taken in the event that the risk crystallised, and the mechanisms by which the risks are managed on a day-to-day basis in the business, including management information, senior management oversight etc.

9.2 Credit Risk

Capital against credit risk of £1.86m has already been set aside under Pillar 1 in Year 1 and this section assesses if the capital set aside under Pillar 1 is adequate or not. If the capital for credit risk under Pillar 1 is determined to be insufficient, additional capital will be allocated under Pillar 2A for credit risk.

Given the business strategy has remained static for a number of years, one approach for the credit risk assessment is to consider historic loss rates. The table below sets out the actual loss experience of Orchard for the last 10 years of trading ending at 31st July 2017.

The actual experience of losses, including the period in the financial crisis, has been very small, with most years having zero losses. Over the planning cycle, Orchard has assumed a loss rate of 1% based on a very prudent approach and in consideration of IFRS 9 requirements on 12 month expected loss on non-default asset and life time loss on defaulted asset. Given the tenor of the assets is less than 12 months, the impairment allowance is based on 12 month expected loss. The 1% loss projections are far in excess of Orchard's actual experience in its market as presented in the table above over the last ten years or the actual experience of the largest lenders in the market, Premium Credit Limited and Close Brothers Bank, who between them wrote over £6.3 billion of business in 2018.

Hence, the annual impairment charge of 1% combined with a capital of 5.6% set aside in Pillar 1 (8% capital requirement on the RWAs on the loan book / Loan assets) far exceeds the actual experience and hence, no additional Pillar 2A capital is deemed necessary.

Table 40: Orchard Historic Losses.

£'000	2007	2008	2009	2010	2011	2012	2013	2014	2015	2016	2017	Average
Total Receivables	15,317	15,710	10,694	9,080	16,234	18,120	17,590	18,019	17,914	22,003	28,523	17,200
3+ arrears	0	0	0	0	0	0	16	26	26	47	106	20
% arrears	0%	0%	0%	0%	0%	0%	0.09%	0.15%	0.15%	0.22%	0.37%	0.12%
Written off	0	552	0	0	0	0	0	0	0	0	26	53
% write-offs		3.51%									0.09%	0.31%
Provision	0	0	0	0	0	0	0	0	0	0	53	5
% provision	0%	0%	0%	0%	0%	0%	0%	0%	0%	0%	0.18%	0.03%

A 'fat tail' event with unprecedented levels of credit losses is considered to be covered in the combined stress event described in section 11.7. Impairment charges over 3 years total £2,433k vs £1,203k in the base case. The difference is less than the Pillar 1 credit risk amount.

9.3 Operational Risk

This section sets out Orchard's approach to the Pillar 2A risk assessment including the risk register, governance process and risk appetite.

The assessment also includes the firm's Pillar 2A operational calculation based on scenario analysis of key operational risks. The Pillar 2A assessment considers each of the items on the firm's risk register.

9.3.1 Risk Register

Each risk registered on the Risk Register (which also serves as a Risk Map) is allocated a total inherent risk score based on consequence (probability x impact) scores, calibrated using the definitions set out in the Residual Heat Map.

Each identified risk is included separately in the Risk Register in a specified category as set out in the Risk & Compliance Management Framework with a full description of the risk and a *probability x impact* inherent score and the residual score after mitigating factors.

9.3.2 Risk Appetite for Operational Risk

Orchard has a low risk appetite for loss from operational failures and seeks to minimise the risk within its business both internally and through suppliers and service providers. Orchard recognises that operational risk cannot be eliminated but has set an appetite to restrict overall losses to £250k per annum.

Orchard has no risk appetite for:

- Incidents of actual or attempted financial or property theft or loss whether it is perpetrated externally or by internal staff.
- Failure of delivery of critical services and systems by third parties. This is pivotal to our operations and, as such, each critical system and supplier operates to appropriate contractual SLAs.
- Any incidence of theft or loss of either customer or Orchard's data.
- Issues caused by inadequate software testing be it new software or an update release.
- Staff health and safety issues.

Orchard will maintain key policies that support the Risk Appetite Statement and provide the staffing, processes and systems infrastructure to operate the business at all times. Risk Committee monitor operational risk and risk appetite limits through reports on:

- The Risk Register and a heat map covering key risks.
- Key Risk Indicators with RAG statuses for early warning indicators.
- Details of limit compliance against policies approved by the Board.
- Any actual losses from operational risk issues.
- Outstanding Internal Audit and External Audit issues.
- The Board will receive a dashboard report on the heat map and key risk indicators together with information on the Risk and Audit Committees' key decisions.

The Board recognises that being small, Orchard may have additional risks compared with larger institutions. The Risk Register has been reviewed by the Board and Risk Committee both for completeness and the probability and impact scores for each operational risk. These risks have then been assessed for potential capital eroding factors over and above that captured by the Pillar 1 operational risk capital resource requirement.

A set of Risk Appetite measures is tracked and measured at least monthly, and any single indicators which reach Amber status provide Early Warning Indicators that the overall appetite measures may be at risk. Escalation to Board is made as appropriate. On reporting to ExCo, corrective actions are proposed/considered and logged as appropriate, allocated to responsible individuals and tracked to closure.

Table 41: Operational Risk Limits RAG Status.

Operational Risk – High level risk limits and KRIs	Green	Amber	Red
Operational Risk Event			
Major	0	0	1
Significant	0	1	2
Important	1	2	>=3
Regrettable Staff Loss	0	2	4
Significant Operational Loss (individual event)	£0	£50k	£62k
Significant Operational Loss (annual total)	£0	£200k	£250k
Satisfactory 1LOD business self-assurance	100%-95%	94%-85%	<85%
Satisfactory 2 LOD business self-assurance	100%-95%	94%-85%	<85%
System (critical) unavailability	0 days	1 day	2 days
Third party SLA violation	0	1 Minor	>1 Minor

9.3.3 Pillar 2A Operational Risk Add-on

Pillar 1 states the minimum capital requirements for operational risk under the Basic Indicator Approach (BIA). In testing the capital adequacy of this amount, the Pillar 1 requirement is compared to the outcome from idiosyncratic stress used in evaluating the impact of stress testing (see section 11.6) and also to the residual risk score from the risk register. If either the idiosyncratic scenario or the risk register is found to be greater than the minimum requirement, then the difference is additional Pillar 2A operational risk capital requirement. If both are greater than the minimum, then the higher value of the two is used to estimate the Pillar 2A requirement, as summarised in the table below and in the detailed assessment presented in the Appendix.

Table 42: Pillar 2A Operational Risk Add-on.

	Year 1 Plan	Year 2 Plan	Year 3 Plan	Year 4 Plan	Year 5 Plan
Pillar 1 Ops Capital requirement (A)	672	750	879	1,135	1,504
Residual Risk score capital requirement (B)	819	860	903	948	996
Scenario outcome (C)	675	675	675	675	675
Pillar 2A: Additional to BIA requirment (B-A)	147	111	25	0	0

It is anticipated that as the Risk & Compliance Management Framework becomes more embedded into the business, then the control framework will become more effective and the risk exposure recorded on the risk register will reduce. For this reason, no scalar has been applied to the residual risk score, and the Pillar 2A requirement reduces over the course of the plan.

9.4 Credit Concentration

Definition and Nature of Risk

Orchard has a low long-term appetite for credit concentration risk and seeks to minimise the risk from excessive concentrations of assets.

Credit concentration risk is the risk of losses to Orchard arising from concentrations of exposures due to imperfect diversification. This imperfect diversification can arise from the small size of a portfolio or a large number of exposures to specific obligors (single name concentration) or from imperfect diversification with respect to economic sectors or geographical regions.

Orchard's appetite for the three types of concentration risk are managed through a set of limits on exposures. The current limits against these three concentration risks are as follows:

- Single name concentration: Orchard only has retail exposure in its loan book. Orchard's only wholesale exposure will be its nostro account bank.
- Sector concentration: this is similar to single name concentration
- Geographic concentration: only UK exposures are permitted.

Following publication of updated PRA's Statement of Policy "The PRA's methodologies for setting Pillar 2 Capital" in April 2018, the PRA now requires firms to submit data to enable them to calculate a credit concentration risk measure, the Herfindahl-Hirschman Index ("HHI") for single name, sectoral and geographical credit concentration risk. The HHI index is based on risk-weighted assets ("RWAs") to reflect a degree of risk sensitivity and is mapped into a capital add-on range for the purposes of calculating the Pillar 2A concentration risk component.

The key drivers of concentration risk and the portfolios in scope under the new Pillar 2 approach are as follows:

- Single name concentration risk: top 20 wholesale credit (non-retail) portfolio exposures excluding intragroup exposures and defaulted assets. For Orchard this includes 'cash at bank' as the loan book is all non-wholesale (either SME or Retail SME).
- Sector concentration risk: wholesale credit (non-retail) portfolio exposures excluding intragroup exposure and defaulted assets. For Orchard this includes exposure arising from 'cash at bank'.
- Geographic (International) concentration risk: wholesale and retail credit portfolio. For Orchard this includes all credit risk exposures in the UK.

In the updated Statement of Policy, the PRA noted that in order to promote consistency of judgement, there will be a default presumption that, unless there are compelling reasons to deviate from it, the credit concentration risk add-on will fall to the mid-point of the capital range for each credit concentration risk bucket. Although single name and sector concentration are applicable only to wholesale credit portfolios (section 6.3 of the SoP), the exposure arising from the banking relationship with its nostro account bank has been considered for these two concentration risk categories.

Mitigation

It should be noted that there a number of mitigants to any concentration risk in the Orchard portfolio:

1. **Single name concentration risk**: All Orchard's loan book exposures are either Retail or Retail SME and are as such not in scope for the single name concentration risk calculation. The only exposures in scope for concentration risks is the exposures to financial institutions (£1m – cash at bank) and the capital add-on has been based on Concentration risk bucket 5 as the concentration is 100%.
2. **Sector risk:** The only exposure is to the Finance Industry and the capital add-on has been based on Concentration risk bucket 5 as the concentration is 100%.
3. **Geographical risk:** All lending is in the UK. The capital add-on has been based on Concentration risk bucket 5 as the concentration is 100%.

The above sets out the applicable risk bucket and the table below from the SoP sets out the applicable range of percentage to apply to the risk weighted assets. The mid-point in the range has been selected. Since the risk bucket applicable to Orchard in all three concentration risks is 5, the mid-point for single name is 3.5%, for sector is 1.75% (2% high point used as the exposure is in financial sector) and for geography, 1.33%.

Table 43: HHI Capital Add-On Ranges.

Concentration Risk Bucket	1		2		3		4		5	
Single name concentration risk (granularity)										
HHI RWA	0%	0.29%	0.29%	0.59%	0.59%	1.15%	1.15%	1.65%	>1.65%	
Capital Add-on (% portfoliio RWA)	0%	0.50%	0.50%	1%	1%	2%	2%	3%	3%	4%
Sector concentration risk										
HHI RWA	11.10%	20.30%	20.30%	25.80%	25.80%	41.70%	41.70%	67.40%	>67.4%	
Capital Add-on (% portfolio RWA)	0%	0.25%	0.25%	0.50%	0.50%	1%	1%	1.50%	1.50%	2.80%
Geographic (international) concentration risk										
HHI RWA	11.10%	24.90%	24.90%	34.50%	34.50%	47.80%	47.80%	77.90%	>77.9%	
Capital Add-on (% portfolio RWA)	0%	0.20%	0.20%	0.50%	0.50%	0.80%	0.80%	1.25%	1.25%	1.40%

Capital Allocation

The analysis below sets out Orchard's total concentration risk add-on (£319k) for the 1st year based on the PRA's HHI methodology. The key outputs are as follows:

1. **Single Name concentration risk:** The only wholesale exposure in scope for this assessment is the £1m exposure to the nostro bank account with a £200k RWA. Consequently, the HHI concentration for this exposure is 100% resulting a mapping to concentration risk bucket 5 as seen in the table above. The mid-point add-on in bucket 5 is 3.5% of RWAs resulting in a single name add-on of £7,000.
2. **Sector concentration risk:** The only wholesale exposure in scope for this assessment is the £1m exposure to the nostro account bank with a £200k RWA. Consequently, the HHI concentration to the financial industry is 100% resulting a mapping to concentration risk bucket 5 as seen in the figure above. The mid-point add-on in bucket 5 is 1.75% of RWAs resulting in a sector add-on of £3,500.
3. **Geographic concentration risk:** Both the wholesale exposures and the unsecured retail/SME exposures (£21.37m RWAs) along with the bank exposures (£200k RWA) are in scope for this assessment. Consequently, the HHI concentration to UK exposures are 100% resulting a mapping to concentration risk bucket 5 as seen in the figure above. The mid-point add-on in bucket 5 is 1.33% of RWAs resulting in a geographic add-on of £308,387.

Pillar 2 A Concentration Risk Add-On Over the Plan Period

The table below sets out the Pillar 2A concentration risk capital requirements over the plan period.

Table 44: Pillar 2A Concentration Risk.

		Year 1		£'000
	Credit Exposure	**RWA**	**Capital add-on %**	**Pillar 2A requirements**
Single Name	1,000	200	3.50%	7
Sector	1,000	200	1.75%	4
Geography	34,075	23,187	1.33%	308
Total				**319**
		Year 2		
	Credit Exposure	**RWA**	**Capital add-on %**	**Pillar 2A requirements**
Single Name	1,000	200	3.50%	7
Sector	1,000	200	1.75%	4
Geography	41,867	28,603	1.33%	380
Total				**391**

Table 44 (continued)

Year 3				
	Credit Exposure	**RWA**	**Capital add-on %**	**Pillar 2A requirements**
Single Name	1,000	200	3.50%	7
Sector	1,000	200	1.75%	4
Geography	53,028	36,360	1.33%	484
Total				**494**
Year 4				
	Credit Exposure	**RWA**	**Capital add-on %**	**Pillar 2A requirements**
Single Name	1,000	200	3.50%	7
Sector	1,000	200	1.75%	4
Geography	69,569	47,855	1.33%	636
Total				**647**
Year 5				
	Credit Exposure	**RWA**	**Capital add-on %**	**Pillar 2A requirements**
Single Name	1,000	200	3.50%	7
Sector	1,000	200	1.75%	4
Geography	94,841	65,419	1.33%	870
Total				**881**

9.5 Interest Rate Risk in the Banking Business

Definition and Nature of Risk

Orchard has a low risk appetite for interest rate risk.

Interest Rate Risk is the risk from changes in market interest rates that adversely impact the Net Interest Income (NII) arising from Orchard's assets and liabilities. The adverse impact on NII can mainly arise from three different risk types.

13. Duration risk

    This risk arises from maturity mismatch of fixed rate assets and liabilities. A shift in market interest rate becomes effective with repricing when the assets and liabilities mature and hence, a mismatch will result in some assets/ liabilities repricing earlier and others later, which will therefore impact the Net Interest Income.

14. Basis risk

    This risk arises from the different market rate basis used as the anchor point to determine the product pricing. Since the different available market rates, e.g., Bank base rate, Libor, do change on a different basis as there is no perfect correlation between the pricing of assets on one market benchmark and the pricing on another. This will therefore give rise to a risk on NII.

15. Optionality
    This risk arises from the flexibility built in to contractual terms, i.e., the flexibility to repay a fixed rate loan earlier or withdraw a fixed rate deposit. In certain instances, the cost of optionality risk is factored into the contractual terms, which will penalise early settlement.

Other interest rate risk is the pipeline risk, which arises from the variation in the expected verses actual business written.

Orchard's lending and deposit taking will all be fixed rate and hence, the duration risk will arise from mismatch in maturity of assets and liabilities. The impact of this risk is determined through a 200bps parallel shift in interest rate.

The assets and liabilities margins at inception of the loans or deposits are based on the same market benchmark, Bank base rate, and hence, basis risk does not arise.

Early repayment on Orchard's deposits is only considered under customer hardship conditions and assessed on a case by case basis. The short term loan tenor means that an early repayment would on average be 6 months. On this basis and rationale, Optionality risk is not considered material to Orchard's current business and the Board considers that no additional capital is required for Optionality risk.

Capital Allocation

Our projections based on form FSA017 indicate an economic value at risk of £165k from a 2% parallel shift in year 1. This approach has been used to derive the impact over the first three years of the plan.

The detail calculations for 2% parallel shift in interest rate in the first year of the plan using the FSA017 table is appended to this document and the table below presents the summary over four years of the plan. The risk appetite for IRRBB has been determined by this assessment.

Table 45: 2% Parallel Shift Impact.

	2 % shift impact		**£'000**	
	+ shift	**– shift**	**CET1**	**% of CET1**
Yr 1	154	(165)	14,878	1.1%
Yr 2	133	(142)	16,251	0.9%
Yr 3	319	(338)	18,295	1.9%
Yr 4	307	(325)	21,394	1.5%

The plan period has been assessed and management have set the risk appetite, that has been approved by the Board.

Table 46: Risk appetite.

Limit category		Target	Early warning indicator (Amber)	Trigger (Red)
Market	Interest Rate Risk Sensitivity – % of CET1	2.3%	2.70%	3%

9.6 Business Risk

Definition and Nature of Risk

Orchard operates in a highly competitive environment particularly around price. Business risk is defined as the potential loss (or inability to realise planned revenues) arising from the inability to properly implement strategic plans.

Table 47: Orchard Business Risks.

Business Risk	Impact on Orchard business
Economic Downturn	Orchard operated its business throughout the Global Financial Crisis (GFC). The insurance premium finance sector remained resilient through the GFC as individuals still needed to insure their vehicles, houses and businesses. Orchard commenced the accountancy fee funding business in 2010 and did not have the benefit of operating the business through the GFC. The professional fee funding business has many similar characteristics to the insurance premium finance business and Orchard believes that the business will behave in the same manner during an economic downturn.
Origination	Orchard has a very small share of the insurance premium finance market and the professions finance market. Orchard grew its lending by over 30% in the year ended July 2017 and believes that it will continue to grow its market share by offering a service orientated relationship to its insurance broker and professional firm clients. No current customer accounts for more than 10% of its business.
Brexit	Brexit could eventually lead to a divergence of regulatory rules, relating to insurance and consumer credit, from the current European-wide legislation. This will be subject to continual review, but Orchard currently sees no reason to regard this as a threat to the business.

Orchard will be exposed to the risk of economic downturn affecting its business lines.

Economic risk directly translates into credit default risk in the lending businesses of Orchard. This risk can be mitigated by the same considerations at a single transactional level – careful assessment of the customer and business written by experienced underwriters. However, mitigating economic risk at its systemic level is more about management of the portfolio of Orchard as a whole. This requires careful monitoring of key economic indicators to predict the likely trends in the economy. The correlation between the business written and the economic cycle will not be perfect and will often be lagged, as customers are able to carry on using their own resources before the real effect of the downturn starts to apply.

The regular management and monitoring of the economic risks faced by Orchard lies with management and the ExCo. The Risk Committee will regularly review and challenge Orchard's exposure to this risk.

The impact of a macroeconomic downturn on the business has been analysed through the stress testing process (described in Section 9 of this document). Under the PRA Anchor Stress, the financial projections show that Orchard maintains capital resources above its proposed TCR. (Therefore, no additional Pillar 2 capital allocation has been made for exposure to an economic downturn).

There is a risk that Orchard fails to originate the planned asset volumes and net interest margins. This is mitigated by proven asset originations over many years and Orchard's modest growth ambitions.

Capital Allocation

No capital is allocated for business and strategic risks from the consideration given to the output of the stress scenarios and impact on capital.

9.7 Reputational Risk

Definition and nature of risk

Reputational risk is the risk of a loss of reputation of Orchard, for example as a consequence of a failure to manage principal risks or from inappropriate conduct by any member of staff – particularly senior management given their relatively higher visibility in the market.

Mitigation

Orchard has an experienced management team and seeks to comply with the letter and spirit of all relevant UK legal and regulatory requirements. Factors that could impact Orchard's reputation are regularly reviewed by the Risk Committee. Under the SMR, Orchard's Responsibility Map identifies the allocation of responsibilities for senior management evidencing complete coverage of accountability and demonstrating that Orchard has robust governance arrangements, a clear organisational structure with well-defined and transparent lines of responsibility.

Capital Allocation

Orchard has considered all potential risks in the risk register, some of which could impact the reputation of the firm. Since, the costs for these risks have all been considered, including the associated reputation risk that would arise as a result, no further capital allocation is required beyond that already included in the operational risk add-on.

9.8 Money Laundering Risk

Definition and nature of risk

Money laundering is the risk of accepting deposits from illegal activities. Orchard will provide certain services, which could be targeted for money laundering purposes. Specifically, these are:

- **Premium Finance/Professions Finance:** Premium finance/Professions finance could be used for money laundering, particularly though the acceleration of the agreed repayment schedule. However, in Orchard's case the money laundering risk is limited since it will predominantly be financing 'small ticket' items where the JMLSG has identified there is usually little incentive for money laundering
- **Retail and SME Savings Accounts:** The JMLSG have identified that there is a high risk that proceeds from illegal activities will pass through retail banking accounts at all stages in the money laundering process

Mitigation

Orchard will ensure that there is a robust system of controls in order to prevent Orchard being used for money-laundering. Key mitigating activities which Orchard will perform to minimise its money laundering risk include:

- **Know your customer (KYC) checks:** customers will be validated using on-line tools, which verify the identity and address of the customer. In the event that online checks are not possible traditional documentary validation processes will be used and supplemented by the use of credit reference agency validation. Where customers are identified as being high risk, then more detailed enhanced due diligence will be undertaken.
- **Customers are either regulated entities or customers of regulated entities:** customers that are regulated entities include insurance brokers and professional firms (which are regulated by their governing bodies such as the ACCA or the Law Society). Each such Customer of Orchard warrants that KYC checks have been conducted in respect of each of its clients to which Orchard provides finance. The CRO, as Head of Compliance, will conduct sample reviews of Orchard's customers, to ensure that their warranty is true and valid.

- **Clear source of funds:** Orchard will only accept funds that emanate from a UK bank account in the name of the customer – either by faster payments or by cheque – never in cash. Similarly, Orchard will only remit funds back to this bank account
- **Monitoring for Politically Exposed Persons (PEPs):** Orchard will undertake a regular scan of all accounts in order to identify any potential matches with screening databases for PEPs, terrorists or other known criminals
- **Transaction Monitoring:** Orchard will ensure that its IT system has monitoring and control disciplines to detect suspicious activity. This will be supported by rigorous training provided to staff. Suspicious transactions will be reported to the MLRO
- **Training:** all staff will receive rigorous training with regard to their AML responsibilities

Capital Allocation

In light of the control environment, which Orchard has in place to prevent money laundering risk, it does not consider that any Pillar 2A capital requirement is necessary to mitigate this risk.

9.9 Insurance Risk

Definition and nature of risk

Orchard will have insurance cover for standard business risks, including buildings and contents, Bankers Blanket Bond, computer crime, professional indemnity and D&O cover. No cover will be taken against commercial risks such as credit, market or residual value exposures, and no form of insurance will be provided to customers.

Capital Allocation

No material insurance risk is expected; therefore, no Pillar 2A capital allocation has been made.

9.10 Pension Obligation Risk

Definition and nature of risk

Orchard is not exposed to any risks relating to pension liabilities. Orchard operates a defined contribution pension scheme where the employees take the investment risk.

Capital Allocation

No pensions risk inherent; therefore, no Pillar 2A capital allocation has been made.

9.11 Securitisation Risk

Definition and nature of risk

Securitisation risk is not applicable to Orchard as it does not securitise assets or participates in any way or form in securitisation.

Capital Allocation

Therefore, no allocation of capital has been assigned under Pillar 2A.

9.12 Key Person Risk

Definition and nature of risk

Key Person risk is the risk that a key person is no longer able to work for Orchard or that a key person leaves the business.

Ravi Takhar has led the Orchard business since its formation in 2002. The 2 other directors in each of the current subsidiaries of Orchard have worked with Ravi for over 10 years each. Each director has a full understanding of all aspects of origination, underwriting, servicing and financing of the current business of Orchard.

[] the current CFO of Orchard was the auditor of the business from its formation to its floatation in 2015, when he was appointed as CFO. Liam will be FD of the new bank.

[], the CFO designate of Orchard, has many years' experience as a senior finance manager in a bank, including deposit-taking experience.

Orchard will also have succession plans in place for key personnel and all executive staff will have notice periods.

Although this risk will be constantly monitored Orchard does believe that it has Key Person Risk that may impact its business plan and this has been considered and a capital charge added in the Operational Risk section above.

Capital Allocation

Capital of £228k has been allocated in Pillar 2A and included in the risk register in the appendix.

9.13 Residual Risk

Definition and nature of risk

Residual risk covers the inadequacy of credit risk mitigation techniques including the residual value of loan collateral and any other unknown risk (including loss of business, internal fraud, external fraud and/or emergency recruiting costs) that might arise in the course of business.

Mitigation

The controls employed by the business to control its operational and other risks are included within the risk register. The "residual risk score" is the estimated exposure to Orchard after the application of these controls. This is compared to the Pillar 1 operational risk capital requirement, and if the total residual risk score is higher than the requirement, the additional amount is included in the Pillar 2A operational risk charge.

Orchard believes that all residual risks referred to above are covered by the Pillar 2A operational risk charge.

Capital Allocation

No capital has been allocated for residual risk.

10 Pillar 2B Capital Requirements

10.1 Calculation of the PRA buffer

Specific guidance for new entrants

In the July 2014 FCA and PRA publication 'A review of requirements for firms entering into or firms expanding in the banking sector: one year on', the approach for setting the Capital Planning Buffer (CPB) for new entrants has been stated. This approach has been adopted by Orchard to determine its Pillar 2B capital requirements. (The Statement of Policy "The PRA's methodologies for setting Pillar 2 capital", published on 30 April 2018 confirms that this method is still valid for Pillar 2B.)

The publication states that where new entrant banks are assessed as resolvable with no systemic impact, the CPB will be set at a level equal to the wind down costs of the new entrant bank. The publication also states that over time the Pillar 2B requirement will be aligned to incumbent firms, in line with what the new entrant bank's board considers to be an appropriate glide path and as reviewed by the PRA through their annual supervisory cycle.

Orchard's Pillar 2B Assessment

As stated above Orchard will base its Pillar 2B capital requirements on an assessment of wind down costs. Existing banks' PRA buffers under Pillar 2B are the highest of the stress testing impacts on the firms' capital and the CRD IV requirements for the capital conservation buffer (CCoB) and the countercyclical buffer (CCyB) plus the systemic buffer. The CCoB is expressed as a percentage of Risk Weighted Assets ('RWAs') and is set at 2.50% of RWAs. The CCyB is expressed as a percentage of RWAs and is currently set at 1%. The systemic buffer is only applicable to systematically important firms and hence, not considered for Orchard.

The Pillar 2B capital is defined as the amount of capital that firms should hold, in addition to their total capital requirement (TCR), to cover losses that may arise under a severe stress scenario, but avoiding duplication with the CRD IV Buffers.

As stated, Orchard as a new bank entrant will determine the wind-down cost and initially set this amount as its Pillar 2B capital. However, for the sake of completeness and to provide a view to the Board, the future glide path of the capital requirements under CRD IV requirements and the stress capital impacts are also presented in this section.

10.2 Approach to Pillar 2B

Orchard's approach to its Pillar 2B capital requirement is to determine the wind-down costs of the firm and set this amount as Pillar 2B capital for the 1st year of the plan, which increases by 5% per annum.

10.2.1 Wind-Down Costs

Timing

The wind-down costs have been calculated through applying scenario analysis to year 2, where no new loans are written and the existing loans amortise over their short-term to zero. No new deposits are taken and existing deposits are repaid as the fixed rate expires and the Bank ceases trading. The business continues for 12 months in year 2 resulting in slightly lower expenses over the base case scenario as certain marketing, underwriting, development and operations expenses will not be incurred. Further, additional expenses arising from the wind-down scenario have also been factored in.

Impairment

Impairment is not expected to be impacted, as very few customers would be likely to be aware of Orchard's situation and customers would always need to maintain payment in order to remain insured. Recourse to the insurance brokers would remain in operation.

Disposal

Given the short tenor of the loan book it is unlikely that a sale of the portfolio would be a sensible or viable option. Loans will simply be collected over their remaining lives.

Cost Savings

The operating costs assumption under this scenario is as follows:

Table 48: Adjustment to operating costs in wind-down.

	Year 1	£'000 Year 2
Total opex (base)	**2,870**	**3,267**
Cost not incurred in wind-down		
Sales force		430
IT development		115
Underwriting		132
Reducing ops headcount		101
Advertising		58
Entertainment		35
Travel		40
Deposit raising expenses		30
Bank charges		86
Bonus		294
Total costs not incurred on wind-down		**1,320**
One off costs in wind-down		
Redundancy/retention (25% of annual salaries)		468
Legal and professional costs		184
3rd party contracts – early termination costs		50
Total additional costs		**702**
Total annual opex on wind-down		**2,649**

The rest of the income statement is driven by the balance sheet, with reducing lending and repayment of the deposits as they mature or early repayment as the cash becomes available.

The output of the scenario is presented below.

Table 49: Wind-down Scenario.

Income Statement	**WINDDOWN Year 2**	***Base Case Year 2***
Interest Receivable	1,627	*6,370*
Interest payable	(204)	*(591)*
Net interest income	**1,422**	***5,779***
Administration expenses	(2,648)	*(3,267)*
Impairment charges	(71)	*(393)*
Operating profit before tax	**(1,296)**	***2,119***

Table 49 (continued)

Income Statement	**WINDDOWN Year 2**	***Base Case Year 2***
Corporation tax	246	*(403)*
Profit after tax	**(1,050)**	***1,716***
Dividends	0	*(343)*
Retained earnings	**(1,050)**	***1,373***
Balance Sheet		
Assets		
Loans and advances	(2)	*40,475*
Cash at bank	1,000	*1,000*
Liquid asset buffer	13,998	*7,612*
Fixed assets	556	*556*
Other assets	158	*158*
Total assets	**15,710**	***49,801***
Liabilities		
Customer deposits	0	*31,000*
Trade creditors	2,051	*2,051*
Tax liabilities	(246)	*403*
Non-current liabilities	78	*96*
Total liabilities	**1,882**	***33,550***
Equity		
Share capital	214	*214*
Share premium	8,692	*8,692*
Merger reserves	891	*891*
Retained earnings	5,081	*5,081*
Current year retained earnings	(1,050)	*1,373*
Total equity	**13,828**	***16,251***
Total equity and liabilities	**15,710**	***49,801***

Based on this scenario, the loss on wind-down (after tax) in year 2 is £1.05m and is used for Orchard's Pillar 2B capital requirement.

10.2.2 CRD IV – Pillar 2B Requirements

The table below sets out the future regulatory requirement for Orchard under CRD IV and is based on the firm's projected RWAs.

All Orchard's exposures are with UK counterparties.

There is an additional Pillar 2B requirement for risk management and governance weaknesses that is determined by the PRA based on their assessment of a firm's risk management and governance (the 'PRA Buffer top-up' in Table 50). Under the guidelines

Table 50: CRD IV buffers.

	CRD IV Buffer (% of RWAs)
Capital Conservation Buffers	2.50%
Countercyclical Buffer	1% (set by FPC)
Systemic Risk Buffer	NA – G-SIBs only
PRA Buffer top-up	NA – Start up banks

in the publication 'A review of requirements for firms entering into or firms expanding in the banking sector: one year on', this is less likely to be applied for new entrants.

Based on the above requirements and assumptions, the future capital required calculation for CCoB and CCyB is presented below:

Table 51: CRD IV Buffer Requirement.

	Year 2	Year 3	Year 4	Year 5
Risk weighted assets	38,039	47,413	62,117	84,294
CCoB %	2.50%	2.50%	2.50%	2.50%
CCyB %	1%	1%	1%	1%
CCoB capital requirement	951	1,185	1,553	2,107
CCyB capital requirement	380	474	621	843
Total CRD IV Pillar 2B capital before PRA buffer	1,331	1,659	2,174	2,950

The requirement under this basis is higher than the wind-down cost of £1.05m and hence, the future requirements will increase slightly on the CRD IV basis. In part, the increase is also driven by the growth in the balance sheet.

10.2.3 Stress Testing Impact on Capital

The impact on regulatory capital available under the stress scenarios, excluding reverse stress is presented in the table below.

Table 52: Stress testing impact on future capital requirements.

	Year 2	Year 3
	£'000	£'000
Stress Test Scenario impact		
– Stress Scenario – Market-wide	1,159	1,523
– Stress Scenario – Idiosyncratic	1,231	1,241
– Stress Scenario – Combined	3,487	4,125

The combined scenario is more severe than the market-wide and the idiosyncratic stresses and results in capital depletion of £4m in year 3. Against the wind-down cost of £1.2m in year 3, the requirement under this basis will be significantly higher.

10.2.4 Pillar 2B Capital Requirement

Based on the above analysis, Orchard intends to allocate £1.05m of capital for Pillar 2B in the first year of the plan, which increases by 5% annually. The capital requirement under Pillar 2B is expected to increase in subsequent ICAAP processes as we move away from the 'new entrants' basis of calculation.

11 Stress Testing and Scenario Analysis

11.1 Stress Testing Framework

An overview of the stress testing process, in chronological order, undertaken by Orchard is as follows:

1. The medium-term corporate plan is produced by management and presented to the Board for approval. Upon Board approval, this becomes the Base Case plan.
2. Executive management will assess the latest Annual Cyclical Scenario ("ACS") issued by the PRA. For this ICAAP the 2019 ACS has been considered.
3. Executive management determines the scenarios for stress testing, taking into account the proposed ACS assumptions issued by the Regulator and propose these to the Risk Committee and ultimately to the Board for approval.
4. The Board will review and challenge the proposed scenarios and agree on final scenarios for stress testing.
5. The scenarios are run against the base case over a three year period, with and without management action in response to each stress, and the output presented to the Board in the form of the ICAAP document for review and approval.

Orchard's approach to stress testing involves applying forward-looking analytical reviews which seek to anticipate possible losses that might occur if an identified economic downturn or risk event crystallises. The approach used is based on PRA Supervisory Statement SS31/15.

Orchard's management has identified several stress testing scenarios to address the impact of an economic down-turn or risk event and these are as follows:

The above stresses start at the beginning of the 2nd year of the plan and where necessary, continue into the 3rd year of the plan. However, management actions would have been instigated to prevent further deterioration.

Table 53: Stress Scenarios.

No	Stress Scenario	Scenario Overview
1	Market-wide (Anchor) stress	The Bank of England's 2019 annual cyclical scenario's key elements of the scenario are deep simultaneous recessions in the UK and global economies, a financial market stress and an independent stress of misconduct costs.
2	Idiosyncratic stress	A number of operational scenarios specific to Orchard have been considered. These have been derived from the Risk Register. In addition, the adverse impact of the operational shortcomings on business drivers has been considered.
3	Combined stress	This stress is a combination of market-wide and idiosyncratic stress. Due to the idiosyncratic stress, the impacts from the market-wide stress have been exacerbated.
4	Reverse stress	The reverse stress is driven by a massive market shock that impacts customers' ability to repay loans and at the same time, the introducing brokers going insolvent, rendering the guarantee worthless. This in turn, results in depositors losing confidence with massive attrition on maturity and no new deposits, resulting in initiating other expensive funding options. This drives the business model to become unviable and at the same time, the capital resources are eroded to below minimum requirements.

11.2 Economic Variables

Economic variables considered for the base financial operating plan, as well as for stresses, are from the PRA ACS 2019 (March 2019 – Key elements of the 2019 stress test (PDF), Variable paths for the 2019 stress test (XLSX)). Management has selected those variables that are considered to be more relevant to Orchard. Given no exposure to international markets, the economic variables have been limited to the UK market. Both the base and anchor variables relevant for Orchard, presented in the PRA ACS 2019 are shown in the tables below. The fourth quarter in each year is presented for ease of reference.

Table 54: Key Economic Indicators.

	Actual	Plan	Plan	Plan
	2018 Q4	**Year 1**	**Year 2**	**Year 3**
Base Case				
Unemployment (%)[1]	4.0	4.1	4.1	3.9
Household income (£bn)[2]	372.0	382.8	394.3	411.0
Base rate (quarterly average – %)[3]	0.75	0.896	1.01	1.11
Consumer credit (%)[4]	6.6	6.1	6	6.1

Table 54 (continued)

Market -Wide	Plan Year 1	Plan Year 2	Plan Year 3
Unemployment (%)[1]	8.3	9.2	8.6
Household income (£bn)[2]	361.4	374.1	394.8
Base rate (quarterly average – %)[3]	4.00	4.00	4.00
Consumer credit (%)[4]	−0.6	−4.7	−0.1

[1]UK unemployment rate (LFS definition, all, aged 16 and over, seasonally adjusted, %). ONS code: MGSX.
[2]UK household nominal income (nominal disposable income, adjusted for pensions contributions, £bn). ONS code: RPQ
[3]Quarterly average of official Bank Rate (%)
[4]Quarterly 12 month growth rate of total (excluding the Student Loans Company) sterling net consumer credit to individuals (in percent) seasonally adjusted.

11.3 Summary of Capital Impact of Scenarios

The base case and each of the scenarios are described in detail below. Table 55 summarises the impact on the key capital ratios (after management action).

Table 55: Scenario summary – key capital ratios.

	Percentage of RWA's			Variance to Base		
	Year 1	Year 2	Year 3	Year 1	Year 2	Year 3
Base						
Total Capital Requirement + Pillar 2B	13.3%	12.6%	12.2%	–	–	–
Regulatory Capital Resources	45.7%	41.4%	37.4%	–	–	–
Surplus / (deficit) regulatory capital	32.4%	28.8%	25.2%	–	–	–
Market-wide (Anchor) Stress						
Total Capital Requirement + Pillar 2B	13.3%	13.6%	13.2%	–	1.0%	1.0%
Regulatory Capital Resources	45.7%	46.5%	36.4%	–	5.1%	(1.0%)
Surplus / (deficit) regulatory capital	32.4%	32.9%	23.2%	–	4.1%	(2.0%)
Idiosyncratic Stress						
Total Capital Requirement + Pillar 2B	13.3%	12.9%	12.8%	–	0.3%	0.5%
Regulatory Capital Resources	45.7%	40.2%	34.6%	–	(1.2%)	(2.8%)
Surplus / (deficit) regulatory capital	32.4%	27.3%	21.8%	–	(1.5%)	(3.4%)
Combined Stress						
Total Capital Requirement + Pillar 2B	13.3%	14.3%	13.7%	–	1.7%	1.5%
Regulatory Capital Resources	45.7%	43.7%	26.3%	–	2.3%	(11.1%)
Surplus / (deficit) regulatory capital	32.4%	29.5%	12.6%	–	0.6%	(12.6%)

Table 55 (continued)

	Percentage of RWA's			Variance to Base		
	Year 1	**Year 2**	**Year 3**	**Year 1**	**Year 2**	**Year 3**
Reverse Stress						
Total Capital Requirement + Pillar 2B	13.3%	15.0%	16.1%	–	2.4%	3.9%
Regulatory Capital Resources	45.7%	37.4%	10.2%	–	(4.0%)	(27.2%)
Surplus / (deficit) regulatory capital	32.4%	22.4%	(5.9%)	–	(6.4%)	(31.1%)

11.4 Base Case

Orchard has selected the more relevant of the ACS variables in constructing its base case. Unemployment has been linked to the level of defaults, household income to the level of savings, base rates to the funding costs (less so, for the gross lending margins) and consumer credit to the overall insurance funding market. It should be noted that past experience (the last financial crisis in 2008) has shown that Orchard's business model is relatively robust in the face of an economic downturn. Insurance is not seen as an expense to be cut back during times of austerity.

Based on these, the business drivers, income statement, balance sheet and capital position under the base case are as follows:

Table 56: Base Case – Key Business Drivers.

Base	**Actual 2018**	**Plan Year 1**	**Plan Year 2**	**Plan Year 3**	**Plan Year 4**	**Plan Year 5**
New Lending – £000	68,730	86,000	107,800	139,400	186,709	259,576
Lending growth %		25%	25%	29%	34%	39%
Lending stock – £000	31,084	32,762	40,475	51,531	67,917	92,953
Lending interest rate (wt. average)		14.53%	14.46%	14.40%	14.32%	14.26%
Net New Deposit – £000		21,000	10,000	10,000	13,000	22,000
Deposit stock – £000		21,000	31,000	41,000	54,000	76,000
Deposit interest rate (wt. average)		2.15%	2.32%	2.43%	2.51%	2.58%
Bank funding – £000		–	–	–	–	–
Funding interest rate		4.30%	4.47%	4.58%	4.66%	4.73%
Operating expenses £000	2,746	2,870	3,267	3,651	4,184	4,820
Operating expenses % uplift YoY		5%	14%	12%	15%	15%
Impairment charge %		1.0%	1.0%	1.0%	1.0%	1.0%

Table 57: Base Case Income Statement and Balance Sheet – Orchard.

			£'000
Base Income Statement	**Plan Year 1**	**Plan Year 2**	**Plan Year 3**
Interest Receivable	4,887	6,370	8,175
Interest payable	(396)	(591)	(870)
Net interest income	**4,491**	**5,779**	**7,305**
Administration expenses	(2,870)	(3,267)	(3,651)
Stresses (idio, conduct, systems	0	0	0
Impairment charges	(312)	(393)	(498)
Operating profit before tax	**1,308**	**2,119**	**3,156**
Corporation tax	(257)	(403)	(600)
Profit after tax	**1,051**	**1,716**	**2,556**
Dividends	(210)	(343)	(511)
Retained Earnings	**841**	**1,373**	**2,045**
Balance Sheet	**Plan Year 1**	**Plan Year 2**	**Plan Year 3**
Assets			
Loans and advances	32,762	40,475	51,531
Cash at bank	1,000	1,000	1,000
Liquid asset buffer	3,867	7,612	8,740
Fixed assets	483	556	621
Other assets	158	158	158
Total assets	**38,270**	**49,801**	**62,049**
Liabilities			
Customer deposits	21,000	31,000	41,000
Bank funding	0	0	0
Trade creditors	2,051	2,051	2,051
Tax liabilities	257	403	600
Non-current liabilities	84	96	103
Total liabilities	**23,393**	**33,550**	**43,754**
Equity			
Share capital	214	214	214
Share premium	8,692	8,692	8,692
Merger reserves	891	891	891
Retained earnings	4,240	5,081	6,454
Current year retained earnings	841	1,373	2,045
Total equity	**14,878**	**16,251**	**18,295**
Total equity and liabilities	38,270	49,801	62,049

Table 58: Base Case – Orchard Capital Position.

Base	Plan Year 1	Plan Year 2	Plan Year 3
Pillar 1			
Credit risk on loan assets	1,839	2,272	2,893
Credit risk on bank balances	16	16	16
Fixed assets	5	5	6
Credit risk on HQLA	0	0	0
Total credit risk	**1,860**	**2,294**	**2,914**
Operational risk basic indicator	672	750	879
Pillar 1 capital requirements	**2,532**	**3,043**	**3,793**
Pillar 2A capital requirements			
Operational risk	147	111	25
Business risk	0	0	0
Reputational risk	0	0	0
Credit concentration risk	319	391	494
Interest rate risk in the banking book (IRRBB)	165	142	338
Residual operational risk from risk register	0	0	0
Pillar 2A capital requirements	**631**	**644**	**857**
Total capital requirement (Pillar 1 + Pillar 2A)	**3,163**	**3,687**	**4,650**
Share capital	9,797	9,797	9,797
Audited retained earnings	5,081	6,454	8,498
DTA on operating losses (Deduction)	0	0	0
Intangible Assets (Deduction)	(421)	(490)	(552)
Total Capital resources	**14,457**	**15,761**	**17,744**
Risk weighted assets (Credit + Ops)	**31,652**	**38,039**	**47,413**
Total Capital requirement % of RWAs	**10%**	**10%**	**10%**
Pillar 2B	**1,050**	**1,102**	**1,158**
TCR + Pillar 2B % of RWAs	**13%**	**13%**	**12%**
CET1 % of RWAs	**47%**	**43%**	**39%**
Regulatory Capital Resources % of RWAs	**46%**	**41%**	**37%**
Surplus / (deficit) regulatory capital	**10,244**	**10,971**	**11,936**

11.5 Market-Wide (Anchor) Stress

From the Bank of England's 2019 ACS, relevant economic variables have been selected that are more relevant to Orchard's business model.

A simple relationship of the selected macroeconomic variables to the business drivers has been designed by associating the relative change between base and stress economic variables to the business drivers. The economic variables applied to the business drivers are as follows:

- Unemployment rate, which is assumed to drive the level of impairment losses;
- Household income, which is assumed to drive the level of savings;
- Base rate assumed to drive both the cost of funds as well as the lending rate, though lending rate increase will be constrained by commercial factors;
- Consumer credit, which is assumed to drive the lending originated by Orchard.

Based on the above assumptions, the impact on the business drivers is presented below. The impact on new lending is more severe than in the last recession in 2008 where lending in the insurance premium funding market did not reduce.

Table 59: Market-wide stress scenario – Impact on key business drivers (before management action).

Anchor no MA	Plan Year 1	Plan Year 2	Plan Year 3
Impact on business drivers			
New lending	0%	(30%)	(20%)
Loan Rate	0.0%	0.0%	0.0%
Net new Deposits volumes	0%	(40%)	(20%)
Deposit rate	0.0%	0.0%	0.0%
Impairment charge % of asset	0.0%	0.5%	0.2%
Expenses increase from prior period	0%	3%	0%
Bank funding margin increase vs plan	0.0%	0.0%	0.0%

Table 60: Market-wide stress scenario – Impact on key business drivers (after management action).

Anchor	Plan Year 1	Plan Year 2	Plan Year 3
Impact on business drivers			
New lending	0%	(20%)	(10%)
Loan Rate	0.0%	(2.0%)	(2.0%)
Net new Deposits volumes	0%	(20%)	(5%)
Deposit rate	0.0%	1.5%	1.0%
Impairment charge % of asset	0.0%	0.5%	0.2%
Expenses increase from prior period	0%	3%	0%
Bank funding margin increase vs plan	0.0%	0.0%	0.0%

Unlike other lending markets, the insurance premium finance market did not suffer in any material manner from the 2008 financial crisis. The actual experience of Orchard and comparable businesses through the downturn, is that loss rates did not exceed 1% of average balances and market volumes did not decrease. In line with other lending businesses, the stress assumes an increase in bad debt and decrease in volumes together with several other adversely affected drivers. The below, provides a reasonable proxy for the impact of the market-wide scenario on the Orchard Base Financial Operating Plan.

Table 61: Market-wide stress scenario (before management action) – Key business drivers.

Anchor no MA	Actual 2018	Plan Year 1	Plan Year 2	Plan Year 3
New Lending – £000	68,730	86,000	75,460	111,520
Lending growth %		25%	(12%)	48%
Lending stock – £000	31,084	32,762	28,163	41,151
Lending interest rate (wt. average)		14.53%	14.46%	14.40%
Net New Deposit – £000		21,000	6,000	8,000
Deposit stock – £000		21,000	27,000	35,000
Deposit interest rate (wt. average)		2.15%	2.32%	2.43%
Bank funding – £000		–	–	–
Funding interest rate		4.30%	4.47%	4.58%
Operating expenses £000	2,746	2,870	3,334	3,721
Operating expenses % uplift YoY		5%	16%	12%
Impairment charge %		1.0%	1.5%	1.2%

Table 62: Market-wide stress scenario (after management action) – Key business drivers.

Anchor	Actual 2018	Plan Year 1	Plan Year 2	Plan Year 3
New Lending – £000	68,730	86,000	86,240	125,460
Lending growth %		25%	0%	45%
Lending stock – £000	31,084	32,762	32,236	46,293
Lending interest rate (wt. average)		14.53%	12.46%	12.40%
Net New Deposit – £000		21,000	8,000	9,500
Deposit stock – £000		21,000	29,000	38,500
Deposit interest rate (wt. average)		2.15%	3.82%	3.43%
Bank funding – £000		–	–	–
Funding interest rate		4.30%	4.47%	4.58%
Operating expenses £000	2,746	2,870	3,334	3,721
Operating expenses % uplift YoY		5%	16%	12%
Impairment charge %		1.0%	1.5%	1.2%

Orchard's lending portfolio consists of only short term products and the company has the ability to wind-down its business within 12 months, as all lending will have matured within that time period. As a result of this, undertaking stress testing beyond two years provides limited benefit.

Lending volumes and deposit volume reductions are based on a scenario where general economic conditions are worsening and as a result, fewer loans are made and less cash is being saved.

The key management actions to mitigate the stress are to reduce loan rates to maintain market share and increase deposit rates to maintain funding. Loan rates have been re-set by looking realistically at the need to reduce lending rates to mitigate any reduction in lending volumes. It should be noted that the 2% stress represents a 14% reduction in rates charged to customers. Deposit rates have been increased to encourage depositors to continue to make deposits with Orchard. It has been assumed that deposit rates will need to be 1.5% higher than base plan in Year 2.

Expense increases have been established by looking at the wider economy (lack of skilled personnel, inflation, general shortage of providers of service and negative exchange rate fluctuations) and applying these factors to Orchard's business.

Based on the change in drivers, the capital requirements under a market-wide stress are tabled below.

Table 63: Market-wide stress scenario (before management action) – Financials.

			£'000
Anchor no MA	**Plan**	**Plan**	**Plan**
Income Statement	**Year 1**	**Year 2**	**Year 3**
Interest Receivable	4,887	4,967	6,415
Interest payable	(396)	(541)	(749)
Net interest income	**4,491**	**4,426**	**5,666**
Administration expenses	(2,870)	(3,334)	(3,721)
Stresses (idio, conduct, systems	0	0	0
Impairment charges	(312)	(444)	(471)
Operating profit before tax	**1,308**	**648**	**1,473**
Corporation tax	(257)	(123)	(280)
Profit after tax	**1,051**	**525**	**1,193**
Dividends	(210)	(105)	(239)
Retained Earnings	**841**	**420**	**955**
Balance Sheet	**Plan Year 1**	**Plan Year 2**	**Plan Year 3**
Assets			
Loans and advances	32,762	28,163	41,151
Cash at bank	1,000	1,000	1,000
Liquid asset buffer	3,867	14,693	10,758
Fixed assets	483	556	621
Other assets	158	158	158
Total assets	**38,270**	**44,570**	**53,689**
Liabilities			
Customer deposits	21,000	27,000	35,000
Bank funding	0	0	0

Table 63 (continued)

Anchor no MA **Income Statement**	**Plan** **Year 1**	**Plan** **Year 2**	**Plan** **Year 3**
Trade creditors	2,051	2,051	2,051
Tax liabilities	257	123	280
Non-current liabilities	84	98	105
Total liabilities	**23,393**	**29,273**	**37,436**
Equity			
Share capital	214	214	214
Share premium	8,692	8,692	8,692
Merger reserves	891	891	891
Retained earnings	4,240	5,081	5,501
Current year retained earnings	841	420	955
Total equity	**14,878**	**15,298**	**16,252**
Total equity and liabilities	38,270	44,570	53,689

Table 64: Market-wide stress scenario (after management action) – Financials.

£'000

Anchor **Income Statement**	**Plan** **Year 1**	**Plan** **Year 2**	**Plan** **Year 3**
Interest Receivable	4,887	4,891	6,204
Interest payable	(396)	(734)	(1,146)
Net interest income	**4,491**	**4,158**	**5,058**
Administration expenses	(2,870)	(3,334)	(3,721)
Stresses (idio, conduct, systems	0	0	0
Impairment charges	(312)	(493)	(532)
Operating profit before tax	**1,308**	**331**	**805**
Corporation tax	(257)	(63)	(153)
Profit after tax	**1,051**	**268**	**652**
Dividends	(210)	(54)	(130)
Retained Earnings	**841**	**214**	**522**
Balance Sheet	**Plan** **Year 1**	**Plan** **Year 2**	**Plan** **Year 3**
Assets			
Loans and advances	32,762	32,236	46,293
Cash at bank	1,000	1,000	1,000
Liquid asset buffer	3,867	12,354	8,351

Table 64 (continued)

Anchor Income Statement	**Plan Year 1**	**Plan Year 2**	**Plan Year 3**
Fixed assets	483	556	621
Other assets	158	158	158
Total assets	**38,270**	**46,304**	**56,423**
Liabilities			
Customer deposits	21,000	29,000	38,500
Bank funding	0	0	0
Trade creditors	2,051	2,051	2,051
Tax liabilities	257	63	153
Non-current liabilities	84	98	105
Total liabilities	**23,393**	**31,212**	**40,809**
Equity			
Share capital	214	214	214
Share premium	8,692	8,692	8,692
Merger reserves	891	891	891
Retained earnings	4,240	5,081	5,295
Current year retained earnings	841	214	522
Total equity	**14,878**	**15,092**	**15,613**
Total equity and liabilities	38,270	46,304	56,423

Table 65: Market-wide stress scenario (before management action) – Orchard Capital Position.

£'000

Anchor no MA	**Plan Year 1**	**Plan Year 2**	**Plan Year 3**
Pillar 1			
Credit risk on loan assets	1,839	1,591	2,314
Credit risk on bank balances	16	16	16
Fixed assets	5	5	6
Credit risk on HQLA	0	0	0
Total credit risk	**1,860**	**1,612**	**2,336**
Operational risk basic indicator	672	682	729
Pillar 1 capital requirements	**2,532**	**2,294**	**3,065**
Pillar 2A capital requirements			
Operational risk	147	178	174
Business risk	0	0	0
Reputational risk	0	0	0
Credit concentration risk	319	278	398
Interest rate risk in the banking book (IRRBB)	165	132	318
Residual operational risk from risk register	0	0	0

Table 65 (continued)

Anchor no MA	Plan Year 1	Plan Year 2	Plan Year 3
Pillar 2A capital requirements	**631**	**588**	**890**
Total capital requirement (Pillar 1 + Pillar 2A)	**3,163**	**2,882**	**3,955**
Share capital	9,797	9,797	9,797
Audited retained earnings	5,081	5,501	6,455
DTA on operating losses (Deduction)	0	0	0
Intangible Assets (Deduction)	(421)	(490)	(552)
Total Capital resources	**14,457**	**14,808**	**15,700**
Risk weighted assets (Credit + Ops)	**31,652**	**28,672**	**38,311**
Total Capital requirement % of RWAs	**10%**	**10%**	**10%**
Pillar 2B	**1,050**	**1,102**	**1,158**
TCR + Pillar 2B % of RWAs	**13%**	**14%**	**13%**
CET1 % of RWAs	**47%**	**53%**	**42%**
Regulatory Capital Resources % of RWAs	**46%**	**52%**	**41%**
Surplus / (deficit) regulatory capital	**10,244**	**10,824**	**10,588**

Table 66: Market-wide stress scenario (after management action) – Orchard Capital Position.

£'000

Anchor	Plan Year 1	Plan Year 2	Plan Year 3
Pillar 1			
Credit risk on loan assets	1,839	1,820	2,603
Credit risk on bank balances	16	16	16
Fixed assets	5	5	6
Credit risk on HQLA	0	0	0
Total credit risk	**1,860**	**1,841**	**2,625**
Operational risk basic indicator	672	669	685
Pillar 1 capital requirements	**2,532**	**2,510**	**3,310**
Pillar 2A capital requirements			
Operational risk	147	192	218
Business risk	0	0	0
Reputational risk	0	0	0
Credit concentration risk	319	316	446
Interest rate risk in the banking book (IRRBB)	166	149	341
Residual operational risk from risk register	0	0	0

Table 66 (continued)

Pillar 2A capital requirements	**632**	**657**	**1,005**
Total capital requirement (Pillar 1 + Pillar 2A)	**3,164**	**3,166**	**4,316**
Share capital	9,797	9,797	9,797
Audited retained earnings	5,081	5,295	5,816
DTA on operating losses (Deduction)	0	0	0
Intangible Assets (Deduction)	(421)	(490)	(552)
Total Capital resources	**14,457**	**14,602**	**15,062**
Risk weighted assets (Credit + Ops)	**31,652**	**31,370**	**41,379**
Total Capital requirement % of RWAs	**10%**	**10%**	**10%**
Pillar 2B	**1,050**	**1,102**	**1,158**
TCR + Pillar 2B % of RWAs	**13%**	**14%**	**13%**
CET1 % of RWAs	**47%**	**48%**	**38%**
Regulatory Capital Resources % of RWAs	**46%**	**47%**	**36%**
Surplus / (deficit) regulatory capital	**10,243**	**10,333**	**9,589**

Capital resources are reduced under the stress scenario but still materially exceed Orchard's TCR and do not erode the PRA Buffer.

Management Action in Anchor Stress Scenario

Management will conduct a full review of its lending products to determine if margin can be maintained at historic levels. Failing this Orchard will consider the introduction of new products which will enable it to retain margins.

Orchard will review its deposit strategy to determine how it can reduce its deposit rates. Orchard will consider introducing shorter-term deposits such as 3 and 6 months terms to reduce its deposit rates, and at the same time raise funding.

It should be noted that the base case projections include a presumed annual dividend of 20% of annual earnings. In situations of capital stress this dividend is unlikely to be paid and this provides an additional capital buffer in the base case.

11.6 Idiosyncratic Stress

For the idiosyncratic stress, management considered both operational risks and credit risk. A credit risk scenario was run with credit losses inflated to 3% from a planned figure of 1% and recent experiences of less than 1%. The operational risks identified in the risk register were considered and appropriate scenarios derived. Over and above the impact of the operational shortcomings, the indirect impact on business drivers was also considered.

11.6.1 Operational Risk Scenario Analysis

An assessment of the potential losses from key operational risks in the Risk Register has been performed. This assessment took the form of a scenario analysis, where the impact of multiple scenarios occurring simultaneously was considered. In analysing the scenario, a number of risks within a chosen ORIX category were presumed to have failed, and the risk exposure calculated to show the increase in the residual risk consequence.

This has been grouped into the relevant Basel Operational Risk Scenario Category:

Table 67: Operational Risk Scenario Categories.

Basel Category	Description	Assessment in scenario
Internal Fraud	Misappropriation of assets, tax evasion, intentional mismarking of positions, bribery	Scenario 5
External Fraud	Theft of information, hacking damage, third party theft and forgery	Scenario 4
Employment Practices and Workplace Safety	Discrimination, workers compensation, employee health and safety	Scenario 1
Clients, Products and Business Practice	Market manipulation, antitrust, improper trade, product defects, fiduciary breaches, account churning	Scenario 2
Business Disruption and Systems Failures	Concerted utility disruptions, software failures, hardware failures	Scenario 3
Execution, Delivery, and Process Management	Data entry errors, accounting errors, failed mandatory reporting, negligent loss of client assets	Scenario 4
Damage to Physical Assets	Natural disasters, terrorism, vandalism	Scenario 3

Table 68: Operational Risk Scenarios.

Scenario 1	Key Management Dependency
Scenario Considered	The Board recognises that Orchard is more dependent on key management than larger banks meaning that when key employees are unexpectedly absent for a period of time, Orchard could be left with a gap that it cannot readily cover or replace internally. In these circumstances an appropriate person has to be hired temporarily, usually at a proportionately higher cost, until a permanent replacement can be found. Additionally, there remains a risk of losses if management don't fully understand or optimally execute their duties. The Exco is small with a broad range of responsibilities across many areas of expertise.

Table 68 (continued)

Trigger	Sudden unforeseen resignation of one or more key members of staff due to conflict related to strategic direction.
Existing Controls	i. Orchard will have a pool of interim skills available in its non-executive directors ("NEDs") who may be able to cover the absence/loss of either of the two Executive Directors whilst a replacement is found. Going forward, as the Board membership evolves, the quality of NEDs brought onto the Board is expected to be such that those interim skills should still be available. ii. Orchard will take out key person insurance cover on the executive directors, CRO and Head of IT & Operations to cover business disruption and recruitment costs. iii. There is sufficient internal cross-training to cover any given individual's unplanned absence for a *short* period of time. iv. Delegated authorities are formally documented.
Management Actions	i. The Board acknowledges that it would need to take into consideration the potential conflict between the oversight role of an NED and the executive decision making role of an executive director. An emergency meeting of the Board would determine an action plan. ii. Use would be made of recruiters specialising in senior management roles for permanent and interim appointments.
Impact	The annual cost of the temporary replacement for any two of the ExCo (Chief Executive, CFO, CRO, Head of IT & Operations, Head of Finance & Operations) has been estimated as follows according to severity: – **Severe:** 2 individuals leaving has been estimated at £298k (Severe impact) being twice the average remuneration package of the two members of key staff concerned (including 20% add-ons). – **Moderate:** 1 individual leaving: £149k (the cost of one key employee leaving)

Scenario 2	**Senior Management Conduct Failure**
Scenario Considered	As a small bank there is an increased risk of weak corporate governance and/or conflict, which could lead to poor strategy and inadequate challenge to the executive, tolerance of poor leadership and potential misunderstanding of regulatory and business issues leading to misperception of risks. A collective failure of the bank's governance could lead to regulatory fines and repayments to customers, as well as the replacement of a tranche of the bank's Board.
Trigger	Incident involving allegations of miss-selling or conduct detrimental to customer interests.
Existing Controls	i. Formal process in place for recruitment and induction of NEDs. ii. NEDs will be provided with support to attend external training courses, which will be complemented with in-house compliance training. iii. A standard review schedule will be in place for Risk Management documents, Business Plan, ICAAP & ILAAP and all Policies. iv. Orchard will develop a new product approval policy and procedure, and apply this retrospectively to existing products

Table 68 (continued)

Scenario 2	**Senior Management Conduct Failure**
Management Actions	Use would be made of recruiters specialising in senior management roles for permanent and interim appointments. Use would be made of a third-party management team to conduct a review and to advise on recruitment.
Impact	Assessment: The annual cost of NED replacement with varying severity is as follows: – **Severe: External review (£200k) and regulatory sanction (£250k) plus** 2 NEDs leaving (£140k) where the replacement per NED is £70k being twice the average NED fee. Total £590k. – **Moderate:** 1 NED leaving (£70k) where the replacement per NED is £70k being twice the average NED fee.

Scenario 3	**Cyber Attack**
Scenario Considered	A concerted cyber-attack on the bank's hosted systems removes the staff's access.
Trigger	Staff cannot access systems.
Existing Controls	i. The Board will vet and approve all significant outsourcing agreements in accordance with its Outsourcing Policy. ii. Regularly monitored Service Level Agreements for IT. iii. Escrow for third party software. iv. Contracts will include Business Continuity by providers. v. Regular testing of Disaster Recovery Plan and staff training regarding business continuity
Management Actions	The Disaster Recovery Plan would be initiated immediately.
Impact	Assessment: – **Severe:** The cost of a skilled person's report requested by the Regulator is estimated to be in the region of £100k with £150k of remediation work required. Total £250k. – **Moderate:** Regulator requesting remediation programme (£50k cost)

Scenario 4	**Third Party & Processing Failure**
Scenario Considered	A major failure of outsourced IT services means that no transactions can be processed.
Trigger	Main IT supplier systems failure.
Existing Controls	i. Critical systems will be outsourced to experienced providers. ii. Systems will be installed on Orchard servers and support will be in place with the providers. Internal systems will continue to be supported by Assign IT, who are experienced and reputable.

Table 68 (continued)

	iii. All systems will be backed up incrementally regularly with regular simulation tests for recovery and contingency sites. Backups will be taken both to local storage and to alternative recovery sites. Customer letters and statements will be backed up daily. iv. Regular testing of Disaster Recovery Plan and staff training regarding business continuity
Management Actions	Management will initiate the Disaster Recovery Plan immediately.
Impact	Impact: – **Severe:** the dependency on a software provider for the system for supporting loans and deposits. i. It is anticipated that, were the software provider to fail to support its systems in any way, it would cost circa £100k (based on the experience of management in implementing 3rd party software systems) to work with an alternative supplier to implement a replacement banking system. ii. Compensation to be paid to customers for delayed payments is estimated at £50k. iii. In addition, a fine could be levied by the PRA and the FCA. The former would be likely to be in the order of £500k, and the latter £250k, based on (respectively) 10% and 5% of the previous year's income. Early cooperation would see a reduction of 30% applied, reducing the fine to approximately £525k. – Total Impact: £675k. – **Moderate:** Significant system downtime (restored after 5 days will result in £150k of IT consultancy cost to enable alternative short-term workaround).

Scenario 5	**Failure of Fraud Prevention**
Scenario Considered	A number of maturing fixed term deposit accounts are re-directed to fraudsters' accounts and customers have to be reimbursed. This would also have an impact of the bank's reputation, with considerable effort required to address customer detriment as well as the issues.
Trigger	Customer complaints that deposits are not being returned to their nominated accounts when the term is due.
Existing Controls	i. Controls over savings account processes will be laid down in Standard Operating Process (SOP) documents. ii. The controls will include an automated 'closed loop' process for deposit account maturities, '4 eyes' checks on any data changes, plus, for individual and batch payments, segregation of duties between payment 'inputter' and 'authoriser' built in to the Agency Banking system which Orchard will use. iii. Detective controls will also be in place reporting movements daily to the Head of Finance and Operations.
Management Actions	Management will immediately suspend all banking operations and initiate verification checks on account details to be performed by members of staff not involved in account processing.

Table 68 (continued)

Impact	The impact is as follows:
	- **Severe** (£490k)
	  - Deposits paid away (£200k)
	  - Compensation (£20k)
	  - Investigation (£20k)
	  - Regulatory Fine (£250k)
	  - Total Impact: £490k.
	- **Moderate** (£240k)
	  - Deposits paid away (£100k)
	  - Compensation (£20k)
	  - Investigation (£20k)
	  - Regulatory Fine (£100k)
	  - Total Impact: £240k

11.6.2 Summary of Operational Risk Scenarios

Management have assessed the operational risk quantitatively via the five scenarios outlined above, and have taken the highest impact scenario for idiosyncratic stress, being scenario 4.

Table 69: Pillar 2B Operational Risk Impacts.

Scenario	Indicated P2B add-on
Base Scenario	–
Scenario 1: Key person	£298k
Scenario 2: Senior Management Conduct Failure	£590k
Scenario 3: Cyber Attack	£250k
Scenario 4: Third Party & Processing Failure	£675k
Scenario 5: Failure of Fraud Prevention	£490k
Maximum	**£675k**

The operational event will have an indirect impact on the business drivers and the table below presents the additional impact arising from the scenario.

Table 70: Idiosyncratic stress op risk scenario – Impact on key business drivers (before management action).

Idio no MA	**Plan Year 1**	**Plan Year 2**	**Plan Year 3**
Impact on business drivers			
New lending	0%	(20%)	(20%)
Loan Rate	0.0%	0.0%	0.0%

Table 70 (continued)

Idio no MA	**Plan Year 1**	**Plan Year 2**	**Plan Year 3**
Net new Deposits volumes	0%	(30%)	(30%)
Deposit rate	0.0%	0.0%	0.0%
Impairment charge % of asset	0.0%	0.0%	0.0%
Expenses increase from prior period	0%	15%	0%
Bank funding margin increase vs plan	0.0%	0.0%	0.0%

Table 71: Idiosyncratic stress op risk scenario – Impact on key business drivers (after management action).

Idio	**Plan Year 1**	**Plan Year 2**	**Plan Year 3**
Impact on business drivers			
New lending	0%	(5%)	(5%)
Loan Rate	0.0%	(1.5%)	(1.5%)
Net new Deposits volumes	0%	(5%)	(5%)
Deposit rate	0.0%	1.0%	1.0%
Impairment charge % of asset	0.0%	0.0%	0.0%
Expenses increase from prior period	0%	15%	0%
Bank funding margin increase vs plan	0.0%	0.0%	0.0%

- As lending volumes suffer, the lending rate is reduced to generate more business. The impact on lending and resultant rate is less severe than the market-wide scenario.
- Deposits rates are increased slightly to attract and retain deposits.
- Expenses are increased by over £800k in aggregate over year 2 and 3 to resolve the underlying issues. This is over and above the £675k impact of the operational issue.

The resultant business drivers are tabled below:

Table 72: Idiosyncratic stress op risk scenario – Key business drivers (before management action).

Idio no MA	**Actual 2018**	**Plan Year 1**	**Plan Year 2**	**Plan Year 3**
New Lending – £000	68,730	86,000	86,000	111,520
Lending growth %		25%	0%	29%
Lending stock – £000	31,084	32,762	32,366	41,224
Lending interest rate (wt. average)		14.53%	14.46%	14.40%
Net New Deposit – £000		21,000	7,000	7,000
Deposit stock – £000		21,000	28,000	35,000
Deposit interest rate (wt. average)		2.15%	2.32%	2.43%

Table 72 (continued)

Idio no MA	Actual 2018	Plan Year 1	Plan Year 2	Plan Year 3
Bank funding – £000		–	–	–
Funding interest rate		4.30%	4.47%	4.58%
Operating expenses £000	2,746	2,870	3,668	4,072
Operating expenses % uplift YoY		5%	28%	11%
Impairment charge %		1.0%	1.0%	1.0%

Table 73: Idiosyncratic stress op risk scenario – Key business drivers (after management action).

Idio	Actual 2018	Plan Year 1	Plan Year 2	Plan Year 3
New Lending – £000	68,730	86,000	102,410	132,430
Lending growth %		25%	19%	29%
Lending stock – £000	31,084	32,762	38,463	48,949
Lending interest rate (wt. average)		14.53%	12.96%	12.90%
Net New Deposit – £000		21,000	9,500	9,500
Deposit stock – £000		21,000	30,500	40,000
Deposit interest rate (wt. average)		2.15%	3.32%	3.43%
Bank funding – £000		–	–	–
Funding interest rate		4.30%	4.47%	4.58%
Operating expenses £000	2,746	2,870	3,668	4,072
Operating expenses % uplift YoY		5%	28%	11%
Impairment charge %		1.0%	1.0%	1.0%

Table 74: Idiosyncratic stress op risk scenario – Financials (before management action).

Idio no MA Income Statement	Plan Year 1	Plan Year 2	Plan Year 3
Interest Receivable	4,887	5,432	6,588
Interest payable	(396)	(554)	(760)
Net interest income	**4,491**	**4,878**	**5,829**
Administration expenses	(2,870)	(3,668)	(4,072)
Stresses (idio, conduct, systems	0	0	0
Impairment charges	(312)	(328)	(398)
Operating profit before tax	**1,308**	**882**	**1,359**
Corporation tax	(257)	(168)	(258)
Profit after tax	**1,051**	**714**	**1,100**
Dividends	(210)	(143)	(220)
Retained Earnings	**841**	**572**	**880**

Table 74 (continued)

Balance Sheet	**Plan Year 1**	**Plan Year 2**	**Plan Year 3**
Assets			
Loans and advances	32,762	32,366	41,224
Cash at bank	1,000	1,000	1,000
Liquid asset buffer	3,867	11,697	10,752
Fixed assets	483	556	621
Other assets	158	158	158
Total assets	**38,270**	**45,776**	**53,755**
Liabilities			
Customer deposits	21,000	28,000	35,000
Bank funding	0	0	0
Trade creditors	2,051	2,051	2,051
Tax liabilities	257	168	258
Non-current liabilities	84	109	116
Total liabilities	**23,393**	**30,327**	**37,425**
Equity			
Share capital	214	214	214
Share premium	8,692	8,692	8,692
Merger reserves	891	891	891
Retained earnings	4,240	5,081	5,652
Current year retained earnings	841	572	880
Total equity	**14,878**	**15,449**	**16,330**
Total equity and liabilities	38,270	45,776	53,755

Table 75: Idiosyncratic stress op risk scenario – Financials (after management action).

			£'000
Idio Income Statement	**Plan Year 1**	**Plan Year 2**	**Plan Year 3**
Interest Receivable	4,887	5,643	6,955
Interest payable	(396)	(705)	(1,170)
Net interest income	**4,491**	**4,938**	**5,785**
Administration expenses	(2,870)	(3,668)	(4,072)
Stresses (idio, conduct, systems	0	(675)	0
Impairment charges	(312)	(377)	(473)
Operating profit before tax	**1,308**	**219**	**1,240**
Corporation tax	(257)	(42)	(236)
Profit after tax	**1,051**	**177**	**1,005**

Table 75 (continued)

Idio Income Statement	**Plan Year 1**	**Plan Year 2**	**Plan Year 3**
Dividends	(210)	(35)	(201)
Retained Earnings	**841**	**142**	**804**
Balance Sheet	**Plan Year 1**	**Plan Year 2**	**Plan Year 3**
Assets			
Loans and advances	32,762	38,463	48,949
Cash at bank	1,000	1,000	1,000
Liquid asset buffer	3,867	7,544	7,498
Fixed assets	483	556	621
Other assets	158	158	158
Total assets	**38,270**	**47,720**	**58,226**
Liabilities			
Customer deposits	21,000	30,500	40,000
Bank funding	0	0	0
Trade creditors	2,051	2,051	2,051
Tax liabilities	257	42	236
Non-current liabilities	84	109	116
Total liabilities	**23,393**	**32,701**	**42,403**
Equity			
Share capital	214	214	214
Share premium	8,692	8,692	8,692
Merger reserves	891	891	891
Retained earnings	4,240	5,081	5,222
Current year retained earnings	841	142	804
Total equity	**14,878**	**15,019**	**15,823**
Total equity and liabilities	38,270	47,720	58,226

Table 76: Idiosyncratic stress op risk scenario – Orchard Capital Position (before management action).

			£'000
Idio no MA	**Plan Year 1**	**Plan Year 2**	**Plan Year 3**
Pillar 1			
Credit risk on loan assets	1,839	1,818	2,314
Credit risk on bank balances	16	16	16
Fixed assets	5	5	6
Credit risk on HQLA	0	0	0
Total credit risk	**1,860**	**1,839**	**2,336**

Table 76 (continued)

Idio no MA	**Plan Year 1**	**Plan Year 2**	**Plan Year 3**
Operational risk basic indicator	672	705	760
Pillar 1 capital requirements	**2,532**	**2,544**	**3,096**
Pillar 2A capital requirements			
Operational risk	147	156	143
Business risk	0	0	0
Reputational risk	0	0	0
Credit concentration risk	319	315	398
Interest rate risk in the banking book (IRRBB)	165	130	311
Residual operational risk from risk register	0	0	0
Pillar 2A capital requirements	**631**	**601**	**852**
Total capital requirement (Pillar 1 + Pillar 2A)	**3,163**	**3,145**	**3,948**
Share capital	9,797	9,797	9,797
Audited retained earnings	5,081	5,652	6,533
DTA on operating losses (Deduction)	0	0	0
Intangible Assets (Deduction)	(421)	(490)	(552)
Total Capital resources	**14,457**	**14,959**	**15,778**
Risk weighted assets (Credit + Ops)	**31,652**	**31,795**	**38,696**
Total Capital requirement % of RWAs	**10%**	**10%**	**10%**
Pillar 2B	**1,050**	**1,102**	**1,158**
TCR + Pillar 2B % of RWAs	**13%**	**13%**	**13%**
CET1 % of RWAs	**47%**	**49%**	**42%**
Regulatory Capital Resources % of RWAs	**46%**	**47%**	**41%**
Surplus / (deficit) regulatory capital	**10,244**	**10,712**	**10,672**

Table 77: Idiosyncratic stress op risk scenario – Orchard Capital Position (after management action).

			£'000
Idio	**Plan Year 1**	**Plan Year 2**	**Plan Year 3**
Pillar 1			
Credit risk on loan assets	1,839	2,159	2,748
Credit risk on bank balances	16	16	16
Fixed assets	5	5	6
Credit risk on HQLA	0	0	0
Total credit risk	**1,860**	**2,181**	**2,769**

Table 77 (continued)

Idio	Plan Year 1	Plan Year 2	Plan Year 3
Operational risk basic indicator	672	708	761
Pillar 1 capital requirements	**2,532**	**2,888**	**3,530**
Pillar 2A capital requirements			
Operational risk	147	153	143
Business risk	0	0	0
Reputational risk	0	0	0
Credit concentration risk	319	372	470
Interest rate risk in the banking book (IRRBB)	165	147	343
Residual operational risk from risk register	0	0	0
Pillar 2A capital requirements	**631**	**672**	**956**
Total capital requirement (Pillar 1 + Pillar 2A)	**3,164**	**3,561**	**4,486**
Share capital	9,797	9,797	9,797
Audited retained earnings	5,081	5,222	6,026
DTA on operating losses (Deduction)	0	0	0
Intangible Assets (Deduction)	(421)	(490)	(552)
Total Capital resources	**14,457**	**14,529**	**15,271**
Risk weighted assets (Credit + Ops)	**31,652**	**36,104**	**44,127**
Total Capital requirement % of RWAs	**10%**	**10%**	**10%**
Pillar 2B	**1,050**	**1,102**	**1,158**
TCR + Pillar 2B % of RWAs	**13%**	**13%**	**13%**
CET1 % of RWAs	**47%**	**42%**	**36%**
Regulatory Capital Resources % of RWAs	**46%**	**40%**	**35%**
Surplus / (deficit) regulatory capital	**10,243**	**9,866**	**9,628**

This resulted in a reduced capital surplus in year 3 of £9,628k (£2,308k lower than base case), detailed in the table above.

Management Action in Idiosyncratic Stress Scenario

Management will initiate the disaster recovery plan immediately.

Although the severity of the idiosyncratic scenario's impact on both lending and deposit volumes is less than the market-wide stress scenario, management action will be similar to that taken under the market-wide scenario. In addition, pro-active communication with brokers and depositors will be undertaken to provide assurance and updates on the status of the business.

11.6.3 Credit Risk Scenario

A scenario was run with impairment costs inflated from 1% of receivables to 3% (current experience is < 1%).

Table 78: Idiosyncratic stress credit risk scenario – Impact on key business drivers.

Credit Idio	Plan Year 1	Plan Year 2	Plan Year 3
Impact on business drivers			
New lending	0%	0%	0%
Loan Rate	0.0%	0.0%	0.0%
Net new Deposits volumes	0%	0%	0%
Deposit rate	0.0%	0.0%	0.0%
Impairment charge % of asset	0.0%	2.0%	2.0%
Expenses increase from prior period	0%	0%	0%
Bank funding margin increase vs plan	0.0%	0.0%	0.0%

The resultant business drivers are tabled below:

Table 79: Idiosyncratic stress credit risk scenario – Key business drivers.

Credit Idio	Actual 2018	Plan Year 1	Plan Year 2	Plan Year 3
New Lending – £000	68,730	86,000	107,800	139,400
Lending growth %		25%	25%	29%
Lending stock – £000	31,084	32,762	39,689	50,535
Lending interest rate (wt. average)		14.53%	14.46%	14.40%
Corporate Insurance Loan stock (£000)		19,484	21,432	23,575
Average loan size (£000)		172	172	172
Number accounts (vols)		113	125	137
Direct Insurance loan stock (£000)		5,124	8,063	14,218
Average loan size (£000)		0.48	0.48	0.48
Number accounts (vols)		10,675	16,799	29,621
Accountancy Loan stock (£000)		8,155	10,193	12,742
Average loan size (£000)		5.10	5.10	5.10
Number accounts (vols)		1,599	1,999	2,498
New Deposit – £000		21,000	22,600	37,000
Deposit stock – £000		21,000	31,000	41,000
Deposit interest rate (wt. average)*		2.15%	2.32%	2.43%
Average deposit (£000)		24	24	24
Number of deposit accounts stock (vol)		875	1,292	1,708
Number of new deposits		875	942	1,542
Number of new deposits per day		3	4	6

This generates an income statement and balance sheet as below:

Table 80: Idiosyncratic stress credit risk scenario – Financials.

			£'000
Credit Idio Income Statement	**Plan Year 1**	**Plan Year 2**	**Plan Year 3**
Interest Receivable	4,887	6,370	8,169
Interest payable	(396)	(591)	(870)
Net interest income	**4,491**	**5,779**	**7,299**
Administration expenses	(2,870)	(3,267)	(3,651)
Stresses (idio, conduct, systems	0	0	0
Impairment charges	(312)	(1,178)	(1,493)
Operating profit before tax	**1,308**	**1,333**	**2,154**
Corporation tax	(257)	(253)	(409)
Profit after tax	**1,051**	**1,080**	**1,745**
Dividends	(210)	(216)	(349)
Retained Earnings	**841**	**864**	**1,396**
Balance Sheet	**Plan Year 1**	**Plan Year 2**	**Plan Year 3**
Assets			
Loans and advances	32,762	39,689	50,535
Cash at bank	1,000	1,000	1,000
Liquid asset buffer	3,867	7,740	8,387
Fixed assets	483	556	621
Other assets	158	158	158
Total assets	**38,270**	**49,142**	**60,701**
Liabilities			
Customer deposits	21,000	31,000	41,000
Bank funding	0	0	0
Trade creditors	2,051	2,051	2,051
Tax liabilities	257	253	409
Non-current liabilities	84	96	103
Total liabilities	**23,393**	**33,401**	**43,564**
Equity			
Share capital	214	214	214
Share premium	8,692	8,692	8,692
Merger reserves	891	891	891
Retained earnings	4,240	5,081	5,944
Current year retained earnings	841	864	1,396
Total equity	**14,878**	**15,741**	**17,137**
Total equity and liabilities	38,270	49,142	60,701

This resulted in a reduced capital surplus in year 3 of £10,774k (£1,161k lower than base case), detailed in the table below:

Table 81: Idiosyncratic stress credit risk scenario – Orchard Capital Position.

			£'000
Credit Idio	**Plan Year 1**	**Plan Year 2**	**Plan Year 3**
Pillar 1			
Credit risk on loan assets	1,839	2,272	2,893
Credit risk on bank balances	16	16	16
Fixed assets	5	5	6
Credit risk on HQLA	0	0	0
Total credit risk	**1,860**	**2,294**	**2,914**
Operational risk basic indicator	672	750	878
Pillar 1 capital requirements	**2,532**	**3,043**	**3,793**
Pillar 2A capital requirements			
Operational risk	147	111	25
Business risk	0	0	0
Reputational risk	0	0	0
Credit concentration risk	319	391	494
Interest rate risk in the banking book (IRRBB)	165	144	342
Residual operational risk from risk register	0	0	0
Pillar 2A capital requirements	**631**	**645**	**861**
Total capital requirement (Pillar 1 + Pillar 2A)	**3,163**	**3,688**	**4,654**
Share capital	9,797	9,797	9,797
Audited retained earnings	5,081	5,944	7,340
DTA on operating losses (Deduction)	0	0	0
Intangible Assets (Deduction)	(421)	(490)	(552)
Total Capital resources	**14,457**	**15,252**	**16,586**
Risk weighted assets (Credit + Ops)	**31,652**	**38,039**	**47,409**
Total Capital requirement % of RWAs	**10%**	**10%**	**10%**
Pillar 2B	**1,050**	**1,102**	**1,158**
TCR + Pillar 2B % of RWAs	**13%**	**13%**	**12%**
CET1 % of RWAs	**47%**	**41%**	**36%**
Regulatory Capital Resources % of RWAs	**46%**	**40%**	**35%**
Surplus / (deficit) regulatory capital	**10,244**	**10,461**	**10,774**

The credit risk scenario had a smaller adverse effect on capital than the worst operational risk scenario. The operational risk scenario was therefore used for idiosyncratic risk.

11.7 Combined Stress

Management has combined the market-wide stress with the idiosyncratic stress, and has assumed that the business drivers will be more adversely impacted by an operational event in very difficult market conditions. The table below provides the impact on the key drivers.

Table 82: Combined stress scenario – Impact on key business drivers (before management action).

Combined no MA	Plan Year 1	Plan Year 2	Plan Year 3
Impact on business drivers			
New lending	0%	(50%)	(30%)
Loan Rate	0.0%	0.0%	0.0%
Net new Deposits volumes	0%	(80%)	(50%)
Deposit rate	0.0%	0.0%	0.0%
Impairment charge % of asset	0.0%	2.0%	2.0%
Expenses increase from prior period	0%	25%	15%
Bank funding margin increase vs plan	0.0%	0.0%	0.0%

Table 83: Combined stress scenario – Impact on key business drivers (after management action).

Combined	Plan Year 1	Plan Year 2	Plan Year 3
Impact on business drivers			
New lending	0%	(30%)	(15%)
Loan Rate	0.0%	(3.0%)	(2.0%)
Net new Deposits volumes	0%	(35%)	(20%)
Deposit rate	0.0%	3.0%	3.0%
Impairment charge % of asset	0.0%	2.0%	2.0%
Expenses increase from prior period	0%	25%	15%
Bank funding margin increase vs plan	0.0%	0.0%	0.0%

- Given the reduction in new lending, the margins have been significantly reduced to attract new business in very difficult market conditions.
- Deposit rates have been increased significantly to manage both retention and new business given that the operational risk event has resulted in some damage to reputation. As the deposits are protected, some depositors will be attracted by the higher rates offered.
- The operating expenses increase to manage the operational event in a timely and efficient manner.

The resultant business drivers are as follows:

Table 84: Combined stress scenario – Key business drivers (before management action).

Combined no MA	Actual 2018	Plan Year 1	Plan Year 2	Plan Year 3
New Lending – £000	68,730	86,000	53,900	97,580
Lending growth %		25%	(37%)	81%
Lending stock – £000	31,084	32,762	19,739	35,426
Lending interest rate (wt. average)		14.53%	14.46%	14.40%
Net New Deposit – £000		21,000	2,000	5,000
Deposit stock – £000		21,000	23,000	28,000
Deposit interest rate (wt. average)		2.15%	2.32%	2.43%
Bank funding – £000		–	–	–
Funding interest rate		4.30%	4.47%	4.58%
Operating expenses £000	2,746	2,870	3,935	4,913
Operating expenses % uplift YoY		5%	37%	25%
Impairment charge %		1.0%	3.0%	3.0%

Table 85: Combined stress scenario – Key business drivers (after management action).

Combined	Actual 2018	Plan Year 1	Plan Year 2	Plan Year 3
New Lending – £000	68,730	86,000	75,460	118,490
Lending growth %		25%	(12%)	57%
Lending stock – £000	31,084	32,762	27,784	42,999
Lending interest rate (wt. average)		14.53%	11.46%	12.40%
Net New Deposit – £000		21,000	6,500	8,000
Deposit stock – £000		21,000	27,500	35,500
Deposit interest rate (wt. average)		2.15%	5.32%	5.43%
Bank funding – £000		–	–	–
Funding interest rate		4.30%	4.47%	4.58%
Operating expenses £000	2,746	2,870	3,935	4,913
Operating expenses % uplift YoY		5%	37%	25%
Impairment charge %		1.0%	3.0%	3.0%

Table 86: Combined stress scenario – Orchard Financials (before management action).

Combined no MA Income Statement	Plan Year 1	Plan Year 2	Plan Year 3 (£'000)
Interest Receivable	4,887	4,024	5,404
Interest payable	(396)	(491)	(615)
Net interest income	**4,491**	**3,533**	**4,789**

Table 86 (continued)

Combined no MA Income Statement	**Plan Year 1**	**Plan Year 2**	**Plan Year 3**
Administration expenses	(2,870)	(3,935)	(4,913)
Stresses (idio, conduct, systems	0	0	0
Impairment charges	(312)	(695)	(994)
Operating profit before tax	**1,308**	**(1,097)**	**(1,118)**
Corporation tax	(257)	208	212
Profit after tax	**1,051**	**(889)**	**(905)**
Dividends	(210)	0	0
Retained Earnings	**841**	**(889)**	**(905)**
Balance Sheet	**Plan Year 1**	**Plan Year 2**	**Plan Year 3**
Assets			
Loans and advances	32,762	19,739	35,426
Cash at bank	1,000	1,000	1,000
Liquid asset buffer	3,867	17,496	5,650
Fixed assets	483	556	621
Other assets	158	158	158
Total assets	**38,270**	**38,948**	**42,855**
Liabilities			
Customer deposits	21,000	23,000	28,000
Bank funding	0	0	0
Trade creditors	2,051	2,051	2,051
Tax liabilities	257	(208)	(421)
Non-current liabilities	84	117	142
Total liabilities	**23,393**	**24,959**	**29,772**
Equity			
Share capital	214	214	214
Share premium	8,692	8,692	8,692
Merger reserves	891	891	891
Retained earnings	4,240	5,081	4,192
Current year retained earnings	841	(889)	(905)
Total equity	**14,878**	**13,989**	**13,084**
Total equity and liabilities	38,270	38,948	42,855

Table 87: Combined stress scenario – Orchard Financials (after management action).

£'000

Combined Income Statement	**Plan Year 1**	**Plan Year 2**	**Plan Year 3**
Interest Receivable	4,887	4,244	5,665
Interest payable	(396)	(858)	(1,600)
Net interest income	**4,491**	**3,387**	**4,065**
Administration expenses	(2,870)	(3,935)	(4,913)
Stresses (idio, conduct, systems	0	(675)	0
Impairment charges	(312)	(890)	(1,231)
Operating profit before tax	**1,308**	**(2,114)**	**(2,080)**
Corporation tax	(257)	402	395
Profit after tax	**1,051**	**(1,712)**	**(1,685)**
Dividends	(210)	0	0
Retained Earnings	**841**	**(1,712)**	**(1,685)**
Balance Sheet	**Plan Year 1**	**Plan Year 2**	**Plan Year 3**
Assets			
Loans and advances	32,762	27,784	42,999
Cash at bank	1,000	1,000	1,000
Liquid asset buffer	3,867	12,933	3,599
Fixed assets	483	556	621
Other assets	158	158	158
Total assets	**38,270**	**42,432**	**48,377**
Liabilities			
Customer deposits	21,000	27,500	35,500
Bank funding	0	0	0
Trade creditors	2,051	2,051	2,051
Tax liabilities	257	(402)	(797)
Non-current liabilities	84	117	142
Total liabilities	**23,393**	**29,266**	**36,896**
Equity			
Share capital	214	214	214
Share premium	8,692	8,692	8,692
Merger reserves	891	891	891
Retained earnings	4,240	5,081	3,369
Current year retained earnings	841	(1,712)	(1,685)
Total equity	**14,878**	**13,166**	**11,481**
Total equity and liabilities	38,270	42,432	48,377

Table 88: Combined stress scenario – Orchard Capital Position (before management action).

£'000

Combined no MA	Plan Year 1	Plan Year 2	Plan Year 3
Pillar 1			
Credit risk on loan assets	1,839	1,136	2,025
Credit risk on bank balances	16	16	16
Fixed assets	5	5	6
Credit risk on HQLA	0	0	0
Total credit risk	**1,860**	**1,157**	**2,046**
Operational risk basic indicator	672	637	641
Pillar 1 capital requirements	**2,532**	**1,795**	**2,687**
Pillar 2A capital requirements			
Operational risk	147	223	263
Business risk	0	0	0
Reputational risk	0	0	0
Credit concentration risk	319	202	350
Interest rate risk in the banking book (IRRBB)	165	105	262
Residual operational risk from risk register	0	0	0
Pillar 2A capital requirements	**631**	**530**	**875**
Total capital requirement (Pillar 1 + Pillar 2A)	**3,163**	**2,325**	**3,562**
Share capital	9,797	9,797	9,797
Audited retained earnings	5,081	4,192	3,287
DTA on operating losses (Deduction)	0	(208)	(421)
Intangible Assets (Deduction)	(421)	(490)	(552)
Total Capital resources	**14,457**	**13,291**	**12,111**
Risk weighted assets (Credit + Ops)	**31,652**	**22,434**	**33,589**
Total Capital requirement % of RWAs	**10%**	**10%**	**11%**
Pillar 2B	**1,050**	**1,102**	**1,158**
TCR + Pillar 2B % of RWAs	**13%**	**15%**	**14%**
CET1 % of RWAs	**47%**	**62%**	**39%**
Regulatory Capital Resources % of RWAs	**46%**	**59%**	**36%**
Surplus / (deficit) regulatory capital	**10,244**	**9,864**	**7,392**

Table 89: Combined stress scenario – Orchard Capital Position (after management action).

£'000

Combined	Plan Year 1	Plan Year 2	Plan Year 3
Pillar 1			
Credit risk on loan assets	1,839	1,594	2,459
Credit risk on bank balances	16	16	16
Fixed assets	5	5	6
Credit risk on HQLA	0	0	0
Total credit risk	**1,860**	**1,616**	**2,481**
Operational risk basic indicator	672	630	597
Pillar 1 capital requirements	**2,532**	**2,246**	**3,078**
Pillar 2A capital requirements			
Operational risk	147	230	306
Business risk	0	0	0
Reputational risk	0	0	0
Credit concentration risk	319	278	422
Interest rate risk in the banking book (IRRBB)	166	148	326
Residual operational risk from risk register	0	0	0
Pillar 2A capital requirements	**632**	**656**	**1,054**
Total capital requirement (Pillar 1 + Pillar 2A)	**3,164**	**2,902**	**4,132**
Share capital	9,797	9,797	9,797
Audited retained earnings	5,081	3,369	1,684
DTA on operating losses (Deduction)	0	(402)	(797)
Intangible Assets (Deduction)	(421)	(490)	(552)
Total Capital resources	**14,457**	**12,274**	**10,132**
Risk weighted assets (Credit + Ops)	**31,652**	**28,070**	**38,473**
Total Capital requirement % of RWAs	**10%**	**10%**	**11%**
Pillar 2B	**1,050**	**1,102**	**1,158**
TCR + Pillar 2B % of RWAs	**13%**	**14%**	**14%**
CET1 % of RWAs	**47%**	**47%**	**30%**
Regulatory Capital Resources % of RWAs	**46%**	**44%**	**26%**
Surplus / (deficit) regulatory capital	**10,243**	**8,270**	**4,843**

- Although there is still surplus capital of £4.8m, this is below the risk appetite target of £5.5m and hence, management action is required to rectify the position.
- Management will also consider moderating the future level of lending. Continuation on the path of the base operating plan in year 4 would result in a funding shortfall that would require drawdown of the bank facilities.

Management Action in Combined Stress Scenario

As the capital position breaches the Board approved risk appetite, management action will be initiated much earlier than the end of year 3 as the management monitoring process would identify the future trajectory of the capital position in years 3. The following actions will be taken to manage the capital position before it breaches the Risk Appetite:

- Reduce lending to lower margin customers;
- Decrease deposit rates at the cost of lower deposits. At the same time, make a concerted effort through pro-active customer contact to retain maturing deposits;
- Non-essential operating expenses would be stopped such as marketing, given the objective of not attracting new business. Expenses and staff recruitment would be deferred where possible.

11.8 Reverse Stress

The Reverse Stress test is viewed separately since it is specifically designed to model circumstances that render the business model unviable.

The reverse stress is driven by a massive market shock that impacts the customers' loan repayment ability severely. At the same time, some brokers go into insolvency and hence, the guarantees no longer safeguard the business from losses. The insurance rebates are reduced significantly and only partially contribute towards impairment reduction.

The escalating losses result in depositors losing confidence in the bank, resulting in only 10% of deposits in Year 2 and no new deposits thereafter. In order to manage retention of existing deposits, interest rates are increased. This action still does not close the funding gap and hence, the lending plan is revised downwards. The remaining funding gap is closed by bank facilities. Given the overall deteriorating position of the business, its inability to assign assets by way of security and inability to pay in priority to depositors, the bank facilities are offered at much higher rates.

Table 90: Reverse stress – Impact on key business drivers.

Reverse	Plan Year 1	Plan Year 2	Plan Year 3
Impact on business drivers			
New lending	0%	(40%)	(40%)
Loan Rate	0.0%	(7.0%)	(7.0%)
Net new Deposits volumes	0%	(90%)	(100%)
Deposit rate	0.0%	5.0%	5.0%
Impairment charge % of asset	0.0%	11.0%	9.0%
Expenses increase from prior period	0%	10%	15%
Bank funding margin increase vs plan	0.0%	7.0%	7.0%

Table 91: Reverse stress – Key business drivers.

Reverse	Actual 2018	Plan Year 1	Plan Year 2	Plan Year 3
New Lending – £000	68,730	86,000	64,680	83,640
Lending growth %		25%	(25%)	29%
Lending stock – £000	31,084	32,762	21,522	28,345
Lending interest rate (wt. average)		14.53%	7.46%	7.40%
Net New Deposit – £000		21,000	1,000	-
Deposit stock – £000		21,000	22,000	22,000
Deposit interest rate (wt. average)		2.15%	7.32%	7.43%
Bank funding – £000		-	-	1,646
Funding interest rate		4.30%	11.47%	11.58%
Operating expenses £000	2,746	2,870	3,534	4,432
Operating expenses % uplift YoY		5%	23%	25%
Impairment charge %		1.0%	12.0%	10.0%

Table 92: Reverse stress – Orchard Financials.

			£'000
Reverse Income Statement	**Plan Year 1**	**Plan Year 2**	**Plan Year 3**
Interest Receivable	4,887	3,048	2,518
Interest payable	(396)	(847)	(1,466)
Net interest income	**4,491**	**2,201**	**1,052**
Administration expenses	(2,870)	(3,534)	(4,432)
Stresses (idio, conduct, systems	0	(675)	0
Impairment charges	(312)	(3,188)	(3,001)
Operating profit before tax	**1,308**	**(5,197)**	**(6,382)**
Corporation tax	(257)	987	1,212
Profit after tax	**1,051**	**(4,209)**	**(5,169)**
Dividends	(210)	0	0
Retained Earnings	**841**	**(4,209)**	**(5,169)**
Balance Sheet	**Plan Year 1**	**Plan Year 2**	**Plan Year 3**
Assets			
Loans and advances	32,762	21,522	28,345
Cash at bank	1,000	1,000	0
Liquid asset buffer	3,867	10,600	0
Fixed assets	483	556	621
Other assets	158	158	158
Total assets	**38,270**	**33,836**	**29,124**

Table 92 (continued)

Reverse Income Statement	Plan Year 1	Plan Year 2	Plan Year 3
Liabilities			
Customer deposits	21,000	22,000	22,000
Bank funding	0	0	1,646
Trade creditors	2,051	2,051	2,051
Tax liabilities	257	(987)	(2,200)
Non-current liabilities	84	104	127
Total liabilities	**23,393**	**23,168**	**23,625**
Equity			
Share capital	214	214	214
Share premium	8,692	8,692	8,692
Merger reserves	891	891	891
Retained earnings	4,240	5,081	871
Current year retained earnings	841	(4,209)	(5,169)
Total equity	**14,878**	**10,668**	**5,499**
Total equity and liabilities	38,270	33,836	29,124

Table 93: Reverse stress – Orchard Capital Position.

£'000

Reverse	Plan Year 1	Plan Year 2	Plan Year 3
Pillar 1			
Credit risk on loan assets	1,839	1,374	1,743
Credit risk on bank balances	16	16	16
Fixed assets	5	5	6
Credit risk on HQLA	0	0	0
Total credit risk	**1,860**	**1,395**	**1,764**
Operational risk basic indicator	672	571	387
Pillar 1 capital requirements	**2,532**	**1,966**	**2,152**
Pillar 2A capital requirements			
Operational risk	147	290	516
Business risk	0	0	0
Reputational risk	0	0	0
Credit concentration risk	319	242	303
Interest rate risk in the banking book (IRRBB)	167	83	212
Residual operational risk from risk register	0	0	0
Pillar 2A capital requirements	**633**	**614**	**1,031**
Total capital requirement (Pillar 1 + Pillar 2A)	**3,166**	**2,580**	**3,183**

Table 93: (continued)

Reverse	**Plan Year 1**	**Plan Year 2**	**Plan Year 3**
Share capital	9,797	9,797	9,797
Audited retained earnings	5,081	871	(4,298)
DTA on operating losses (Deduction)	0	(987)	(2,200)
Intangible Assets (Deduction)	(421)	(490)	(552)
Total Capital resources	**14,457**	**9,191**	**2,748**
Risk weighted assets (Credit + Ops)	**31,652**	**24,574**	**26,895**
Total Capital requirement % of RWAs	**10%**	**10%**	**12%**
Pillar 2B	**1,050**	**1,102**	**1,158**
TCR + Pillar 2B % of RWAs	**13%**	**15%**	**16%**
CET1 % of RWAs	**47%**	**43%**	**20%**
Regulatory Capital Resources % of RWAs	**46%**	**37%**	**10%**
Surplus / (deficit) regulatory capital	**10,241**	**5,509**	**(1,593)**

- The capital buffer has been depleted to zero.
- The capital resource (Regulatory CET1) is short by £0.4m relative to the TCR of £3.2m.
- Impairment charge increases as broker guarantees are not effective due to broker insolvency. The FSCS protection on insurance companies' insolvency is limited.
- No liquidity available and very expensive bank borrowing is initiated in year 3.

Management Action in Reverse Stress Test scenario.

The Reverse Stress Test scenario has been designed to create several unprecedented and very severe stresses to the Orchard business, to determine the level of stress that would effectively make the business insolvent.

Potential management actions that can be taken are as follows:

- Initiate wind-down as this still ensures that depositors are repaid.
- Shut down of all non-essential activities to manage down the costs and preserve as much of the capital as possible.
- Reduce new lending to zero in year 3.
- Although unlikely to materialise, assess the possibility of further capital injections from investors.

Appendix 1 Risk Register

Nature of Risk	Enterprise Risk	Level 2	Risk (Level 2)	Risk Summary	Inherent			Controls	Residual		
					Likelihood	Impact	Score		Likelihood	Impact	Score
Conduct	**Con1. Conduct**	Con1.1	Product Design	Failure to design products that meet our customer's needs and expectations. Products or services that do not meet customer needs or are targeted inappropriately.	3	5	£100,000	New Product policy. CEO on the New Product committee and will need to recommend new products for Board approval. External legal counsel drafted all documentation. CR review on all customer facing documents. T&Cs made clear to all customers in advance. Products meet regulatory requirements. 3rd party introducers regularly reviewed. Compliance and legal part of new product process. Detailed complaints process following best practice. CR requirements are incorporated into strategy and business planning process. CEO with CR responsibility. Governance committees receive regular TCF MI. The Board and ExCo receive and review regular briefings on CR requirements.	2	3	£18,960

	Con1.2	Distribution	The Bank's distribution processes result in the customer selecting a product or service which is inappropriate for their needs or circumstances.	3	5	£100,000	Appropriate conduct detailed in the Compliance Manual and Staff Handbook. High levels of initial and ongoing recorded training provided to staff. Legal and compliance sign off on all marketing material. Due diligence conducted on all intermediaries and reviewed on annual basis. Staff do not receive commissions. Internal Audit to monitor conduct. Complaints MI monitored.	3	4	£12,000
	Con1.3	Governance, Culture	The Bank's governance processes fail to identify, manage, or reduce conduct risk. Also includes conduct risks stemming from an inappropriate strategy or culture which places insufficient emphasis on good customer outcomes.	4	5	£500,000	Internal Audit will be conducted by an independent accountancy practice. The Board will independently review their performance.	2	4	£2,250
	Con1.4	Governance Structures	Failure to practice good governance due to a weakness in the design or execution of the governance structures.	4	4	£60,000	Clear governance and management structure. CR metrics reviewed and signed off monthly and subject to committee review. Committee TOR include requirement to oversee and challenge CR requirements.	4	2	£2,400

(continued)

Nature of Risk	Enterprise Risk	Level 2	Risk (Level 2)	Risk Summary	Inherent			Controls	Residual		
					Likelihood	Impact	Score		Likelihood	Impact	Score
	Con2. Legal	Con2.1	Legal	Failure to comply with any legislative requirements which apply to the Bank such as breaches of OFT guidelines, Consumer Credit requirements and Environmental and Corporate Responsibility requirements. Breaches of the Data Protection Act should be captured under "Ops 4.1 Information Management".	3	5	£100,000	CRO and CFO to attend Regulator briefings and updates and obviated by forming a pro-active relationship with the Regulator particularly during the initial set up period. Business already has experience as an FCA regulated entity. External legal counsel drafted all documentation. CR review on all customer facing documents. T&Cs made clear to all customers in advance. Products meet regulatory requirements. 3rd party introducers regularly reviewed. Compliance and legal part of new product process. Detailed complaints process following best practice. The Bank's clearing bank is Barclays which is a Global-SIFI whose payment facilities should not be disrupted. The Bank will hold separate accounts with other banks to be opened in Mobilisation.	2	3	£2,340

	Con3. Regulatory Compli-ance	Con3.1	Regulatory – Prudential	Failure to comply with EU or UK prudential, securities or markets (PSM) regulation issued or supervised by the PRA or FCA; or European authorities such as the EC, EBA and ESMA.	4	5	£500,000	Detailed controls and monitoring set out in ICAAP/ILAAP. The Liquidity Contingency Plan (approved by the Board) will set out the steps to be followed to manage Orchard's liquidity. The Finance team will provide on a regular basis, a report showing the predicted cashflow.	3	3	£2,400
		Con3.2	Regulatory – Conduct	Failure to comply with any Financial Conduct Authority (FCA) regulatory requirement applicable to the Bank or its subsidiaries.	4	5	£500,000	The compliance manual clearly states the high standards of integrity and customer service that Orchard expects. This is augmented by initial and regular recorded training. The manual also lists the record keeping requirements and the CEO has to jointly sign off any destruction. The permissions are also set out on the compliance manual. New products/ activities have to be approved by the Board . All of the above will be monitored by Internal Audit.	3	5	£100,000
Credit	**Crd1. Credit**	Crd1.1	Wholesale Credit Risk	Failure to limit credit exposures associated with counterparty failure.	Calculated in line with CRD requirements		£-	Orchard will not hold any trading book.	Calculated in line with CRD requirements		£-

(continued)

Nature of Risk	Enterprise Risk	Level 2	Risk (Level 2)	Risk Summary	Inherent			Controls	Residual		
					Likelihood	Impact	Score		Likelihood	Impact	Score
		Crd1.2	Credit Losses	Failure to control retail credit activities such that losses are outside of Risk Appetite.	Calculated in line with CRD requirements		£-	Risk appetite for individual Bank credit risk to be set by Board to be mitigated by depositing only with highly rated banks. Large sums will be split across several entities	Calculated in line with CRD requirements		£-
Financial	**Fin1. Financial Reporting & Tax**	Fin1.1	Financial Accounting & Tax Errors	Failures in financial management. Failure to calculate, report or disclose the Bank's tax liabilities.	3	5	£100,000	The internal financial controls will be audited and approved by the Audit committee and Orchard's auditors to ensure they are robust.	2	4	£2,250
		Fin1.2	Internal / External Financial Reporting	Failures to produce timely and accurate and complete reporting both internally and externally.	3	5	£100,000	Comprehensive training programme for CFO with additional training for Head of Finance to provide back up support. Head of Finance will assist with regulatory reporting.	2	4	£2,250
	Fin2. Model	Fin2.1	Business Models	The risk that Models are applied to activities for which they are inappropriate or are implemented or operated incorrectly.	3	5	£100,000	Use of 4 eyes checks.	2	3	£450

		Fin2.2	Capital Adequacy Risk	Failure to hold an adequate capital position to meet our regulatory requirements.	3	5	£100,000	Experienced Board, including NEDs selected for their wide ranging experience in banking, regulatory, financial and business matters.	1	5	£5,000
		Fin2.3	Liquidity and Funding	Failure to maintain sufficient liquidity and a stable funding profile of appropriate duration to meet adverse outflows.	3	5	£100,000	Detailed controls and monitoring set out in ICAAP/ILAAP. The Liquidity Contingency Plan (approved by the Board) will set out the steps to be followed to manage Orchard's liquidity. The Finance team will provide on a regular basis, a report showing the predicted cashflow.	2	5	£18,750
		Fin2.4	Interest Rate Risk on the Banking Book	Failure to manage the potential impact on both Net Interest Income and Economic Value.	4	3	£12,000	Orchard will not hold any trading book.	1	1	£2,400
Opera-tional	**Ops1. People**	Ops1.1	Employment diversity, discrimination and harassment	The Bank's governance processes fail to identify, manage, or reduce discrimination and harassment or fail to support promote employment diversity.	3	3	£2,400	Board is aware of the importance of the HR function. Outside experts will be used where circumstances dictate. HR Advisory firm appointed who supply detailed HR Manual and guidance notes with prepaid support package. Recruitment policy and procedure. Job descriptions/person specifications. Appraisal process. Training and development process.	3	3	£2,400

(continued)

Nature of Risk	Enterprise Risk	Level 2	Risk (Level 2)	Risk Summary	Inherent			Controls	Residual		
					Likelihood	Impact	Score		Likelihood	Impact	Score
		Ops1.2	Business Disruption – Employee Related	Risk of business disruption due to workforce unavailability.	4	5	£500,000	Board and senior management responsible for relaying culture of business to staff on a regular basis. Staff bonus structure, discretionary and not based on sales generated. Strong culture developed through many years of conducting business of putting service to customer as key priority of the business. Orchard will have succession plans in place for key personnel, and all staff will have notice periods. i) Formal process for recruiting NEDs. Robust Board appraisal process. CPD programme covering key regulatory requirements. Embedded ethics statement. Formal strategies, Business Plan, ICAAP & ILAAP processes. Standard review schedule in place for Risk framework appetite and policies. ii) The succession plan is reviewed annually alongside appraisal of NED's and includes a discussion regarding their planned departure. The Board can agree with individuals an extension to the stated maximum term to manage planned departures.	3	4	£228,750

The Bank and the current Directors are occasionally approached by or meet potential independent directors whose details are retained for future use. The Bank could use specialist recruitment professionals to identify candidates with the appropriate skillset.

i) Internal cross-training would provide short term cover. Salaries are reviewed annually against the market.

Key Man life insurance on key managers holding SMF responsibilities. Interim skill available for advice from the Board.

Policy to ensure staff travel independently.

Succession plan is in place within the Business Continuity Plan for the Executive Committee.

ii) Delegated authorities formally documented. Procedure manuals. Regular appraisals for all staff, including review of training requirements.

Intend to use experienced staff with initial and ongoing recorded training a priority.

The Compliance Manual will set out all staff's obligations and they be required to sign to say that they understand their responsibilities. Comprehensive training programme for CFO with additional training for Head of Finance to provide back up support. Head of Finance will assist with regulatory reporting.

(continued)

Nature of Risk	Enterprise Risk	Level 2	Risk (Level 2)	Risk Summary	Inherent			Controls	Residual		
					Likelihood	Impact	Score		Likelihood	Impact	Score
	Ops2. Business Continuity	Ops2.1	IT Architecture Design and Development	Inappropriate architecture (e.g., systems integration through merger); strategic risk (platform / supplier / outsourcing); Inadequate systems capacity planning; obsolescence of hardware or software; lack of alignment with business strategy; business requirement inconsistent with strategic IT architecture.	5	5	£1,250,000	Systems are covered by support contract which enables quick identification of any problems. Remote support access enables prompt resolution of incidents. Internet connection provides guaranteed access.	5	3	£30,000

	Ops2.2	IT Availability Network / Hardware / Software	Failures in the delivery of IT services; change control failures; failures in incident management; IT system failure and business disruption for all aspects of IT infrastructure and operating systems (including network, hardware and software failure).	5	5	£1,250,000	Core systems and data are backed up overnight to a remote location. Firewalls in place to prevent hacking.	5	3	£30,000
	Ops2.3	Change	Risks associated with individual projects, programmes of change and the portfolio of change (i.e., all projects and programmes).	4	4	£60,000	Orchard experience in designing, developing, testing and implementing the IT required for its business requirements.	2	4	£ 2,250
Ops3. Data manage-ment	Ops3.1	Failure to maintain the accuracy of data	The risk that reports are delivered based on data which are inappropriate or inaccurate.	3	5	£100,000	Focus is on employing experienced staff with a heavy emphasis on initial and regular training	3	4	£12,000

(continued)

Nature of Risk	Enterprise Risk	Level 2	Risk (Level 2)	Risk Summary	Inherent			Controls	Residual		
					Likelihood	Impact	Score		Likelihood	Impact	Score
	Ops4. Infor-mation Security (including Cyber)	Ops4.1	Information Management	Failure to manage the confidentiality, integrity and availability of information or personal data in use within the Bank whether physical of electronic in format. This includes the failure to manage the storage and destruction of data and information.	4	5	£500,000	Simple and stable business model which does not push regulatory boundaries. Small, stable and experienced staff team. Distance Learning training package completed by all staff.Implementation Plan to comply with GDPR including cross-business representation.	5	4	£ 150,000
		Ops4.2	System Security	Failure to manage the confidentiality, integrity and availability of the systems that provide access to data and information. This includes the failure to manage against the threat of Internal and External attack against the Bank.	4	5	£500,000	System is monitored on a regular basis. Detailed incident reporting process. Governance oversight and monitoring.	3	4	£12,000

Ops4. Infor-mation Security (including Cyber)	Ops4.3	End User Computing and Application Failure	Failure to manage the confidentiality, integrity and availability of the data and information on the Bank's systems deployed to third parties, e.g., intermediaries.	3	4	£12,000	All hard disks and network servers are encrypted. Access to systems is via a limited number of password-protected accounts.	2	2	£ 90
Ops5. Physical Security and Safety	Ops5.1	Business Disruption – Workplace Related	Risk of disruption to the Bank due to issues affecting access to the Bank's premises or the premises impacting the staff within its building(s).	4	5	£500,000	Fire and Safety Audits reviewed annually. Health & Safety Policy, reviewed annually. Managed by staff member on an ongoing basis. Annual staff training. Disaster recovery plan is in place and will be tested on a regular basis. Staff training.	2	5	£23,750
	Ops5.2	Malicious Damage / Physical Security	Malicious damage to the Bank's property or reputation. This includes malicious comment or publicity against the Bank	3	4	£12,000	Limited sign posting of the Bank's location with very few expected customer visits. The Bank has a Business Continuity Plan with a contract for emergency off-site location in place which can be invoked if necessary. The Emerging Risk register would highlight and then monitor any potential threats to the business with appropriate actions taken to mitigate the risk. Comprehensive insurance in place. Business Continuity contract in place for emergency cover.	3	4	£ 4,650

(continued)

Nature of Risk	Enterprise Risk	Level 2	Risk (Level 2)	Risk Summary	Inherent			Controls	Residual		
					Likelihood	Impact	Score		Likelihood	Impact	Score
	Ops6. Third Party	Ops6.1	Procurement	The failure of third party supplier (external) to provide the service required by the Bank (either through their own organisational failure or substandard performance).	4	4	£60,000	Systems are covered by support contract which enables quick identification of any problems. Remote support access enables prompt resolution of incidents. Internet connection provides guaranteed access.	2	2	£90
		Ops6.2	Supplier Management / Delivery	Failure to identify, select and set up appropriate contracts and agreements with suppliers of goods and services to the Bank.	4	4	£60,000	All introducers credit approved. All introducers are checked for regulatory status if applicable. All introducers are subject to annual review and are subject to audit visit on an annual basis. Board vets and approves all significant outsourcing agreements in accordance with Outsourcing Policy. Major software providers are all market standard, with regular updates. Regularly monitored Service Level Agreements for IT. Escrow for banking software and regulatory reporting software. Contracts include Business Continuity by providers.	3	4	£14,400

Ops7. Financial Crime	Ops7.1	Financial Crime	Non-compliance with legal and regulatory obligations (including Money Laundering Regulations, Proceeds of Crime Act and Terrorism Act) leading to failure to prevent and detect money laundering and other financial crimes not covered under bribery, competition or fraud.	3	5	£100,000	The Board will review AML procedures adopted and ongoing account monitoring. New customers will be vetted including identity checks and credit checks, prior to approval by the company. Financial Crime Policy sets out customer due diligence requirements both at take on and annual review. Mirrored in the Compliance Manual. Internal audit to monitor.	2	5	£18,750
	Ops7.2	Bribery & Corruption	The Bank fails to prevent bribery and corruption.	3	5	£100,000	Anti-bribery policy approved by the Board, read and accepted by all staff in Compliance Manual. Clear guidelines given on accepting gifts and hospitality and disclosure requirements. Ad-hoc monitoring by Internal Audit. Suppliers reviewed annually by the Board	2	4	£2,250

(continued)

Nature of Risk	Enterprise Risk	Level 2	Risk (Level 2)	Risk Summary	Inherent			Controls	Residual		
					Likelihood	Impact	Score		Likelihood	Impact	Score
	Ops8. Fraud	Ops8.1	Internal Fraud	Abuse of position committed by an employee(s) through the deliberate misuse or misapplication of the Bank's resources or assets, usually for personal gain.	3	4	£12,000	Controls over account processes set out in Standard Operating Process documents. Closed loop, 4 eye checks. The conflict of interest policy is set out in our compliance manual so that staff are clearly aware of their responsibilities. Internal audit will monitor. Controls will be set through treasury mandates, management controls, limit monitoring Account terms and conditions will contain clauses to cover misdirected payments. Use of 4 eyes for payments, PA dealing code; compliance framework; training; culture	2	3	£14,898
		Ops8.2	External Fraud	Fraud perpetrated against the Bank and/or customers by an external party, usually for personal gain. Includes third party fraud (committed by a person with no obvious connection to the Bank) and first party fraud (committed by a customer), including benefit fraud.	4	4	£60,000	Payment procedures policy is set by the Board to ensure no one party can set up and approve a payment. Payments require two people to authorise it against appropriate documentation.	3	4	£12,000

Ops9. Trans-action Processing	Ops9.1	Post Sales Product Delivery and Operation	Customers are not treated fairly after the point of sale, service or transaction. Also covers failures in complaints handling process.	3	4	£12,000	Credit Policy is set by the Board and reviewed at least annually. More often if adverse reports are being received from credit committee. In particular bad debt reporting is reviewed by the Board quarterly to enable changes to credit policy as necessary. Full transparency and communication of Ts and Cs and fees and charges to customers. Review, sign off and committee oversight of CR MI on a monthly basis.	3	4	£14,250
	Ops9.2	Financial Transaction Payment Processing	Mistakes, errors and/or process failures related to the management and execution of all customer financial transactions. This includes “Manual data entry errors”.	4	5	£500,000	Reconciliations, confirmations, transaction checks carried out by trained staff. Resourcing with expertise to manage DD exceptions. Head of Credit will be copied with all new approvals. Internal Audit will sample new and existing credits.	3	4	£14,250
	Ops9.3	Customer on-boarding and account management	Failures in non-payment administration processes. This includes delivery of the administration process and customer relationship management.	4	4	£60,000	Appropriate conduct detailed in the Compliance Manual and Staff Handbook. High levels of initial and ongoing training provided, experienced staff to be recruited. Internal Audit to monitor. Approval limits set by Board monitored by internal audit-higher value credits to be approved by the Credit Committee Internal audit will sample and review new approvals and sample the lending book. Historic losses de minimis.	3	3	£2,650

(continued)

Nature of Risk	Enterprise Risk	Level 2	Risk (Level 2)	Risk Summary	Inherent			Controls	Residual		
					Likelihood	Impact	Score		Likelihood	Impact	Score
		Ops9.4	Lending Quality	Failure to to lend in line with Policy objectives and to maintain sufficient quality to withstand macro-economic stresses.	3	4	£12,000	Loan process set by Board in Credit Policy and administered through the Credit Committee. This includes approval, facility documentation and security processes. Internal Audit will monitor. Onboarding process in place for each new client. Senior management sign off required for new accounts. 1. Lending is throughout the UK 2. Geographic and sector risk is not considered a material risk for insurance premium finance and professions fee finance. 3. Board to set limit of exposure to any one client/group. 4. Managed by robust credit approval procedures with credit policy set and monitored by the Board	2	4	£16,500
Strategic	**Stg1. Strategic Risk**	Stg1.1	Concentration	Lack of sufficient product diversity. Business concentrated via a small number of intermediaries.	2	5	£18,750	Detailed controls and monitoring set out in ICAAP/ILAAP. The Liquidity Contingency Plan (approved by the Board) will set out the steps to be followed to manage Orchard's liquidity. The Finance team will provide on a regular basis, a report showing the predicted cashflow	2	4	£2,250

Stg1.2	Changes in Business Conditions	Failure to plan for changes in business conditions	3	4	£12,000	The CRO and CEO will keep abreast of potential Regulatory changes and the impact it may have on the business and will inform the Board, in order that appropriate timely changes can be made to the business plan. Experienced Board, including NEDs selected for their wide ranging experience in banking, regulatory, financial and business matters. ALCO will review competitiveness of interest rates. Where necessary Board will review new products and/or amend interest rate policy. ALCO/Credit Committee will manage new loans authorisations accordingly. Long trading history indicates steady non-volatile demand for the company's products ALCO/Credit Committee will manage new loan deals to match deposits. Deposit rates will be set in declining tranches to reduce demand once target levels are reached The Board will review detailed cost forecasts prior to incurring expenditure materially outside of budgets.	2	4	£27,750
Stg1.3	Changes in Market Competition	Failure to plan for new competition	4	5	£500,000	Regular competitor analysis will be undertaken and the Board will review its impact on the business and make changes to strategy as appropriate	4	3	£12,000
				Total inherent risk:	**£8,565,150**			**Total residual risk:**	**£819,378**

Appendix 2

FSA017
Interest rate gap report

		A	B	C	D	E	F	G	H	J	K	L	M	N	P	Q
1	Gap sensitivity to parallel shift of:	2														
	Assets	Totals	Overnight to 3 months	3-6 months	6-12 months	1-2 years	2-3 years	3-4 years	4-5 years	5-6 years	6-7 years	7-8 years	8-9 years	9-10 years	Over 10 years	No specific re-pricing
2	Monetary balance sheet assets (non-optional) as per contractual re-pricing date	£ 1,84,65,798	£ 64,85,147	£ 80,14,737	£ 39,65,914	£ -	£ -	£ -	£ -	£ -	£ -	£ -	£ -	£ -		
3	> Adjustments for actual expected re-pricing date	£ -	£ -	£ -	£ -	£ -	£ -	£ -	£ -	£ -	£ -	£ -	£ -	£ -	£ -	£ -
4	> Pipeline products	£ -	£ -	£ -	£ -	£ -	£ -	£ -	£ -	£ -	£ -	£ -	£ -	£ -	£ -	£ -
5	Monetary balance sheet assets with option features and with re-pricing maturity determined as per note 1 below	£ -	£ -	£ -	£ -	£ -	£ -	£ -	£ -	£ -	£ -	£ -	£ -	£ -	£ -	£ -
6	> Adjustments for actual expected re-pricing date	£ -	£ -	£ -	£ -	£ -	£ -	£ -	£ -	£ -	£ -	£ -	£ -	£ -	£ -	£ -
7	> Pipeline products	£ -	£ -	£ -	£ -	£ -	£ -	£ -	£ -	£ -	£ -	£ -	£ -	£ -	£ -	£ -
8	Net Trading Book asset	£ -	£ -													
9	Non-monetary and other assets	£ 8,68,668	£ -	£ -	£ -	£ -	£ -	£ -	£ -	£ -	£ -	£ -	£ -	£ -	£ -	£ 8,68,668
10	Asset sub-total	£ 1,93,34,465	£ 64,85,147	£ 80,14,737	£ 39,65,914	£ -	£ -	£ -	£ -	£ -	£ -	£ -	£ -	£ -	£ -	£ -
11	> Linear derivative contracts	£ -	£ -	£ -	£ -	£ -	£ -	£ -	£ -	£ -	£ -	£ -	£ -	£ -	£ -	£ -
12	> Non-linear derivative contracts	£ -	£ -	£ -	£ -	£ -	£ -	£ -	£ -	£ -	£ -	£ -	£ -	£ -	£ -	£ -
13	Asset totals	£ 1,93,34,465	£ 64,85,147	£ 80,14,737	£ 39,65,914	£ -	£ -	£ -	£ -	£ -	£ -	£ -	£ -	£ -	£ -	£ 8,68,668
	Liabilities															
14	Monetary balance sheet liabilities (non-optional) as per contractual re-pricing date	£ 21,50,000	£ 2,40,000	£ 3,15,000	£ 6,30,000	£ 8,95,000	£ 70,000	£ -	£ -	£ -	£ -	£ -	£ -	£ -	£ -	£ -
15	> Adjustments for actual expected re-pricing date	£ -	£ -	£ -	£ -	£ -	£ -	£ -	£ -	£ -	£ -	£ -	£ -	£ -	£ -	£ -
16	> Pipeline products	£ -	£ -	£ -	£ -	£ -	£ -	£ -	£ -	£ -	£ -	£ -	£ -	£ -	£ -	£ -
17	Monetary balance sheet liabilities with option features and with re-pricing maturity determined as per	£ -	£ -	£ -	£ -	£ -	£ -	£ -	£ -	£ -	£ -	£ -	£ -	£ -	£ -	£ -
18	> Adjustments for actual expected re-pricing date	£ -	£ -	£ -	£ -	£ -	£ -	£ -	£ -	£ -	£ -	£ -	£ -	£ -	£ -	£ -
19	> Pipeline products	£ -	£ -	£ -	£ -	£ -	£ -	£ -	£ -	£ -	£ -	£ -	£ -	£ -	£ -	£ -
20	Net Trading Book Liability	£ -	£ -													
21	Non Monetary and other Liabilities	£ 24,74,485	£ -	£ -	£ -	£ -	£ -	£ -	£ -	£ -	£ -	£ -	£ -	£ -	£ -	£ 24,74,485
22	Capital and Reserves	£ 1,35,83,263	£ -	£ -	£ -	£ -	£ -	£ -	£ -	£ -	£ -	£ -	£ -	£ -	£ -	£ 1,35,83,263
23	> Adjustments for capital investement term assumptions	£ -	£ -	£ -	£ -	£ -	£ -	£ -	£ -	£ -	£ -	£ -	£ -	£ -	£ -	£ -
24	Liability sub-total	£ 1,82,07,749	£ 2,40,000	£ 3,15,000	£ 6,30,000	£ 8,95,000	£ 70,000	£ -	£ -	£ -	£ -	£ -	£ -	£ -	£ -	£ 1,60,57,749
25	> Linear derivative contracts	£ -	£ -	£ -	£ -	£ -	£ -	£ -	£ -	£ -	£ -	£ -	£ -	£ -	£ -	£ -
26	> Non-linear derivative contracts	£ -	£ -	£ -	£ -	£ -	£ -	£ -	£ -	£ -	£ -	£ -	£ -	£ -	£ -	£ -
27	Liability totals	£ 1,82,07,749	£ 2,40,000	£ 3,15,000	£ 6,30,000	£ 8,95,000	£ 70,000	£ -	£ -	£ -	£ -	£ -	£ -	£ -	£ -	£ 1,60,57,749
	Gap sensitivity															
28	Net Gap	£ 11,26,717	£ 62,45,147	£ 76,99,737	£ 33,35,914	-£ 8,95,000	-£ 70,000	£ -	£ -	£ -	£ -	£ -	£ -	£ -	£ -	-£ 1,51,89,081
29	*Gap limits (optional)*															
30	Cumulative gap		£ 62,45,147	£ 1,39,44,884	£ 1,72,80,798	£ 1,63,85,798	£ 1,63,15,798	£ 1,63,15,798	£ 1,63,15,798	£ 1,63,15,798	£ 1,63,15,798	£ 1,63,15,798	£ 1,63,15,798	£ 1,63,15,798	£ 1,63,15,798	
31	Reverse cumulative gap		£ 1,63,15,798	£ 1,00,70,651	£ 23,70,914	-£ 9,65,000	-£ 70,000	£ -	£ -	£ -	£ -	£ -	£ -	£ -	£ -	
32	*Cumulative gap limits (optional)*		£ -	£ -	£ -	£ -	£ -	£ -	£ -	£ -	£ -	£ -	£ -	£ -	£ -	
33	*Reverse cumulative gap limits (optional)*		£ -	£ -	£ -	£ -	£ -	£ -	£ -	£ -	£ -	£ -	£ -	£ -	£ -	
34	Period to reprice (mid-point, in years)		0.125	0.375	0.750	1.500	2.500	3.500	4.500	5.500	6.500	7.500	8.500	9.500	12.500	
43	Discount rate/rates (or forward yield curve)		2.75	2.75	2.75	2.75	2.75	2.75	2.75	2.75	2.75	2.75	2.75	2.75	2.75	
44	Discount factors for central rate		0.99661	0.98988	0.97986	0.96012	0.93443	0.90942	0.88508	0.86139	0.83834	0.81590	0.79406	0.77281	0.71241	
45	Discount factors for + shift		0.99422	0.98275	0.96579	0.93276	0.89046	0.85008	0.81153	0.77473	0.73960	0.70607	0.67405	0.64348	0.55985	
46	Discount factors for - shift		0.99907	0.99720	0.99441	0.98885	0.98149	0.97419	0.96693	0.95974	0.95259	0.94550	0.93846	0.93148	0.91083	
47	PV of net gap at central rate		£ 62,24,005	£ 76,21,803	£ 32,68,725	-£ 8,59,311	-£ 65,410	£ -	£ -	£ -	£ -	£ -	£ -	£ -	£ -	
48	PV of net gap with + shift		£ 62,09,025	£ 75,66,903	£ 32,21,805	-£ 8,34,818	-£ 62,332	£ -	£ -	£ -	£ -	£ -	£ -	£ -	£ -	
49	PV of net gap with - shift		£ 62,39,317	£ 76,78,193	£ 33,17,272	-£ 8,85,025	-£ 68,705	£ -	£ -	£ -	£ -	£ -	£ -	£ -	£ -	
38	NPV Sensitivity to + shift (as derived from above data)	-£ 89,230	- 14,980.01	-£ 54,900	-£ 46,920	£ 24,492	£ 3,078	£ -	£ -	£ -	£ -	£ -	£ -	£ -	£ -	
39	NPV Sensitivity to - shift (as derived from above data)	£ 91,239	£ 15,312	£ 56,390	£ 48,546	-£ 25,714	-£ 3,295	£ -	£ -	£ -	£ -	£ -	£ -	£ -	£ -	
40	Alternative estimate of NPV sensitivity to + shift															
41	Alternative estimate of NPV sensitivity to - shift															
42	*NPV Sensitivity limits (optional)*	£ 78		£ 1	£ 2	£ 3	£ 4	£ 5	£ 6	£ 7	£ 8	£ 9	£ 10	£ 11	£ 12	

Note An option that is IN the money or would be in the event of the parallel shift calculated in 45 or 46 or more should be assigned a maturity (i.e re-pricing) date equal to the expiry date of the contract This affects data elements 12 and 26 (options).

1 An option that is OUT of the money and
An option within these two bounds should have its re-pricing date determined by simple straight line interpolation - e.g. an option exactly at the money, would be assigned a notional maturity date halfway between overnight and the contract expiry date

4 Internal Liquidity Adequacy Assessment Plan (the 'ILAAP')

4.1 Outline of the ILAAP

The third core document in a bank application is the Internal Liquidity Adequacy Assessment Plan ('ILAAP').

As demonstrated in every banking crisis, most latterly in the GFC, liquidity and not credit is the key risk that will bring down a bank and in turn bring down the whole financial system.

Interestingly the bank crisis of the 1920s was caused by a liquidity crisis due to depositors demanding a repayment of their deposits. As part of the New Deal, F. D. Roosevelt's administration introduced rules which would protect banks from similar runs by introducing the Federal Deposit Insurance Scheme. Problem solved. Not so much. Roll on to 2008 and despite the lack of queues outside banks (save for Northern Rock) due to deposit insurance, we still had a bank liquidity crisis.

The 2008 crisis on liquidity was more structured. In those vulnerable banks in the GFC, liquidity moved away from being something that banks relied on depositors for to something that they relied on other banks for through the long-term and short-term bond markets. When some banks stopped revolving their bonds to other banks, the bond issuing banks suddenly did not have the liquidity they required to fund their assets.

Suffice it to say that new bank applicants will not be able to explore the capital markets wonderland that large banks played in prior to the GFC. New bank applicants will simply have to demonstrate how they will avoid the 1920s type liquidity crisis on their business. As all new bank applicants will have the benefit of deposit insurance the management of liquidity should be a relatively simple exercise.

The PRA does not however, distinguish between a small new bank and a large global bank in its requirement for the production of an ILAAP. The document is therefore by definition far too complex for the simple and straightforward analysis of liquidity required for new bank applications.

4.2 Background to Bank's Business Activities

As per the Regulatory Business Plan & the ICAAP, the ILAAP will set out the background to the bank's business activities. As explained above although this seems like an inordinate waste of time and paper, a separate department will be looking at the ILAAP and therefore the inclusion of this section makes reference more efficient.

https://doi.org/10.1515/9783111101545-004

4.3 Business Viability

Again, as per the RBP & the ICAAP, the ILAAP will set out why the business of the bank is viable.

4.4 Liquidity Risk Ratio Reporting

There are two key Liquidity Ratios, the Liquidity Cash Ratio ('LCR') and the Net Stable Funding Ratio ("NSFR").

The key elements to calculate LCR for a bank are the stock of high-quality liquid assets it holds, the expected cash inflows and the expected cash outflows arising from bank's base plan projections. The PRA's minimum requirement is that a bank will have an LCR ratio of at least 100%.

The Liquidity Cash Ratio

The LCR calculation will look at the following items in detail:

1. The liquidity asset buffer. This buffer is usually made up of High Quality Liquid Assets (for example, Treasury Bonds, which can be quickly turned into cash).
2. Cash sitting at the bank. This is the simple calculation that every business has to run, i.e., how much cash is sitting in the bank accounts.
3. A deduction is made for outflows of deposits, which is assumed to be a minimum of a 20% run-off rate. A greater deduction will have to be assumed if the deposits are greater than the insured maximum of £85k, where there is a general assumption that all can be withdrawn at short notice or where the bank has committed facilities.

Therefore, the bank should be able to demonstrate whether its liquidity assets buffer will support a demand for the repayment of deposits at any given time. This buffer should help to prevent the bank suffering a 1920s style bank run.

As a further check a bank will model the cash inflows it will benefit from the repayment of its banking book. For bank modelling purposes the cash inflows are limited to 75% of the cash outflows.

Again, the net sum of the outflows vs. the inflows will be measured against the stock of liquidity in the form of HQLAs and cash to determine whether the bank will have enough liquidity to meet its cash outflow requirements.

Net Stable Funding Ratio

A bank applicant will be required to use the Net Stable Funding Ratio to analyse the stability of its funding profile.

Available Stable Funding is measured based on the broad characteristics of the relative stability of bank's funding sources, including contractual maturities of all its liabilities. For new bank applicants the funding sources should be relatively simple comprising equity and deposits from new customers.

A bank's deposit will be broken down into a number of categories depending on the maturity of those deposits, for example:
- Term deposits of greater than 1-year term
- Term deposits of less than 1-year term
- Deposits which are repayable on demand

A percentage is applied to those deposits to determine the amount of such deposits that are available to the bank to fund its requirements. For example, the percentage applied to term deposits of over 1-year term is 100%, i.e., 100% of term deposits of over 1 year are available for the bank's funding requirements.

The Available Stable Funding is then compared to the Required Stable Funding.

Required Stable Funding will be broken down into a number of categories, for example:
- Funding required for the purposes of acquiring HQLAs
- Funding to remain as cash in the bank's accounts
- Funding required to fund the bank's loan book

As should be expected, the PRA requires banks to have a minimum NSFR of 100% to ensure that it has adequate funding for all parts of its business.

4.5 Risk Management Assessment

Each bank will be required to demonstrate how it will manage its liquidity from a risk perspective.

This demonstration will be broken down into a number of areas.

Liquidity Risk Appetite

Each bank will be required to demonstrate that it will maintain adequate liquidity resources to meet its maturing obligations at all times, as and when they fall due. The bank will set out its methods for managing liquidity risk, examples of which are listed below:

- Maintenance of cash balances – banks will be required to maintain cash balances at all times to meet short-term liquidity requirements
- Survival days – a bank will be required to demonstrate that it has sufficient liquidity to meet all its liquidity requirements over a 30-day horizon
- Liquidity Key Risk Indicators. A bank will monitor the performance of its risk appetite statement through a number of primary and secondary risk indicators. The key liquidity risk metrics will be measured against green/amber/red criteria to ensure that necessary action is taken, where appropriate. Example liquidity KRIs could include:
  - Liquidity Coverage Ratio – for example there could be a target of 150% LCR, with Amber and Red triggers set at 125% and 110% respectively;
  - Net Stable Funding Ratio – for example there could be a target NSFR of 125%, with Amber and Red triggers set at 110% and 105% respectively;
  - Survival horizon under stress – for example there could be a target period of 90 days, with Amber and Red triggers set at 75days and 60 days respectively;
  - HQLAs to Deposits – for example this could be set at 14%, with Amber and Red triggers at 12% and 8% respectively;
  - Increase in cost of funds for depositors above average rates paid in market – for example the target could be set at the average of the rates offered by the top 10 providers in the market, with Amber and Red Triggers set if the bank has to pay 100 to 200 basis points more than the average.
- The bank will also have a number of secondary risk metrics, which it will also monitor to determine the level of liquidity risk in its business. Examples of secondary risk metrics are set out below:
  - A bank may monitor the deposit inflows it is receiving, setting for example Red Triggers at deposit inflows less than 70% or over 130% of its budgeted inflow assumptions;
  - A bank may monitor the retention rates of maturing fixed rate deposits, setting Red Triggers if the retention rates are below 50% of the maturing deposits;
  - A bank may monitor deposits over £85k and set a Red Trigger limit of 5% of such deposits;

4.6 Governance & Risk

As per the RBP and the ICAAP, the ILAAP will set out verbatim the Governance & Risk sections from those documents.

4.7 Liquidity Risk Management

The PRA has outlined 14 liquidity risk drivers in its stress testing guidelines set out in Chapter 11 of the ILAAP Rules.

Each of the risk drivers is set out below.

1. Retail funding liquidity risk
The bank will set out its plans for retail deposit raising and why those plans are viable. New applicant banks will generally only target deposits below the FSCS limit therefore lowering the risk of large-scale outflows in a stress scenario.

2. Wholesale secured and unsecured funding risk
New applicant banks will not in practice be able to rely on wholesale secured and unsecured funding facilities from third-party financial institutions. This will therefore not be a risk relevant to new bank applications.

3. Risk of correlation between funding markets and lack of diversification
As new bank applicants will seek to achieve a diversified depositor base, they will not be exposed to the risk of correlation and lack of diversification from their depositor base.

4. Off-Balance sheet funding risk.
Committed facilities, where the bank is exposed to providing liquidity do not appear on the balance sheet. New bank applicants will avoid this type of funding risk in their product set.

Further new bank applicants will rely on depositors for their liquidity and not on off-balance sheet structures such as securitisation vehicles to provide the liquidity for balance sheet assets.

The lack of management of this risk was one of the main reasons for the global financial crisis in 2008 and although of fundamental importance to larger banks is all but irrelevant for new applicant banks.

Books of many thousands of pages have been written on this subject and can be simplified as follows. Larger financial institutions packaged their loans and sold them to off balance sheet special purpose vehicle (SPVs), which in turn funded the acquisition through issuing bonds. This released the capital that the financial institutions were required to hold against their loans, whilst enabling the financial institutions to still receive income from the loans (after bond costs). This was a way for a financial institution with limited capital to benefit from the income from a huge loan book and not have to set aside capital for that loan book.

The problem occurred when the bonds did not renew. The loans had to be funded through other forms of liquidity, which were simply not available to the financial institutions that needed that liquidity. One of those financial institutions was Lehman Brothers, the now infamous US investment bank.

5. Funding tenor risk
This is the risk that the loans made by the bank have different tenors (or are of a different term in months) than the deposits funding those loans. As one of the key functions of a bank is to transform deposits into loan assets of longer maturities this appears to

be an important risk to consider. In summary, the bank runs of the past have made this an important risk to be managed by banking institutions.

In simple terms there is a risk that short-term deposits, which can be called at any time, are relied upon to fund longer-term loans. A bank has to consider how it will manage if a proportion of its deposits are called at any one time. The management of this risk was the precise reason why FD Roosevelt's New Deal introduced the Federal Deposit Insurance Corporation ('FDIC'). The FDIC and other types of deposit insurance give depositors the comfort that a bank failure will not mean the loss of their deposits. Banks still have to consider the impact of a deposit call. In the main this is managed through always having a liquidity buffer to meet any unexpected demands for cash by depositors.

6. Risk of deterioration of credit rating
As new bank applicants will generally not have a credit rating. This is only really relevant to large rated banks that rely on the capital markets, usually the bond markets for liquidity as well as retail deposits.

7. Cross-currency funding risk
As new bank applicants will in the main be taking UK sterling deposits to fund UK loan assets the liquidity risk arising from currency fluctuations is not considered relevant for new bank applicants.

8. Risk that liquidity resources cannot be transferred across entities, sectors and countries
Again, this risk will not be generally relevant to new bank applications which will be stand-alone entities or group entities, where all the subsidiaries of the bank are wholly owned or where a parent entity to the bank has no access to the liquid assets of the bank.

9. Funding risk resulting from estimates of future balance sheet growth
If the balance sheet projections are lower or higher than plan, there will either be a greater demand for liquidity than projected or there will be a lower level of assets to generate the servicing of the liquidity raised by the bank. In the earlier case, the bank will need to demonstrate its ability to raise a higher level of deposits than originally projected, which in turn may have an impact on the cost of deposits and the net interest margin achieved by the bank.

In the case of less asset origination than projected, the bank will have to set out how it will service the deposits raised.

Both risks will generally be simple to manage and the implications of either scenario relatively simple to model. In short, new banks will either step up or step down their deposit-raising strategies and will have to demonstrate that the liquidity required in either scenario is manageable through its capital positions.

10. Franchise risk
This risk examines the impact on liquidity of a deterioration of the bank's business. A bank will be required to demonstrate how such risk will be monitored through the bank's KRIs and ultimately in the Recovery Plan and the Resolution Plan, how the bank will wind down its business and service all its liquidity requirements. For a new bank, the material adverse consequences of a risk that impacts a brands franchise are dealt with in the Recovery Plan and the Resolution Plan.

11. Marketable assets risk
New banks will generally not engage in market trading of assets such as the buying and selling of bonds and therefore such risk will not be relevant to their business model.

12. Non-marketable assets risk
A new banks core non-marketable asset will be its loan book. There is historically a secondary loans market and banks may also be able to sell their assets into securitised structures. A new bank will plan to hold assets to maturity or pre-payment.

If a bank is forced into a situation that requires the sale of its loan book assets, this may trigger the provisions of the Recovery Plan or the Resolution Plan and is therefore considered in detail in those documents.

13. Internalisation risk
As new banks will generally be smaller financial institutions this risk is not relevant to new bank applications.

14. Intra-day liquidity risk
A new bank will have to consider daily cash requirements and the risk that it does not have sufficient liquidity to meet intra-day liquidity risk. A new bank will consider its maximum projected daily outflows and will seek to hold liquid funds equal to a multiple of such daily outflows.

15. Other liquidity risks
New banks will be required to consider other risks that may impact the liquidity requirements of their business, such as impacts on the liquidity requirements due to increases or reductions in projected loans origination, or pro-cyclicality where demands for loans goes up, when liquidity does down (such as occurred in the Global Financial Crisis).

4.8 Liquidity Stress Testing

As per capital stress testing, new banks are expected to conduct stresses on their business relating to market-wide events, idiosyncratic events and a combination of such events. A new bank will generally model such stress based on the period 12 months after the date it starts raising deposits and the stress period will for example range from 2 weeks to 12 weeks.

An example of the liquidity stresses that can be modelled by a new bank are summarised below:

- A stress can be applied to the assumed level of deposits actually raised by a new bank. For example, the base case model may assume a 100%, a market-wide, idiosyncratic and combined stress may reduce the level of deposits raised to 25%, 20% and 5% respectively.
- A stress can be applied to the assumed renewal of fixed rate deposits. For example, the base case model may assume an 80% retention rate of deposits, a market-wide, idiosyncratic and combined stress may reduce this retention to 75%, 50% and 25% respectively.
- A stress can be applied to the value of HQLAs, which in turn will impact the liquidity generated by the realisation of those HQLAs. The base case model may assume 100%, a market-wide, idiosyncratic and combined stress may reduce the value of HQLAs by 5% respectively. As HQLAs are by definition unlikely to be impacted by a stress event the 5% haircut is acceptable across the different stress scenarios.
- A stress can be applied to the levels of new loans written by the bank. The base case model will assume 100%, a market-wide, idiosyncratic and combined stress may reduce the level of loans by 80%, 60% and 65% respectively
- A stress can be applied to the performance of the bank's portfolio with a stress on the arrears/loss rates experienced by a new bank. The base case scenario will remain unchanged, a market-wide, idiosyncratic and combined stress may increase losses by 5%, 3% and 5% respectively. In this case simply the higher loss rate may be taken from the 2 scenarios in the combined scenario.

Market-Wide Stress Scenario (Including Retail Funding Risk)

The bank will model a severe recession over a 12-week period to determine the impact to liquid resources of the bank and the impact to the balance sheet of the bank.

The bank will determine the impact of the stresses on the bank's key liquidity ratios and example of such ratios is listed out below:

1. Liquid Assets to Loans
2. Liquid Assets to Deposits
3. HQLAs to Deposits
4. Liquidity Coverage Ratio
5. Net Stable Funding Ratio

Further Stress Tests

Idiosyncratic stress, combined stress and reverse stress.

As per the capital stresses the bank will model the stresses to determine the impact on the bank's liquid resources and also its key liquidity ratios as set out above.

4.9 Liquidity Contingency Plan

An applicant bank is required to demonstrate its understanding of the importance of liquidity for its day-to-day operations and set out a detailed plan for addressing liquidity requirements in times of crisis. The plan should recognise that a liquidity crisis can arise due to either an internal or external event or a combination of both and the plan should address both contingencies.

Invocation of Liquidity Contingency Plan

A bank applicant is required to demonstrate that it will monitor its liquidity through regular and timely management information ('MI').

The bank will monitor primary and secondary liquidity risk metrics and where there are breaches in those metrics the bank will demonstrate that it has a detailed escalation process related to the said breaches.

An example escalation process is set out below:

1. Early Warning Indicator breach noted in KRI report.
   The Key Risk Indicator report will highlight an Early Warning Indicator ("EWI") in respect of liquidity. For example, the LCR may be 125%, representing an Amber risk and below the target of 150%.
   In this event the CRO will ensure that the Assets & Liability Committee is notified of the breach.
   The ALCO will then determine whether the breach can be remediated and if it cannot be remediated the breach is redesignated as a Trigger Breach, such that ALCO will be required to report to the Risk Committee.
   The Risk Committee will report to Board on outstanding breaches.
   If a breach is outstanding for 6 months, the Board must extend the remediation period or alternatively redesignate the breach as a Trigger Breach.
2. Trigger Breach highlighted in KRI Report. ALCO or Risk Committee redesignates EWI as a Trigger Breach. Board redesignates persistent EWI breach as a Trigger Breach.
   A Trigger Breach is immediately escalated to the Board. The Board determines on the basis of the severity and ability to repair the breach, the required classification of the breach between Level 1, Level 2 and Level 3.

3. Level 1 Trigger Breach. A Level 1 Trigger Breach is one that is expected to be resolved within the bank's capital and liquidity limits. The Board will approve and monitor the management actions required to resolve the breach.
4. Level 2 Trigger Breach. A Level 2 Trigger Breach is one that is expected to be resolved, but not within the bank's capital and liquidity limits.
   The Board will instruct the CEO to convene EXCO, which in turn will implement the Recovery Plan and/or the Liquidity Contingency Plan. The Board will instruct the CEO to immediately notify the regulatory authorities.
5. Level 3 Trigger Breach. A Level 3 Trigger Breach is one that is not expected to be resolved. The Board will instruct the CEO to immediately notify the regulatory authorities of the Breach

Governance for Liquidity Contingency Plan

When the LCP is invoked, the bank will form an emergency ALCO, chaired by the CEO, to evaluate the steps required to contain a crisis event on the basis of the perceived nature, severity and duration of the situation. The CEO is responsible for executing the LCP, detailing projections, steps to be taken, timescales, risk assessment and escalation to the Board.

The Emergency ALCO will perform an assessment of the situation and prioritise the tasks necessary to achieve a recovery. In addition, it will be responsible for ongoing monitoring and the submission of detailed, timely reports on the situation to the Board. The Board will convene as required during the crisis. Any decision to initiate the Resolution Plan resides with the Board.

Communications

Invocation of the LCP is predicated on an actual or prospective breach of regulatory requirements. It is the responsibility of the CEO to promptly notify the Regulator that the LCP has been invoked and to agree communication and reporting requirements for the duration of the crisis period.

An important goal of a bank during the period the LCP is invoked is to communicate stability to its customers. A bank will not only be seeking funds to cover its obligations, but also to finance new assets for business continuity.

Recent events have shown that concerns about a bank's solvency can arise quickly. Attempting to access new markets or sources of liquidity where a bank has not previously been a regular and active participant may exacerbate existing concerns.

The CEO, in consultation with the Board, will manage external communications during this period in order to mitigate any adverse reputational consequences arising from steps taken under the LCP.

Implementation of the LCP

Prior to the meeting of the Emergency ALCO, the Finance team of a bank will be required to produce the following MIS reports:

- Deposit analysis
- Maturity analysis
- Cash flow projections
- A schedule of any committed payments

The Emergency ALCO will make an initial consideration of the circumstances and review the sources of liquidity that are available in the market to classify the issue as:

1. Short-term liquidity crisis
2. Long-term liquidity crisis
3. The issue is not yet critical but enhanced vigilance is required.

Actions required for a Short-Term Liquidity Crisis

A short-term liquidity issue is likely to arise from a shock to the financial system which disrupts funding operations. Such a crisis would be temporary in nature and would most likely not involve a significant change to the credit standing of the bank.

The Emergency ALCO will inform the Board of Directors and set out the circumstances and the recommended measures.

Actions available to the Emergency ALCO to resolve the crisis:

- Draw down any of the bank's borrowing facilities
- Reduce lending
- Prioritise payments:
  - repayment of depositors
  - interbank payments
  - expenses
  - new lending already confirmed
- Increasing the rates offered on deposits to increase retention as well as new business
- Increasing the rates on loans to reduce the lending volumes

Actions Required for a Long-Term Liquidity Crisis

The Emergency ALCO will similarly convene a meeting of the Executive Committee and inform it that there is a Long-Term Liquidity problem, set out the circumstances, the expected duration of the issue, and the recommended measures. The Executive Committee will inform the Board and the PRA of the nature of the problem and the bank's proposed actions.

The finance team will produce a run-off schedule of assets and liabilities setting out the contractual cash-flows and the supplementary actions to be taken under the LCP through to the conclusion of the crisis. The run-off schedule will be produced regularly until the crisis has been resolved.

Actions available / required to deal with a long-term liquidity crisis will include all those available under a short-term crisis, and in addition the following:

- Cease taking on new lending customers
- Cease new lending to existing customers
- Review deposit pricing in order to stimulate deposit flows
- Negotiate new bank facilities
- Seek to raise additional capital
- Enter into a repurchase agreement with the Bank of England in respect of its assets, subject to the rules of the Sterling Monetary Framework
- Sale of loan assets
- Arrange meetings or other communications with certain depositors. Such meetings or communications should be used to reassure depositors and to determine their intent at rollover
- Commence an orderly wind-down of the bank's operations

4.10 Template ILAAP

Contents

Tables

Figures

1 Executive Summary

1.1 Introduction

The Board of Orchard Funding Group PLC ("Orchard") is responsible for ensuring that the institution maintains sufficient liquidity to manage its day to day operations in normal business conditions, as well in periods of stress. The Board will also ensure compliance with the regulatory liquidity framework currently set out in the following rules and guidelines:

- The Internal Liquidity Adequacy Assessment Process, part of the PRA Rulebook (ILAAP rules),
- The 'Liquidity Coverage Requirement — UK Designated Investment Firms' part of the PRA Rulebook;
- The PRA's approach to banking supervision;
- The PRA's approach to supervising liquidity and funding risks (Supervisory Statement 24/15)
- Part Six (Liquidity) of the Capital Requirements Regulation (CRR) and the European Commission Delegated Act with regards to the liquidity coverage requirement (LCR) for credit institutions ('Delegated Act').
- Titles 8 and 9 of the EBA SREP Guidelines In respect of liquidity and funding risk management and control.

The ILAAP is proportionate to Orchard's business model, scale, complexity and risk appetite, and takes into account all sources of liquidity. Its key purpose is to document and demonstrate overall liquidity adequacy of the business.

The ILAAP will be updated annually or more frequently if changes in Orchard's business strategy, balance sheet, the nature or scale of its activities, or its operational environment suggest that its level of liquidity resources has changed significantly.

Monitoring and reporting of liquidity parameters will take place regularly and at least monthly, to ExCo and the Board.

The assessment set out in this document is undertaken on a forward looking basis over the Base Financial Operating Plan period.

For the purposes of this ILAAP, Orchard should be read as Orchard Funding Group PLC or the newly authorised Orchard Bank, as the context so requires.

1.2 ILAAP Purpose and Use

The key functions of Orchard's ILAAP are as follows:

1. To assess:
   a. the sources of liquidity risks to Orchard which arise from the proposed business model;

   b. any mitigating factors which may reduce either the likelihood of the liquidity risks identified occurring or their impact on liquidity;
   c. the adequacy of Orchard's liquidity resources to meet its payment obligations as they fall due in both normal market conditions and periods of stress.
2. To inform the Board of the liquidity risks in a) above, and how Orchard proposes to manage them;
3. To enable the Board to set a recommended level of liquidity asset buffer which will comply with:
   a. Orchard's own internal liquidity risk appetite, as set out in the overall Risk Appetite Statement that has been approved by the Board;
   b. Regulatory liquidity adequacy rule.
4. To enable the PRA to assess Orchard's liquidity resources and risks more effectively, both in normal market conditions and in a stressed environment.

1.3 Governance, Challenge and Approval by Board

Orchard has established a Liquidity Risk Management Framework (LRMF), which is included in this ILAAP and provides detailed approach to managing and mitigating liquidity risk. Decision making responsibility at Orchard rests ultimately with the Board. This is cascaded down through the organisation by delegation of responsibility to the main committees and through individuals' documented responsibilities. Although responsibility is delegated for some day-to-day activities, the Board retains overall responsibility for the Orchard's strategy and its compliance with all laws and regulations.

The Asset & Liability Committee (ALCO) is responsible for the management of liquidity in Orchard. The Individual Liquidity Adequacy Assessment Process (ILAAP), requiring involvement of the Board and management team, supplies the backdrop and context for ALCO and Orchard to review the status of its liquidity adequacy. The ILAAP will also help the management team and Board to conduct liquidity planning exercises.

This ILAAP document was reviewed and challenged by the Board on 16 July 2019 and comments on the draft document (version of 20.06.2019) received from the INEDs. Post the Board challenge, the document was updated and issued to BDO on 16 September 2019 for comments. The ILAAP was formally challenged by the Board on 17th October 2019 and reviewed again on 14th November 2019.

1.4 Risk Appetite

It is Orchard's policy to maintain sufficient liquidity at all times to meet any obligations as and when they fall due, including under severe yet plausible stress. Orchard's Board has set four risk appetite targets to manage liquidity risks and these are:

1. Liquidity Coverage Ratio of 150% against the regulatory requirement of 100%,
2. Net Stable funding Ratio of 125% against the regulatory requirement of 100%,
3. Survival Horizon under stress of 90 days against the regulatory requirement of 30 days, and
4. High Quality Liquid Assets of 14% of the deposit base with funds placed in the Bank of England Reserve Account. Prior to the establishment of this account funds will be invested in short term (<3 months maturity) UK Government Gilts.

All the key liquidity ratios have a very conservative voluntary buffer that is built into the risk appetite as the Board considers this to be appropriate for a new entrant into the deposit market. The table below sets out the Board approved liquidity risk appetite.

Table 1: Liquidity Risk Appetite.

Limit category		Target	Early warning indicator (Amber)	Trigger (Red)
Liquidity	Liquidity Coverage Ratio (LCR PRA min 100%)	150%	125%	110%
	Net Stable Funding Ratio (NSFR 100%)	125%	110%	105%
	Survival Horizon under stress (PRA min 30days)	90 days	75 days	60 days
	HQLAs to Deposits	14%	12%	8%
	Increase in cost of fundsfor deposits above the average of top ten providers on Money.co.uk website	Av. Of top ten providers for 1 year and 2 year fixed rate deposits	= or >100 basis points	= >200 basis points

The Pillar 1 liquidity ratios under the Base Financial Operating Plan are presented below:

Table 2: Base Plan Pillar 1 Liquidity Ratios.

	Target	Year 1	Year 2	Year 3	Year 4	Year 5
LCR	150%	3069%	4093%	3553%	2690%	2406%
NSFR	125%	154.3%	160.3%	160.3%	153.9%	154.2%
% Liquid Assets to Loans		15%	21%	19%	14%	13%
% HQLA to Deposits	14%	18%	25%	21%	16%	14%

1.5 Stress Testing

Orchard has completed a number of stress tests in respect of its future business projections to assess the impact of such stresses on the liquidity of the business.

The 3 key stress tests conducted by Orchard are as follows:

5. Market-wide (anchor) stress has been designed to test the impact of a deep recession, with high unemployment that results in lower lending volumes, increased impairment charges, lower new deposit volumes and much higher attrition of maturing deposits.
6. Idiosyncratic stress has been designed around adverse press coverage of increasing losses at the bank, which results in a substantial increase in deposit withdrawal and reduced new deposits.
7. Combined stress takes account of more severe market-wide impacts and the idiosyncratic stress scenario.

The impact on the business drivers has been assessed from the end of year 1, with the stress time period of 2 weeks and 12 weeks for idiosyncratic and the other two stresses, respectively.

Table 3: Impact on business drivers under each stress scenario.

	Base	Market wide	Idiosyncratic	Combined
Deposit retention rate at maturity	80%	75%	50%	25%
New deposits as a percentage of plan	100%	25%	20%	5%
Liquid assets buffer haircut	0%	5%	5%	5%
New loans as a percentage of plan	100%	80%	60%	65%
Loan default rates	0%	5%	3%	5%
Period of stress (weeks)	–	12	2	12

The impact on the key liquidity ratios after the period of stress are tabled below.

Table 4: Liquidity ratios post the stress period.

	Base Plan	Market wide	Idiosyncratic	Combined
Period of stress (weeks)	**Year 1**	**Post 12 weeks**	**Post 2 weeks**	**Post 12 weeks**
Ratios				
LCR	**3069%**	**2586%**	**3528%**	**3407%**
NSFR	**154%**	**158%**	**164%**	**160%**
% Liquid Assets to Loans	15%	13%	17%	16%
% Liquid Assets to Deposits	23%	21%	26%	27%
% HQLA to Deposits	18%	16%	21%	20%

1.6 Cash Balances

Orchard will place all surplus cash up to £1m with its clearing bank as 'Cash at Bank' and the balance will be placed in a reserve account with the Bank of England. In the interim, before getting the Bank of England Reserve account set up, the funds will be invested in short term (< 3 months maturity) UK Gilts.

Orchard's Pillar 1 (LCR) adequately covers the liquidity risk inherent in its simple business model. Detailed calculations of the LCR are set out in Table 11 below. Orchard's risk appetite for LCR of 150% sufficiently covers the liquidity risk and Orchard does not, therefore, intend to hold additional liquidity under Pillar 2.

1.7 NSFR

Orchard's Net Stable Funding Ratio (NSFR) is set out in Table 12 below. Due to Orchard's business model, which funds short-term loans with longer term deposits, the NSFR will be materially in excess of standard regulatory requirements.

1.8 Liquidity Contingency Plan

Orchard believes that advance preparations and contingency plans for potential liquidity needs are vital components of liquidity risk management. Accordingly, Orchard has developed:

- Identification of specific triggers that prompt heightened liquidity management activity;
- Specific guidelines for the management of a liquidity crisis – Liquidity Contingency Plan ("LCP");
- A methodology for the formulation of Orchard's Liquidity Crisis Team;
- A methodology for allocating specific roles, responsibilities and time frames for the required operational and other actions.

The LCP comes into force in times of potential crisis, either due to a specific-bank event, or due to market-wide conditions, or a combination of both.

The LCP is summarised in this ILAAP (Section 12 below) and incorporated in the Bank's Recovery Plan. The LCP will be reviewed at least on an annual basis when updating the ILAAP or as the market and economic situation dictates. During times of crisis the LCP will be reviewed on an on-going basis and testing will be performed for the readiness and suitability of mechanisms under the given market conditions.

The purpose of Early Warning Indicators in the Risk Appetite is to provide early warnings of a potential liquidity problem in order to take appropriate actions before the problem escalates. These will be reviewed on a regular basis by senior management and presented to ALCO, with the reporting frequency dependent on the prevailing market conditions.

Orchard has also identified specific management actions that it will implement in cases of a liquidity crisis, together with expected cash-flows, time-lines, responsible personnel and an assessment as to the firm's ability to implement the proposed actions.

1.9 Conclusion

Orchard will maintain liquidity resources that are adequate, both as to amount and quality, to ensure that there is no significant risk that its liabilities cannot be met as they fall due. This is in line with the PRA's overall liquidity adequacy rule (OLAR).

As set out in this ILAAP document, Orchard's LCR and NSFR will be materially above the regulatory benchmarks for liquidity. This is the case even under stressed market conditions.

The following liquidity risk metrics will be monitored:

Table 5: Primary Liquidity Risk Metrics.

Limit category		**Target**	**Early warning indicator (Amber)**	**Trigger (Red)**
Liquidity	Liquidity Coverage Ratio (LCR PRA min 100%)	150%	125%	110%
	Net Stable Funding Ratio (NSFR 100%)	125%	110%	105%
	Survival Horizon under stress (PRA min 30days)	90 days	75 days	60 days
	HQLAs to Deposits	14%	12%	8%
	Increase in cost of fundsfor deposits above the average of top ten providers on Money.co.uk website	Av. Of top ten providers for 1 year and 2 year fixed rate deposits	= or >100 basis points	= >200 basis points

The ILAAP will also demonstrate that, due to the conservative cash balances that will be maintained by Orchard and due to the short-term and amortising nature of its lending products, Orchard will always be able to ensure that it meets any reasonably expected liquidity demands placed on its business over the plan period.

2 Background to Orchard Business Activities

2.1 Historic Financial Performance

Orchard specialises in the insurance premium finance and the professions finance market. The group lent £68m in the 12 months to 31 July 2018, generated revenue of £5.2m and generated a profit before tax of £1.9m. The group's lending book was c. £31.0m as of the end of July 2018. The published key financials of the group, income statement and balance sheet, over the last three years to July 2018 are presented below.

The accounts to 31 July 2019, which are subject to approval at Orchard's AGM, show lending book growing to £32.1m at the end of the financial year, revenue of £5.5m and profit before tax of £2.0m.

Table 6: Orchard Historic Financials – year ended July.

			£'000
Income Statement	**Actual 2016**	**Actual 2017**	**Actual 2018**
Revenue	3,469	4,560	5,174
Finance costs	(238)	(329)	(452)
Other operating costs	(76)	(78)	(83)
Gross Profit	**3,155**	**4,153**	**4,639**
Administration expenses	(1,884)	(2,512)	(2,746)
Operating profit before tax	**1,271**	**1,641**	**1,893**
Corporation tax	(267)	(303)	(381)
Profit after tax	**1,004**	**1,338**	**1,512**

Balance Sheet	**Actual 2016**	**Actual 2017**	**Actual 2018**
Assets			
Loans and advances	22,004	28,523	31,084
Cash at bank	1,390	1,728	1,286
Fixed assets	95	77	59
Other assets	44	98	60
Total assets	**23,533**	**30,426**	**32,489**
Liabilities			
Bank borrowing	9,208	13,734	16,008
Trade creditors	1,657	3,181	2,051
Tax liabilities	289	279	339
Non-current liabilities	37	65	54
Total liabilities	**11,191**	**17,259**	**18,452**
Equity			
Share capital	214	214	214
Share premium	8,692	8,692	8,692
Merger reserves	891	891	891

Table 6 (continued)

Balance Sheet	Actual 2016	Actual 2017	Actual 2018
Retained earnings	2,545	3,370	4,240
Total equity	**12,342**	**13,167**	**14,037**
Total equity and liabilities	**23,533**	**30,426**	**32,489**

2.1.1 Key Objectives

Key objectives of Orchard over the next five years are:

- to create a bank focused on providing consistent, reliable and cost-effective liquidity to borrowers deserving of such liquidity in the insurance premium finance market and the professions finance market;
- to conduct its business with integrity and ensure that customers are always treated fairly;
- to offer fair rates to depositors and provide transparency and clarity to all stakeholders in respect of the business of the bank;
- to protect depositors by writing prudent and conservative business in its chosen markets;
- to establish a board and executive management team, with strong, complementary non-executive directors and executive directors having a strong track record in specialist lending, deposit taking and risk management;
- to implement a risk management framework, supported by an operational platform with strong systems and controls, to enable effective operations, oversight, regulatory compliance and excellent service to the bank's depositors and borrowers;
- to grow Orchard's share of its chosen markets by continuing to build long term partnerships with key industry players in insurance and professional services. Orchard will utilise the unparalleled expertise of its management team and experienced sales team to achieve its business plan projections;
- to achieve targeted/projected pre- and post-tax profit and return on capital employed (RoCE)
- to deliver good customer outcomes to all stakeholders – depositors, borrowers, staff and shareholders.

2.1.2 Business Proposition

Orchard provides finance in the insurance premium finance market and the professions finance market in the UK. Finance is provided to SMEs and consumers typically over a 10-month term on a fully amortising basis. All finance provided by Orchard is guaranteed by the introducing professional firm or insurance broker. The directors believe that the lending undertaken by the group is very low risk, demonstrated by the fact that Orchard has suffered minimal arrears and loan losses over the last seven years. A banking licence will allow Orchard to tap into the UK deposits market and obtain access to a more stable, reliable, cost-effective and scalable source of funding, enabling it to support SMEs and consumers with better access to financing.

Orchard has been trading since 2002 and operates an efficient and profitable lending model. Orchard has developed its own bespoke software, LendXP, to allow it to conduct day-to-day lending operations. The software has been used by the group for over eight years and has proven to be reliable and with appropriate levels of control. The group was shortlisted as finalist for "Outsourced Partner of the Year 2016" by British Insurance Awards and "Service Provider of the Year 2016" by The Insurance Times. Orchard has been awarded "Intermediary of the Year" by Commercial Broker Awards 2017.

2.2 Lending Target Market

Insurance Premium Financing

The insurance premium finance market is a large and active market, which is driven by the general insurance market. The general insurance market is estimated to be currently worth over £35bn p.a. (measured in terms of gross written premium). Based on historic growth rates in the market from the Association of British Insurers (ABI), management have estimated that the annual growth rate has averaged c. 20% over the last ten years. The proportion that is financed is c. 38%. Management expect this growth to continue over the next 5 years.

The market is dominated by Premium Credit and Close Brothers, who lent a combined £6.3bn in 2018, representing approximately 47% of the £13.3bn insurance premium finance market in the United Kingdom. There are over 3,800 insurance broker firms in the UK regulated by the Financial Conduct Authority (FCA). Premium Credit and Close Brothers focus on larger volume-driven insurance brokers. Despite its historic funding constraints, Orchard has lent successfully into the market and has contractual relationships with over 100 insurance brokers for direct facilities and for in house premium finance facilities. Through these contracts Orchard lent c. £58m into the premium financing market in 2018 and plans to grow annual lending to c. £201m at the end of its five year plan, still less than 1% of the entire market.

Professions Financing

There are over 6,600 accountancy firms in the UK according to data published by the Annual Survey of the Office of National Statistics with over 335,000[7] individual members registered with the seven UK accountancy bodies according to the Financial Reporting Council. At the smaller end of the market 52% of accountancy firms are sole

7 Key facts and trends in the Accountancy Profession, June 2015, Financial Reporting Council

practitioners, and another 44% have between 2 and 6 principals. The accountancy fee finance market is currently estimated to be worth £300m per year and the professions finance working capital market is estimated by the directors to be worth over £3bn p.a.

The group currently has contractual relationships with over 400 accountancy firms. Through these contracts Orchard provided c. £10m of financing in 2018, and looks to grow annual lending to c. £59m at the end of five years.

2.3 Lending Products

2.3.1 Existing Lending Product Lines

The Bank proposes to have the following business lines. All of the business lines are currently being originated and administered by Orchard:

1. Orchard provides finance to limited companies ("Broker Finance Companies"), which are owned and operated by insurance brokers. Broker Finance Companies provide finance to the clients of the related insurance broker to finance the insurance premiums of those clients. Orchard provides its finance to Broker Finance Companies, based upon and secured by the credit agreements between each Broker Finance Company and its client. Orchard takes a debenture from the Broker Finance Company and also a guarantee from the related insurance broker for all the obligations of the Broker Finance Company. Orchard's lending is for a maximum term of 12 months and is repaid on a fully amortising basis. Broker Finance Companies assign the benefit of all their credit agreements to Orchard and Orchard undertakes the collection and administration of the credit agreements;
2. Orchard provides finance to the clients of insurance brokers. The clients of insurance brokers are introduced to Orchard by the insurance broker. The clients can be consumers and non-consumers. A guarantee of the obligations of the clients is obtained from the introducing insurance broker;
3. Orchard provides finance to the clients of professional services firms, which are mainly accountancy practices. The clients of professional services firms are introduced to Orchard by the firms. The clients can be consumers and non-consumers. Orchard's lending is for a term of 12 months or less and is repaid on a fully amortising basis. A guarantee of the obligations of the clients is obtained from the introducing professional firm;
4. Orchard provides finance to professional services firms directly. This is all non-consumer business. The lending is for a term of 12 months or less and is repaid on a fully amortising basis. Guarantees are also provided by the partners of the professional firm;
5. Orchard provides a nominal amount of finance in adjacent markets to its core markets, such as golf fees, school fees and football season ticket fees. This is a relatively embryonic market and the current lending is very small. Orchard's core

focus as a bank will continue to be the insurance premium finance market and professions finance market.

2.3.2 Lending Product Features

Structure

Bexhill – Insurance Premium Financing

Bexhill is currently a wholly owned subsidiary of Orchard. The Bexhill business will be folded into the new bank. Bexhill was established in 2002 and has achieved consistent revenue growth between 2002 and 2018. However, due to the global financial crisis, Bexhill's funding became significantly restricted in 2008. Bexhill continued to trade through the difficult period and supported its client base despite scarcity of available funding. Currently Bexhill has over 100 insurance broker clients.

Bexhill typically lends through a finance company owned and operated by an insurance broker (corporate insurance) for the purpose of providing finance to the clients of the insurance broker. All Bexhill's lending is guaranteed by the insurance broker and all credit agreements entered into by the finance company are assigned to Bexhill and Bexhill undertakes the collection and administration of those credit agreements.

Orchard – Professions Financing and Direct Insurance Lending

Orchard Funding Limited (OFL) is currently a wholly owned subsidiary of Orchard. The OFL business will be merged into the new bank. OFL was established in 2010 in order to take advantage of the withdrawal of one of the largest funders in the market for smaller professional practices. OFL's lending book has grown since its launch, despite its funding being relatively expensive and constrained. OFL has over 400 professional firm clients as at July 2018, most of which are accountancy firms. OFL's professional firm clients introduce their clients to OFL to finance their professional fees. OFL also provides facilities to a number of professional firms directly. OFL's insurance broker clients introduce their clients to OFL to finance their insurance premiums. OFL's client list has grown consistently year-on-year.

OFL typically lends directly to the client of the insurance broker (direct insurance), client of the professional firm; or the professional firm directly.

Product Terms

Orchard's lending products will have the following terms, which replicate the terms of the products currently originated and administered by the group:

- APR – target 15–18%;
- Maximum term – 12 months;
- Fully amortising over the term of the credit;

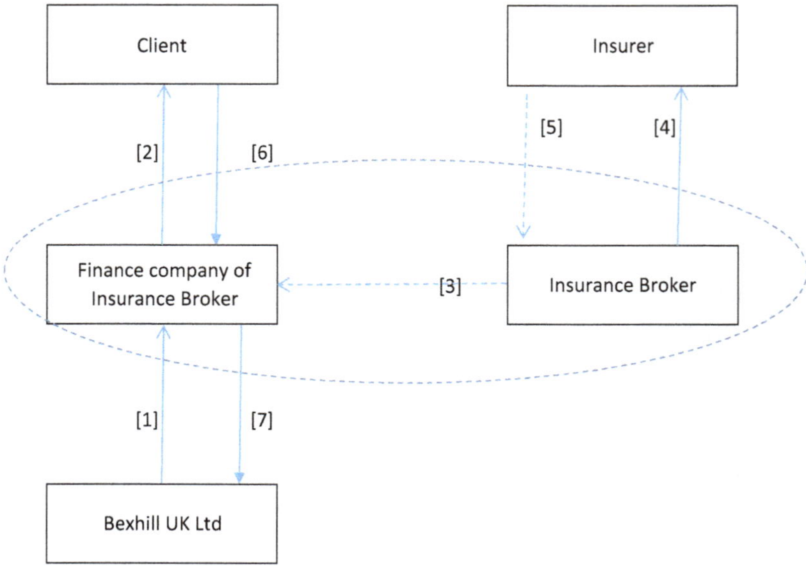

[1] Funding to financing company
[2] White-labeled finance agreement
[3] Guarantee from insurance broker
[4] Premium paid to the insurer
[5] Unearned premium on cancellation
[6] Monthly instalments
[7] Loan repayment

Figure 1: Corporate insurance structure.

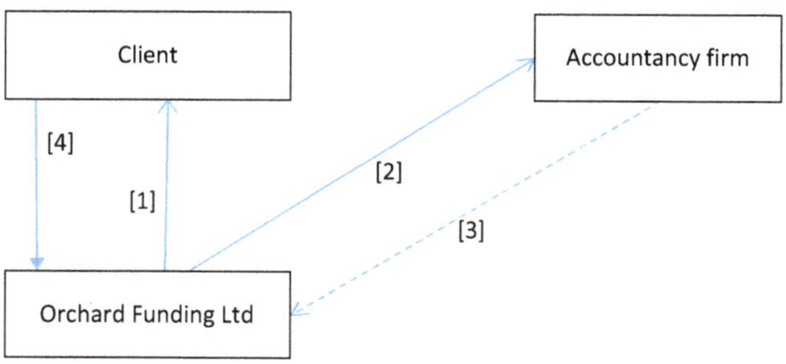

[1] Funding agreement
[2] Fees paid to the accountancy firm
[3] Guarantee from accountancy firm
[4] Monthly instalments

Figure 2: Accountancy fee funding structure.

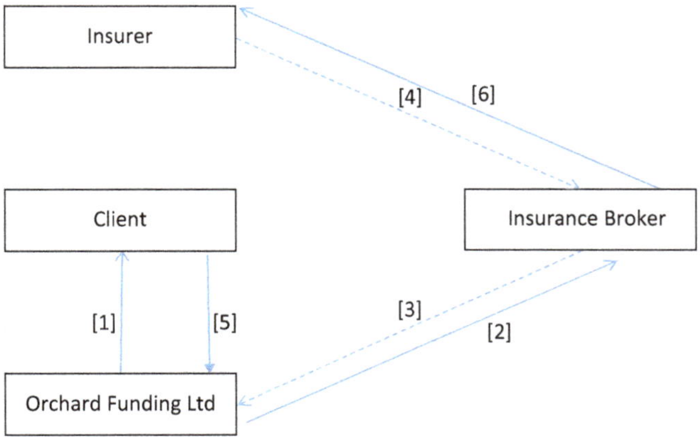

[1] Funding agreement
[2] Premium paid to the broker
[3] Guarantee from insurance broker
[4] Unearned premium
[5] Monthly instalments
[6] Premium paid to insurer

Figure 3: Direct insurance structure.

- Full agreement to pay from the introducing insurance broker or professional firm.

Although in isolation an APR of 15–18% appears relatively high, there are a number of factors, which suggest the rate is sustainable and fair to the borrower, including inter-alia:

- There are very limited sub-12 month amortising credit products available in the market. The larger financial institutions, including the banking market find the short-term nature and relatively small ticket size of this type of credit product unattractive;
- Unsecured overdrafts from banks can be over 20% APR and often over 30% APR;
- Credit card rates for borrowing are generally over 20% APR;
- Non-bank short-term credit terms can be punitively expensive;
- The rate paid by the Customer is often less than 10% APR, but Orchard is able to increase its IRR to over 15% by managing its settlement dates to the Introducer.

Financing through Orchard enables a borrower to still have the option of using its other credit providers for alternative spending.

Delivery Channels

Orchard currently uses a relationship-based model for lending origination which it plans to continue after authorisation.

Origination

Orchard has over 17 years of experience in its lending markets. The senior members of the sales team have decades of experience in the short-term financing market working with Orchard and previously with the leading competitors in the market. They have long-standing relationships with key players in the insurance brokerage sector and accountancy/law firms. The in-house solution offered by Bexhill allows insurance brokers to white-label the financing of insurance premiums to their clients, which is particularly attractive to a number of larger insurance brokers and may potentially lead to opportunities to scale up the lending business further in the future. Ongoing communication with the borrowers about loan administration is carried out over phone/email. An outline of a loan customer's journey with Orchard is set out in Appendix 1.

2.3.3 Lending Products – Conduct Risk

All new products are assessed for conduct risks, to ensure fair customer outcomes, and are signed off in accordance with the product approval policy. This includes:

- Product Characteristics
- Incentives/Income
- Pricing Structure
- Barriers to Exit
- Product Complexity
- Target Market
- Customer risk (performance metrics)
- Staff Competency
- Soft launch
- Monitoring
- Financial Promotions

All financial promotions require sign off from senior management and Compliance prior to publication.

2.3.4 Future Lending Products

Orchard has, in line with its key competitors, conducted test marketing in adjacent markets to its core insurance premium finance and accountancy fee funding market. The test marketing is currently less than 5% of Orchard's lending book and is not considered material. The adjacent markets are in service fee markets with similar characteristics, documentation and system requirements to its core markets, i.e., short-term credit where there is recourse to the introducer or a there are compelling reasons for the customer to ensure that its payments are made. Currently adjacent markets that are being tested are school fees, club fees and site fees. Orchard will continue to focus on the insurance premium market and accountancy fee funding market and consider adjacent markets where it can use its existing documentation, systems and expertise to ensure effective, profitable and controlled lending.

2.4 Deposit Target Market

Deposits Market

The total deposit base in the UK is over £2.9trn[8] of which the share of notice accounts is 12% (£350bn) and the share of fixed rate deposits is 7% (£200bn). The rate-sensitive share of the deposit market that is prone to switching is about 10% or £35bn and £20bn respectively for notice and fixed rate deposits according to market estimates of PBF Solutions (an outsourced deposit management provider). Assuming the average behavioural maturity of fixed term deposits is 2 years (realistic as most of the fixed term deposits are of 1 year maturity), £10bn of fixed rate deposits migrate looking for attractive rates in the market. By all measures, the market is vast and Orchard's share (projected to be c. £76m even after five years of operation) will be a very small fraction of the total available market.

Orchard intends to raise liabilities in the retail deposits market and understands it is difficult to offer a deposit proposition which is significantly differentiated from that of the competition. However, Orchard will offer a simple set of deposit products with attractive interest rates and a simple postal application process, through conventional best-buy tables.

Details in respect of the projected deposits to be raised by Orchard are set out in the base financial operating plan. Our deposit raising numbers (amounts and customers) are extremely conservative. We are confident that such deposit levels will be capable of being raised through a prominent exposure on best buy tables.

In the context of Orchard's conservative deposit raising aspirations, we believe the following research we have undertaken is sufficient to determine whether there is a market for our deposit taking plans. We have reviewed a number of publicly available research documents on the subject, including the FCA's Cash Savings Market Study of the UK deposit market and believe that such research enables us to conclude that there is a deep enough deposit market for the numbers set out in our Plan.

The current rates offered in the market place have been studied through the best buy tables to assess the margins above the bank base rates for the top ten providers. The base plan has assumed similar margins above the base rate, which is presented below. The time period in the chart is the period post mobilisation and authorisation as a bank.

8 Cash Savings – An International Comparison, A Study for the FCA, PwC, Sep 2014

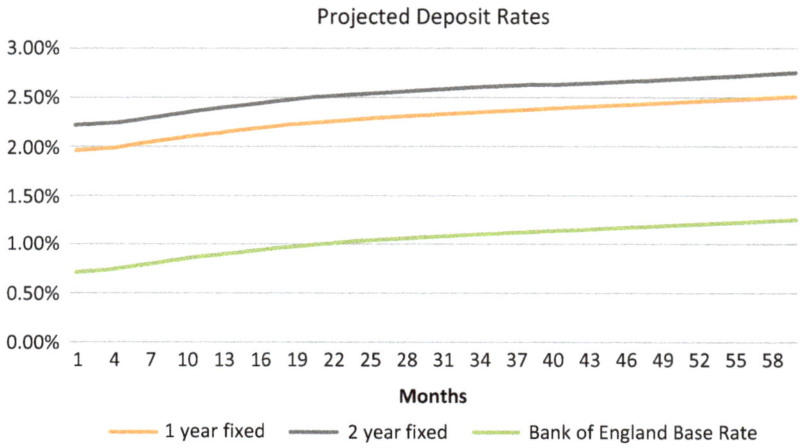

Figure 4: Deposit Rates.

2.5 Deposit Products

2.5.1 New Deposit Products

Orchard will initially have 2 deposit products:

1. 1 year fixed rate deposit
2. 2 year fixed rate deposit.

The proposed new bank will operate nationally across the UK from its base in Luton. Staff with relevant experience will be recruited to run the new retail deposits operation. As noted above, the markets in which the group currently lends are very large and provide ample opportunities for growth over the time horizon envisaged in this plan. The group's proposed new deposit taking activities will similarly form an even smaller share of the target market.

Orchard plans to have a low-risk liability strategy focusing on a limited product set (1 year and 2 year fixed rate deposit accounts) initially offered in tranches to retail customers, combined with a simple postal application process, attractive and consistently fair rates and targeted customer retention schemes. There are no plans to offer instant access or current accounts, but other term deposit products may be considered. Initially the Bank will develop brand awareness through prominence on the best-buy tables. Given the modest deposit raising plans in the projection (Orchard plans to have just over £76m in its deposit book at the end of year 5) these marketing efforts are considered to be adequate and proportionate.

Orchard will utilise the savings module of a proven software house, Mutual Vision Limited, for its deposit business. This software is used by a number of small building societies and banks.

2.5 2 Deposit Product Features

Structure

The fixed rate, fixed term deposits will have a minimum of £1K to cover operational costs and a maximum set to stay within the FSCS guarantee limit. Money will only be returned to the UK bank account where the deposit was credited from, with the option to roll over. Fixed term deposits will not be withdrawable before contractual maturity except in hardship conditions.

Product Terms

1-year fixed rate deposit
We have assumed a margin above base rate of 1.25% and average deposit size of £24,000. In year 1 we will therefore have approximately 525 depositors and this will increase to 1,900 over the 5-year life of the plan.

2-year fixed rate deposit
We have assumed a margin above base rate of 1.5% and average deposit size of £24,000. In year 1 we will therefore have approximately 336 depositors and this will increase to 1,216 over the 5-year life of the plan.

Deposit Delivery – Channels, Origination and Retention

Orchard initially intends to raise deposits through postal applications. It plans to offer simple deposit products with market-leading rates and a simple postal application process. Orchard will be a new entrant into the deposits market and intends to market its products through the best-buy tables. This will help build brand recognition among the target market of depositors (high net worth, cash-rich individuals such as pensioners) and will result in lower costs of customer acquisition, higher retention and lower deposit rates over time given the modest deposit requirements planned in the projections.

Monthly tranche limits will be set by ALCO in order to avoid peaks in funds inflows and, therefore, funds outflows at maturity. Deposit applications will be made by filling out a form downloaded from the Orchard website. The number of downloads will be monitored automatically in order to estimate the expected inflow of funds and flag where run-rates exceed or fall short of preset parameters. This will prompt adjustment to pricing or temporary withdrawal of products where necessary. Orchard recognises that the appearance of deposit products in the best buy tables could lead to increases in inflows of deposits in excess of the levels required leading to excess liquidity and thereby creating a negative carry cost and spikes in outgoing funds at maturity. Orchard will carefully manage this risk by closely monitoring the application activity by number of downloads of the application forms from the website to project expected volume and amend the interest rates on the deposit products to reduce new business levels if required.

Orchard recognises that the cost of acquiring new deposits is significantly higher than the cost of retaining existing deposits, and will design tailored retention schemes (depositors contacted 4–6 weeks prior to deposit maturity, offered market leading rates that are the same as what is offered to new customers) to preserve them.

In the event that customers are met with financial difficulties leading them to want to withdraw their deposit, Orchard will review each application to withdraw deposits prior to the contractual maturity date. As Orchard's assets are amortising and the liquidity buffers are extremely conservative throughout the term of the plan, Orchard will act in the manner of a reasonably prudent financial institution to determine whether a contractual deposit term can be broken. Our Deposit Hardship Policy sets out the basis on which each case will be determined, ensuring a fair and equitable outcome for the customer. It is anticipated that less than 1% (by value) of depositors will request a withdrawal of deposits prior to the contractual term date. An outline customer journey for Deposit customers with Orchard is attached in the Appendix.

All new products will be reviewed by EXCO, with oversight from Compliance, and submitted to the Board for sign-off where appropriate.

Redemption Profile of Deposits

The majority of deposit stock will be below the FSCS limit lowering the risk of large-scale outflow in a stress scenario. Liability origination will be spread across the year by flexing the rate relative to competition to ensure no more than 12% of the existing liability stock contractually matures in a given month. Daily applications and new business will be tracked to manage the future maturity profile. At maturity, tailored retention schemes focused on a simple experience and consistently fair rates will help retain deposits and result in lower behavioural outflows. The terms of the deposit will clearly state that upon redemption a deposit will be rolled over for the same term at a rate that will be communicated to the depositor 4–6 weeks before the maturity of the deposit, and the depositor will be given an option to either switch to another deposit product or withdraw the proceeds altogether.

2.6 Competitive Advantages

The directors believe Orchard has the following key differentiators vis-à-vis its competitors:

- Orchard has been operating in the insurance premium finance market and professions finance market since 2002. In that time its senior management team has remained in place and developed strong and trusted relationships with its existing clients and with other key parties in its markets. The length of time that Orchard has operated in the market provides confidence to insurance brokers and professional firms that Orchard is a constant and reliable player in the market. This is very important as a number of companies have entered and exited the market since Orchard commenced its business.

- Orchard's senior management team has unparalleled experience in the premium finance and professions finance market. Unlike the management teams in the other leading competitors in the market, the management team has been exclusively focused on its markets since 2002 and in the case of some of the team since the late 1990s. Again, this depth of expertise provides a high level of confidence to insurance brokers and professional firms seeking a funding partner.
- The group understands the needs and requirements of insurance broker firms and professional firms and offers a fully tailored solution to the target market. The larger dominant market players are less focused on the smaller end of the lending market creating an opportunity for the group.
- Orchard is in regular contact with all its clients and strives to ensure that a high-quality service is consistently delivered. The larger players in both the insurance premium finance and professions finance market have in the past provided limited services to certain parts of the market allowing the group to build up a loyal customer base.
- The group's in-house premium finance product is unique and enables insurance brokers to take greater control and provide unparalleled service in the provision of premium finance to their clients. This product is very attractive to well capitalised insurance brokers who wish to ensure the highest levels of service are provided to their clients. No other company offers this product to insurance brokers and the product is attractive to some of the largest insurance brokers in the UK.
- The group does not impose any fees or require minimum levels of business for the availability of its facility to insurance brokers or professional firms.
- The group's online platform has the functionality to support white-label and direct financing and is simple to navigate and use. The system enables quick and efficient data entry for its insurance broker and professional firm clients, effective credit and affordability assessment and efficient production of compliant legal documentation for a client to sign either by hand or electronically.
- Senior management of the group is involved in all aspects of the business and in particular maintain close and strong relationships with the group's clients. The personal involvement of senior management in the needs and concerns of the group's client base is very important to the clients of the group. The group has always regarded itself as an SME and is therefore sympathetic to the needs and aspirations of insurance brokers and professional firms, many of which are themselves SMEs.
- The ability, given the pricing of its lending, to offer consistently attractive rates on a simple and transparent deposit range to raise and retain the requisite deposit base to develop its business.

Due to the simplicity of its lending products Orchard will provide transparency and openness to depositors and all other stakeholders on all aspects of its business.

3 Business Viability

The Bank intends to provide unsecured short-term credit to limited companies, partnerships and consumers in the insurance premium finance market and the professions finance market, funding itself with a strong capital base and a stable stock of retail deposits. The loan book is projected to grow at a steady pace (from c. £33m at the end of year 1 to c. £93m at the end of year 5) and provide a commercially viable net interest margin (c. 14%-15%). Robust underwriting and guarantees from introducing insurance brokers and professional firms are expected to keep the loan loss rate low (assumed at 1% compared to the historic experience of very low levels of losses in the past eight years). Operating overheads in salaries and investments in better systems and controls are projected to grow from c. £2.8m in year 1 to £4.8m in year 5, allowing the capital resources to grow from c. £14.8m at the end of year 1 to c. £26.2m at the end of the fifth year of the business plan. Consequently, no plan for additional capital raising has been included in the projections.

3.1 Projections

The base financial operating plan is based on a fully operative bank and the first year equates to the first twelve months as a deposit taking bank. Hence, the plan is not presented in calendar years but presented from the time of bank inception.

As Orchard currently runs a profitable financing business, even after absorbing the additional investments and expenditure during the Bank building phase it is expected that the Bank will be profitable in its first year of operation. The high-level assumptions behind the projections are as follows:

- The direct insurance business will start from a small base of £5.4m in year 1 and will grow during the five years of projection horizon to £45.4m at the end of the period.
- The corporate insurance business where Orchard has a more established presence in the market will start at £19.5m in year 1 and will grow to £28.5m at the end of the period.
- The professional fee financing business will grow from a base of £8.1m in year 1 to £19.9m at the end of the period.
- Deposit issuance will start at £1.7m per month (c.71 accounts per month) and will continue for a year to replace existing bank facilities and total £21m at the end of Year 1 of the Plan. Net new deposits will total £10m in each of Years 2 and 3 of the Plan and then rise to £13m in Year 4 and £22m in year 5 of the Plan.
- Only 1 year and 2 year fixed rate deposits will be offered at 60:40 split, respectively.
- At the end of the projection horizon the balance sheet will have £93m of loans and £12m of liquid assets and £1m of fixed and other assets that will be funded by £76m of deposits, £4m of other trade creditors and £26m of shareholder capital.

Orchard's Board reviewed the base operating plan on the 30th May 2019 and provided feedback. The final plan was approved by the Board on 16 July, 2019.

3.1.1 Loan Book Growth

Based on the origination experience of Orchard's management team it is expected that the Bank will grow the direct insurance business at the fastest pace as this is the largest segment of the insurance premium financing market. This is followed by moderate projected growth in the accountancy business and the corporate insurance business. Lending interest rates are expected to remain steady.

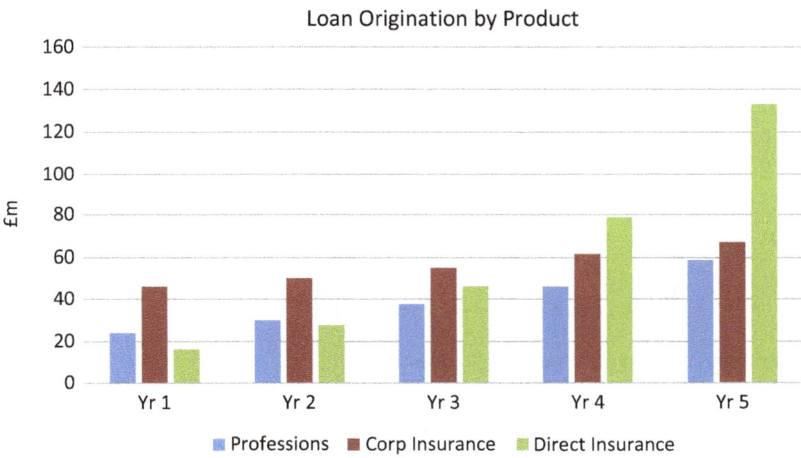

Figure 5: Loan origination volume (by loan type).

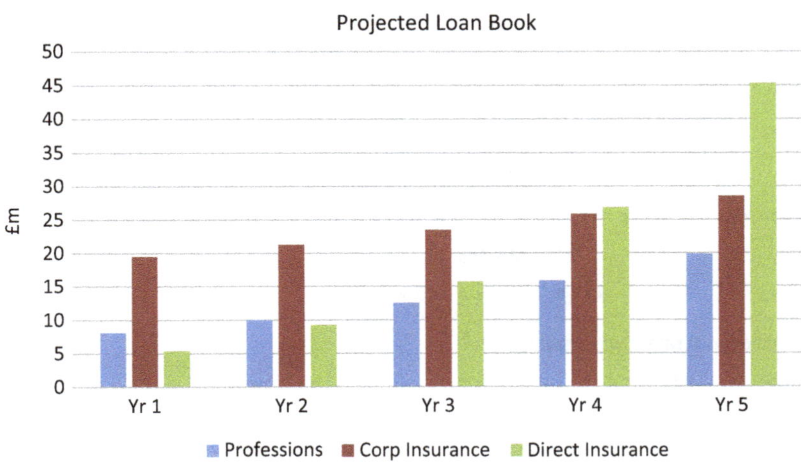

Figure 6: Projected loan book on balance sheet (by loan type).

3.1.2 Deposit Book Growth

The deposit book is projected to grow from £21m at the end of year 1 to c. £76m at the end of year 5. The liquidity strategy is maintained at low risk by offering only 1 year and 2 year fixed rate deposits that are contractually not withdrawable before maturity. The deposit rates are projected to go up in line with Bank of England base rate projections.

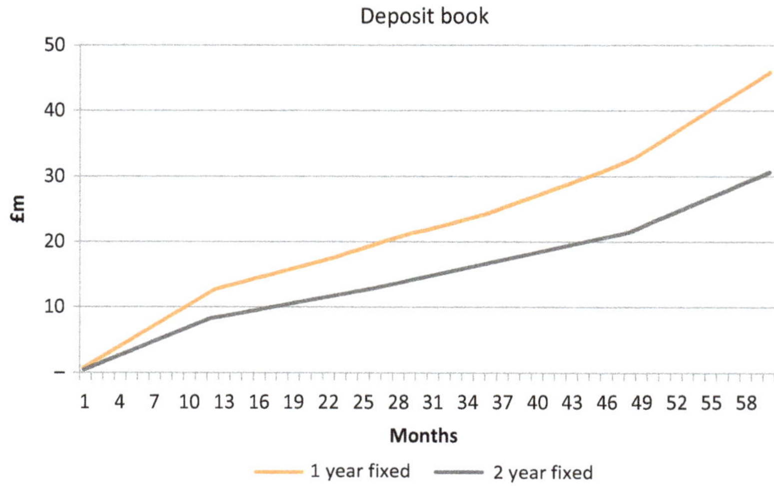

Figure 7: Projected deposit book on balance sheet (by deposit type).

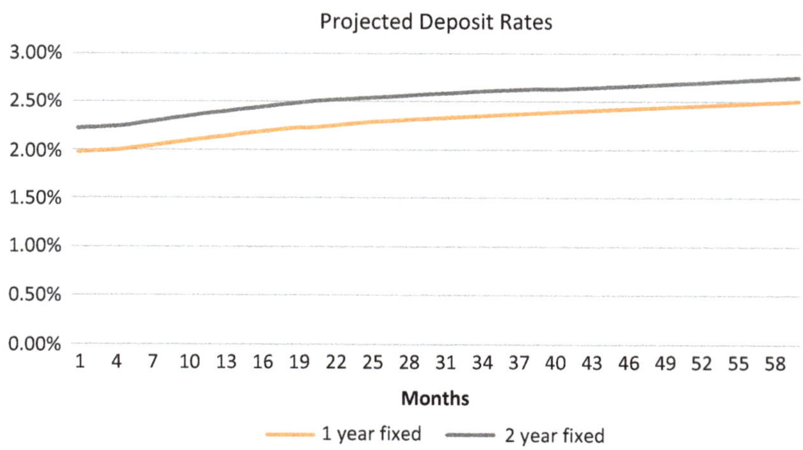

Figure 8: Projected deposit rates (by deposit type).

3.1.3 Income Statement, Balance Sheet & KPIs

The base financial operating plan that was reviewed by the Board on the 30 May 2019 and approved on the 16 July 2019 is presented below.

The financial operating plan is based on a fully operative bank and the first year equates to the first twelve months as a bank. Hence, the plan is not presented in calendar years but presented from the time of the Bank being able to take deposits.

Table 7: Orchard Projected Financials.

£'000

Income Statement	**Actual 2018**	**Plan Year 1**	**Plan Year 2**	**Plan Year 3**	**Plan Year 4**	**Plan Year 5**	**CAGR**
Interest Receivable	5,174	4,887	6,370	8,175	10,817	14,856	23.5%
Interest payable	(535)	(396)	(591)	(870)	(1,198)	(1,702)	26.0%
Net interest income	4,639	4,491	5,779	7,305	9,619	13,154	23.2%
Administration expenses	(2,746)	(2,870)	(3,267)	(3,651)	(4,184)	(4,820)	11.9%
Impairment charges	0	(312)	(393)	(498)	(653)	(888)	
Operating profit before tax	**1,893**	**1,308**	**2,119**	**3,156**	**4,782**	**7,446**	**31.5%**
Corporation tax	(381)	(257)	(403)	(600)	(909)	(1,415)	
Profit after tax	**1,512**	**1,051**	**1,716**	**2,556**	**3,874**	**6,031**	**31.9%**
Dividends	(642)	(210)	(343)	(511)	(775)	(1,206)	
Retained earnings	**870**	**841**	**1,373**	**2,045**	**3,099**	**4,825**	

£'000

Balance Sheet	**2018**	**Year 1**	**Year 2**	**Year 3**	**Year 4**	**Year 5**
Assets						
Loans and advances	31,084	32,762	40,475	51,531	67,917	92,953
Cash at bank	1,286	1,000	1,000	1,000	1,000	1,000
Liquid asset buffer	0	3,867	7,612	8,740	8,717	10,972
Fixed assets	59	483	556	621	681	737
Other assets	60	158	158	158	158	158
Total assets	**32,489**	**38,270**	**49,801**	**62,049**	**78,472**	**105,819**
Liabilities						
Customer deposits	16,008	21,000	31,000	41,000	54,000	76,000
Bank funding						
Trade creditors	2,051	2,051	2,051	2,051	2,051	2,051
Tax liabilities	339	257	403	600	909	1,415
Non-current liabilities	54	84	96	103	118	134
Total liabilities	**18,452**	**23,393**	**33,550**	**43,754**	**57,078**	**79,600**

Table 7 (continued)

Balance Sheet	2018	Year 1	Year 2	Year 3	Year 4	Year 5
Equity						
Share capital	214	214	214	214	214	214
Share premium	8,692	8,692	8,692	8,692	8,692	8,692
Merger reserves	891	891	891	891	891	891
Retained earnings	3,370	4,240	5,081	6,454	8,498	11,597
Current year retained earnings	870	841	1,373	2,045	3,099	4,825
Total equity	**14,037**	**14,878**	**16,251**	**18,295**	**21,394**	**26,219**
Total equity and liabilities	**32,489**	**38,270**	**49,801**	**62,049**	**78,472**	**105,819**

Table 8: Orchard Projected KPIs.

Key Ratios	unit	Year 1	Year 2	Year 3	Year 4	Year 5
Average interest earning assets (monthly weighted)	£'000	31,230	38,805	49,091	64,238	87,249
Gross interest margin	%	15.6%	16.4%	17%	16.8%	17.0%
Average cost of funds	%	2.1%	2.3%	2.4%	2.5%	2.6%
NIM	%	14.4%	14.9%	14.9%	15.0%	15.1%
Cost:Income ratio	%	64%	57%	50%	44%	37%
PAT growth YoY	%	-30%	63%	49%	52%	56%
Dividend per share (pence per share)	pence	1.0	1.6	2.4	3.6	5.6
ROE (PAT)	%	7.1%	10.6%	14.0%	18.1%	23.0%

The underlying business drivers, with volume assumptions and key financial assumptions are tabled below:

Table 9: Orchard Projected Volumes.

Base	Actual 2018	Plan Year 1	Plan Year 2	Plan Year 3	Plan Year 4	Plan Year 5
New Lending (£'000)	68,730	86,000	107,800	139,400	186,709	259,576
Lending growth %		25%	25%	29%	34%	39%
Lending stock (£'000)	31,084	32,762	40,475	51,531	67,917	92,953
Lending interest rate (wt. average)		14.53%	14.46%	14.40%	14.32%	14.26%
Corporate Insurance Loan stock (£'000)		19,484	21,432	23,575	25,933	28,526
Average loan size (£'000)		172	172	172	172	172
Number accounts (vols)		113	125	137	151	166
Direct Insurance loan stock (£'000)		5,124	8,849	15,213	26,057	44,517
Average loan size (£'000)		0.48	0.48	0.48	0.48	0.48
Number accounts (vols)		10,675	18,436	31,695	54,285	92,745

Table 9 (continued)

Base	**Actual 2018**	**Plan Year 1**	**Plan Year 2**	**Plan Year 3**	**Plan Year 4**	**Plan Year 5**
Accountancy Loan stock (£'000)		8,155	10,193	12,742	15,927	19,909
Average loan size (£'000)		5.10	5.10	5.10	5.10	5.10
Number accounts (vols)		1,599	1,999	2,498	3,123	3,904
New Deposits (inc rollovers) (£'000)		21,000	22,600	37,000	41,600	66,800
Deposit stock (£'000)		21,000	31,000	41,000	54,000	76,000
Deposit interest rate (wt. average)*		2.15%	2.32%	2.43%	2.51%	2.58%
Average deposit (£'000)		24	24	24	24	24
Number of deposit accounts stock (vol)		875	1,292	1,708	2,250	3,167
Number of new deposits		875	942	1,542	1,733	2,783
Number of new deposits per day		3	4	6	7	11

*Based on the Bank of England inflation report, February 2019.

Table 10: Key Financial Assumptions.

Base	**Plan Year 1**	**Plan Year 2**	**Plan Year 3**	**Plan Year 4**	**Plan Year 5**
Annual losses % receivables (IFRS 9)	1.0%	1.0%	1.0%	1.0%	1.0%
Base rate (end of year)	0.9%	1.0%	1.1%	1.2%	1.3%
Corporation tax rate	19.7%	19.0%	19.0%	19.0%	19.0%

*Based on the Bank of England inflation report, February 2019.

4 LCR Reporting

4.1 LCR reporting

Orchard's risk appetite for its LCR is 150%. This will be regularly monitored and reported to senior management and form part of the Exco monthly management report.

4.2 Liquidity Asset Buffer

All surplus cash, after holding a maximum of £1m in Orchard's bank account, will be held in a Bank of England Reserve Account. In the interim before the account is set up, surplus cash will be invested in short term (<3 months maturity) UK Government Gilts. This will represent the Liquid Asset Buffer (LAB) that will provide liquidity resources even in severe yet plausible stress scenarios.

4.3 Liquidity Coverage Ratio (LCR)

The key elements to calculate LCR are the stock of high quality liquid assets, cash inflows and outflows arising from Orchard's base plan projections.

Orchard more than adequately covers the liquidity risks reflected by its simple business model. Orchard will maintain a liquidity buffer that ensures an LCR that is materially higher than the PRA's requirement of 100%.

Table 11: LCR calculation.

£'000

Category	Asset / Liability	Split (>85k)	Run off rate	%age <30days	Plan Year 1	Plan Year 2	Plan Year 3	Plan Year 4	Plan Year 5
Liquid asset	Liquid asset buffer		na		3,867	7,612	8,740	8,717	10,972
Liquid asset	Cash at bank		na		1,000	1,000	1,000	1,000	1,000
Outflow	less stable retail deposits insured	100%	20%	12%	504	744	984	1,296	1,824
Inflows	loan repayments (P&I) direct		50%	11%	302	513	873	1,484	2,523
Inflows	loan repayments (P&I) corporate		50%	11%	1,082	1,191	1,310	1,441	1,585
Inflows	loan repayments (P&I) accountant		50%	11%	453	566	708	885	1,106
	Subtotal inflows				1,837	2,270	2,890	3,809	5,213
	Stock of HQLA				3,867	7,612	8,740	8,717	10,972
	Cash outflow				504	744	984	1,296	1,824
	Cash inflow (capped at 75% of outflows)				378	558	738	972	1,368
	LCR				**3069%**	**4093%**	**3553%**	**2690%**	**2406%**

Orchard's modelling demonstrates that Orchard's LCR will always be materially above the regulatory minimum requirement of 100%. This is driven by the very short tenor of the loans, which generates a significant amount of cash inflows and the level of HQLA maintained by the business. The inflows have been restricted to a maximum of 75% of the outflows.

- A 20% run-off rate has been used for deposit balances, in line with Article 28, paragraph 1 of the Delegated Act.

- A 12% percentage < 30 days has been used for deposit balances, in line with the maximum maturities in one month allowed in the treasury policy.
- A 50% run-off rate has been used for loan repayments in line with Article 32 paragraph 3(a) of the Delegated Act.
- An 11% percentage < 30 days has been used for loan repayments, reflecting a minimum 9 month term.

The liquidity buffer will be held in a Bank of England Reserve Account.

The Board's view is that there is no need to hold any additional liquidity buffer over and above that calculated under Pillar 1. This is due to:
1. Orchard's simple short-term amortising lending products;
2. The fact that all deposits are below the FSCS limit;
3. The fact that Orchard's Risk Appetite for liquidity is considerably higher than the minimum regulatory requirements.

Orchard plans to raise all its deposits through postal applications, which it believes will enhance the stickiness of its deposits in comparison to on-line deposits. Orchard also believes that postal deposits will reduce IT risk and control burdens on the new bank and help in providing more visibility and control over the quantum of new deposits placed at Orchard.

5 Liquidity Risk Assessment

5.1 Overall Liquidity

Orchard's liquidity requirements have been set by assessing the output of a number of stress tests undertaken on the Base Financial Operating Plan.

There is no seasonality in the core insurance premium funding market. Other non-core markets, such as school fees and football club season ticket loans, are seasonal in nature but make up less than 5% of the portfolio.

5.2 Evaluation of Intra-Day Liquidity Risk

Intra-day liquidity will be monitored by a regular cash report produced by the Finance team in conjunction with the CFO.

On the new deposit side of its business, the savings module of a proven software house, Mutual Vision Limited will be implemented, subject to due diligence. This software is used by a number of small building societies and banks to manage their deposit taking business.

Orchard will have a policy of maintaining liquidity equal to a minimum of 3 days of its projected loan outflows held as 'Cash at Bank' with Orchard's clearing bank. The first year's lending is assumed to be £86m. This equates to £1m for 3 business days (£86m / 52 weeks / 5 days * 3 days).

The Finance team will be responsible for real-time monitoring of intra-day liquidity risk. The Finance team will be mandated to inform the CFO immediately should there be any threat that the liquidity coverage ratio will be breached.

5.3 Evaluation of Liquidity Buffer

The Board approved ratio of HQLA to deposits has been set at 14%, which provides adequate liquidity as observed through the actual LCR and NSFR. The liquid assets buffer will be held in a Bank of England Reserve Account. Additional liquidity of at least £1m will be held as 'Cash at Bank' with Orchard's clearing bank.

6 Inherent Funding Risk Assessment

6.1 Evaluation of Risks to the Stability of the Funding Profile

Orchard has used the Net Stable Funding Ratio to analyse the stability of its funding profile.

Available Stable Funding is measured based on the broad characteristics of the relative stability of Orchard's funding sources, including contractual maturities of all its liabilities.

Required Stable Funding is measured based on the broad characteristics of the liquidity risk profile of Orchard's assets.

Orchard's Net Stable Funding Ratio is materially higher than regulatory requirements as demonstrated in the table below.

Orchard's reliance upon undated capital and term deposits for funding together with the short-term nature of its loans and its conservative cash position means that it comfortably exceeds the required NSFR limits in all time horizons.

Table 12: Net Stable Funding Ratio Calculations.

Asset / Liability Category	Asset and liability allocation						Available Stable Funding						£'000
	Actual 2018	**Plan Year 1**	**Plan Year 2**	**Plan Year 3**	**Plan Year 4**	**Plan Year 5**		**Actual 2018**	**Plan Year 1**	**Plan Year 2**	**Plan Year 3**	**Plan Year 4**	**Plan Year 5**
Capital	14,037	14,878	16,251	18,295	21,394	26,219	**100%**	14,037	14,878	16,251	18,295	21,394	26,219
Deposits > 1 year	0	8,400	4,000	12,400	9,200	21,200	**100%**	0	8,400	4,000	12,400	9,200	21,200
Stable retail demand deposits	0	0	0	0	0	0	**95%**	0	0	0	0	0	0
Stable retail term deposits <1 year	0	0	0	0	0	0	**95%**	0	0	0	0	0	0
Type 2 retail demand deposits	0	0	0	0	0	0	**90%**	0	0	0	0	0	0
Type 2 retail term deposits < 1 year	0	12,600	27,000	28,600	44,800	54,800	**90%**	0	11,340	24,300	25,740	40,320	49,320
Other funding > 12 months maturity	0	0	0	0	0	0	**100%**	0	0	0	0	0	0
Other funding > 6 months maturity	0	0	0	0	0	0	**50%**	0	0	0	0	0	0
Other funding < 6months maturity	16,008	0	0	0	0	0	**0%**	0	0	0	0	0	0
All other liabilities	2,444	2,393	2,550	2,754	3,078	3,600	**0%**	0	0	0	0	0	0
Total equity and liabilities	**32,489**	**38,270**	**49,801**	**62,049**	**78,472**	**105,819**							

(continued)

Table 12 (continued)

Asset / Liability Category	**Asset and liability allocation**						**Available Stable Funding**						**£'000**
	Actual 2018	**Plan Year 1**	**Plan Year 2**	**Plan Year 3**	**Plan Year 4**	**Plan Year 5**		**Actual 2018**	**Plan Year 1**	**Plan Year 2**	**Plan Year 3**	**Plan Year 4**	**Plan Year 5**
							Available Stable Funding	**14,037**	**34,618**	**44,551**	**56,435**	**70,914**	**96,739**
							Required Stable Funding						
Liquid asset buffer	1,286	3,867	7,612	8,740	8,717	10,972	**5%**	64	193	381	437	436	549
Cash at bank	0	1,000	1,000	1,000	1,000	1,000	**15%**	0	150	150	150	150	150
Unencumbered loans	9,601	32,762	40,475	51,531	67,917	92,953	**65%**	6,240	21,296	26,308	33,495	44,146	60,419
Encumbered loans (warehouse facility)	21,344	0	0	0	0	0	**100%**	21,344	0	0	0	0	0
	0	0	0	0	0	0	**100%**	0	0	0	0	0	0
Non-performing loans	0	312	393	498	653	888	**100%**	0	312	393	498	653	888
Other assets	100	483	556	621	681	737	**100%**	100	483	556	621	681	737
	32,331	38,425	50,036	62,389	78,967	106,550	**Required Stable Funding**	**27,749**	**22,435**	**27,788**	**35,201**	**46,065**	**62,743**
							NSFR	**51%**	**154.3%**	**160.3%**	**160.3%**	**153.9%**	**154.2%**

7 Risk Management Assessment

7.1 Assessment of Risk Strategy and Risk Appetite

7.1.1 Risk Appetite

Orchard will take a conservative approach to liquidity management. Surplus funds will be placed with Orchard's clearing bank as 'Cash at Bank' up to £1m and any excess, will be held in a Bank of England Reserve Account and in the interim before the account is set up, will be held in short term (<3 months maturity) UK Government Gilts.

Orchard's cash reserves will at all times be in excess of that required by relevant regulatory rules.

Orchard will ensure that it maintains adequate liquidity resources to meet its maturing obligations at all times, as and when they fall due. The primary methods for managing liquidity risk are listed below:

7.1.2 Maintenance of Cash Balances

Orchard will maintain a cash balance of £1m in Orchard's clearing bank as 'Cash at Bank' and hold surplus cash in the Bank of England Reserve Account. In the interim, before getting the Bank of England Reserve account opened, surplus funds will be invested in short term (<3 months maturity) UK gilts to fulfil the liquidity requirements in respect of holding HQLA.

7.1.3 Cash Buffer

Orchard's liquidity stress-testing methodology and analysis report details the generation and outputs of a range of stress scenarios designed to identify the minimum level of highly liquid assets necessary to counter severe yet plausible stressed scenarios over two time horizons – two weeks and twelve weeks.

Orchard will not offer undrawn committed facilities to its customers. Any stress scenario lasting more than one week is likely to result in a decision to reduce the volume of lending and after one month, the consideration of whether new loans should be suspended.

Given the specific position and operations of Orchard, the liquidity horizons will be two and twelve weeks (10 and 60 working days) respectively.

The table below demonstrates the high level of liquid cash balances that Orchard will maintain over its 3 year plan.

Table 13: Liquidity Ratios to Loans and Deposits.

					£'000
	Plan Year 1	**Plan Year 2**	**Plan Year 3**	**Plan Year 4**	**Plan Year 5**
Funding Source					
Deposits	21,000	31,000	41,000	54,000	76,000
Equity	14,878	16,251	18,295	21,394	26,219
Bank Loans	-	-	-	-	-
Total Funding	**35,878**	**47,251**	**59,295**	**75,394**	**102,219**
Funding Consumption					
Loans	**32,762**	**40,475**	**51,531**	**67,917**	**92,953**
Liquid assets					
Cash at bank	1,000	1,000	1,000	1,000	1,000
Liquid asset buffer	3,867	7,612	8,740	8,717	10,972
Other Corp. bonds	-	-	-	-	-
Total liquid assets	**4,867**	**8,612**	**9,740**	**9,717**	**11,972**
Ratios					
% Liquid Assets to Loans	15%	21%	19%	14%	13%
% Liquid Assets to Deposits	23%	28%	24%	18%	16%
% HQLA to Deposits	18%	25%	21%	16%	14%
NSFR	154%	160%	160%	154%	154%
LCR	3069%	4093%	3553%	2690%	2406%

7.1.4 Survival Days

A survival horizon is a time period during which Orchard is capable of meeting its obligations as and when these obligations fall due and has been included in its liquidity risk appetite. Although the regulatory minimum is a 30 day horizon, the Board has set a risk appetite of 90 days. Orchard's projections indicate that it would at all times have adequate liquidity to meet the combined liquidity stress scenarios for a period 90 days.

7.1.5 Risk Targets Based on Risk Drivers

In addition to the foregoing measures overseen by the Board, Orchard has also set measures and targets to be regularly monitored by the Finance Team and ALCO, based on the key liquidity risks outlined in section 10.

7.1.6 Liquidity Key Risk Indicators (KRIs)

Orchard will monitor the performance of its risk appetite statement through its Primary and Secondary key risk indicators where the key liquidity risk metrics are measured against green/amber/red criteria to ensure that necessary action is taken, where appropriate. The Firm's KRIs are set out in the tables below.

Table 14: Primary Liquidity Risk Metrics.

Limit category		Target	Early warning indicator (Amber)	Trigger (Red)
Liquidity	Liquidity Coverage Ratio (LCR PRA min 100%)	150%	125%	110%
	Net Stable Funding Ratio (NSFR 100%)	125%	110%	105%
	Survival Horizon under stress (PRA min 30days)	90 days	75 days	60 days
	HQLAs to Deposits	14%	12%	8%
	Increase in cost of fundsfor deposits above the average of top ten providers on Money.co.uk website	Av. Of top ten providers for 1 year and 2 year fixed rate deposits	= or >100 basis points	= >200 basis points

Table 15: Secondary Risk Metrics.

Metric	Trigger (Red)
Deposit Inflows as proportion of budgeted inflows	Min 70%, Max 130%
Retention rate of maturing fixed term deposits	Min 50%
Proportion of deposits which are 'high risk'	Max 5%
Number of payment systems	Min 2
Savings Operational Trigger per month in Year 1 of the plan	Postal applications volume >75 (value – £1.8m) Web application form downloads >300

8 Governance & Risk

8.1 Board Composition

The directors recognise the importance of sound corporate governance and comply with the QCA Corporate Governance Code (as devised by the QCA in consultation with a number of significant institutional small company investors). In addition, the PRA and FCA set standards for Board Governance in Banks, which Orchard will comply with.

Orchard recognises the concerns that the PRA has over 'dominant individuals' on bank boards and has put together a committee structure and recruited suitable INED's to help mitigate this risk. The Board of the Bank will comprise five directors of which two will be executives and three will be independent non-executives. The Board reflects a blend of different experience and backgrounds.

The objective of the Board will be to enhance the long-term success of the Bank by developing a sustainable business model. This will be supported by approving and setting strategy, risk appetite and culture in line with the business model and in light of changing business opportunities, environment and risk.

The Board will delegate the day to day implementation of the strategy, business plans, policies, procedures and risk appetite within the approved policy statements to the Executive Committee and it will be the responsibility of the Board to monitor the overall performance of the business. In addition, the risk management framework and control environment will enable the Board (through the oversight of the Audit and Risk Committees) to gain assurance that it is operating as designed and within the tolerances set by its risk appetite.

Orchard has a full and detailed Corporate Governance Policy, which will be finalised during Mobilisation.

Brief biographies of the directors are shown in Table 16 below.

Board roles and responsibilities are detailed in the table 18 below.

Table 16: Brief biography of the directors.

Name	Board Membership	Brief Biography
	Independent Non-Executive Chairman	
Ravi Takhar	Chief Executive Officer	Mr Ravi Takhar has over 25 years' experience in the acquisition, growth, financing and disposal of financial businesses. Mr Takhar founded the business in 2002 and has led the growth of the UK business to its current size. Prior to creating the group, Ravi was an investment banker and Head of Financial Services investment at Nikko, the Japanese investment bank, from 1998 to 2002 as well as Chairman of Mortgages PLC, the mortgage lender. Mr Takhar was also Head of Mortgage Principal Finance at Investec Bank PLC from 2005 to 2008. He qualified as a banking solicitor at Clifford Chance, a leading international law firm, and has an MA from the University of Oxford.
	Chief Financial Officer	
	Non-Executive Director	
	Non-Executive Director	

Table 17: Brief biography of the CRO.

Name	Senior Management Role	Brief Biography
	Chief Risk Officer	

Table 18: Orchard Funding Group PLC – Board Roles & Responsibilities.

Role	Key Responsibilities	Appointment
Chief Executive and Board Director SMF1 SMF 3 SMF 24	The CEO is responsible for: – effective day to day management of the business – operating the business in accordance with board approved strategies, plans and policies – ensuring an effective systems and control environment – managing overall enterprise risk and returns – setting the corporate culture – primarily responsible for the relationship with the relevant regulatory bodies and for all other stakeholders in the business – compliance with Board Risk Appetite Statement The CEO is Chairman of the Executive Committee and member of ALCO and Credit Committee. The CEO is also responsible for ensuring that the board members are: – able to sufficiently challenge the executive and understand the business model – provided with a full understanding of higher risk activities and products – in receipt of appropriate management information to be able to carry out their oversight role The CEO will have oversight responsibility for HR and marketing. The CEO also has oversight responsibility for: – the effective development of the bank's retail savings business in terms of its administration functions, ensuring that high standards of performance and service are achieved at all times and that it operates at all times within the policies and parameters set by the board – ensuring that all staff members within the retail savings business act at all times in compliance with the letter and the spirit of all laws and regulations applying to the business The CEO also holds primary responsibility for: – management, stability, security and effectiveness of the systems and communications used in the bank – operating within parameters and budgets set by the Board and the Executive Committee – ensuring the Bank remains appropriately positioned to address its business needs, provide operational resilience, security risks and to respond to identified opportunities and threats relevant to IT and Communications	Ravi Takhar

Table 18 (continued)

Role	Key Responsibilities	Appointment
	– managing the secure delivery of the bank's website and email communications. – Business Continuity and Disaster Recovery Plan, maintaining it up to date at all times and ensuring it is subject to appropriate and regular testing – Bank-wide project management – Outsourcing arrangements – Facilities management	
Chief Financial Officer and Board Director SMF2, SMF3	The CFO has overall responsibility for: – overseeing the Finance and Treasury functions of the Bank and ensuring that each operates within the parameters and policies set by the Board and Executive Committee – primary accountability for the quality of the business-wide financial and management information – all statutory and regulatory reporting – oversight of the principal financial systems and controls of the business – the preparation of the ILAAP, ICAAP, Recovery Plan and Resolution Plan – the financial and treasury related risks of the Bank on a day to day basis including capital management, liquidity management and compliance with IFRS. – managing the production of and present the medium term financial plan for approval to the Board – compliance with Board Risk Appetite Statement As a member of the Executive Committee the CFO is responsible for contributing to overall direction of the business in terms of its strategies, performance, systems and controls. The CFO is a member of the Executive Committee and Credit Committee and Chair of ALCO. Working with the CEO, the CFO will take primary responsibility for the delivery of the bank's deposit strategy, ensuring that the Bank achieves the right mix of funding across its target customer segments and at an acceptable cost of funds. The CFO is also responsible for: – the production of all financially related statutory and regulatory returns in accordance with prescribed timetables – production of timely management information, pulling this together from across all areas of the bank – operation of the payments and reconciliations of the Bank which is a key area of control – ensuring that finance operations function within Board and Executive Committee approved parameters and policies	

Table 18 (continued)

Role	Key Responsibilities	Appointment
CRO SMF4, SMF 16 & 17	The CRO has primary responsibility to the Board on the quality of the Bank's overall risk management framework. He is a key link between the Board and the business with the ability to translate what is at times highly technical and often detailed reporting of risk into high level information for the Board to understand and interpret at a strategic level. The CRO attends all the executive committees of the Bank providing internal challenge and is a Member of ALCO and Credit Committee. As a member of the Executive Committee the CRO is responsible for contributing to the overall direction of the business in terms of its strategies, performance, systems and controls. In addition to enterprise-wide risk management, the CRO has primary oversight responsibility for: – legal and compliance (including conduct risk) – financial crime prevention – fraud management – Credit risk and credit systems – Operational risk – compliance with Board Risk Appetite Statement The CRO will be responsible for: – ensuring the Bank meets all its statutory and regulatory requirements relating to the operation of the Bank other than the financial ones undertaken by the Finance Director and CFO – ensuring compliant procedures are in place to enable the business operations to comply with current legislation and regulations – taking responsibility for the effective management, measurement and monitoring of exposure to Conduct Risk – monitoring compliance with Complaints Handling and Treating Customers Fairly – documenting and reporting results of legal and compliance monitoring to the Board, Audit& Risk and Executive Committees as appropriate – compliance with Board Risk Appetite Statement He also acts as Money Laundering Reporting Officer (MLRO). As MLRO he has responsibility for: – ensuring all statutory and regulatory responsibilities are discharged on behalf of the bank – the implementation of and compliance with anti-money laundering procedures and policies – receiving and reviewing suspicious transaction reports and advising SOCA as necessary	

Table 18 (continued)

Role	Key Responsibilities	Appointment
	He is responsible for developing and delivering all compliance training requirements. His legal responsibilities relate to taking primary responsibility for: – reviewing all terms and conditions of products, third party contracts for services and business relationships and ensuring that they are appropriate within the context of the board approved policies and parameters and applicable laws and regulations.	
Chairman (Board) & Chairman of Noms and Rems INED SMF 9 SMF 12 SMF 13	Responsible for leading the Board and ensuring effective direction and challenge for Management Setting Board Agenda (in consultation with Management) Chair of Noms and Rems Committee Setting tone from the top in terms of the Culture of the Organisation Board training agenda Board evaluation (annual) Appraisal of performance of Board members and CEO Ensuring appropriate balance of skills and diversity of Board	
Chair of Audit INED SMF 10	Responsible for ensuring an effective Audit Committee operating in the interests of all stakeholders Ensuring regulatory and listing responsibilities are discharged effectively Audit Committee Agenda (in consultation with Management) Oversight of Internal Audit (including assessing performance in conjunction with CEO) Liaising with External Auditors Audit Committee Evaluation (annual)	
Chair of Risk INED SMF 11	Responsible for ensuring an effective Risk Committee in accordance with its terms of reference Setting Risk Committee Agenda Oversight of CRO (including assessing performance in conjunction with CEO) Risk Committee evaluation (Annual) Responsible for the maintenance of an appropriate Whistleblowing process for customers, staff and other stakeholders of the business.	

8.2 Improvement of Governance Structure

The corporate governance structure has been enhanced to prepare for Orchard becoming a bank as follows:

1. The appointment of an independent non-executive Chairman and independent non-executive directors with many years of recent and current banking experience in SMF designated roles;

2. The independent non-executive directors comprising a majority of the Board and supported by an appropriate quorum voting structure;
3. A new Board Risk Committee and continuance of the Board Audit Committee and the Board Nominations & Remuneration Committee comprised only of independent non-executive directors.
4. The appointment of a new CFO and new CRO with recent bank experience, who will provide an executive balance to the CEO.
5. The Board will appoint an external party to carry out its internal audit function.
6. The enhancement of the governance structure with more detailed and regular board and committee meetings, supplemented with enhanced regular management information, to ensure effective corporate governance.

The Board is satisfied that the profile and experience of the independent NEDs and the new executive appointments, together with the enhanced corporate governance structure will be provide effective and controlled governance of Orchard as a bank.

8.3 Assessment of Board Skills and Experience

Orchard has been operating in its core market for 17 years and the Board and senior management have a strong understanding of (i) the risks associated with Orchard's regulated activities and (ii) the regulatory requirements which govern the way in which Orchard conducts its regulated activities.

The Board and senior management recognise that, as a Bank, Orchard will be subject to additional regulatory requirements and are confident that they have the experience and skills to ensure compliance with these new obligations. We have undertaken an assessment for the Board and senior management to identify areas where skills and knowledge can be further enhanced.

Orchard's board is now comprised of senior individuals with many years of recent experience in the banking industry. Gaps in the skills and experience of individual directors and senior managers will continue to be addressed through an ongoing training program. The Skills and Experience Matrix in the table below summarises the current assessment of the Board.

8.3.1 Skills and Experience Matrix

Table 19: Orchard Funding Group PLC – Board Skills Matrix.

Code: 1-Specialist experience (eg executive function holder within past 5 years CRO, CFO, CIO etc) 2- Good Experience (but not specialist function holder in past 5 years) 3- Knowledgeable but no direct experience (capable of development with support/training) 4- Not considered essential as sufficiently covered by others	Ravi Takhar CEO	CFO	CRO	INED Chairman	INED Chairman of Audit Committee	INED Chairman of Risk Committee
Risk Management and setting risk appetite	1	3	1	2	2	1
Technology including Business continuity, resilience and security	2	2	2	2	1	2
Treasury management including asset and liability management	1	2	2	2	1	2
Operations and project management	1	2	2	2	2	1
Financial statements and reporting, including regulatory	2	1	4	1	1	2
Prudential and Conduct regulation, including conduct, SYSC, threshold conditions (PRA and FCA), SMCR	1	2	1	1	1	1
Business strategy, including for Orchard's chosen markets	1	2	2	1	2	2
Retail deposits marketing and operations	3	2	2	1	1	2

Table 20: Orchard Funding Group PLC – Board Behaviours Matrix for Performance Evaluation.

Code: 1-Strong requirement 2- Requirement 3- Not required	Ravi Takhar CEO	CFO	CRO	INED Chairman	INED Chairman of Audit Committee	INED Chairman of Risk Committee
Customer Focus	1	1	1	1	1	1
Challenges Executives	NA	NA	NA	1	1	1
Actively participates in debates	1	1	1	1	1	1
Prepares properly for meeting and reads papers	1	1	1	1	1	1
Up to date in own area of expertise	1	1	1	1	1	1
Board Committees Chairman – Leadership qualities/effectiveness/potential	1	1	2	1	1	1

8.4 Board Structure

The Orchard Board at launch of the Bank and during mobilisation will have the following composition:

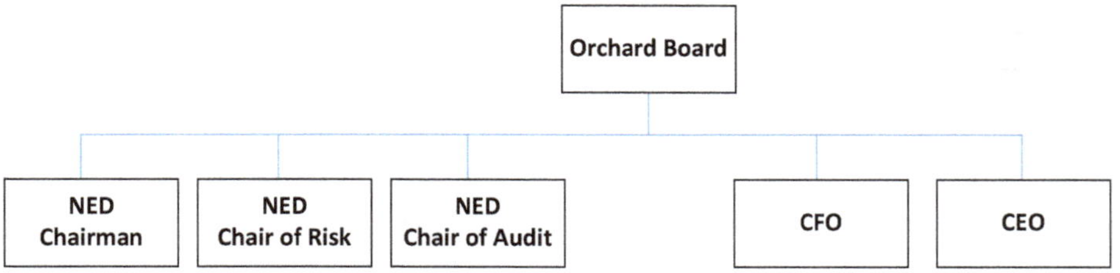

Figure 9: Orchard Board Composition.

8.5 Committee and Management Structure Charts

The following section describes the relationships and functions of the key governance committees proposed for Orchard.

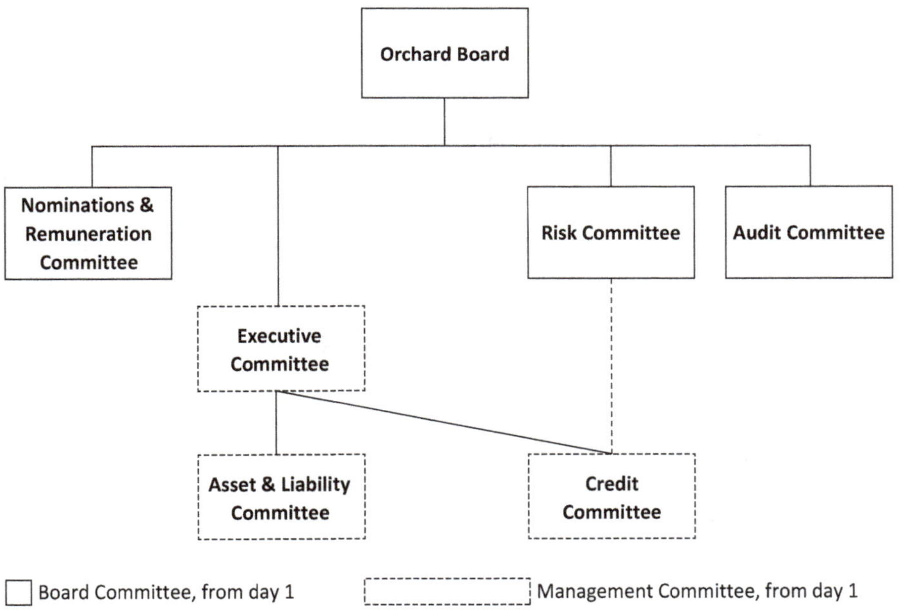

Figure 10: Orchard Governance Committees.

8.6 Governance Framework – Board and Board Sub-Committees

A summary table of the Board and Board Sub-Committees is presented below:

Table 21: Orchard Board and Board Sub-Committees.

Committee	Quorum	Members	Frequency
Board	3(at least 2 INEDs)	Chairman CEO CFO INEDs	Ten times a year, or more frequent if required by the Chairman
Risk Committee	2	Chair of Risk, INEDs (inc Board Chairman) [CEO, CFO and CRO standing invitees]	Four times a year, or more frequent if required by the committee chair
Audit Committee	2	Chair of Audit, INED [Internal Audit, External Audit, Chairman of the Board, CEO, CFO and CRO standing invitees]	Four times a year, or more frequent if required by the committee chair
Nominations & Remuneration Committee	3	Chairman CEO (non-voting) INEDs	At least twice a year, or more frequent if required by committee chair

8.6.1 Board

The Board's primary role is to provide leadership, ensure that the Bank is appropriately managed and deliver long term shareholder value. It sets the strategic objectives and provides direction.

The Board is responsible for managing the Bank on behalf of its shareholders and each Director must act in a manner that he/she considers promotes effective working of the Board and the long term success of the Bank for the benefit of those shareholders, its employees and all of its customers. The Board will meet as necessary, but typically on a monthly basis, with the exception of August and December months (to allow for holidays).

The Board will ensure there are appropriate controls in place and that there is a healthy balance between promoting long term growth and delivering short term performance, but it will place the emphasis on the longer term health and sustainability of the Bank.

The Board delegates responsibility for the day-to-day management of the Bank to the executive management team, led by the Chief Executive and through the Executive Committee. However, certain matters are specifically reserved for the Board and these include the approval, monitoring and review of:

- Setting business strategy, plans and budgets from time to time
- Monitoring business performance and effectiveness
- Oversight of regulatory compliance and internal controls
- Financial statements and significant changes to accounting policies and practices
- Board terms of reference, membership and powers including the appointment and removal of board members
- Principal policies of the Bank, committee terms of reference and the overall governance framework, systems and controls
- Risk appetite, risk management, insurance and mitigation
- Corporate initiatives such as mergers and acquisitions or significant business partnerships.
- Culture, values and attitudes of the management and staff of the Bank towards both its customers and the risks that are taken
- Remuneration, benefits and incentive policy and appointment of senior management
- Regulatory and statutory compliance
- Prudential and regulatory matters including but not limited to ICAAP, ILAAP and RRP.

Board performance will be reviewed at least annually. The Chairman will meet annually with the non-executive directors. The non-executive directors will meet annually to appraise the Chairman's performance.

At each regular scheduled meeting the board will receive reports from the Chief Executive and Chief Financial Officer on the performance, results, strategic developments and initiatives, operating functions, legal, compliance, human resources and corporate development matters.

There will be an annual schedule of rolling agenda items to ensure that all matters are given due consideration and are reviewed at the appropriate point in the financial and regulatory cycle.

Meetings will be structured to ensure that there is sufficient time for consideration and debate of all matters.

8.6.2 Risk Committee

The Committee will assist the Board to manage the risks faced by the Bank and is responsible for the identification, management and mitigation of risk and will review the effectiveness of the risk management and the compliance frameworks of the Bank. The Committee plays an important role in setting the tone and culture that promotes effective risk management across Orchard. The Risk Committee will typically meet quarterly.

8.6.3 Audit Committee

The Committee is responsible for oversight of the systems of internal control in operation in the Bank, the integrity of its financial statements and regulatory reports and the oversight of both external and internal audit. The Audit Committee will meet quarterly.

8.6.4 Nominations and Remuneration Committee

The Committee is responsible for ensuring the recruitment and selection of appropriately qualified experienced and skilled individuals into senior positions within the organisation and the setting of remuneration, rewards and benefits at levels which attract, retain and motivate employees, whilst being affordable and appropriate. The Committee will meet as required, but a minimum of once per year.

The Committee must ensure that the Bank conforms in all respects with the recruitment policies set out in the staff handbook particularly with regard to the avoidance of unfair discrimination in the recruitment of employees and Board members, and also ensuring that it conforms to the CRD IV proposals regarding diversity in board composition.

8.7 Governance Framework –Management Committees

Summary tables of the Management Committees are presented below:

Table 22: Orchard Management Committees.

Committee	Quorum	Members	Frequency
Executive Committee	3	CEOCFO CRO Head of Finance & Operations Head of Credit & Operations	Once a fortnight, or more frequent if required by committee chair
Asset & Liability Committee (ALCO)	3 with CFO	CEO CFOCRO Head of Finance & Operations Head of Credit & Operations	Once a month, or more frequent if required by committee chair
Credit Committee	3 with CRO	CEO CFO CRO Head of Finance & Operations Head of Credit & Operations	Twice a month, or more frequent if required by the committee chair

8.7.1 Executive Committee

The Executive Committee has its authority delegated to it by the Board of Directors. It represents the principal forum for conducting the business of the Bank and takes day to day responsibility for the efficient running of the business. In addition, the Executive Committee is responsible for the formulation and implementation of Board approved strategies and plans. It is responsible for ensuring the performance of the business in accordance with plans. It will review prudential and regulatory matters including but not limited to ICAAP, ILAAP and other reviews.

8.7.2 Asset and Liability Committee

The Asset and Liability Committee's (ALCO's) purpose is to manage the assets and liabilities of the Bank in respect of duration, interest rate and liquidity risk. It is responsible for determining the Bank's strategy in respect to its balance sheet assets, capital, funding and liquidity profiles, seeking to understand and anticipate future market and economic developments affecting the Bank and considering these in the context of the Bank's ILAAP.

8.7.3 Credit Committee

The Credit Committee is the body charged with the transactional credit responsibility for the Bank. It operates within policy parameters approved by the Board in carrying out the approval and monitoring of the credit business of the Bank.

8.8 Board and Committee Membership

Orchard's Board and committee membership is summarised in the table below:

Table 23: Orchard SMR Responsibilities Map.

8.9 SMR Responsibilities

The allocation of Senior Management Regime responsibilities is summarised in the table below:

Table 24: Orchard SMR Responsibilities Map.

8.10 Management of Conflict of Interest of Ravi Takhar as CEO and Majority Shareholder of Orchard

Ravi Takhar has been CEO and majority shareholder of Orchard since its flotation in 2015. In that time, the potential conflict between his actions as CEO and his actions as a shareholder has been managed and controlled by Orchard's governance being comprised of: a Board with 2 independent non-executive directors; a Board Committee structure of Audit & Risk Committee and Remuneration and Nominations Committee, comprising only NEDs.

The management and control of the potential conflicts of interest will be enhanced when Orchard becomes a bank as follows:

1. The appointment of an independent non-executive Chairman and independent non-executive directors with recent and current banking experience;
2. The independent non-executive directors comprising a majority quorum of the Board;
3. A new Board Risk Committee and continuance of the Board Audit Committee and Board Remuneration Committee comprised only of independent non-executive directors.
4. The appointment of a new CFO and new CRO with recent bank experience, who will provide executive balance to the CEO.
5. The enhancement of the governance structure with more detailed and regular board and committee meetings to ensure that potential conflicts are managed in a timely manner.
6. The introduction of a clear and transparent approach to Conflicts of Interest with a register of interests maintained for the Board and Board and Committee procedures which call out any actual or potential conflicts which may arise.

The Board is satisfied that the profile and experience of the independent NEDs and the new executive appointments, together with the enhanced corporate governance structure will be able to manage any potential conflicts of interest between the CEO's position as an executive and majority shareholder of Orchard.

Orchard also recognizes that Ravi Takhar has not held a CEO position at a deposit taking institution, and hence, the composition of the Board, both executive as well as non-executive, has been strengthened to include individuals with strong banking experience.

8.11 Risk Appetite

The level of risk that Orchard is prepared to accept and the tolerance limits around the acceptable risk is set out in the risk appetite. The risk appetite is both qualitative and quantitative and covers the risks identified in the business. These are categorised as level 1 risks, with more granularity under level 2. The identified risks are set out in the table below:

Table 25: Orchard Level 1 and Level 2 Risks.

Level 1	Credit Risk	Financial Risk	Conduct Risk	Strategic Risk	Operational Risk
Level 2	Credit	Financial Reporting and tax Model	Conduct Legal Regulatory Compliance	Strategic	Business continuity Data management Financial crime Fraud Information security (incl. Cyber) People Physical security and safety Third party Transaction processing

The Board is responsible for setting Orchard's risk appetite and delegates the responsibility for the setting of limits and policies and monitoring of processes, systems and reporting to the Risk Committee. Orchard's risk appetite sets out the level of risk that it is willing to accept in pursuit of its business objectives.

Risk appetite statements have been created for each Level 1 and Level 2 Risk category and provide an articulation of Orchard's tolerance for risk in both quantitative measures and qualitative terms. They have been created following discussions among Orchard's executive management and with members of the Risk Committee and the Board. They are used in mapping key risks and assessing their materiality and ultimately underpin Orchard's overall risk management framework.

The risk appetite statements are reviewed formally on an annual basis by the Board as part of budget setting and the review of Orchard's medium-term strategy. They combine a top-down view of Orchard's overall risk capacity with a bottom-up view of the risk profile requested and recommended by the business area (which will be previously discussed and reviewed by the Risk Committee).

Throughout the year all aspects of the risk appetite statement (which will be monitored by the CRO) will be reported to the Risk Committee and Board. In particular, the CRO will be responsible for assessing the impact on Orchard's risk appetite of any changes in circumstances (internal or external) that may warrant a change to the risk appetite statements and recommending any consequent changes to the Risk Committee and the Board ahead of the scheduled annual review.

8.11.1 Overarching Risk Appetite Statements

A set of overarching principles has been established, which govern the articulation of the lower-level risk appetite statements. These principles are that Orchard's risk appetite should:

- Reflect the bank's strategy and its culture;
- Focus on manageable, forward looking measures of risk, rather than on backward looking measures of loss;
- Include qualitative description, quantitative measures and prescribed behaviours;
- Facilitate understanding of why limits have been set at the level determined;

These will be communicated, throughout the organisation, in a way that enables each individual to see how risk appetite influences the way they carry out their job responsibilities.

The qualitative Board Risk Appetite statements:

- Cover each level 1 and Level 2 risk category;
- Are approved by the Board and reviewed at least annually in consultation with all key stakeholders taking into account business changes and reported at least quarterly.

Overarching statements as detailed below express Orchard's broad risk appetite at a whole business level, whilst underlying limits cover specific aspects of Orchard's operations.

We will maintain stakeholder confidence – by operating the business in such a way that we deliver against key objectives, both financial and non-financial and remain within our risk appetite;

We will maintain adequate capital and liquid resources – we will maintain a sufficient level of capital and liquidity to effectively support the lending activity of the business and ensure that all liabilities will be met as they fall due under both normal conditions and under a range of stress scenarios and regulatory guidance;

We will protect our reputation – we will be a safe haven for retail depositors and can be seen as an organisation that treats all our customers and employees fairly. We have no appetite for material negative or adverse reputational events;

We will limit the potential for credit losses – by being aware of and managing key concentrations, lending in markets where we can demonstrate expertise to credit worthy borrowers where affordability can be demonstrated and consistent with risk adjusted returns;

We will effectively manage our operational risks and operational resilience – we have a low tolerance of operational risk failures (including IT systems failures and cyber-crime) and will ensure that all our people are properly trained, procedures are thoroughly documented and supervisory controls and reporting methodologies are in place and minimize the impact of adverse operational risk events that disrupt customer service;

We will demonstrate high standards of conduct and compliance – we have a low tolerance for material conduct and compliance related adverse events, or breaches of a regulatory or legal nature and will operate the business in such a way as to minimise the potential for such adverse events to occur.

8.12 Risk Management Framework

8.12.1 Overview of Three Lines of Defence

Orchard is working to establish a Risk Management Framework (RMF) that provides guidance for cohesive and consistent risk management activity across the whole business. The aim of the RMF is to ensure that all types of risk are identified and managed in a consistent manner across Orchard. The RMF sets the standard approach for the management of each Principal Risk and comprises the following components:

- Risk Culture;
- Risk Governance and Control;
- Risk Strategy and Appetite;
- Risk Measurement and Reporting; and
- Stress Testing and Contingency Planning

The RMF will be enacted through a series of policies and processes, setting out our risk management approach and appetite in respect of each of the major risks identified. The adherence to each policy and risk appetite limit will be monitored by management through the establishment of a formal governance process. Performance is measured for, and reported to, ExCo and the Risk Committee, with material risk issues explicitly highlighted as they arise and formally reported on a monthly basis.

The RMF will be submitted to the Risk Committee for challenge and debate, following which it will be submitted to the Board for formal approval and adoption. It will be reviewed at least annually by the Risk Committee.

8.12.2 Three Lines of Defence Model

To manage its risks, Orchard will operate a Three Lines of Defence model which segregates risk management by each of the three distinct categories.

8.12.3 First Line of Defence

Operationally, Management have primary responsibility for the identification, measurement and management of all risks. Clear ownership of each specific risk is set out in the Board approved RMF policy documents which establish the limit structures within which Orchard operates. In addition to the day to day risk management processes of Orchard, risk management is overseen through a number of management committees.

The table below provides a more detailed responsibility map against each activity.

Table 26: 1st Line (Ownership and Control) Business Units.

Role	Responsibility
Provision of risk management and control	Implementation of risk policies Ensuring compliance with policy across the business Identification and escalation of incidents, in line with policy Operation of controls
Development of the understanding of risk	Development and management of risk mitigation plans Undertaking scenario analysis
Engagement with the business and customers	Understanding of, and provision of input to, risk policies Educating staff in the need for risk awareness
Definition and defence of a risk strategy	Input to risk appetite definition through Credit Committee Implementation of policies, framework and methodology in line with defined appetite and strategy
Taking responsibility for regulatory compliance	Ensuring that Orchard remains compliant with all relevant laws and regulations Implementation of changes and enhancements to risk management methodology

8.12.4 Second Line of Defence

The Risk and Compliance function has responsibility for owning Orchard's RCMF, developing the usability of the RCMF and for the oversight and challenge of the day to day management, control and reporting of risks. In addition, the function is responsible for providing advisory support to the business on risk- and compliance- related matters, and for supporting the Governance Oversight of the Bank.

The Risk and Compliance function is responsible for collating and aggregating risk reporting to support the function with regards to forming an independent view of Orchard's overarching risk and compliance profile. The Risk and Compliance function is responsible for creating and managing the Compliance Monitoring Plan, and for reporting on the Bank's adherence to this at the Audit Committee. Oversight of the Bank's implementation of policies against financial crime, money laundering and terrorist financing is provided by the Risk and Compliance function.

The Risk Committee, supported by the Risk and Compliance function:

- assists the Board in the formulation of Orchard's desired risk culture, risk appetite, risk management strategies, policies and limit structures;
- ensures that Orchard has the processes and internal controls to meet the requirements imposed by governmental bodies, regulators, industry mandates or internal policies;
- leads the overall design, implementation and ongoing maintenance of Orchard's RCMF;

- monitors the performance and delivery of the Compliance Monitoring Plan; and
- oversees and objectively challenges the management, control and reporting of risks.

The Risk and Compliance function is responsible for the timely identification of key regulatory changes impacting Orchard, and the development of the Risk, Compliance & Governance Culture as well as Legal and Regulatory Compliance.

The CRO has a reporting line to the Chairman of the Risk Committee, with a dotted line to the CEO. The table below provides more detailed responsibility map against each activity.

Table 27: 2nd Line (Risk and Compliance).

Role	Responsibility
Policies	Update and challenge of risk and compliance policies Update and provision of financial crime, etc. policies
Methodology and Tools	Ownership, development and maintenance of the Risk and Compliance Framework
Training and Communications	Delivery of regular communication to the business on risk-, compliance- and crime-related topics Provision of risk and compliance training to the business
Oversight	Oversight and challenge of the business on the adequacy and effectiveness of the use of the risk and compliance management and methodology in the business The provision of expert support and advice to the business on risk management, including how to interpret and comply with the risk and compliance policies and to meet the requirements of the respective frameworks
Financial Crimes	Independent oversight and reporting on Money Laundering Provision of support and guidance on requirements for monitoring against financial crime, criminal activity, terrorist financing, bribery, corruption and identification of PEPs
Governance	Communication of concerns to the appropriate manager and of unresolved concerns to the Risk Committee

8.12.5 Third Line of Defence

Internal Audit is responsible for independent review of the effectiveness of risk management and the control environment at Orchard. Internal Audit report directly to the Chairman of the Audit Committee and have a dotted line to the CEO for day to day operational purposes.

Orchard intends to outsource this work to third party specialists in Internal Audit on an on-going basis. By bringing in an outsourced facility, the following benefits will be realised:

- Suitably qualified and experienced resources from a reputable firm;
- Depth of resources from an outsourced provider available when required and with a greater potential for specific experience in Orchard's specialist business activities;

- Access to external benchmarking and experience through the outsource provider into practices in other banks in the industry as well as expertise in advising on trends and regulatory developments; and
- Appropriate balance of cost against benefit.

The Internal Auditor is required to undertake a program of audit work on a planned and ad hoc basis under the direction of the Audit Committee. They act independently, but will meet with the senior management of Orchard prior to the commencement of any particular audit to discuss their specific audit plans and to ensure that they also address areas of particular concern to management.

Internal audit will further investigate any actual or suspected frauds and any serious control failures under the direction of the CEO and/or the Audit Committee as a third line after Risk. Internal Audit will attend each Audit Committee meeting.

The outsourcing arrangements will remain under review as the business evolves and grows in the future to ensure that it remains the best option. A future solution may be co-sourcing between in-house resources and third parties for specialist capabilities such as IT and cyber risk.

8.12.6 Primary Board Risk Appetite Metrics and Reporting

Periodically the Board and management will review the corporate plan, performance against the plan and the key underpinning assumptions. Reviews can take place more frequently if circumstances change although typically the formal annual review of the Corporate Plan alongside Risk Appetite provides the foundation for review of the ILAAP and other key prudential documents.

The risk profile will be reported monthly to the ExCo, the Audit Committee, the Risk Committee and the Board supported by commentary on an exception basis (Amber and Red indicators) where they are subject to review and challenge.

The metrics will provide both a point in time position (current month RAG) and an indication of direction of travel versus short and medium term plans. As a consequence, the Board and Executive management are better equipped to decide, at an early stage, whether changes to the plan or to levels of appetite require further consideration.

Full details of the Liquidity Risk Appetite metrics are set out in section 7.1.6.

9 Liquidity Risk Management

9.1 Liquidity Risk Management Framework

Orchard will maintain liquidity resources that are adequate, both as to amount and quality, to ensure that there is no significant risk that its liabilities cannot be met as they fall due. This is in line with the PRA's overall liquidity adequacy rule (OLAR).

Orchard has in place a Liquidity Risk Management Framework (LRMF) that enables monitoring and management of Orchard's liquidity risk. The overall objective of the LRMF is to ensure that Orchard has adequate liquid resources to meet its obligations as and when they fall due, at all times.

9.1.1 The Framework Elements

Board & Management Governance and Oversight

The Board sets the overall risk appetite for the Bank and approves the ILAAP. The ILAAP documents Orchard's approach to liquidity management and forms the foundation of the company's liquidity risk policies, which are subject to review, challenge and approval by the Board.

Liquidity risk is the risk that Orchard's cash may be insufficient to meet its payment obligations as they fall due. On a regular basis, senior management will review liquidity reports. In accordance with the PRA's Liquidity Regime, Orchard will produce an ILAAP, which is reviewed and approved by the Board at least annually. The ILAAP will include stress testing to be undertaken to assess and plan for the impact of a range of scenarios on Orchard's liquidity along with the planned management actions to be taken to mitigate the effects of the stress scenarios.

Identification, Measurement and Monitoring of Liquidity Risk

Internal reporting systems will monitor and manage the identified liquidity risk metrics, outlined in Section 7. These overall limits and early warning indicators will be monitored regularly by the Finance team and senior management (ALCO and EXCO monthly or as required) and overseen by the Board.

The liquidity risk metrics will be monitored on a regular basis. The Finance team will be responsible for producing the required reports and distributing them to EXCO on a regular and timely basis. The Finance team will be responsible for ensuring that the values are within the set internal early warning indicator limits. These limits will be independently monitored by the CFO. In cases where the actual values exceed the internal early warning indicator limits, escalation will take place, dependent on the severity of the breach, in line with the process described in the Liquidity Contingency Plan (see section 12).

Careful liquidity management will be underscored and reinforced by the liquidity policy which requires that all surplus cash is held in the nostro account (up to a balance of £1million) and in the Bank of England Reserve Account. ALCO will be responsible for liquidity management and this will be considered at its monthly meetings.

Stress Testing

Orchard will conduct stress tests based on severe yet plausible scenarios in order to evaluate the liquidity profile and analyse management actions to be taken in the event of a stress situation. Orchard will carry out stress tests that consider the potential impact of idiosyncratic, market-wide and combined stress scenarios. These tests will assist in the evaluation of mismatch gaps and survival periods under stress, cash buffer sufficiency, and also in the development of and updating of the Recovery Plan and the Resolution Plan. Taken together these stress tests, based on the stress scenarios and assumptions reviewed and approved by the Board, provide informed quantitative feedback on the key liquidity risks faced by Orchard.

Cash Buffer

The LAB will be composed of cash held in the Bank of England Reserve Account. In the interim, before the Reserve Account is opened, cash will be invested in short term (<3 months maturity) UK Government Gilts.

Recovery Plan and Resolution Plan

Both the Recovery Plan and the Resolution Plan are prepared following internal discussions by the management team, based on stress testing results. They address the bank's strategies and procedures in the event of liquidity shortfalls in emergency situations.

Orchard will actively manage its liquidity through the following measures:

- Liquidity risk tolerance/appetite, set by the Board and supported by policies that are approved by the Board;
- Limits and early warning indicators that will be monitored using internal reporting systems to identify adverse indicators and prompt action to mitigate any potential breaches;
- Identification, and continual measurement, monitoring and control of liquidity risk in conformity with the bank's own and the PRA's specific rules and guidance;
- Stress testing of the cash flows based on various scenarios to ensure that the LAB is maintained at appropriate levels to withstand stresses on Orchard's business;
- Monitoring EWIs and stress triggers. Development and maintenance of the Liquidity Contingency Plan (LCP) (summarised in this ILAAP and within the Recovery Plan and Resolution Plan).

9.2 Treasury Management

At the commencement of business of Orchard Bank and due to its relatively modest deposit taking aspirations at launch, the Finance team will be responsible for funding and related risk management. The Finance team will also initially be responsible for managing the cash at bank with Orchard's clearing bank and cash held at the Bank of England Reserve Account. Initially, excess funds will be invested in short term (<3 months) UK Government gilts until the Bank of England Reserve Account becomes operational. During its first year of operations Orchard will start to build a separate Treasury team, which will take over these responsibilities from the Finance team. Orchard will not have a trading book or any FX swaps, interest rate swaps or forward transactions. Orchard has no current plans to trade on its own account.

Initially, the Finance team is responsible for funding/product strategy (1st line of defence) while ALCO is responsible for monitoring compliance with risk appetite and limits. The 2nd line defence under the risk management framework will provide challenge to the Management regarding adequacy, accuracy and effectiveness of treasury risk management.

9.3 Pricing Liquidity Risk

The main source of funding for Orchard will be retail deposits. These deposits will only be transacted at agreed fixed rates, and only if it is reasonably determined that the funds can be lent at higher rates than the borrowing cost plus the carrying cost of the cash buffer.

9.4 Management of Liquidity Across Business Lines and Currencies

Due to the simple nature of its business model, and the relatively small size of the business, the Finance team will carry out management of the bank's liquidity across business lines.

9.5 Funding Diversification and Market Access

Orchard will set up an agency banking relationship to support deposit taking and get access to additional payment mechanisms. Application will be made to the Bank of England during the mobilisation phase to get membership to the Sterling Monetary Framework (SMF) to enable the deposit of excess cash in the reserve account, with accompanying access to BoE EnquiryLink either directly through SWIFT or via Bottomline.

10 Liquidity Risk Identification, Measurement, Management, Monitoring and Reporting

Orchard has analysed the 14 liquidity risk drivers outlined in the PRA stress testing guidelines (Chapter 11 of the ILAA Rules).

Regular monitoring of liquidity positions will be carried out as part of normal operations by the Finance team within the Board approved risk appetite/tolerance. Any breaches of these limits will be escalated to the CFO immediately and to ALCO and the Board. Any regulatory breaches will immediately be notified to the PRA along with the corrective action plans.

The different risk drivers and their analysis are outlined in the sub-sections below.

10.1 Retail Funding Liquidity Risk

10.1.1 Risk in Raising Deposits

Orchard plans to have a low-risk liability strategy focusing on limited products (1 year and 2 year fixed term deposit accounts initially) combined with a simple customer journey, attractive and consistently fair rates and targeted customer retention schemes.

There are no plans to offer instant access or current accounts. Orchard will seek to place its deposit products in the middle of the best buy tables. Given the modest deposit raising plans in the projections (Orchard plans to have just over £76m in its deposit book at the end of year 5) this strategy is considered to be adequate and proportionate.

Orchard intends to require new depositors to download a deposit application form from its website and send the application form with deposit cheque to Orchard through the post. Orchard considers that this form of application will enable it to conduct all relevant checks on a manual basis prior to opening a new account and therefore reduces risk from fraud or misrepresentation from on-line applications.

10.1.2 Redemption Profile of Deposits

All of the deposit stock will be below the FSCS limit lowering the risk of large-scale outflow in a stress scenario. Liability origination will be spread out to ensure no more than 12% of the existing liability stock contractually matures in a given month. Tailored retention schemes focused on a simple experience and consistently fair rates will help retain deposits and result in lower behavioural outflows. The terms of the deposit will clearly state that upon redemption a deposit will be rolled over for the same term at a rate that will be communicated to the depositor 4-6 weeks before the maturity of the deposit and the depositor will be given an option to either switch to another deposit product or withdraw the proceeds altogether.

Key controls and Mitigants

The deposit administration team will ensure that all the deposits are below the FSCS limit of £85k.

Additionally, Orchard will be monitoring the maturity of deposits using its own management information and the C66 Maturity Ladder return in the COREP suite of returns to ensure that there are no large volumes of deposits maturing on a particular date or that there is no risk of a significant funding maturity mismatch between loans and deposits.

10.2 Wholesale Secured and Unsecured Funding Risk

Orchard has historically used a wholesale funding facility from Barclays Bank PLC to part finance its lending business. Whilst Orchard plans to retain the facility to diversify funding sources subject to appropriate covenants after approval, Orchard plans for funding to be provided through a mixture of its capital and retained earnings and retail deposits.

Key controls and Mitigants
The wholesale funding risk is managed by the Bank by setting a cap on wholesale funding equivalent to 25% of the Bank's total liabilities.

10.3 Risk of Correlation Between Funding Markets and Lack of Diversification

Orchard plans to have a diversified depositor base, and therefore will not be exposed to risk of correlation and lack of diversification from its depositor base. Further Orchard will maintain its wholesale funding facilities with Barclays Bank PLC, or a financial institution of similar standing subject to appropriate covenants.

Key controls and Mitigants
The wholesale funding diversification is managed by the Bank by setting a cap on wholesale funding equivalent to 25% of the Bank's total liabilities.

10.4 Off-Balance Sheet Funding Risk

Orchard does not plan to provide guaranteed undrawn facilities to its borrowers in exchange for a fee. Facilities, which are made available, will not be guaranteed and disbursement will be subject to final approvals and can be withdrawn at the absolute discretion of Orchard.

The bank's business model does not anticipate the use of other off-balance sheet products.

Key controls and Mitigants
New product approval processes will have controls in place to ensure no off balance sheet exposure is generated through guaranteed facility provision in the contractual terms.

10.5 Funding Tenor Risk

Orchard plans to have a low-risk funding profile at inception and also on an ongoing basis. At inception it plans to launch fixed rate deposits (split 60:40 between 1 year and 2 year products contractually non-withdrawable before maturity). The projected average tenor of the deposit book will be 17 months, which is higher than the average tenor of 5–6 months for the loan book (typical original tenor of 10 months, maximum 12 months). This will ensure a steady supply of liquidity available to lend with a high degree of certainty and very low liquidity mismatch on the balance sheet.

Key controls and Mitigants

The Firm will monitor the maturity of deposits using its own management information and the C66 Maturity Ladder return in the COREP suite of returns to ensure that there are no large volumes of deposits maturing or a significant funding maturity mismatch between loans and deposits.

A large liquidity buffer will be maintained throughout the plan period and will be held in a Bank of England Reserve Account and with a balance of up to £1million also held in Orchard's clearing bank. The liquidity buffer combined with the fact that Orchard's loans will have no contractual forward lending commitments will further bolster the available liquidity to meet lending and deposit redemption obligations.

10.6 Risk of Deterioration in Orchard's Credit Rating

Orchard does not plan to raise funding in the near future by issuing bonds or commercial paper. Orchard has therefore not considered this as a relevant risk in stress tests.

10.7 Cross-Currency Funding Risk

All of Orchard's business will be in the UK and sterling based. Orchard has therefore not considered this as a relevant risk.

10.8 Risk That Liquidity Resource Cannot Be Transferred Across Entities, Sectors and Countries

This is not considered a relevant risk to Orchard. Both current trading entities will be 100% owned by the Bank and the same individuals are listed on the bank mandates of each subsidiary.

10.9 Funding Risk Resulting From Estimates of Future Balance Sheet Growth

A longer tenor of liabilities than assets will benefit Orchard in a positive growth scenario where the loan book grows steadily. However, this will expose the Bank to risk if the loan book growth slows down. While on an on-going basis the liability book can be adjusted downward by lowering deposit interest rates, a short-term negative carry on excess liabilities will adversely affect the bank's net interest margin. The Bank will maintain high capital ratios throughout to ensure such stresses to NIM can be absorbed. If Orchard is unable to originate new loans for a period of six months, with a £76m deposit book (at the end of year 5) at an average deposit rate of 3% p.a. the Bank will incur £1.14m in negative carry cost or about 4.3% of the c. £26m capital resources. A similar stress scenario at the end of year 1 of operation (£21m projected deposits at deposit rate of 3% p.a.) would result in a carrying cost of 2.3% of the £14m projected capital resources.

Initially, funding using own funds mitigates the funding concentration risk. As the balance sheet grows the large number of individual depositors will mitigate funding concentration risk.

Key controls and Mitigants

Orchard will manage any mismatch due to balance sheet growth by monitoring the Firm's cash to deposit ratio in line with its risk appetite. This will ensure that any rapid balance sheet growth or contraction will be adequately managed as the appropriate action on the asset/liability side will be taken.

10.10 Franchise Risk

If during a stress event Orchard deleverages through its loan book, and loan production is not maintained at a sufficient level due to liquidity constraints, Orchard's franchise will diminish. Net interest margin and fee income will deteriorate, funding costs will increase, tenors and volumes will decrease and insolvency pressures build. It is accepted that if Orchard was obliged to entirely cease its lending activities due to a liquidity crisis, it is likely that this would severely impair its franchise value and lead to a winding down of the business. Orchard's balance sheet maturity profile is structured so that it will be able to achieve such a wind down in an orderly manner.

Orchard's potential market is very large, comprising of SMEs and retail borrowers throughout the UK. A stress event that causes Orchard to reduce one of its business lines, e.g., new lending can be expected to damage the franchise as existing borrowers will be unable to obtain new credit and many will take their business elsewhere. However, given the overall size of the market, the damage should not make Orchard unviable. There are an estimated 5.2 million businesses in the UK, insurance market turnover is £35 billion, and the professional fee market is £300 million. Orchard's activities represent a very small proportion of the overall markets in which it operates.

Similarly, should Orchard need to temporarily cease taking new deposits, it should not impact a significant portion of the addressable market which comprises many millions of individual depositors. Orchard's business plan envisages 861 deposit accounts at the end of year 1. Orchard could achieve a sharp reduction in new deposits by temporarily reducing its interest rates below market levels for new customers. This would not impact the existing customer deposits which would continue to receive the original contractual rate.

Key controls and Mitigants

This risk is monitored through multiple KRIs that the Firm has designed covering profitability, growth, loan-to-deposit ratio, maturity mismatch, survivability days and the LCR. Any breaches of the EWI triggers for these KRIs should assist in identifying the Franchise Viability Risk so the appropriate action can be taken.

10.11 Marketable Assets Risk

Orchard will not hold any marketable assets as all excess cash will be placed with the Bank of England.

10.12 Non-Marketable Assets Risk

The only non-marketable assets on the Bank's balance sheet will be those in the loan portfolio. At the end of year 1 these are forecast to have a weighted average maturity of 6 months. Although a securitisation programme may be a possibility at some point in the future once volumes have increased sufficiently, currently Orchard has no plans to sell these loans into the secondary market or securitise them and would seek to allow them to run off on maturity

A stress scenario that required the liquidation of the loan portfolio via a sale or collateral structure would also be likely to trigger a wind down of Orchard in line with the Recovery and Resolution Plan.

10.13 Internalisation Risk

Given the small scale and simplicity of Orchard's business this risk item is not considered relevant.

10.14 Intra-Day Liquidity Risk

Orchard, through its Finance team, will manage intraday payments and receipts to maintain a balance of cash-flow.

Our cash-flow modelling indicates maximum daily outflows of £300,000 at the end of year one, which include projected loan and deposit outflows. It should be noted that Orchard's loan outflows are never committed so that such outflows can be managed if there is a liquidity constraint. In order to support these projected cash-flows the Finance team will position an overnight cash balance equal to 3 days of these outflows at the close of each business day. This is a conservative assumption which ignores the positive impact of cash inflows from maturing loans.

It is recognised that at this stage, the above figures are forecasts based on the financial projections and certain other assumptions. Once Orchard is operating as a bank, the Finance team will acquire empirical evidence to manage intra-day liquidity on a more active basis.

Key Controls and Mitigants

Intraday liquidity is managed by holding cash balances to support 3 consecutive days of the £300,000 gross regular outflows. This buffer ensures that the Firm has enough funds available to meet an intraday liquidity stress scenario.

10.15 Other Risks

Orchard Bank has identified a number of additional liquidity risk drivers in addition to those identified in the ILAA rules which are considered below.

Risk

A reduction in origination of new loans may be interpreted by the market as signalling that Orchard is in a distressed situation and, thus, could exacerbate funding pressures.

Key controls and Mitigants

Orchard's deposit funding will all be fixed term, with maturities of 1 year and 2 years designed to over compensate the maturity profile of the loan assets. Depositors will be permitted to break their funding commitment but only at the discretion of the Bank in hardship cases. Such discretion would only be exercised in unstressed scenarios where adequate alternative funding is available to Orchard. Additionally, the insurance status of deposits is an important determinant of deposit run-off rates. Since all of Orchard's deposits will be below the FSCS limits, the deposits run off rates should be lower in stress conditions.

Risk

In periods of liquidity stress Orchard may elect to reduce its lending appetite. However, this could give rise to loss of more business due to reputation and breakdown in relationship with brokers.

Key controls and Mitigants
Orchard will systematically manage down new lending without damaging broker relationships. Orchard will engage in more active interaction with brokers to ensure they understand the changes necessitated in lending criteria.

Risk
Pro-cyclicality – market-wide liquidity stresses are likely to increase the demand for loans whilst simultaneously reducing the availability of funding to Orchard.

Key controls and Mitigants
Broker facilities are not committed and the level of lending can be managed by tightening the lending criteria and/ or the rates.

Risk
The rapid usage of liquidity buffer assets during a stress scenario may result in a force sale value for the asset, with a discount to the book value and thus damage the solvency of the Bank.

Key controls and Mitigants
This risk is limited, as Orchard will not invest excess cash in securities, simply holding the cash in its bank account (up to a balance of £1 million) or in Bank of England Reserve Account.

11 Liquidity Stress Testing

11.1 Methodology and Approach

Orchard has modelled a market-wide, an idiosyncratic and a combined stress scenario to determine the impact on the liquidity position of Orchard in each scenario. The stress is undertaken after month 12 and the stress period ranges from 2 weeks to 12 weeks.

For each of the stresses, the base plan drivers were flexed and daily cash-flow modelled to assess the impact. The drivers for the stresses are tabled below:

11.2 Market-Wide Stress Scenario (Including Retail Funding Risk)

Orchard modelled the impact of a severe recession over the course of three months with negative growth. We used as the baseline Balance Sheet the position at the end of year 1.

Table 28: Business drivers impact under stress.

	Base	Market wide	Idiosyncratic	Combined
Deposit retention rate at maturity	80%	75%	50%	25%
New deposits as a percentage of plan	100%	25%	20%	5%
Liquid assets buffer haircut	0%	5%	5%	5%
New loans as a percentage of plan	100%	80%	60%	65%
Loan default rates	0%	5%	3%	5%
Period of stress (weeks)	–	12	2	12

The assumptions made are set out in the table above.

11.2.1 Deposits

We have assumed that deposit rollover rates would fall to 75%, i.e., 25% of deposits would be withdrawn at maturity and accounts closed. This reflects the assumption that (a) in times of severe recession whilst there are no adverse credit events specifically impacting Orchard, it may nevertheless be the case that some depositors move their funds to highly capitalised banks; and (b) with SMEs and consumers stressed by falling sales, unemployment etc. we could anticipate that some of the savings on our balance sheet may be drawn down at rollover.

The recession is assumed to reduce all economic activity and combined with a flight to quality which we anticipate would disproportionately impact new entrant banks, we have assumed that new deposits will be obtained at only 25% of the original planned rate.

11.2.2 Loans

We have assumed that loan default rates spike from planned levels to 5%, reflecting the increased level of insolvencies during a recession. Additionally, we assume that the level of new lending declines from 100% to 80% of the planned levels. The level of 80% is consistent with retaining an adequate level of surplus cash (3 days outflows) in accordance with the banks risk appetite statement. Lending has been reduced to 80% and not to a lower level in order (i) to preserve the banks franchise and protect long term customer relationships, and (ii) to recognise that a reduction in economic activity may also lead to an increase in demand for credit from our customers.

11.2.3 Results of the Market-Wide Stress

The base case liquid resources available to meet liabilities as they fall due are £4.8m. Post stress, the level of liquidity resources available are slightly lower at £4.1m.

The bank's capital base is reduced from £14.9m to £13.2m, mainly due to impairment charges for bad loans.

Table 29: Balance Sheet post stress.

Balance Sheet	**Base Plan**	**Market wide**
	Year 1 **£'000**	**Post 12 weeks** **£'000**
Assets		
Loans and advances	32,762	30,924
Cash at bank	1,000	1,000
Liquid asset buffer	3,867	3,111
Fixed assets	483	483
Other assets	158	158
Total assets	**38,270**	**35,676**
Liabilities		
Customer deposits	21,000	20,050
Bank funding	0	0
Trade creditors	2,051	2,051
Tax liabilities	257	257
Non-current liabilities	84	84
Total liabilities	**23,393**	**22,443**
Equity		
Share capital	214	214
Share premium	8,692	8,692
Merger reserves	891	891
Retained earnings	4,240	4,240
Current year retained earnings	841	(803)
Total equity	**14,878**	**13,234**
Total equity and liabilities	**38,270**	**35,676**

Table 30: Funding and ratios.

	Base Plan	**Market wide**
Period of stress (weeks)	**Year 1** **£'000**	**Post 12 weeks** **£'000**
Funding Source		
Deposits		625
Loan Repayment		20,947
Total Funding		**21,572**
Funding Consumption		
Loans		(20,753)
Deposit attrition		(1,575)
Total funding consumption		**(22,328)**

Table 30 (continued)

	Base Plan	Market wide
Period of stress (weeks)	**Year 1** **£'000**	**Post 12 weeks** **£'000**
Net funding surplus / (consumption)		**(756)**
Liquid assets		
Cash at bank	1,000	1,000
Liquid asset buffer	3,867	3,111
Total liquid assets	**4,867**	**4,111**
Loan asset	**32,762**	**30,924**
Deposits	**21,000**	**20,050**
Ratios		
% Liquid Assets to Loans	15%	13%
% Liquid Assets to Deposits	23%	21%
% HQLA to Deposits	18%	16%
LCR %	3069%	2586%
NSFR %	154%	158%

11.3 Idiosyncratic Stress Scenario (Franchise Risk)

Orchard has modelled a scenario in which there are widespread reports in the media that the Bank has experienced severe credit losses on loans, which although as yet uncrystallised are believed to have eliminated a significant portion of the Bank's regulatory capital. The Bank is perceived to be a new and relatively inexperienced institution and as a result the press comment leads to significant deposit outflows.

The bank's balance sheet one-year post authorisation has been used as the baseline for modelling the outcome. Such a scenario at this early stage of the banks development might be expected to result in the closure of the institution.

11.3.1 Deposits

As a result of the crisis we assume that new deposit business runs at only 20% of the previously planned level and that as deposits mature 50% are removed from the Bank to be placed at other institutions for the period of stress. These assumptions are relatively severe, however for a name specific stress on a new entrant to the deposit market we can assume considerable risk aversion from depositors notwithstanding the availability of FSCS insurance.

11.3.2 Loans

We have assumed that the Bank would cease 40% of its new loan business, making new loans only in exceptional cases for existing relationships, and the Bank should therefore benefit from a steady net inflow of funds from maturing loans. As the stress scenario is bank specific there is no expectation that our customers would experience increased rates of insolvency. Nevertheless, it is likely that we would not receive all the funds due in for a variety of reasons such as (i) realising that the bank/customer relationship has likely terminated, borrowers may delay repayment (ii) some borrowers may seek to exploit the bank's difficulties and offer to repay on time, but only if they are given a financial incentive. (iii) some borrowers may be unable to repay as they had been budgeting to rollover the loans on maturity. To account for these factors, we have modelled a collection rate of 97% of the sums due.

11.3.3 Results of the Idiosyncratic Stress

The available liquidity after the stress period increases to £5.3m from £4.8m at the start of the stress. This is mainly driven by the short tenor of loans that give rise to £3.5m of repayments that support both the new lending and deposit attrition, leaving a surplus of £0.48m.

Shareholders' equity is reduced from £14.9 million to £13.9 million over the 2-week period as full impairment charges are raised for bad loans.

We considered the relatively short time frame would not permit the realisation of any of our loan assets, either via a trade sale or some form of securitisation.

11.4 Combined Stress Scenario

Orchard has modelled the impact of a recession coupled with press speculation that Orchard Bank has suffered large losses on its loan portfolio, which has significantly reduced its regulatory capital.

The assumptions made are set out in Table 28 above.

11.4.1 Deposits

The deposit attrition at maturity has increased considerably to 75% and very little new deposits expected.

11.4.2 Loans

The default rates have increased significantly and the level of new business has reduced to 65% of the plan lending.

Table 31: Balance Sheet post stress.

Balance Sheet	Base Plan	Idiosyncratic
	Year 1 £'000	Post 2 weeks £'000
Assets		
Loans and advances	32,762	30,871
Cash at bank	1,000	1,000
Liquid asset buffer	3,867	4,352
Fixed assets	483	483
Other assets	158	158
Total assets	**38,270**	**36,864**
Liabilities		
Customer deposits	21,000	20,558
Bank funding	0	0
Trade creditors	2,051	2,051
Tax liabilities	257	257
Non-current liabilities	84	84
Total liabilities	**23,393**	**22,951**
Equity		
Share capital	214	214
Share premium	8,692	8,692
Merger reserves	891	891
Retained earnings	4,240	4,240
Current year retained earnings	841	(124)
Total equity	**14,878**	**13,913**
Total equity and liabilities	**38,270**	**36,864**

11.4.3 Results of the Combined Stress

Liquidity under this scenario is slightly lower at £4.3m from £4.8m in the base case. Clearly, the short loan tenor assists greatly in managing liquidity under severe market conditions, whilst enabling the management of new lending to conserve the franchise.

The bank's capital base is reduced from £14.9m at the onset of the scenario to £13.4m at the end of 12 week period due to the credit losses on the loan portfolio.

11.5 Reverse Stress Test

No reverse stress test has been undertaken. Given the short tenor of the loans giving rise to cash inflows and low experience of losses, it is unlikely that a liquidity crisis

Table 32: Funding and ratios.

	Base Plan	Idiosyncratic
Period of stress (weeks)	**Year 1** **£'000**	**Post 2 weeks** **£'000**
Funding Source		
Deposits		83
Loan Repayment		3,565
Total Funding		**3,648**
Funding Consumption		
Loans		(2,638)
Deposit attrition		(525)
Total funding consumption		**(3,163)**
Net funding surplus / (consumption)		**485**
Liquid assets		
Cash at bank	1,000	1,000
Liquid asset buffer	3,867	4,352
Total liquid assets	**4,867**	**5,352**
Loan asset	**32,762**	**30,871**
Deposits	**21,000**	**20,558**
Ratios		
% Liquid Assets to Loans	15%	17%
% Liquid Assets to Deposits	23%	26%
% HQLA to Deposits	18%	21%
LCR %	3069%	3528%
NSFR %	154%	164%

would impact the bank. Notwithstanding this fact, in the unlikely event that such a crisis were to arise, the following management actions would be implemented:

- Reduce lending at the cost of the franchise. This is a simple option to implement as no loans or facilities are guaranteed to customers and underwriting criteria can be tightened or rates increased to lower the intake of new business.
- Proactive deposit retention campaign, clarifying the rules on FSCS protection and offering marginally better rates on maturity.
- Defer any capital investments
- Defer costs, where possible and within legal rights to do so.

Table 33: Balance sheet post stress.

Balance Sheet	Base Plan	Combined
	Year 1 £'000	Post 12 weeks £'000
Assets		
Loans and advances	32,762	27,227
Cash at bank	1,000	1,000
Liquid asset buffer	3,867	3,352
Fixed assets	483	483
Other assets	158	158
Total assets	**38,270**	**32,221**
Liabilities		
Customer deposits	21,000	16,400
Bank funding	0	0
Trade creditors	2,051	2,051
Tax liabilities	257	257
Non-current liabilities	84	84
Total liabilities	**23,393**	**18,793**
Equity		
Share capital	214	214
Share premium	8,692	8,692
Merger reserves	891	891
Retained earnings	4,240	4,240
Current year retained earnings	841	(609)
Total equity	**14,878**	**13,428**
Total equity and liabilities	**38,270**	**32,221**

Table 34: Funding and ratios.

	Base Plan	Combined
Period of stress (weeks)	Year 1 £'000	Post 12 weeks £'000
Funding Source		
Deposits		125
Loan Repayment		20,947
Total Funding		**21,072**
Funding Consumption		
Loans		(16,862)
Deposit attrition		(4,725)
Total funding consumption		**(21,587)**
Net funding surplus / (consumption)		**(515)**

Table 34 (continued)

	Base Plan	Combined
Period of stress (weeks)	**Year 1** **£'000**	**Post 12 weeks** **£'000**
Liquid assets		
Cash at bank	1,000	1,000
Liquid asset buffer	3,867	3,352
Total liquid assets	**4,867**	**4,352**
Loan asset	**32,762**	**27,227**
Deposits	**21,000**	**16,400**
Ratios		
% Liquid Assets to Loans	15%	16%
% Liquid Assets to Deposits	23%	27%
% HQLA to Deposits	18%	20%
LCR %	3069%	3407%
NSFR %	154%	160%

12 Liquidity Contingency Plan

12.1 Overview and Principles

The CEO is responsible for executing the Liquidity Contingency Plan.

Orchard recognises the importance of liquidity for its day-to-day operations and believes it is essential to have a plan for addressing liquidity requirements in times of crisis. A liquidity crises can arise due to either an internal or external event or a combination of both and our plan addresses both contingencies.

This Liquidity Contingency Plan ('LCP') will be further developed during mobilisation and signed off by the Board as part of the Recovery Plan. It will be updated and approved by the Board annually unless a significant change in the business should warrant an earlier review.

The LCP is a dynamic document and will be updated in light of changes to the Bank's risk profile, regulation, markets and competition. The growth in the Bank's business from £33million of loan assets in year 1 to a projected £93m of loan assets in year 5 will result in significant changes to the funding profile, with early reliance upon capital giving way to retail deposits.

At least once a year, the CFO will initiate a dummy run of the liquidity contingency plan to assess the continued readiness for invocation in response to a real crisis.

12.2 Invocation

Liquidity will be monitored through regular, timely MI, generated by the Finance department and distributed to Exco.

The primary and secondary liquidity risk metrics will be published within the MI. Breach levels and the related escalation process are described in detail in the Recovery Plan, and summarised below.

12.3 Escalation Process

This process has the following stages:

- EWI breach
- Persistent EWI breach
- Level 1 Trigger Breach
- Level 2 Trigger Breach- Recovery Plan/Liquidity Contingency Plan
- Level 3 Trigger Breach-possible Resolution Plan

Responsibilities for oversight and action are determined by the classification of the breach.

The classification of the breach is initially determined by the CRO and is subject to subsequent review and potential reclassification by the relevant committee and the Board.

A breach classified as a Level 2 Trigger Breach leads to immediate implementation of the Bank's Recovery Plan and/or Liquidity Contingency Plan.

The table below illustrates how the escalation process works in practice for a liquidity EWI breach:

Table 35: Escalation Process.

Step	Event	Step actions	Key responsibility
1	EWI breach noted in KRI Report	CRO ensures relevant committee (ALCO for liquidity issues) is notified	CRO
		ALCO determines whether breach can be remediated and, if not, breach is redesignated as a Trigger Breach. ALCO informs Risk Committee.	ALCO
		Risk Committee report to Board on all unremediated breaches	Risk Committee
		Breaches unremediated after 6 months require Board approval of extension of remediation period or alternatively redesignation as Trigger Breach	Board

Table 35 (continued)

Step	Event	Step actions	Key responsibility
2	Trigger Breach noted in KRI Report Risk Committee/ALCO redesignates EWI Breach as a Trigger Breach Board redesignates persistent EWI Breach or combination of EWI Breaches as a Trigger Breach	Escalated immediately to the Board Board determines on the basis of the severity and remediability of the breach, the required classification of the breach between Level 1, Level 2 and Level 3	Board
3	Level 1 Trigger Breach-expected to be resolvable within regulatory capital and liquidity limits	Board approves and monitors management actions	Board
4	Level 2 Trigger Breach-expected to be resolvable but not within regulatory capital and liquidity limits	Board instructs CEO to convene EXCO which in turn implements the Recovery Plan and/or the Liquidity Contingency Plan. Board instructs CEO to immediately notify the regulatory authorities	EXCO
5	Level 3 Trigger Breach-not expected to be resolvable	Board instructs CEO to immediately notify the regulatory authorities	Board

12.4 Governance

When the LCP is invoked, Orchard will form an emergency ALCO, chaired by the CEO, to evaluate the steps required to contain a crisis event on the basis of the perceived nature, severity and duration of the situation. The CEO is responsible for executing the LCP, detailing projections, steps to be taken, timescales, risk assessment and escalation to the Board.

The Emergency ALCO will perform an assessment of the situation and prioritise the tasks necessary to achieve a recovery. In addition, it will be responsible for on-going monitoring and the submission of detailed, timely reports on the situation to the Board. The Board will convene as required during the crisis. Any decision to initiate the Resolution Plan resides with the Board.

12.5 Communications

Invocation of the LCP is predicated on an actual or prospective breach of regulatory requirements. It is the responsibility of the CEO to promptly notify the Regulator that the LCP has been invoked and to agree communication and reporting requirements for the duration of the crisis period.

An important goal of the Bank during the period the LCP is invoked is to communicate stability to its customers. The Bank will not only be seeking funds to cover its obligations, but also to finance new assets for business continuity.

Recent events have shown that concerns about a bank's solvency can arise quickly. Attempting to access new markets or sources of liquidity where the Bank has not previously been a regular and active participant may exacerbate existing concerns.

The CEO, in consultation with the Board, will manage external communications during this period in order to mitigate any adverse reputational consequences arising from steps taken under the LCP.

12.6 Implementation of the Plan

Prior to the meeting of the Emergency ALCO, the Finance team will produce the following MIS reports:
- Deposit analysis;
- Maturity analysis;
- Cash flow projections;
- A schedule of any committed payments.

The Emergency ALCO will make an initial consideration of the circumstances and review the sources of liquidity that are available in the market to classify the issue as:
4. Short term liquidity crisis;
5. Long term liquidity crisis; or
6. The issue is not yet critical but enhanced vigilance is required.

Actions required for a Short-Term Liquidity Crisis

A short-term liquidity issue is likely to arise from a shock to the financial system which disrupts funding operations. Such a crisis would be temporary in nature and would most likely not involve a significant change to the credit standing of the Bank.

The Emergency ALCO will inform the Board of Directors and set out the circumstances and the recommended measures.

Actions available to the Emergency ALCO to resolve the crisis:
- Draw down any of the Bank's borrowing facilities;
- Reduce lending;
- Prioritise payments:
  - repayment of depositors
  - interbank payments
  - expenses
  - new lending already confirmed

- Increasing the rates offered on deposits to increase retention as well as new business;
- Increasing the rates on loans to reduce the lending volumes;

Actions Required for a Long-Term Liquidity Crisis

The Emergency ALCO will similarly convene a meeting of the Executive Committee and inform it that there is a Long- Term Liquidity problem, set out the circumstances, the expected duration of the issue, and the recommended measures. The Executive Committee will inform the Board and the PRA of the nature of the problem and the Bank's proposed actions.

The Finance team will produce a run off schedule of assets and liabilities setting out the contractual cash-flows and the supplementary actions to be taken under the LCP through to the conclusion of the crisis. The run off schedule will be produced regularly until the crisis has been resolved.

Actions available / required to deal with a long-term liquidity crisis will include all those available under a short-term crisis, and in addition the following:

- Cease taking on new lending customers;
- Cease new lending to existing customers;
- Review deposit pricing in order to stimulate deposit flows;
- Negotiate new bank facilities;
- Seek to raise additional capital
- Enter into a repurchase agreement with the Bank of England in respect of its assets, subject to the rules of the Sterling Monetary Framework;
- Sale of loan assets;
- Arrange meetings or other communications with certain depositors. Such meetings or communications should be used to reassure depositors and to determine their intent at rollover;
- Commence an orderly wind down of Orchard's operations.

5 The Recovery Plan

5.1 Outline of Recovery Plan

A new bank's Recovery Plan will need to cover the following matters:

- Provide assurance that the bank has a documented plan setting out how it will respond progressively to deteriorating conditions.
- Demonstrate that the recovery options available in periods of extreme stress are credible and adequate in terms of their timing and their effect on capital and liquidity.
- Explain the way in which the recovery options would be implemented and demonstrate that there will be appropriate governance around their execution.
- Demonstrate how the process for execution of the recovery plan is embedded in the bank's Risk Management Framework.
- Show how recovery planning is integrated with the bank's strategic planning, risk appetite, risk management and stress testing.
- Explain and set out the governance relating to the preparation and finalisation of the Recovery Plan.

Recovery Plan's will be formulated with reference to the PRA Policy Statement SS9/17.2 Recovery Plan Overview.

An applicant bank is expected to consider a range of scenarios and develop a range of recovery options that would enable it to recover from modelled shocks and preserve the continuity of any critical functions provided by the bank. The plan will seek to clearly identify the trigger points that would require a decision to be taken on activating one or more recovery options and will describe the recovery options themselves.

Recovery options might escalate, dependent on the nature of the trigger and the efficacy of the action taken to date. The plan will describe the required escalation process.

The applicant bank will identify specific supplementary actions which can be taken in times of extreme stress to supplement day-to-day management actions. The impact of these actions on the bank's liquidity and capital positions will be quantified, allowing for appropriate asset price discounts, and likely realistic timing will be estimated. These supplementary actions will be described in the plan.

Recovery actions will be subject to a clearly defined governance and decision-making process and, where applicable, to internal and external communication requirements. These will be described in the plan.

Early Warning Indicators and recovery actions will the seek to cover all risks to which the bank will be exposed, including liquidity risks. This plan therefore incorporates the bank's liquidity contingency plan (which is also incorporated in the ILAAP).

Recovery planning is a prescribed responsibility under the SMR. The bank's executive accountable for the recovery plan pack and for overseeing the internal processes

https://doi.org/10.1515/9783111101545-005

regarding their governance is the CEO. The CEO will be responsible for overseeing the testing of the Recovery Plan, as far as is practicable, on an annual basis.

5.2 Overview of the Business Model and Key Risks

As per the RBP, ICAAP and ILAAP document, the Recovery Plan will set out an overview of the business of the bank applicant.

5.3 Stress Scenarios

The plan will set out the capital and liquidity stress scenarios set out in the ICAAP and ILAAP document.

5.4 Recovery Planning and the Risk Management Framework

The Recovery Plan will set out how key elements of the RMF are relevant to the Recovery Plan, namely:

- A schedule of Key Risk Indicators (KRIs) linked to each of the key risks identified in the business.
- Allocation of responsibility for all KRIs to first line of defence (front office individuals) and second line of defence (Executive Committee or Asset and Liability Committee (ALCO)).
- For each KRI, a defined risk measure comprising a target, an EWI, and a Trigger indicator, based on the company's risk appetite and as defined in the Risk Appetite Statement.
- A documented process, overseen by the CRO, for the reporting of actual and projected performance relative to each KRI to the second line of defence.
- A clearly defined escalation process to ensure that any breaches are dealt with in accordance with the Board's requirements.

5.4.1 Key Risk Indicators

EWIs and Trigger Events will be established by the Board for each of the key risks faced by the business.

The EWIs will focus on manageable, forward-looking measures of risk and will be linked to the bank's risk appetite.

The EWI structure will be intended to be both proportionate to the bank's business model but also to encompass fully the range of risks faced by the business. Risks to be monitored will include market-wide indicators as well as bank-specific indicators.

A bank's management will be expected to also proactively monitor the market for early warning signs that might lead to a general market deterioration, or situations that might have a particular impact on the bank, such as signalling a worsening of stress conditions or warning about an imminent issue.

A bank will also employ internal EWIs and triggers to identify and monitor significant and unexplained negative movements. When these EWIs are breached, predetermined reporting and oversight processes will be initiated to investigate and establish the cause, which will then determine the course of action to be taken.

EWIs are expected to provide a forewarning before a Trigger Event occurs and provide the management team with the required cushion to take action before such an event.

EWI thresholds will be calibrated to take into account how long it might take for remedial management actions to have an effect.

Table 13 is extracted from an example Risk Appetite Statement and sets out the bank's EWIs and triggers. The EBA has released its guidelines on the minimum indicators that firms should include in Recovery Plans. Whilst a large number of these will be used by most banks within their EWI framework, a few may not be included as they will not be relevant to the bank. Table 14 provides a list of Secondary Liquidity Risk Metrics.

The rationale for and determination of the level of these EWIs and triggers will be an annual process linked to the ICAAP and ILAAP and will be fully described in the Risk Management Framework.

Table 13: Example Table of Risk Metrics.

Limit category		**Target**	**Early warning indicator (Amber)**	**Trigger (Red)**	**Primary Responsibility**
Financial	Return on Equity (PAT)	7%	>6%	>5%	CFO
	Net Interest Margin (monthly wt. average assets)	14.5%	>12%	>10%	CFO
	Average cost of funds higher than Plan	0%	>2%	>3%	CFO
	Cost: Income ratio	64%	>70%	>75%	CFO
	Net lending balances v Plan	100%	>80%	>70%	CFO
Economic	GDP Growth Rate (quarterly)	0%	=>0%	=>-0.25%	CFO
	Unemployment rolling 12m change	4%	>5.5%	>6.5%	CFO
	Base Rate	0.75%	1.25%	1.50%	CFO

Table 13 (continued)

Limit category		Target	Early warning indicator (Amber)	Trigger (Red)	Primary Responsibility
Capital	CET1 Ratio (PRA min 8%)	30%	22.50%	20%	CFO
	Leverage Ratio (PRA min 3.25%)	28%	25%	22%	CFO
	Surplus Capital over TCR & Pillar 2B	£5.5m	>£5.5m	>£2.5m	CFO
Liquidity	Liquidity Coverage Ratio (LCR PRA min 100%)	150%	125%	110%	CFO
	Net Stable Funding Ratio (NSFR 100%)	125%	110%	105%	CFO
	Survival Horizon under stress (PRA min 30days)	90 days	75 days	60 days	CFO
	HQLAs to Deposits	14%	12%	8%	CFO
	Increase in cost of fundsfor deposits above the average of top ten providers on Money.co.uk website	Av. Of top ten providers for 1 year and 2 year fixed rate deposits	= or >100 basis points	= >200 basis points	CFO
Market	Interest Rate Risk Sensitivity – % of CET1	2.3%	2.70%	3%	CFO

Table 14: Example Table of Secondary Liquidity Risk Metrics.

Metric	Trigger (Red)
Deposit Inflows as proportion of budgeted inflows	Min 70%, Max 130%
Retention rate of maturing fixed term deposits	Min 50%
Proportion of deposits which are 'high risk'	Max 5%
Number of payment systems	Min 2
Savings Operational Trigger per month in Year 1 of the plan	Postal applications volume >75 (value – £1.8m) Web application form downloads >300

5.4.2 Monitoring, Reporting & Escalation

KRI Reporting

Reporting of actual and projected outcomes relative to expectations is a fundamental part of a bank's control structure. A Key Risk Indicator Report (KRI Report) is prepared to compare actual and projected risk measures and qualitative indicators with the company's documented risk appetite.

The Risk Appetite Statement sets out for each risk measure a target, an EWI, and a Trigger indicator. The KRI Report sets out the actual outcomes for each risk measure and compares them with the Target, the EWI and the Trigger.

The KRI Report is produced on a monthly basis under the direction of the CRO and is presented to the Executive Committee and to the Asset and Liability Committee (ALCO). Each committee will be delegated responsibility for oversight of certain of the risk measures as a key element of their second line of defence oversight responsibilities. Details of this delegation will be set out in the Risk Management Framework.

Metrics are also reported to the Risk Committee which has an oversight role (see Table 15 for the escalation process).

All Risk Appetite risks are considered by either the Exco or the ALCO.

The committees are also required to consider whether there are any other risks not currently covered by the KRI Report which should be escalated to the Board. This would include, for example, specific consideration of emerging risks requiring Board attention.

The risk measures set out in a bank's RAS should fully cover the mandatory and discretionary indicators set out in the EBA Guidelines (capital, liquidity, profitability, asset quality, market-based, macroeconomic).

By linking the indicators to the bank's Risk Management Framework, a bank is able to demonstrate that the implementation of recovery options is an integral part of its risk management processes.

Escalation Process

A bank's Risk Management Framework will set out the escalation process around breach and prospective breach of the limits set out in the company's risk appetite statement. This process will normally have the following stages:

- EWI breach
- Persistent EWI breach
- Level 1 Trigger Breach
- Level 2 Trigger Breach-Crisis Recovery Plan/Liquidity Contingency Plan
- Level 3 Trigger Breach-possible regulatory resolution plan

Responsibilities for oversight and action are determined by the classification of the breach.

The classification of the breach is initially determined by the CRO and is subject to subsequent review and potential reclassification by the relevant committee and the Board.

A breach classified as a Level 2 Trigger Breach leads to immediate implementation of the company's Recovery Plan and/or Liquidity Contingency Plan. These are described in more detail elsewhere in this book.

Table 15 illustrates how the escalation process works in practice.

Table 15: The Escalation Process.

Step	Event	Step actions	Key responsibility
1	EWI breach noted in KRI Report	CRO ensures relevant committee (Exco or ALCO dependent on the related risk) is notified	CRO
		Exco/ALCO concludes whether breach can be remediated and if not breach is redesignated as a Trigger Breach. Exco/ALCO inform Risk Committee.	Exco or ALCO
		Risk Committee reports to Board on all unremediated breaches	Risk Committee
		Breaches unremediated after 6 months require Board approval of extension of remediation period or alternatively redesignation as Trigger Breach	Board
2	Trigger Breach noted in KRI Report Risk Committee redesignates EWI Breach as a Trigger Breach Board redesignates persistent EWI Breach or combination of EWI Breaches as a Trigger Breach	Escalated immediately to the Board with management recommendations from Exco/ALCO Board determines on the basis of the severity and remediability of the breach the required classification of the breach between Level 1, Level 2 and Level 3	ALL
3	Level 1 Trigger Breach-expected to be resolvable within regulatory capital and liquidity limits	Board approves and monitors management actions	Board
4	Level 2 Trigger Breach-expected to be resolvable but not within regulatory capital and liquidity limits	Board instructs CEO to convene Exco which in turn implement the Recovery Plan and/or the Liquidity Contingency Plan Board instructs CEO to immediately notify the regulatory authorities	Exco
5	Level 3 Trigger Breach-not expected to be resolvable	Board instructs CEO to immediately notify the regulatory authorities	Board

Table 15 is described in more detail in the following sections.

EWI Breach

Each committee of a bank is required to review each risk measure for which it is responsible. For any measure where an EWI measure has been breached, the committee is required to consider whether remedial actions are necessary, to determine what these actions should be and their likely efficacy, in particular that the actions are expected to resolve the breach before a Trigger Breach occurs, and to report their conclusions and actions to the Risk Committee. Committee deliberations will be recorded in the minutes of the relevant committee meeting.

The committees will determine the future frequency of monitoring of any EWI that has been breached (and any other measure that the committee might wish to monitor more frequently than usual). The CRO is responsible for ensuring that the required reporting is put in place.

The CEO is responsible for coordinating the Exco and ALCO meetings and for ensuring that the required remedial actions are communicated to the relevant front line executives.

The CEO is also responsible for ensuring all EWI breaches, actions, and matters requiring Board consideration are duly escalated to the Risk Committee or Board as appropriate.

Any EWI breach will remain as an agenda item for review at each subsequent Exco, ALCO, Risk Committee and Board meeting until such time as the breach has been remediated.

The KRI reporting process follows the company's regular monthly reporting cycle within the delegated committees and the quarterly reporting cycle for oversight by the Board, unless the CRO considers that a matter should be escalated to the Board at any other time. KRIs for management review will be produced more frequently. This might include, for example, instances of an EWI breach where the relevant committees conclude (whether at that the time of the initial breach or on subsequent review) that remedial actions are unlikely to resolve the breach before a Trigger Breach occurs.

In the early stages of the bank's operation there is likely to be a de facto escalation to the Board earlier than in the prescribed escalation, as governance structures and reporting routines are being bedded in.

Persistent EWI Breach

Any EWI breaches not remediated within a reasonable period of months (for example 6 months) will be specifically considered by the Board which must decide whether the relevant committee should continue to oversee the remedial action plan, or whether the breach should be escalated, meaning that the breach will be reclassified as a Trigger Breach and responded to accordingly.

The CRO is responsible for ensuring persistent breaches are escalated to the Board.

Trigger Breach

A Trigger Breach can be defined as one of the following:

- An EWI Breach where remedial action has been in-effective and the Board has determined that further action is required
- An EWI Breach where the Risk Committee has determined that remedial action is unlikely to be effective in preventing a future Trigger Breach, in which case the EWI Breach is escalated to the Board and reclassified as a Trigger Breach
- An immediate breach of a trigger limit without a prior EWI Breach. If such a Trigger Breach occurs, the CRO is responsible for immediate communication of the breach to the Board. A Trigger Breach requires the Board to meet to review the breach within 48 hours of notification.

The Board will immediately consider the remedial action and determine the required classification of the breach into one of 3 different levels, each of which has a different required response. An example of Breach Levels is set out in Table 16.

Management Actions

Overview

In conjunction with its stress testing process, a bank will be expected to undertake an exercise to define likely remedial management actions in response to EWI and Trigger breaches, or variances from Target. These actions are part of the bank's Recovery Plan and are intended to demonstrate the recovery options that would be implemented in the initial stages of any deterioration.

The intention also is to be able to define how the bank would be able to respond to a continuing deterioration illustrating how additional recovery options would be implemented should a deterioration become more severe, including the specific triggers for such actions.

In combination, this schedule of actions constitutes the framework of indicators which identifies the points at which appropriate actions referred to in the plan may be taken, together with a description of the decision-making process relating to the activation of the recovery plan (EBA Guidelines on the minimum list of qualitative and quantitative recovery plan indicators).

Finally, management actions are cross-referenced to the stress scenarios described in the ICAAP and ILAAP to illustrate how the recovery plan would respond to a combination of breaches of increasing severity.

As such, the recovery plan covers a diverse and credible 'menu of financial options' available to the bank to action in order to address a severe stress scenario impact which

Table 16: Levels of Escalation.

Description	Further Explanation	Example
Level 1 Breach expected to be resolvable within regulatory capital and liquidity requirements (albeit outside risk appetite tolerances) with no impact on the bank's critical functions	Management actions expected to remediate the breach Actions would comprise adjustments to the company's strategy, with a likely impact on profitability but with the company remaining within regulatory requirements Actions would be taken under the direction of the Board Bank continues to operate all critical functions	The stress scenarios considered in the company's ICAAP and ILAAP would fall into this category, indicating the impact of these stresses and related management actions can be absorbed within existing projected capital and liquidity resources The bank's Pillar 2B capital is not affected by these stress scenarios Management actions in the ICAAP and ILAAP stress tests were as follows- Anchor scenario – reduce lending rates to counter loan volume reduction caused by economic downturn; maintain deposit inflows by increasing deposit rates; tighten credit processes to reduce bad debt rate back down to planned level
Level 2 Breach expected to be resolvable but not within regulatory capital and liquidity requirements	Crisis Recovery Plan and/or Liquidity Contingency Plan is implemented Management actions expected to remediate the breach but not without breaching regulatory capital and/or liquidity requirements Actions would comprise adjustments to the company's strategy with a likely impact on profitability but and with the company temporarily breaching regulatory requirements Supplementary actions necessary Bank continues to operate all critical functions Regulator communication necessary	Capital and liquidity projections indicate the severity of the events is such that regulatory capital and liquidity requirements will not be met. However the projected impact of management actions (including the supplementary actions) expected to be sufficient to restore the company's capital and liquidity within a timescale acceptable to the regulatory authorities Such an event would be more severe than the stress scenarios considered in the company's ILAAP and ICAAP

may and can be caused by either idiosyncratic problems, a larger financial system failure or a combination of the two.

Ladder of Actions

A bank will be expected to identify a range of actions that could be taken, together or in isolation, in response to variances to Target EWI and Trigger Breaches.

The extent of each action can be varied as necessary to remediate the breach.

Examples of actions are set out below –

Adjustments to commercial operating terms – raise/lower lending rates; raise/lower deposit rates; tighten/loosen underwriting criteria; extend/reduce range of lending products; extend/reduce range of deposit products

Adjustments to operations – align costs with revenues, e.g., cost reduction programme; revise operating strategy and reforecast profit, capital and liquidity requirements

Supplementary actions – if a wholesale lending facility is in place, draw down on the facility to supplement liquidity; draw down on liquidity buffer; reduce/suspend dividend payments to supplement liquidity and/or conserve CET 1 capital; use loan book as collateral for central bank funding drawdown; use loan book as collateral for third party funding; sale of loan book; fund raising from shareholders; changes to company strategy

It is envisaged that Supplementary Actions would only be taken in response to a Trigger Breach.

Table 17 illustrates the management actions that could be taken in response to risk events.

These risk events can be cross-referenced to the company's ICAAP and ILAAP, where they support the development of the company's capital and liquidity stress scenarios.

In practice, required management actions and any enhanced monitoring processes will be determined at the time by the committees responsible for oversight of the risk being measured.

5.5 Invocation of Recovery Plan and Liquidity Contingency Plan

The Recovery Plan and the Liquidity Contingency Plan will be invoked immediately after it has been concluded by the Board that a Trigger Breach cannot be remediated without the company breaching regulatory capital and liquidity requirements.

This consideration may be in response to an escalation of an existing breach or breaches, where management actions have already proved ineffective.

If the Board concludes that the Trigger Breach can be remediated, the CEO will be instructed to invoke the Recovery Plan and/or the LCP.

Table 17: Example of Management Actions in response to liquidity risk events.

Event	EWI Metrics/Potential Breach Impacted by Event	Management Actions in Response to EWI Breach	Possible Constraints
Lending volumes reduction	Net lending balances reduce v plan Cash to loans ratio increases Loans to deposit ratio reduces LCR increases as HQLA increases as deposit inflows unchanged but lending outflows reduce. Net outflows unchanged as inflows in the calculation limited to 75% of outflows NSFR increases as Required Stable Funding reduces Regulatory capital requirement reduces as RWAs reduce	Reduce loan rates to increase volumes, if related reduction in profits/capital allows capital margins to be maintained within risk appetite tolerances Reduce deposit rates to scale back deposit volumes proportionately Reforecast capital and liquidity positions and monitor	Projected capital/liquidity position limits extent to which rates can be reduced; market conditions limit impact of reduced loan rates Projected profitability adversely affected Projected Trigger breach
Loan rates reduction	Net interest margin reduces LCR reduces as HQLA reduces due to reduced interest income NSFR reduces as reduced profits reduce capital which in turn reduces Available Stable Funds	Reduce deposit rates in order to preserve net interest margins Reproject capital and liquidity positions and monitor	Market conditions preclude reduction in deposit rates Projected profitability adversely affected Projected Trigger breach
Deposit volume reductions	Deposit inflows below Plan Loan to deposit ratio increases Cash to deposit ratio increases LCR reduces as HQLA reduces, partially offset by reduction in projected Funding Outflows NSFR reduces as Available Stable Funding reduces	Increase deposit flows through rate increases Increase loan rates to scale back lending volumes proportionately Draw down wholesale bank facilities enabling continuation of lending albeit at higher cost Reduce projected shareholder dividends thus retaining liquidity to support continuation of lending Reproject capital and liquidity positions and monitor	Material rate increases necessary due to adverse market conditions Volume reductions linked to company specific concerns, eg credit quality Projected capital/liquidity position limits extent to which rates can be reduced; market conditions limit impact of reduced loan rates Projected profitability adversely affected

(continued)

Table 17 (continued)

Event	EWI Metrics/Potential Breach Impacted by Event	Management Actions in Response to EWI Breach	Possible Constraints
Deposit rate increases	Net interest margin reduces LCR reduces as HQLA reduces due to increased interest expense NSFR reduces as reduced profits reduce capital which in turn reduces Available Stable Funds	Increase loan rates to maintain net interest margin	Market conditions preclude increase in loan rates Projected profitability adversely affected
Cost of risk increases	Loan losses as % of loan portfolio increase Payment delay as % of loan portfolio increases LCR reduces as HQLA reduces due to increased loan losses NSFR reduces as reduced profits reduce capital which in turn reduces Available Stable Funds	Review lending policy and tighten lending and underwriting criteria Increase loan rates to compensate	Tighter lending criteria and increased loan rate reduce loan volumes Increased cost of risk attributable to general economic conditions Projected profitability adversely affected
Expenses increase	Cost to income ratio exceeds plan LCR reduces as HQLA reduces due to increased expense outgoings NSFR reduces as reduced profits reduce capital which in turn reduces Available Stable Funds	Implement cost saving plan Increase loan rates/reduce deposit rates to maintain profitability	Market conditions preclude rate changes; cost increases structural/ market-wide Projected profitability adversely affected

If the Board concludes that the Trigger Breach cannot be remediated, the CEO will be required to immediately contact the regulatory authorities with a view to the Regulator invoking the resolution plan.

The operation of the Recovery Plan and the LCP is described in the following sections of this book.

Recovery Plan

The CEO is responsible for creating an emergency Exco or emergency ALCO, depending on the nature of the incident, that is responsible for crisis management and the return to a 'business as usual' state. In an extreme situation, where recovery is not possible, the emergency Exco will oversee an orderly wind-down of the bank's business.

Governance

The bank will be expected to form an emergency Exco/ALCO, chaired by the CEO and comprising other ALCO and Exco members, to evaluate the action steps required to contain a crisis event on the basis of the perceived nature, severity and duration of the situation. The Board will be informed immediately about the crisis, will be asked to agree the Recovery Plan and then will be regularly updated on the progress made against the agreed Recovery Plan. The CEO is responsible for executing the Recovery Plan, detailing projections, steps to be taken, timescales and risk assessment.

The emergency Exco/ALCO will comprise their usual membership, plus guests as required. Example individual responsibilities are outlined below.

Emergency Exco/ALCO Member Responsibilities

Table 18 sets out example responsibilities for the CEO, CFO, CRO and Head of IT.

Other staff members or Board members can also be included as part of the emergency committee, depending on the severity and type of crisis.

Communications With Regulatory Authorities

Invocation of the Recovery Plan is predicated on an actual or prospective breach of regulatory requirements. It is the responsibility of the CEO to promptly notify the Regula-

Table 18: Emergency Exco/ALCO Member Responsibilities.

Title	Responsibility
CEO	Overall responsibility for development and execution of the Recovery Plan. Primary responsibility for all internal (Board, Staff & Suppliers) and external (Regulators, Shareholders, Orchard, Customers) communication. Monitor and evaluate regulatory issues including communications with the Regulators. Ensure franchise viability based on the actions proposed by the committee.
CFO and CRO	Manage liquidity positions. Analyse the impact of potential actions on cash positions and on the quality of the securities portfolio. Analyse the impact of potential actions on the credit quality of the asset portfolio. Report financial statements and positions against internal and regulatory triggers, cash-flows and financial implications. Analyse the accounting information, monitor and evaluate risks and regulatory compliance issues.
Head of IT	Ensure IT systems and controls are robust and can meet the requirements of the Recovery Plan.

tor that the Recovery Plan has been invoked and to agree communication and reporting requirements for the duration of the crisis period.

Other Communication

Timely internal and external communication is very important in managing a crisis. The extent of the communication and the parties to be informed will vary based on the severity and nature of the crisis. This section outlines an example of how internal and external communication can be managed during a crisis.

Internal Communication

Internal communication ensures relevant staff members, especially staff interacting with customers and funding providers, are briefed concerning the way to manage stakeholders' expectations, most importantly the expectations of the bank's customers. The emergency committee will be responsible for overall co-ordination of the internal communication, and managers will manage it within their teams, reporting into the committee on its effectiveness.

External Communication

The significant parties to be informed in the event of a crisis are the bank's Board members, customers, shareholders and regulators. Each of these external stakeholders has different information requirements and the emergency committee should ensure that they are informed in a timely manner. An example of how the responsibility for communication with each of these stakeholders is outlined in Table 19:

Table 19: Stakeholder Responsibility.

Stakeholder	Key person responsible
Board of Directors and Shareholders	CEO
Regulatory Authorities	CEO
Depositors	CFO
Borrowers	CEO

Implementation of the Plan

The management course of action outlined by the emergency committee should for example include:

a) Action plan, including plan to increase funding and/or Capital
   a. Clarification and assessment of the problem
   b. Proposed actions
   c. Identification of funding and/or capital providers (if appropriate)
   d. Amount intended to be raised and timing
   e. Regulatory and legal issues
   f. Dependencies/pre-requisites
b) Timescale for actions and key personnel responsible for implementing each one
c) Assessment of risks and the likelihood of successful mitigation
d) Forward liquidity and capital projections including:
   a. Evolution of the size of the capital and liquidity buffer to restore stability
   b. Changes to the bank's funding profile
   c. Changes to the bank's business model
   d. Stress test results to evaluate impact due to various scenarios

The list above is the basic information to be considered by the emergency committee and if necessary additional steps and actions will have to be considered based on the severity and nature of the crisis.

Reporting During Crisis

Daily reports will be created and provided to the emergency committee by the Finance, Treasury and Credit teams. They will highlight the objectives and the impact of actions taken. They will also measure the effects of actions on the bank's continued observance or compliance with internal and regulatory limits.

In the case of a severe crisis, extra reporting should be provided by the Finance and Credit teams to the emergency committee on an intra-day basis.

In line with the severity of the crisis and the reporting requirements, the emergency committee will disseminate internal information to the management team and Board members as the situation unfolds. Reporting frequency affected both by the severity of the problems and time required to action the Recovery Plan, will be decided by the emergency committee.

Over and above internal reporting bank should also take measures to communicate with and provide updates to its regulators and shareholders.

Recovery Plan Options

The bank should consider a number of credible recovery options, which can be applied to a number of varied stress scenarios that may impact its business. It has to be noted that in certain stress scenarios some of these recovery plan options might not be feasible and the business of bank, in such scenarios, will be wound up. Management should believe that the Recovery Plan sets out a reasonable range of options proportionate to the bank's business model.

The recovery options considered are listed below:

1) borrowing against or selling part of its loan book
2) raising additional wholesale funding
3) raising additional capital from its shareholders
4) adjustment of its business model and reduction of operating costs

Summary of Options

Set out below is a menu of credible Recovery Plan options available to a bank. A bank will consider the impact of such actions, how such actions will be executed and whether the actions are in fact credible.

1. Sale of all or part of the debtor book
2. Raise wholesale funding
3. Raise additional capital from shareholders
4. Adjust business model and reduce operating costs
5. Disposal – orderly wind-down or sale of bank to a third party

Return to a Business-as-Usual State

On return to a 'business-as-usual' state (i.e., measures and metrics are once again within tolerable limits), the emergency committee should continue to monitor the liquidity position closely for a period of at least a month, to assess the enduring impact of actions taken. Such continuous monitoring will also assist in the post-mortem of the crisis event and the implementation of steps to avoid a recurrence.

The emergency committee will usually be disbanded after one month of returning to the 'business-as-usual' state and the final report of the incident will be submitted to the Board.

Two potential final resolutions for the business are:
1. A sale of the bank to a third party
2. An orderly wind-down of the bank's business

For new applicant banks, generally in the event of a resolution, no UK economic functions will be impacted and no demands will be made on UK public funds.

Liquidity Contingency Plan

The Recovery Plan usually simply sets out the LCP in the ILAAP details of which are set out in the ILAAP chapter.

5.6 Template Recovery Plan

Table of Contents

Table of Tables

1 Covid-19

This document was well advanced in its review process at the start of the Covid-19 pandemic. No attempt has been made to revise the document, reforecast any macroeconomic model parameters or predict specific impacts on the insurance industry or any of the other markets served by Orchard. Nor have any counter-cyclical buffers been deducted from our capital requirement calculations.

As a non-discretionary item of expenditure we do not expect Covid-19 to materially affect spend on insurance premiums, which remains the main focus of Orchard's business. Customers' ability to pay will doubtless be impacted by the current crisis but Orchard believes that constructive engagement in forbearance arrangements and, ultimately, its ability to rely on recourse arrangements will limit impairment downsides to below the levels already modelled in the ICAAP stress tests. With regard to short-term liquidity, Orchard believes that its short-term amortising loan book and existing bank liquidity facilities will allow Orchard to trade through the immediate impact of the pandemic.

2 Introduction

This document is Orchard's Recovery Plan. It is intended to

- Provide assurance that Orchard has a documented plan setting out how the firm will respond progressively to deteriorating conditions.
- Demonstrate that the recovery options available in periods of extreme stress are credible and adequate in terms of their timing and their effect on capital and liquidity.
- Explain the way in which the recovery options would be implemented and to demonstrate that there will be appropriate governance around their execution.
- Demonstrate how the process for execution of the recovery plan is embedded in the company's Risk Management Framework.
- Show how recovery planning is integrated with the company's strategic planning, risk appetite, risk management and stress testing.
- Explain governance around the preparation of this document.

The Recovery Plan has been formulated with reference to SS9/17.2 Recovery Plan Overview.

This Recovery Plan ("RP") is prepared by Orchard Funding Group PLC ("Orchard"), as part of its annual recovery plan review, as a standalone entity that is self-sufficient in managing its capital and liquidity. The RP is part of Orchard's Risk Management Framework. Unless otherwise noted, values are presented in pounds sterling.

Orchard is expected to consider a range of scenarios and develop a range of recovery options that would enable the firm to recover from these shocks and preserve the continuity of any critical functions provided by the bank. The plan seeks to clearly identify the trigger points that would require a decision to be taken on activating one or more recovery options, and describes the recovery options themselves.

Recovery options might escalate, dependent on the nature of the trigger and the efficacy of the action taken to date. The RP describes the required escalation process.

Orchard has identified specific supplementary actions which can be taken in times of extreme stress to supplement day-to-day management actions. The impact of these actions on the company's liquidity and capital positions has been quantified, allowing for appropriate asset price discounts, and likely realistic timing has been estimated. These supplementary actions are described in this RP.

Recovery actions are subject to a clearly defined governance and decision-making process and, where applicable, to internal and external communication requirements. These are described in this RP.

EWIs and recovery actions cover all risks to which Orchard is exposed, including liquidity risks. This document therefore also now incorporates Orchard's liquidity contingency plan (also incorporated in the ILAAP).

Recovery planning is a prescribed responsibility under the SMR. The Orchard executive accountable for the recovery plan pack and for overseeing the internal processes regarding their governance is the CEO. The CEO will be responsible for overseeing the testing of this Recovery Plan, as far as is practicable, on an annual basis.

The draft Recovery Plan was issued to the Board on 6 March 2020, discussed at Board on 12 March 2020, revised in light of challenge/feedback and reissued for final approval in early April 2020.

3 Overview of Business Model and Key Risks

3.1 Business Model

Orchard's business model is more fully described in the Regulatory Business Plan.

In summary, the company will be undertaking the following:

Orchard provides finance in the insurance premium finance market and the professions finance market. Finance is provided to SMEs and consumers, typically over a 10-month term on a fully amortising basis. The majorty of finance provided by Orchard is guaranteed by the introducing professional firm or insurance broker. The directors believe that the lending undertaken by the group is of a high quality, demonstrated by the fact that there have been de minimis loan losses over the last seven years.

The directors believe that the group lends into relatively safe credit markets as borrowers from the group are strongly motivated to meet their credit obligations. Failure to pay insurance premium finance obligations may leave the borrower uninsured and therefore unable, for example, to drive a vehicle or to conduct business. Similarly, firms are required to satisfy their accountancy fee obligations in order to complete and file important documentation, such as tax returns.

With regard to deposits, Orchard plans to have a low-risk liability strategy focusing on a limited product set (12 month and 24 month fixed term accounts) offered to retail customers, combined with a simple application process, attractive and consistently fair rates and targeted customer retention schemes. There are no plans at the moment to offer instant access or current accounts. Initially the bank will develop brand awareness through publicity in best-buy tables. Given the modest deposit raising plans in the projection (Orchard plans to have just over £65m in its deposit book at the end of year 5) the limited marketing resources are considered to be adequate and proportionate.

3.2 Stress Scenarios

Capital Stresses

Orchard has considered a range of stresses on its capital and liquidity, covering scenarios of systemic market-wide events, idiosyncratic events and combinations thereof. In addition, a reverse stress has also been considered. The PRA's ACS 2019, published in March 2019, has been considered for the economic variables for the market-wide stress and the combined stress. Orchard has endeavoured to build a bank with strong capital and liquidity ratios that will be able to withstand most stress scenarios with a high degree of confidence. It has identified key risk indicators and thresholds that would signify the occurrence of stress scenarios and will adopt invocation protocols documented with identified accountable individuals who would oversee the execution of pre-agreed management actions to alleviate the stress on the bank and achieve recovery. In the event of extreme stress, a clearly delineated path to resolution is charted out and high capital ratios make an orderly resolution possible.

Systemic Market-Wide Stresses

Management has considered the impact on Orchard's business drivers during the last global financial crisis ("GFC") in 2008. The key adverse impact experienced by Orchard was an impact on available liquidity to fund its business. Orchard experienced limited impact on its lending volumes and the margins achieved on its lending business. Notwithstanding the limited impact on Orchard's business in the GFC, we have applied the following stresses to Orchard's business resulting from market-wide stresses:

- Base rates increase to 4%, with unemployment rising to a peak of 9.2% and consumer credit shrinking.
- Consumer credit shrinkage has been assumed to result in lower aggregate demand for lending.
- To attract new lending, rates are reduced.
- Higher unemployment drives higher loss rates.

- With high unemployment and less growth in household income, the level of savings reduces and hence, the level of new deposits.
- To be more competitive in the deposit market, rates are increased.

Idiosyncratic Stresses

Five scenarios, all around the idiosyncratic risk to Orchard were modelled for the idiosyncratic stresses. These scenarios relate to

1. Key person risk
2. Senior management conduct failure (ACS 2019 focuses on conduct risk)
3. Cyber risk, given recent market incidents
4. Third party and processing failure, again from recent market failures
5. Failure of fraud prevention

The highest impact of the idiosyncratic stresses resulted in a cost impact of £675k to Orchard.

Combined Stress

The combined stress takes account of the idiosyncratic stress as well as more severe market-wide stress variables, in part due to idiosyncratic stress driving a bigger impact on the business volumes. The combined stress is much more severe.

Reverse Stress

The reverse stress is driven by a massive market shock, with high unemployment that severely impacts the customer's ability to repay the loan. At the same time, some brokers go into insolvency and hence, the guarantee no longer provides a safeguard against the losses. The escalating losses result in loss of confidence by depositors, resulting in little or no new deposits and very high attrition at maturity. Deposit rates are increased to manage both attrition and new business. However, this action does not close the funding gap and hence, bank borrowing is incepted. Given the weak trading position and the inability to charge assets, the margins charged above base rate on the borrowing are extremely high.

Stress scenario Results

- The capital surplus position under the combined stress is still at least £9.4m above the total capital required (TCR) plus the Pillar 2B capital requirements over the five year period. This is in excess of the risk metric target approved by the Board of £5.5m.
- Orchard's Total Capital Requirement remains at 9%-10% of RWAs throughout the term of the five-year plan under base case. Orchard's CET 1 percentage of RWAs will reduce from 51% to 30% over the plan period as the growth in lending exceeds the build-up of capital through retained earnings.

Table 1: Summary Stress Scenario Results.

	Percentage of RWA's					Variance to Base				
	Year 1	Year 2	Year 3	Year 4	Year 5	Year 1	Year 2	Year 3	Year 4	Year 5
Base										
Total Capital Requirement + Pillar 2B	15.8%	14.8%	14.0%	13.0%	12.9%	–	–	–	–	–
Regulatory Capital Resources	51.0%	45.5%	39.4%	34.2%	29.7%	–	–	–	–	–
Surplus / (deficit) regulatory capital	35.2%	30.7%	25.4%	21.1%	16.8%	–	–	–	–	–
Market-wide (Anchor) Stress										
Total Capital Requirement + Pillar 2B	15.9%	15.0%	14.1%	13.0%	12.9%	0.1%	0.2%	0.1%	0.0%	(0.0%)
Regulatory Capital Resources	50.8%	45.6%	38.4%	32.8%	28.1%	(0.2%)	0.1%	(1.0%)	(1.4%)	(1.5%)
Surplus / (deficit) regulatory capital	35.0%	30.7%	24.3%	19.8%	15.3%	(0.3%)	(0.1%)	(1.1%)	(1.4%)	(1.5%)
Idiosyncratic Stress										
Total Capital Requirement + Pillar 2B	16.2%	15.3%	14.2%	13.1%	12.9%	0.4%	0.5%	0.2%	0.1%	0.0%
Regulatory Capital Resources	51.2%	47.2%	40.8%	36.4%	30.3%	0.2%	1.7%	1.4%	2.3%	0.6%
Surplus / (deficit) regulatory capital	35.0%	31.9%	26.5%	23.3%	17.3%	(0.2%)	1.1%	1.1%	2.2%	0.6%
Combined Stress										
Total Capital Requirement + Pillar 2B	16.5%	15.8%	14.7%	13.3%	13.0%	0.8%	1.0%	0.7%	0.3%	0.2%
Regulatory Capital Resources	49.2%	45.2%	38.5%	33.2%	29.5%	(1.8%)	(0.4%)	(1.0%)	(1.0%)	(0.2%)
Surplus / (deficit) regulatory capital	32.6%	29.4%	23.8%	19.9%	16.4%	(2.6%)	(1.4%)	(1.6%)	(1.3%)	(0.3%)
Reverse Stress										
Total Capital Requirement + Pillar 2B	18.4%	18.6%	20.0%			2.6%	3.9%	6.0%		
Regulatory Capital Resources	54.3%	23.6%	(12.5%)			3.3%	(21.9%)	(51.9%)		
Surplus / (deficit) regulatory capital	35.9%	5.0%	(32.6%)			0.7%	(25.8%)	(58.0%)		

– Reverse stress arises from multiple events and results in breaching the required CET 1 ratio.

3.3 Liquidity Stresses

Orchard has modelled a market-wide, an idiosyncratic and a combined stress scenario to determine the impact on the liquidity position of Orchard under each stress scenario. The stress is undertaken after month 12 and the stress period ranges from 2 weeks to 12 weeks.

For each of the stresses, the base plan drivers were flexed and daily cashflow modelled to assess the impact. The business driver under the base plan and the stresses are presented below:

Table 2: Liquidity Stresses Parameters.

	Base	Market wide	Idiosyncratic	Combined
Deposit retention rate at maturity	80%	75%	50%	25%
New deposits as a percentage of plan	100%	25%	20%	5%
Liquid assets buffer haircut	0%	5%	5%	5%
New loans as a percentage of plan	100%	80%	60%	65%
Loan default rates	0%	5%	3%	5%
Period of stress (weeks)	–	12	2	12

Systemic Market-Wide Stresses

Orchard modelled the impact of a severe recession over the course of six months with negative growth. We used as the baseline Balance Sheet the position at the end of year 1.

– Deposit rollover rates would fall to 75%, i.e., 25% of deposits would be withdrawn at maturity and the accounts closed. This reflects the assumption that (a) in times of severe recession whilst there are no adverse credit events specifically impacting Orchard, it may nevertheless be the case that some depositors move their funds to highly capitalised banks such as HSBC; and (b) with consumers stressed by recession and unemployment we could anticipate that some of the savings on our balance sheet may be drawn down at rollover.
– The recession is assumed to reduce all economic activity and combined with a flight to quality which we anticipate would disproportionately impact new entrant banks, we have assumed that new deposits will be obtained at only 25% of the original planned rate
– Loan default rates spike from planned levels to 5%, reflecting the increased level of insolvencies during a recession.
– New lending declines from 100% to 80% of the planned levels. The level of 80% is consistent with retaining an adequate level of surplus cash (3 days outflows) in

accordance with the bank's risk appetite statement. Lending has been reduced to 80% and not to a lower level in order (i) to preserve the bank's franchise and protect long term customer relationships, and (ii) to recognise that a reduction in economic activity will also lead to an increase in demand for credit from our customers.

Idiosyncratic Stresses

Orchard has modelled a scenario in which there are widespread reports in the media that the bank has experienced severe credit losses on loans, which although as yet uncrystallised are believed to have eliminated a significant portion of the bank's regulatory capital. The bank is perceived to be a new and relatively inexperienced institution and as a result the press comment leads to significant deposit outflows.

- New deposit business runs at only 20% of the previously planned level and maturing deposits have a 50% attrition rate. These assumptions are relatively severe as a name specific stress on a new entrant to the deposit market, risk aversion from depositors will be high notwithstanding the availability of FSCS insurance.
- 40% of new loan business will cease, making new loans only in exceptional cases for existing relationships, and the bank will therefore benefit from a steady net inflow of funds from maturing loans. As the stress scenario is bank specific there is no expectation that our customers would experience increased rates of insolvency. Nevertheless, it is likely that we would not receive all the funds due in for a variety of reasons such as (i) realising that the bank/customer relationship has likely terminated, borrowers may delay repayment (ii) some borrowers may seek to exploit the bank's difficulties and offer to repay on time, but only if they are given a financial incentive. (iii) some borrowers may be unable to repay as they had been budgeting to rollover the loans on maturity. To account for these factors, we have modelled a collection rate of 97% of the sums due.

Combined Stress

Orchard has modelled the impact of a recession coupled with press speculation that Orchard bank had suffered large losses on its loan portfolio, which had significantly reduced its regulatory capital.

- The deposit attrition at maturity has increased considerably to 75% and very few new deposits are expected.
- The default rates have increased significantly and the level of new business has reduced to 65% of the planned lending.

Reverse Stress

No reverse stress test has been undertaken given the short-term nature of the Orchard's lending book which drives considerable cash inflows as demonstrated in the stresses above and the significantly higher Pillar 1 ratios maintained, with high level of liquidity.

Stress Scenario Results

The impact on the liquidity position under each scenario relative to base is as follows:

Table 3: Liquidity Stresses Summary.

	Base Plan	Market wide	Idiosyncratic	Combined
Period of stress (weeks)	**Year 1** **£'000**	**Post 12 weeks** **£'000**	**Post 2 weeks** **£'000**	**Post 12 weeks** **£'000**
Funding Source				
Deposits		625	83	125
Loan Repayment		20,947	3,565	20,947
Total Funding		**21,572**	**3,648**	**21,072**
Funding Consumption				
Loans		(20,753)	(2,638)	(16,862)
Deposit attrition		(1,579)	(526)	(4,736)
Total funding consumption		**(22,332)**	**(3,165)**	**(21,598)**
Net funding surplus / (consumption)		**(760)**	**484**	**(526)**
Liquid assets				
Cash at bank	1,000	1,000	1,000	1,000
Liquid asset buffer	7,038	6,278	7,521	6,512
Total liquid assets	**8,038**	**7,278**	**8,521**	**7,512**
Loan asset	**32,759**	**30,921**	**30,868**	**27,224**
Deposits	**21,050**	**20,096**	**20,607**	**16,439**
Ratios				
% Liquid Assets to Loans	25%	24%	28%	28%
% Liquid Assets to Deposits	38%	36%	41%	46%
% HQLA to Deposits	33%	31%	36%	40%
LCR %	5572%	5207%	6083%	6602%
NSFR %	161%	166%	172%	169%

Base equates to the start position before the stress and is as at the end of year 1.

4 Recovery Planning and the Risk Management Framework

4.1 Overview

The company's Risk Management Framework has the following key elements relevant to the Recovery Plan:

– A schedule of Key Risk Indicators (KRIs) linked to each of the key risks identified in the business.

- Allocation of responsibility for all KRIs to first line of defence (individual) and second line of defence (Executive Committee or Asset and Liability Committee (ALCO)).
- For each KRI, a defined risk measure comprising a target, an EWI, and a Trigger indicator, based on the company's risk appetite and as defined in the Risk Appetite Statement.
- A documented process, overseen by the CRO, for the reporting of actual and projected performance relative to each KRI to the second line of defence.
- A clearly defined escalation process to ensure that any breaches are dealt with in accordance with the Board's requirements.

4.2 Key Risk Indicators

EWIs and triggers have been established by the Board for each of the key risks faced by the business.

The EWIs focus on manageable, forward looking measures of risk and are linked to Orchard's risk appetite.

The EWI structure is intended to be both proportionate to Orchard's business model, which is relatively simple, but also to encompass fully the range of risks faced by the business. Risks monitored include marketwide indicators as well as Orchard-specific indicators.

Orchard's management will also proactively monitor the market for early warning signs that might lead to a general market deterioration, or situations that might have a particular impact on Orchard, such as signalling a worsening of stress conditions or warning about an imminent issue.

Orchard will employ internal EWIs and triggers to identify and monitor significant and unexplained negative movements. When these EWIs are breached, predetermined reporting and oversight processes will be initiated to investigate and establish the cause, which will then determine the course of action to be taken.

EWIs provide a forewarning before a trigger is breached and provide the management team with the required cushion to take action before a breach occurs

EWI thresholds have been calibrated taking into account how long it might take for remedial management actions to have an effect.

The following table is extracted from Orchard's Risk Appetite Statement and sets out Orchard's EWIs and triggers. Orchard acknowledges that the EBA has released its guidelines on the minimum indicators that firms should include in Recovery Plans. Whilst a large number of these will be used by Orchard within its EWI framework, a few are not included as they are not considered relevant.

The rationale for and determination of the level of these EWIs and triggers is an annual process linked to the ICAAP and ILAAP and is fully described in the Risk Management Framework.

Table 4: Risk Metrics.

Limit category		Target	Early warning indicator (Amber)	Trigger (Red)	Primary Responsibility
Financial	Return on Equity (PAT)	7%	>6%	>5%	CFO
	Net Interest Margin (monthly wt. average assets)	14.5%	>12%	>10%	CFO
	Average cost of funds higher than Plan	0%	>2%	>3%	CFO
	Cost: Income ratio	64%	>70%	>75%	CFO
	Net lending balances v Plan	100%	>80%	>70%	CFO
Economic	GDP Growth Rate (quarterly)	0%	=>0%	=>-0.25%	CFO
	Unemployment rolling 12m change	4%	>5.5%	>6.5%	CFO
	Base Rate	0.75%	1.25%	1.50%	CFO
Capital	CET1 Ratio (PRA min 8%)	30%	22.50%	20%	CFO
	Leverage Ratio (PRA min 3.25%)	28%	25%	22%	CFO
	Surplus Capital over TCR & Pillar 2B	£5.5m	>£5.5m	>£2.5m	CFO
Liquidity	Liquidity Coverage Ratio (LCR PRA min 100%)	150%	125%	110%	CFO
	Net Stable Funding Ratio (NSFR 100%)	125%	110%	105%	CFO
	Survival Horizon under stress (PRA min 30days)	90 days	75 days	60 days	CFO
	HQLAs to Deposits	14%	12%	8%	CFO
	Increase in cost of fundsfor deposits above the average of top ten providers on Money.co.uk website	Av. Of top ten providers for 1 year and 2 year fixed rate deposits	= or >100 basis points	= >200 basis points	CFO
Market	Interest Rate Risk Sensitivity – % of CET1	2.3%	2.70%	3%	CFO

Credit	Loan losses as percentage of total loan portfolio	1%	Equal to or >1.5%	Equal to or >2%	CEO
	60 days arrears % of loan asset	<3%	Equal to or >3%	Equal to or >5%	CEO
Operations	Monthly Operational Losses (inc Fraud)	£0	>£200k <£250k	>£250k	CEO
	Rolling 12 months Operational Losses (inc Fraud)	£0	>£600k <£750k	>£750k	CEO
	Operation Risk – Unavailability of Systems	0 days	1 day	2 days	CEO
	Loss of IT equipment (no reportable data breach)	0	2	3	CEO
	Reportable Data Breach	0	1	2	CEO
	Operational Risk – Loss of Key Personnel (Board Directors and direct reports) over six month rolling period	0 persons	2 persons	4 persons	CEO
	Operational Risk – Loss due to failure of Controls	£0 loss	Near miss or potential loss of any amount	An actual loss of >=£62,000	CEO
	1st LOD Control Assurance Plan Results	100–95%	94–85%	<85%	CEO
	2nd LOD Control Assurance Plan Results	100–95%	94–85%	<85%	CRO
	Third Party SLA violation	0	1 Minor	>1 minor	CRO
Conduct & Compliance	Current Complaints as %age customer base	0	0.50%	1%	CRO
	Compliance Training Programme	100–95%	94–85%	<85%	CRO
	Compliance Monitoring Programme	100–95%	94–85%	<85%	CRO

(continued)

Table 4 (continued)

Limit category	Target	Early warning indicator (Amber)	Trigger (Red)	Primary Responsibility
Total Upheld FOS complaints as %age customer base	0	0.25%	0.50%	CRO
Reportable Compliance Breaches Rolling 12 months	0	1	2	CRO
Regulatory Permission – Sanction or Withdrawal of Permission	0	Major systems or controls breakdown. Going concern issue.	Notice from PRA	CRO

Table 5: Secondary Liquidity Risk Metrics.

Metric	Trigger (Red)
High Quality Liquid Assets (HQLA) to Deposits	Minimum of 8% of deposits
Deposit Inflows as proportion of budgeted inflows	Min 70%, Max 130%
Retention rate of maturing fixed term deposits	Min 50%
Proportion of deposit maturing within any 3 month rolling period	Max 25%
Number of payment systems	Min 2
Savings Operational Trigger per month in Year 1 of the plan	Postal applications volume >75 (value – £1.8m) Web application form downloads >300

5 Monitoring, Reporting and Escalation

5.1 KRI Reporting

Reporting of actual and projected outcomes relative to expectations is a fundamental part of the firm's control structure. The Key Risk Indicator Report (KRI Report) is prepared to compare actual and projected risk measures and qualitative indicators with the company's documented risk appetite.

The Risk Appetite Statement sets out for each risk measure a target, an EWI, and a Trigger indicator. The KRI Report sets out the actual outcomes for each risk measure and compares them with the Target, the EWI and the Trigger.

The KRI Report is produced on a monthly basis under the direction of the CRO and is presented to the Executive Committee and to the Asset and Liability Committee (ALCO). Each committee has been delegated responsibility for oversight of certain of the risk measures as a key element of their second line of defence oversight responsibilities. Details of this delegation are set out in the Risk Management Framework.

Metrics are also reported to the Risk Committee which has an oversight role (see Table 6 for the escalation process).

All Risk Appetite risks are considered by either the Exco or the ALCO.

The committees are also required to consider whether there are any other risks not currently covered by the KRI Report which should be escalated to the Board. This would include, for example, specific consideration of emerging risks requiring Board attention.

The company considers that the risk measures set out in its RAS fully cover the mandatory and discretionary indicators set out in the EBA Guidelines (capital, liquidity, profitability, asset quality, market-based, macroeconomic).

By linking the indicators to the company's Risk Management Framework the company is able to demonstrate that the implementation of recovery options is an integral part of risk management processes.

5.2 Escalation Process

The Risk Management Framework sets out the escalation process around breach and prospective breach of the limits set out in the company's risk appetite statement. This process has the following stages:
- EWI breach
- Persistent EWI breach
- Level 1 Trigger Breach
- Level 2 Trigger Breach-Crisis Recovery Plan/Liquidity Contingency Plan
- Level 3 Trigger Breach-possible regulatory resolution plan

Responsibilities for oversight and action are determined by the classification of the breach.

The classification of the breach is initially determined by the CRO and is subject to subsequent review and potential reclassification by the relevant committee and the Board.

A breach classified as a Level 2 Trigger Breach leads to immediate implementation of the company's Recovery Plan and/or Liquidity Contingency Plan. These are described in more detail elsewhere in this document.

The table below illustrates how the escalation process works in practice:

The above is described in more detail in the following sections:

5.3 EWI Breach

Each committee is required to review each risk measure for which it is responsible. For any measure where an EWI measure has been breached, the committee is required to consider whether remedial actions are necessary, to determine what these actions should be and their likely efficacy, in particular that the actions are expected to resolve the breach before a Trigger Breach can occur, and to report their conclusions and actions to the Risk Committee. Committee deliberations will be recorded in the minutes of the relevant committee meeting.

The committees will determine the future frequency of monitoring of any EWI that has been breached (and any other measure that the committee might wish to monitor more frequently than usual). The CRO is responsible for ensuring that the required reporting is put in place.

Table 6: Escalation Process.

Step	Event	Step actions	Key responsibility
1	EWI breach noted in KRI Report	CRO ensures relevant committee (Exco or ALCO dependent on the related risk) is notified	CRO
		Exco/ALCO concludes whether breach can be remediated and if not breach is redesignated as a Trigger Breach. Exco/ALCO inform Risk Committee.	Exco or ALCO
		Risk Committee reports to Board on all unremediated breaches	Risk Committee
		Breaches unremediated after 6 months require Board approval of extension of remediation period or alternatively redesignation as Trigger Breach	Board
2	Trigger Breach noted in KRI Report Risk Committee redesignates EWI Breach as a Trigger Breach Board redesignates persistent EWI Breach or combination of EWI Breaches as a Trigger Breach	Escalated immediately to the Board with management recommendations from Exco/ALCO Board determines on the basis of the severity and remediability of the breach the required classification of the breach between Level 1, Level 2 and Level 3	ALL
3	Level 1 Trigger Breach-expected to be resolvable within regulatory capital and liquidity limits	Board approves and monitors management actions	Board
4	Level 2 Trigger Breach-expected to be resolvable but not within regulatory capital and liquidity limits	Board instructs CEO to convene Exco which in turn implement the Recovery Plan and/or the Liquidity Contingency Plan Board instructs CEO to immediately notify the regulatory authorities	Exco
5	Level 3 Trigger Breach-not expected to be resolvable	Board instructs CEO to immediately notify the regulatory authorities	Board

The CEO is responsible for coordinating the Exco and ALCO meetings and for ensuring that the required remedial actions are communicated to the relevant executives.

The CEO is also responsible for ensuring all EWI breaches, actions, and matters requiring Board consideration are duly escalated to the Risk Committee or Board as appropriate.

Any EWI breach will remain as an agenda item for review at each subsequent Exco, ALCO, Risk Committee and Board meeting until such time as the breach has been remediated.

The KRI reporting process follows the company's regular monthly reporting cycle within the delegated committees and the quarterly reporting cycle for oversight by the Board, unless the CRO considers that a matter should be escalated to the Board at any other time. KRI's for management review will be produced more frequently. This might include, for example, instances of an EWI breach where the relevant committees conclude (whether at that the time of the initial breach or on subsequent review) that remedial actions are unlikely to resolve the breach before a Trigger Breach occurs.

In the early stages of the bank's operation there is likely to be a de facto escalation to the Board earlier than in the prescribed esclalation, as governance structures and reporting routines are bedding in.

5.4 Persistent EWI Breach

Any EWI breaches not remediated within six months will be specifically considered by the Board which must decide whether the relevant committee should continue to oversee the remedial action plan, or whether the breach should be escalated, meaning that the breach will be reclassified as a Trigger Breach and responded to accordingly.

The CRO is responsible for ensuring persistent breaches are escalated to the Board.

5.5 Trigger Breach

A Trigger Breach can be defined as one of the following-

- An EWI Breach where remedial action has been ineffective and the Board has determined that further action is required
- An EWI Breach where the Risk Committee has determined that remedial action is unlikely to be effective in preventing a future Trigger Breach, in which case the EWI Breach is escalated to the Board and reclassified as a Trigger Breach
- An immediate breach of a trigger limit without a prior EWI Breach. If such a Trigger Breach occurs, the CRO is responsible for immediate communication of the breach to the Board. A Trigger Breach requires the Board to meet to review the breach within 48 hours of notification.

Table 7: Breach Levels.

Description	Further Explanation	Example
Level 1 Breach expected to be resolvable within regulatory capital and liquidity requirements (albeit outside risk appetite tolerances) with no impact on the bank's critical functions	Management actions expected to remediate the breach Actions would comprise adjustments to the company's strategy, with a likely impact on profitability but with the company remaining within regulatory requirements Actions would be taken under the direction of the Board Bank continues to operate all critical functions	The stress scenarios considered in the company's ICAAP and ILAAP would fall into this category, indicating the impact of these stresses and related management actions can be absorbed within existing projected capital and liquidity resources Orchard's Pillar 2B capital is not affected by these stress scenarios Management actions in the ICAAP and ILAAP stress tests were as follows- Anchor scenario – reduce lending rates to counter loan volume reduction caused by economic downturn; maintain deposit inflows by increasing deposit rates; tighten credit processes to reduce bad debt rate back down to planned level
Level 2 Breach expected to be resolvable but not within regulatory capital and liquidity requirements	Crisis Recovery Plan and/or Liquidity Contingency Plan is implemented Management actions expected to remediate the breach but not without breaching regulatory capital and/or liquidity requirements Actions would comprise adjustments to the company's strategy with a likely impact on profitability but and with the company temporarily breaching regulatory requirements Supplementary actions necessary Bank continues to operate all critical functions Regulator communication necessary	Capital and liquidity projections indicate the severity of the events is such that regulatory capital and liquidity requirements will not be met. However the projected impact of management actions (including the supplementary actions) expected to be sufficient to restore the company's capital and liquidity within a timescale acceptable to the regulatory authorities Such an event would be more severe than the stress scenarios considered in the company's ILAAP and ICAAP

(continued)

Table 7 (continued)

Description	Further Explanation	Example
Level 3 Breach not expected to be resolvable	Immediate notification to the regulatory authorities Management actions including supplementary actions not expected to remediate the breach In conjunction with regulatory authorities, invoke Resolution Plan	Capital and liquidity projections indicate the severity of the events is such that regulatory capital and liquidity requirements will not be met and that projected impact of management actions (including the supplementary actions) will not be sufficient to restore the company's capital and liquidity within a timescale acceptable to the regulatory authorities Example would be the company's reverse stress test scenario

The Board will immediately consider the remedial action and determine the required classification of the breach into one of 3 different levels, each of which has a different required response. These are set out in the following table-

6 Management Actions

6.1 Overview

In conjunction with its stress testing process, Orchard has undertaken an exercise to define likely remedial management actions in response to EWI and Trigger breaches, or variances from Target. These actions are part of the company's Recovery Plan and are intended to demonstrate the recovery options that would be implemented in the initial stages of any deterioration.

The intention also is to be able to define how the company would be able to respond to a continuing deterioration illustrating how additional recovery options would be implemented should a deterioration became more severe, including the specific triggers for such actions.

In combination this schedule of actions constitutes the framework of indicators which identifies the points at which appropriate actions referred to in the plan may be taken, together with a description of the decision-making process relating to the activation of the recovery plan (EBA Guidelines on the minimum list of qualitative and quantitative recovery plan indicators).

Finally, management actions are cross referenced to the stress scenarios described in the ICAAP and ILAAP to illustrate how the recovery plan would respond to a combination of breaches of increasing severity.

As such, the recovery plan covers a diverse and credible 'menu of financial options' available to the Bank to action in order to address a severe stress scenario impact which may and can be caused by either idiosyncratic problems, a larger financial system failure or a combination of the two.

6.2 Ladder of Actions

The company has identified a range of actions that could be taken, together or in isolation, in response to variances to target, EWI and trigger Breaches.

The extent of each action can be varied as necessary to remediate the breach.

Actions are set out below-

Adjustments to commercial operating terms – raise/lower lending rates; raise/lower deposit rates; tighten/loosen underwriting criteria; extend/reduce range of lending products; extend/reduce range of deposit products

Adjustments to operations – align costs with revenues, eg cost reduction programme; revise operating strategy and reforecast profit, capital and liquidity requirements

Supplementary actions – if a wholesale lending facility is in place, draw down on the facility to supplement liquidity; draw down on liquidity buffer; reduce/suspend dividend payments to supplement liquidity and/or conserve CET 1 capital; use loan book as collateral for central bank funding drawdown; use loan book as collateral for third party funding; sale of loan book; fund raising from shareholders; changes to company strategy

It is envisaged that Supplementary Actions would only be taken in response to a Trigger Breach.

The table below illustrates the management actions that could be taken in response to risk events.

These risk events can be cross-referenced to the company's ICAAP and ILAAP, where they support the development of the company's capital and liquidity stress scenarios.

In practice, required management actions and any enhanced monitoring processes will be determined at the time by the committees responsible for oversight of the risk being measured.

7 Invocation of Recovery Plan and Liquidity Contingency Plan

The Recovery Plan and the Liquidity Contingency Plan must be invoked immediately after it has been concluded by the Board that a Trigger Breach cannot be remediated without the company breaching regulatory capital and liquidity requirements.

This consideration may be in response to an escalation of an existing breach or breaches, where management actions have already proved ineffective.

If the Board concludes that the Trigger Breach can be remediated, the CEO will be instructed to invoke the Recovery Plan and/or the LCP.

If the Board concludes that the Trigger Breach cannot be remediated, the CEO will be required to immediately contact the regulatory authorities with a view to the Regulator invoking the resolution plan.

The operation of the Recovery Plan and the LCP is described in the following sections of this document.

8 Recovery Plan

The CEO is responsible for creating an emergency Exco or emergency ALCO, depending on the nature of the incident, that is responsible for crisis management and the return to 'business as usual' state. In an extreme situation, where recovery is not possible, the emergency Exco will oversee an orderly wind-down of Orchard's business.

Table 8: Management Actions in response to liquidity risk events.

Event	EWI Metrics/Potential Breach Impacted by Event	Management Actions in Response to EWI Breach	Possible Constraints
Lending volumes reduction	Net lending balances reduce v plan Cash to loans ratio increases Loans to deposit ratio reduces LCR increases as HQLA increases as deposit inflows unchanged but lending outflows reduce. Net outflows unchanged as inflows in the calculation limited to 75% of outflows NSFR increases as Required Stable Funding reduces Regulatory capital requirement reduces as RWAs reduce	Reduce loan rates to increase volumes, if related reduction in profits/capital allows capital margins to be maintained within risk appetite tolerances Reduce deposit rates to scale back deposit volumes proportionately Reforecast capital and liquidity positions and monitor	Projected capital/liquidity position limits extent to which rates can be reduced; market conditions limit impact of reduced loan rates Projected profitability adversely affected Projected Trigger breach
Loan rates reduction	Net interest margin reduces LCR reduces as HQLA reduces due to reduced interest income NSFR reduces as reduced profits reduce capital which in turn reduces Available Stable Funds	Reduce deposit rates in order to preserve net interest margins Reproject capital and liquidity positions and monitor	Market conditions preclude reduction in deposit rates Projected profitability adversely affected Projected Trigger breach
Deposit volume reductions	Deposit inflows below Plan Loan to deposit ratio increases Cash to deposit ratio increases LCR reduces as HQLA reduces, partially offset by reduction in projected Funding Outflows NSFR reduces as Available Stable Funding reduces	Increase deposit flows through rate increases Increase loan rates to scale back lending volumes proportionately Draw down wholesale bank facilities enabling continuation of lending albeit at higher cost Reduce projected shareholder dividends thus retaining liquidity to support continuation of lending Reproject capital and liquidity positions and monitor	Material rate increases necessary due to adverse market conditions Volume reductions linked to company specific concerns, eg credit quality Projected capital/liquidity position limits extent to which rates can be reduced; market conditions limit impact of reduced loan rates Projected profitability adversely affected

(continued)

Table 8 (continued)

Event	EWI Metrics/Potential Breach Impacted by Event	Management Actions in Response to EWI Breach	Possible Constraints
Deposit rate increases	Net interest margin reduces LCR reduces as HQLA reduces due to increased interest expense NSFR reduces as reduced profits reduce capital which in turn reduces Available Stable Funds	Increase loan rates to maintain net interest margin	Market conditions preclude increase in loan rates Projected profitability adversely affected
Cost of risk increases	Loan losses as % of loan portfolio increase Payment delay as % of loan portfolio increases LCR reduces as HQLA reduces due to increased loan losses NSFR reduces as reduced profits reduce capital which in turn reduces Available Stable Funds	Review lending policy and tighten lending and underwriting criteria Increase loan rates to compensate	Tighter lending criteria and increased loan rate reduce loan volumes Increased cost of risk attributable to general economic conditions Projected profitability adversely affected
Expenses increase	Cost to income ratio exceeds plan LCR reduces as HQLA reduces due to increased expense outgoings NSFR reduces as reduced profits reduce capital which in turn reduces Available Stable Funds	Implement cost saving plan Increase loan rates/reduce deposit rates to maintain profitability	Market conditions preclude rate changes; cost increases structural/market-wide Projected profitability adversely affected

8.1 Governance

Orchard will form an emergency Exco/ALCO, chaired by the CEO and comprising other ALCO and Exco members, to evaluate the action steps required to contain a crisis event on the basis of the perceived nature, severity and duration of the situation. The Board will be informed immediately about the crisis, will be asked to agree the Recovery Plan and then will be regularly updated on the progress made against the agreed recovery plan. The CEO is responsible for executing the Recovery Plan, detailing projections, steps to be taken, timescales and risk assessment.

The emergency Exco/ALCO will comprise their usual membership, plus guests as required. Individual responsibilities are outlined below.

Table 9: Emergency Exco/ALCO Member Responsibilities.

Title	Responsibility
CEO	Overall responsibility for development and execution of the Recovery Plan. Primary responsibility for all internal (Board, Staff & Suppliers) and external (Regulators, Shareholders, Orchard, Customers) communication. Monitor and evaluate regulatory issues including communications with the Regulators. Ensure franchise viability based on the actions proposed by the committee
CFO and CRO	Manage liquidity positions. Analyse the impact of potential actions on cash positions and on the quality of the securities portfolio. Analyse the impact of potential actions on the credit quality of the asset portfolio. Report financial statements and positions against internal and regulatory triggers, cash-flows and financial implications. Analyse the accounting information, monitor and evaluate risks and regulatory compliance issues.
Head of IT	Ensure the systems and controls are robust and can meet the requirements of the Recovery Plan.

Other staff members or Board members can also be included as part of the emergency committee, depending on the severity and type of crisis.

8.2 Communication With Regulatory Authorities

Invocation of the Recovery Plan is predicated on an actual or prospective breach of regulatory requirements. It is the responsibility of the CEO to promptly notify the Regulator that the Recovery Plan has been invoked and to agree communication and reporting requirements for the duration of the crisis period.

8.3 Other Communication

Timely internal and external communication is very important in managing a crisis. The extent of the communication and the parties to be informed will vary based on the severity and nature of the crisis. This section outlines how internal and external communication will be managed during a crisis.

Internal Communication

Internal communication ensures relevant staff members, especially staff interacting with loan customers and funding providers, are briefed concerning the way to manage stakeholders' expectations, most importantly the expectations of Orchard's customers. The emergency committee will be responsible for overall co-ordination of the internal communication, and managers will manage it within their teams, reporting into the committee on its effectiveness.

External Communication

The significant parties to be informed in the event of a crisis are Orchard's Board members, customers, shareholders and regulators. Each of these external stakeholders has different information requirements and the emergency committee should ensure that they are informed in a timely manner. The responsibility for communication with each of these stakeholders is outlined in the table below:

Table 10: Stakeholder Responsibility.

Stakeholder	Key person responsible
Board of Directors and Shareholders	CEO
Regulatory Authorities	CEO
Depositors	CFO
Borrowers	CEO

8.4 Implementation of the Plan

The management course of action outlined by the emergency committee should include:

e) Action plan, including plan to increase funding and/or Capital
   a. Clarification and assessment of the problem
   b. Proposed actions
   c. Identification of funding and/or capital providers (if appropriate)
   d. Amount intended to be raised and timing
   e. Regulatory and legal issues
   f. Dependencies/pre-requisites

f) Timescale for actions and key personnel responsible for implementing each one
g) Assessment of risks and the likelihood of successful mitigation
h) Forward liquidity and capital projections including:
   a. Evolution of the size of the capital and liquidity buffer to restore stability
   b. Changes to Orchard's funding profile
   c. Changes to Orchard's business model
   d. Stress test results to evaluate impact due to various scenarios

The list above is the basic information to be considered by the emergency committee and if necessary additional steps and actions will have to be considered based on the severity and nature of the crisis.

Reporting During Crisis

Daily reports will be created and provided to the emergency committee by the Finance, Treasury and Credit teams. They will highlight the objectives and the impact of actions taken. They will also measure the effects of actions on Orchard's continued observance or compliance with internal and regulatory limits.

In the case of a severe crisis, extra reporting will be provided by the Finance and Credit teams to the emergency committee intra-day. Orchard will put in place the necessary IT and operational infrastructure to supply these additional reports during mobilisation.

In line with the severity of the crisis and the reporting requirements, the emergency committee will disseminate internal information to the management team and Board members as the situation unfolds. Reporting frequency affected both by the severity of the problems and time required to action the Recovery Plan, will be decided by the emergency committee.

Over and above internal reporting Orchard will also take measures to communicate with and provide updates to the regulators and shareholders.

8.5 Recovery Plan options

Orchard has considered a number of credible recovery options, which can be applied to a number of varied stress scenarios that may impact its business. It has to be noted that in certain stress scenarios some of these recovery plan options might not be feasible and the business of Orchard, in such scenarios, will be wound up. Management believes that this document sets out a reasonable range of options proportionate to Orchard's business model.

The recovery options considered are listed below:

5) borrowing against or selling part of its loan book;
6) raising additional wholesale funding;

7) raising additional capital from its shareholders; and
8) adjustment of its business model and reduction of operating costs.

8.6 Summary of Options

This section outlines the menu of credible Recovery Plan options available to Orchard. Orchard's projected first year balance sheet and profit and loss statement were used as the basis to assess the impact of the various Recovery Plan options. Note that normal business as usual actions, e.g., utilising funds in the nostro account would have already been considered before taking the recovery options.

Sale of All or Part of the Debtor Book

Impact and Assessment

At the end of year 1 gross receivables are projected to be £33.1m.

The sale of these assets may incur a haircut ranging from 50% to 75% and Orchard could be able to realise between £16.5m and £24.8m.

Execution/Implementation Issues

The debtor book could be liquidated within one month after suitable discounting. The CEO will be responsible for implementing this option, based on the action plan initiated by the emergency committee.

Potential purchasers would be finance companies, smaller banks and listed debt funds, who would be interested to acquire the assets given their short-term nature and attractive yields. Approaches would be made to Orchard's two main competitors.

Credibility

In a market-wide stress scenario, the population of buyers for the debtor book may be impacted. Orchard considers that there will always be a buyer for a high quality, short-term and yielding debtor book.

In an idiosyncratic stress scenario, the population of buyers for the debtor book should not be impacted and Orchard considers that there will be a number of potential buyers.

Raise Additional Wholesale Funding

Impact and Assessment

Orchard currently relies on wholesale funding to fund its business. When operating as a bank, this will be replaced with a cheaper source of funds in retail deposits. However,

Table 11: Recovery Plan Options – Market-wide scenario.

Recovery option	Core tier 1 capital impact (in nominal amount and bps/%)	Risk-weighted asset impact (in nominal amount and %)	Liquidity Impact (£m)	Assumptions to quantify liquidity/ capital impact	Timing to realisation of the benefits	Summary of hurdles/risks to implementation	Franchise Impact (Low, Medium, High)	Likely effectiveness (Low, Medium, High)	Owner
Sale of debtor book @ 50% discount	£16.5m (96% reduction)	£38.4m (100% reduction)	+£16.5m	Able to sell the assets. Market players willing to take assets at significant haircut	2 days to 1 month	Market-wide crisis causes severe haircuts as population of potential buyers reduced	High	High	CEO
Raise additional wholesale funding			Variable	Ability to raise funds on commercially viable terms	1 month	Market-wide crisis could impact availability of funds to lend and risk appetite of lenders	Low	High	CEO
Raise additional capital from public markets	Intention to raise capital to pre-crisis levels	RWAs will be increased based on usage of new capital		Ability to raise capital in public markets.	Up to 3 months.	Not available if no appetite from public market shareholders, which will be impacted by market-wide stress	High	High	CEO
Adjust business model		Based on strategic business plan/ model approved by the Board		Orchard will continue to be a going concern under an adjusted model.	3–4 months	Willingness of shareholders to support a new business model	Low	Low	CEO

Table 12: Recovery Plan Options – Idiosyncratic scenario.

Recovery option	Core tier 1 capital impact (in nominal amount and bps/%)	Risk-weighted asset impact (in nominal amount and %)	Liquidity Impact (£m)	Assumptions to quantify liquidity/ capital impact	Timing to realisation of the benefits	Summary of hurdles risks to implementation	Franchise Impact (Low, Medium, High)	Likely effectiveness (Low, Medium, High)	Owner
Sale of debtor book @ 25% discount	£8.2m (48% reduction)	£38.4m (100% reduction)	+£24.8m	Able to sell the assets Market players willing to take assets at significant haircut	2 days to 1 month	Idiosyncratic crisis should not cause severe haircuts as population of potential buyers should not be affected	High	High	CEO
Raise additional wholesale funding			Variable	Ability to raise funds on commercially viable terms	1 month	Idiosyncratic crisis could impact willingness to lend or prompt significant risk premium	Low	High	CEO
Raise additional capital from public markets	Intention to raise capital to pre-crisis levels	RWAs will be increased based on usage of new capital		Ability to raise capital in public markets.	Up to 3 months	Idiosyncratic crisis should not cause lack of appetite in public markets	High	High	CEO
Adjust business model		Based on strategic business plan/ model approved by the Board		Orchard will continue to be a going concern under an adjusted model.	3–4 months	Willingness of shareholders to support a new business model	Low	Low	CEO

Table 13: Recovery Plan Options – Combined scenario.

Recovery option	Core tier 1 capital impact (in nominal amount and bps/%)	Risk-weighted asset impact (in nominal amount and %)	Liquidity Impact (£m)	Assumptions to quantify liquidity/ capital impact	Timing to realisation of the benefits	Summary of hurdles risks to implementation	Franchise Impact (Low, Medium, High)	Likely effectiveness (Low, Medium, High)	Owner
Sale of debtor book @50% discount	£16.5m (96% reduction)	£38.4m (100% reduction)	+£16.5m	Able to sell the assets Market players willing to take assets at significant haircut	2 days to 1 months	Combined crisis causes severe haircuts as population of potential buyers reduced	High	High	CEO
Raise additional wholesale funding			Variable	Ability to raise funds on commercially viable terms	1 month	Idiosyncratic crisis could impact willingness to lend or prompt significant risk premium	Low	High	CEO
Raise additional capital from public markets	Intention to raise capital to pre-crisis levels	RWAs will be increased based on usage of new capital		Ability to raise capital in public markets.	Up to 3 months.	Not available if no appetite from public market shareholders, which will be impacted by market-wide stress	High	High	CEO
Adjust business model	Adjust business model			Orchard will continue to be a going concern under an adjusted model	3–4 months	Willingness of shareholders to support a new business model	Low	Low	CEO

wholesale funding would remain as a contingency option if retail deposits were unavailable or inadequate.

Execution/Implementation Issues

Any approach for funding would be subject to the lending banks' appetite for the business and underwriting criteria. Credit committee approval at the lending bank would be required. Approaches would not be limited to Orchard's current providers but its recent history as a customer would be expected to work in its favour with Barclays.

Credibility

In a market-wide stress scenario, the population of banks with an appetitie to lend will be impacted.

In an idiosyncratic stress scenario, underwriting criteria may not be met or the cost of funds may include a significant risk premium.

Raise Additional Capital from Shareholders

Impact and Assessment

Orchard is currently adequately capitalised with £15 million of Common Equity Tier 1 Capital.

At the end of year 1 of trading as a bank, assets will comprise:

1. Amounts receivable from customers;
2. HQLAs, which will all be cash;
3. Cash held in its nostro account or its account at the Bank of England.

In the event that an unprecedented number of customers fail to pay their obligations under their credit agreements Orchard may be in a situation where it is exposed to a loss of its capital resources. In this case Orchard may be able to raise additional capital from the shareholders subject to the conditions specified in the credibility sub-section below.

Execution/Implementation Issues

The lead time required to raise the additional capital could be 6 months or longer and would be dependent on the appetite for further investment and capital position of the shareholders.

Credibility

Recapitalisation by shareholders would depend on the appetite for further capital investment and capital available to the shareholders to re-invest in Orchard, which could be impacted by a market-wide crisis.

Adjust Business Model and Reduce Operating Costs

Impact and Assessment

In the case of a significant crisis, such as the unprecedented failure of the majority of its customers to pay their obligations under credit agreements with Orchard, an adjustment to the firm's business model would be necessary. There would be a contraction in the number of business lines and a commensurate reduction in staff costs and other operating expenses to reduce outward cash flows.

Execution/Implementation Issues

Currently Orchard's employment contracts do not include provision for guaranteed bonuses. Accordingly redundancy costs would not include bonuses or other variable components of remuneration. In order to operate with reduced capital Orchard's business would be limited in the amount of lending it could conduct. The operating expenses for the first year of operations are forecast to total £3.4 million, and a reduction of operating expenses by 20% to 50% can be achieved, subject to a change in Orchard's business model.

Credibility

While trimming its business model and reducing costs Orchard would have to maintain sufficient revenue generating activities to maintain critical mass as a bank and ensure that regulatory and compliance standards were not compromised.

Disposal – Orderly Wind-Down or Sale of Orchard to Third Party

Please note that this is not a specific recovery option and is more of a resolution option, but listed here for completeness.

In the unprecedented event of a large scale failure by Orchard's debtors to pay their obligations to Orchard and where further support is not available from the shareholders, an orderly wind-down of Orchard may be required, or the sale of Orchard considered within a short period. During this period costs would be reduced, in particular staff costs, in line with the contraction of business. The key steps to be executed by the emergency Exco, with reference to capital and liquidity flows, are outlined below:

1) All credit agreements will be collected in, or sold if a buyer is found for them at an acceptable price;
2) Once credit agreements are converted to cash the liquidator would pay off creditors in order of legal priority.

In the event that it was considered that Orchard's authorisation/licence, core staff, systems and infrastructure may be of value to a third party looking to establish a UK bank as quickly as possible, Orchard could be offered for sale. Orchard's Board has an in-depth understanding of the procedures and processes involved in selling a bank.

Remediation Measures

The recovery options identified are, in management's view, the full set of possible options based on Orchard's existing business model.

The Recovery Plan will be reviewed and updated at least on an annual basis. It will also be reviewed and updated, if considered necessary, in the wake of changes to Orchard's business model, risk appetite, concentration of funding sources or changes in stress assumptions.

8.7 Return to Business as Usual State

On return to a 'business-as-usual' state (i.e., measures and metrics are once again within tolerable limits), the emergency committee will continue to monitor the liquidity position closely for a period of at least a month, to assess the enduring impact of actions taken. Such continuous monitoring will also assist in the post-mortem of the crisis event and the implementation of steps to avoid a recurrence.

The emergency committee will be disbanded after one month of returning to the 'business-as-usual' state and the final report of the incident will be submitted to the Board.

Two potential final resolutions for the business are:

3. A sale of Orchard to a third party; and
4. An orderly wind-down of Orchard's business.

In the event of a resolution, no UK economic functions will be impacted and no demands will be made on UK public funds.

We therefore assert that to the best of our knowledge and belief that this document will provide a credible and executable plan in any severe stress scenarios affecting the business of Orchard.

9 Liquidity Contingency Plan

9.1 Overview and Principles

The CEO is responsible for executing the Liquidity Contingency Plan.

Orchard recognises the importance of liquidity for its day-to-day operations and believes it is essential to have a plan for addressing liquidity requirements in times of crisis. A liquidity crisis can arise due to either an internal or external event or a combination of both and our plan addresses both contingencies.

This Liquidity Contingency Plan ('LCP') will be further developed during mobilisation and signed off by the Board as part of the Recovery Plan. It will be updated and approved by the Board annually unless a significant change in the business should warrant an earlier review.

The LCP is a dynamic document and will be updated in light of changes to the Bank's risk profile, regulation, markets and competition. The growth in the Bank's business from £33million of loan assets in year 1 to a projected £93m of loan assets in year 5 will result in significant changes to the funding profile, with early reliance upon capital giving way to retail deposits.

At least once a year, the CFO will initiate a dummy run of the liquidity contingency plan to assess the continued readiness for invocation in response to a real crisis.

9.2 Invocation

Liquidity will be monitored through regular, timely MI, generated by the Finance department and distributed to Exco.

The primary and secondary liquidity risk metrics will be published within the MI. Breach levels and the related escalation process are described in detail in the Recovery Plan, and summarised below.

9.3 Escalation Process

This process has the following stages:
- EWI breach
- Persistent EWI breach
- Level 1 Trigger Breach
- Level 2 Trigger Breach- Recovery Plan/Liquidity Contingency Plan
- Level 3 Trigger Breach-possible Resolution Plan

Responsibilities for oversight and action are determined by the classification of the breach.

The classification of the breach is initially determined by the CRO and is subject to subsequent review and potential reclassification by the relevant committee and the Board.

A breach classified as a Level 2 Trigger Breach leads to immediate implementation of the Bank's Recovery Plan and/or Liquidity Contingency Plan.

The table below illustrates how the escalation process works in practice for a liquidity EWI breach:

Table 14: Escalation Process.

Step	Event	Step actions	Key responsibility
1	EWI breach noted in KRI Report	CRO ensures relevant committee (ALCO for liquidity issues) is notified	CRO
		ALCO determines whether breach can be remediated and, if not, breach is redesignated as a Trigger Breach. ALCO informs Risk Committee.	ALCO
		Risk Committee report to Board on all unremediated breaches	Risk Committee
		Breaches unremediated after 6 months require Board approval of extension of remediation period or alternatively redesignation as Trigger Breach	Board
2	Trigger Breach noted in KRI Report Risk Committee/ALCO redesignates EWI Breach as a Trigger Breach Board redesignates persistent EWI Breach or combination of EWI Breaches as a Trigger Breach	Escalated immediately to the Board Board determines on the basis of the severity and remediability of the breach, the required classification of the breach between Level 1, Level 2 and Level 3	Board
3	Level 1 Trigger Breach-expected to be resolvable within regulatory capital and liquidity limits	Board approves and monitors management actions	Board
4	Level 2 Trigger Breach-expected to be resolvable but not within regulatory capital and liquidity limits	Board instructs CEO to convene Exco which in turn implements the Recovery Plan and/or the Liquidity Contingency Plan. Board instructs CEO to immediately notify the regulatory authorities	Exco
5	Level 3 Trigger Breach-not expected to be resolvable	Board instructs CEO to immediately notify the regulatory authorities	Board

9.4 Governance

When the LCP is invoked, Orchard will form an emergency ALCO, chaired by the CEO, to evaluate the steps required to contain a crisis event on the basis of the perceived nature, severity and duration of the situation. The CEO is responsible for executing the LCP, detailing projections, steps to be taken, timescales, risk assessment and escalation to the Board.

The Emergency ALCO will perform an assessment of the situation and prioritise the tasks necessary to achieve a recovery. In addition, it will be responsible for on-going monitoring and the submission of detailed, timely reports on the situation to the Board. The Board will convene as required during the crisis. Any decision to initiate the Resolution Plan resides with the Board.

9.5 Communications

Invocation of the LCP is predicated on an actual or prospective breach of regulatory requirements. It is the responsibility of the CEO to promptly notify the Regulator that the LCP has been invoked and to agree communication and reporting requirements for the duration of the crisis period.

An important goal of the Bank during the period the LCP is invoked is to communicate stability to its customers. The Bank will not only be seeking funds to cover its obligations, but also to finance new assets for business continuity.

Recent events have shown that concerns about a bank's solvency can arise quickly. Attempting to access new markets or sources of liquidity where the Bank has not previously been a regular and active participant may exacerbate existing concerns.

The CEO, in consultation with the Board, will manage external communications during this period in order to mitigate any adverse reputational consequences arising from steps taken under the LCP.

9.6 Implementation of the Plan

Prior to the meeting of the Emergency ALCO, the Finance team will produce the following MIS reports:
- Deposit analysis;
- Maturity analysis;
- Cash flow projections;
- A schedule of any committed payments.

The Emergency ALCO will make an initial consideration of the circumstances and review the sources of liquidity that are available in the market to classify the issue as:
1. Short term liquidity crisis;
2. Long term liquidity crisis; or
3. The issue is not yet critical but enhanced vigilance is required.

Actions required for a Short-Term Liquidity Crisis

A short-term liquidity issue is likely to arise from a shock to the financial system which disrupts funding operations. Such a crisis would be temporary in nature and would most likely not involve a significant change to the credit standing of the Bank.

The Emergency ALCO will inform the Board of Directors and set out the circumstances and the recommended measures.

Actions available to the Emergency ALCO to resolve the crisis:

- Draw down any of the Bank's borrowing facilities;
- Reduce lending;
- Prioritise payments:
  - repayment of depositors
  - interbank payments
  - expenses
  - new lending already confirmed
- Increasing the rates offered on deposits to increase retention as well as new business;
- Increasing the rates on new loans to reduce the lending volumes.

Actions Required for a Long-Term Liquidity Crisis

The Emergency ALCO will similarly convene a meeting of the Executive Committee and inform it that there is a long-term liquidity problem, set out the circumstances, the expected duration of the issue, and the recommended measures. The Executive Committee will inform the Board and the PRA of the nature of the problem and the Bank's proposed actions.

The Finance team will produce a run off schedule of assets and liabilities setting out the contractual cash-flows and the supplementary actions to be taken under the LCP through to the conclusion of the crisis. The run off schedule will be produced regularly until the crisis has been resolved.

Actions available / required to deal with a long-term liquidity crisis will include all those available under a short-term crisis, and in addition the following:

- Cease taking on new lending customers;
- Cease new lending to existing customers;
- Review deposit pricing in order to stimulate deposit flows;
- Negotiate new bank facilities;
- Seek to raise additional capital;
- Enter into a repurchase agreement with the Bank of England in respect of its assets, subject to the rules of the Sterling Monetary Framework;
- Sale of loan assets;
- Arrange meetings or other communications with certain depositors. Such meetings or communications should be used to reassure depositors and to determine their intent at rollover;
- Commence an orderly wind down of Orchard's operations.

6 The Resolution Plan

A bank will be required to prepare a Resolution Plan in line with PRA Supervisory Statement SS19/13. The Resolution Plan will set out the steps the bank will take to wind down and close its business operations.

6.1 Ownership and Legal Structure

As per the RBP, ICAAP, ILAAP and Recovery Plan the Resolution Plan will set out the ownership and legal structure of a bank.

6.2 Business Model

Again, as per the RBP, ICAAP, ILAAP and Recovery Plan the Resolution Plan will set out the ownership and legal structure of a bank.

6.3 Capital and Funding

As per the RBP, ICAAP and ILAAP, the Recovery Plan will set out the capital plan of the bank and the liquidity plan for the bank.

6.4 Economic Functions

Each bank will be required to set out its 'Economic Functions' and metrics around each of those Economic Functions. Economic Functions can include:
- Deposit Taking and Savings
- Lending and Loan Servicing
- Capital Markets & Investment
- Wholesale Funding Markets
- Payments, Clearing, Custody and Settlement

There are further requirements to provide details on the following matters:
- Derivatives
- Trading Portfolio
- Securities Financing
- Cash Services

https://doi.org/10.1515/9783111101545-006

- ATMs or Branches
- Legal Entities

The bank will be required to set out the inter-relationship of each of the Economic Functions, between legal entities and business units within the bank.

The bank will be required to set out the impact of the cessation of Economic Functions on the wider financial markets.

The party who is responsible for the Resolution Plan will be set out in the Plan. This is usually the CFO.

6.5 Template Resolution Plan

Table of Contents

Table of Tables

Table of Figures

Phase 1 Part A – Corporate Structure & Significant Legal Entity Information

This Resolution Plan has been prepared in line with PRA Supervisory Statement SS19/13.

1 Covid-19

This document was well advanced in its review process at the start of the Covid-19 pandemic. No attempt has been made to revise the document, reforecast any macroeconomic model parameters or predict specific impacts on the insurance industry or any of the other markets served by Orchard. Nor have any counter-cyclical buffers been deducted from our capital requirement calculations.

As a non-discretionary item of expenditure we do not expect Covid-19 to materially affect spend on insurance premiums, which remains the main focus of Orchard's business. Customers' ability to pay will doubtless be impacted by the current crisis but Orchard believes that constructive engagement in forbearance arrangements and, ultimately, its ability to rely on recourse arrangements will limit impairment downsides to below the levels already modelled in the ICAAP stress tests. With regard to short-term liquidity, Orchard believes that its short-term amortising loan book and existing bank liquidity facilities will allow Orchard to trade through the immediate impact of the pandemic.

2 Orchard Ownership and Legal Structure

Orchard's ownership and legal structure and business model are set out in Orchard's Regulatory Business Plan and are repeated below.

Currently, primarily for historic reasons, the group operates through two wholly owned subsidiaries Orchard Funding Limited (OFL) and Bexhill UK Limited (Bexhill). The current structure of the group is set out in Figure 1 below.

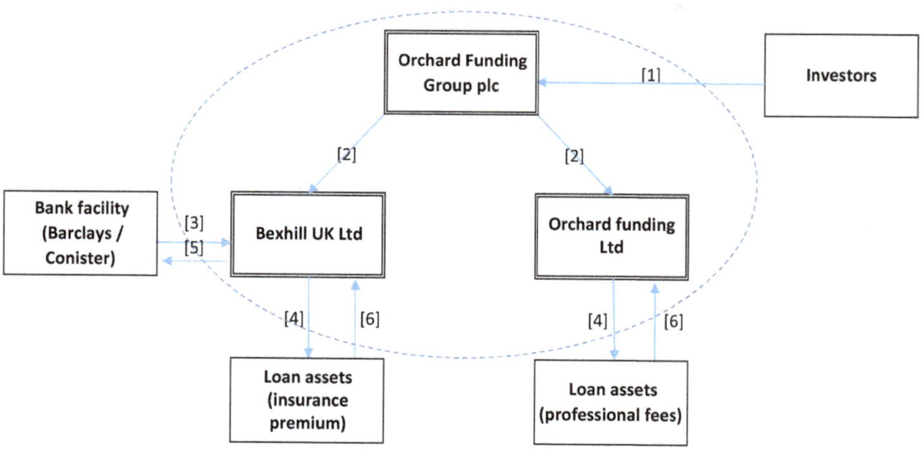

[1] Capital
[2] Intercompany loans from Group plc
[3] £17 million Barclays warehouse facility secured on loan assets
[4] Customer loans
[5] Charge over the loan agreements
[6] Monthly instalments

Figure 1: Orchard Funding Group – current structure chart.

Subject to tax and legal considerations the intention is that the 3 legal entities (within the dotted line) will be merged into one with all operational activities transferred into Orchard Funding Group PLC (Orchard) as reflected in Figure 2. Orchard Funding Group PLC will seek authorisation as a bank. The existing businesses carried on through OFL and Bexhill will continue to operate as profit centres within the merged legal entity.

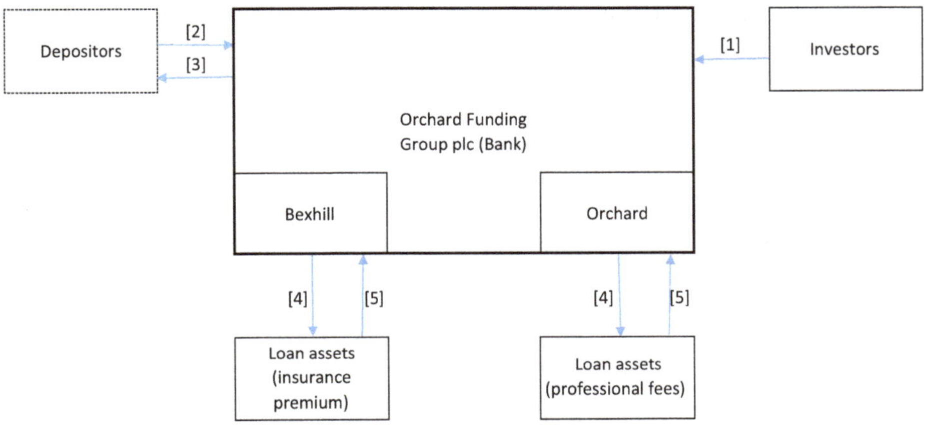

[1] Capital
[2] Proposed new fixed term deposits - 1 and 2 years
[3] Repay deposit with interest
[4] Customer loans
[5] Monthly instalments

Figure 2: Orchard Funding Group – target structure chart.

These changes are intended to reduce the administrative burden of having multiple legal entities and allow resources to be shared across the company's divisions thus reducing risk and increasing efficiency. Bexhill and Orchard are currently authorised by the FCA as consumer credit lenders and credit brokers. Application will be made to pass on these authorisations to the new bank. Reducing the number of regulated entities from 2 to 1, which will streamline the FCA and PRA's regulatory processes.

The move from the current structure to the new banking structure will be planned in detail during mobilisation. It will include procedures to ring fence the encumbered assets against the bank borrowing as the loan assets are repaid and the bank facility is reduced. All new lending with related deposits will be recorded in the bank, separate from the historic asset.

Orchard also have some minority investments in a number of corporates which are not material and which will be retained post authorisation. These include a 20% stake in Accolade Education Finance Limited, a 30% stake in Open B Gateway Limited (a software development firm) and a 35% stake in Zebra Finance Limited (financing golf membership and season ticket loans).

3 Business Model

3.1 Historic Financial Performance

Orchard specialises in the insurance premium finance and the professions finance market. The group lent £73m in the 12 months to 31 July 2019, generated revenue of £5.5m and generated a profit before tax of £2.0m. The group's lending book was c. £32.3m as of the end of July 2019. The published key financials of the group, income statement and balance sheet, over the last four years to July 2019 are presented below.

Table 1: Orchard Historic Financials – year ended July.

				£'000
Income Statement	**Actual 2016**	**Actual 2017**	**Actual 2018**	**Actual 2019**
Revenue	3,469	4,560	5,174	5,481
Finance costs	(238)	(329)	(452)	(558)
Other operating costs	(76)	(78)	(83)	(72)
Gross Profit	**3,155**	**4,153**	**4,639**	**4,851**
Administration expenses	(1,884)	(2,512)	(2,746)	(2,830)
Operating profit before tax	**1,271**	**1,641**	**1,893**	**2,021**
Corporation tax	(267)	(303)	(381)	(387)
Profit after tax	**1,004**	**1,338**	**1,512**	**1,634**

Balance Sheet	**Actual 2016**	**Actual 2017**	**Actual 2018**	**Actual 2019**
Assets				
Loans and advances	22,004	28,523	31,084	32,297
Cash at bank	1,390	1,728	1,286	2,139
Fixed assets	95	77	59	129
Other assets	44	98	60	28
Total assets	**23,533**	**30,426**	**32,489**	**34,593**
Liabilities				
Bank borrowing	9,208	13,734	16,008	16,218
Trade creditors	1,657	3,181	2,051	3,015
Tax liabilities	289	279	339	370
Non-current liabilities	37	65	54	20
Total liabilities	**11,191**	**17,259**	**18,452**	**19,623**
Equity				
Share capital	214	214	214	214
Share premium	8,692	8,692	8,692	8,692
Merger reserves	891	891	891	891
Retained earnings	2,545	3,370	4,240	5,173

Table 1 (continued)

Balance Sheet	Actual 2016	Actual 2017	Actual 2018	Actual 2019
Total equity	12,342	13,167	14,037	14,970
Total equity and liabilities	23,533	30,426	32,489	34,593

3.1.1 Key Objectives

Key objectives of Orchard over the next five years are:

- to create a bank focused on providing consistent, reliable and cost-effective liquidity to borrowers deserving of such liquidity in the insurance premium finance market and the professions finance market;
- to conduct its business with integrity and ensure that customers are always treated fairly;
- to offer fair rates to depositors and provide transparency and clarity to all stakeholders in respect of the business of the bank;
- to protect depositors by writing prudent and conservative business in its chosen markets;
- to establish a board and executive management team, with strong, complementary non-executive directors and executive directors having a strong track record in specialist lending, deposit taking and risk management;
- to implement a risk management framework, supported by an operational platform with strong systems and controls, to enable effective operations, oversight, regulatory compliance and excellent service to the bank's depositors and borrowers;
- to grow Orchard's share of its chosen markets by continuing to build long term partnerships with key industry players in insurance and professional services. Orchard will utilise the unparalleled expertise of its management team and experienced sales team to achieve its business plan projections;
- to achieve targeted/projected pre- and post-tax profit and return on capital employed (RoCE)
- to deliver good customer outcomes to all stakeholders – depositors, borrowers, staff and shareholders.

3.1.2 Business Proposition

Orchard provides finance in the insurance premium finance market and the professions finance market in the UK. Finance is provided to SMEs and consumers typically over a 10-month term on a fully amortising basis. All finance provided by Orchard is guaranteed by the introducing professional firm or insurance broker. The directors believe that the lending undertaken by the group is very low risk, demonstrated by the fact that Orchard has suffered minimal arrears and loan losses over the last seven years. A banking licence will allow Orchard to tap into the UK deposits market and obtain access to a more stable, reliable, cost-effective and scalable source of funding, enabling it to support SMEs and consumers with better access to financing.

Orchard has been trading since 2002 and operates an efficient and profitable lending model. Orchard has developed its own bespoke software, LendXP, to allow it to conduct day-to-day lending operations. The software has been used by the group for over eight years and has proven to be reliable and with appropriate levels of control. The group was shortlisted as finalist for "Outsourced Partner of the Year 2016" by British Insurance Awards and "Service Provider of the Year 2016" by The Insurance Times. Orchard has been awarded "Intermediary of the Year" by Commercial Broker Awards 2017.

3.2 Lending Target Market

3.2.1 Insurance Premium Financing

The insurance premium finance market is a large and active market, which is driven by the general insurance market. The general insurance market is estimated to be currently worth over £35bn p.a. (measured in terms of gross written premium). Based on historic growth rates in the market from the Association of British Insurers (ABI), management have estimated that the annual growth rate has averaged c. 20% over the last ten years. The proportion that is financed is c. 38%. Management expect this growth to continue over the next 5 years.

The market is dominated by Premium Credit and Close Brothers, who lent a combined £6.3bn in 2018, representing approximately 47% of the £13.3bn insurance premium finance market in the United Kingdom. There are over 3,800 insurance broker firms in the UK regulated by the Financial Conduct Authority (FCA). Premium Credit and Close Brothers focus on larger volume-driven insurance brokers. Despite its historic funding constraints, Orchard has lent successfully into the market and has contractual relationships with over 100 insurance brokers for direct facilities and for in house premium finance facilities. Through these contracts Orchard lent c. £64m into the premium financing market in 2019 and plans to grow annual lending to c. £201m at the end of its five year plan, still less than 1% of the entire market.

3.2.2 Professions Financing

There are over 6,600 accountancy firms in the UK according to data published by the Annual Survey of the Office of National Statistics with over 335,000[9] individual members registered with the seven UK accountancy bodies according to the Financial Reporting Council. At the smaller end of the market 52% of accountancy firms are sole practitioners, and another 44% have between 2 and 6 principals. The accountancy fee finance market is currently estimated to be worth £300m per year and the

9 Key facts and trends in the Accountancy Profession, June 2015, Financial Reporting Council

professions finance working capital market is estimated by the directors to be worth over £3bn p.a.

The group currently has contractual relationships with over 400 accountancy firms. Through these contracts Orchard provided c. £7m of financing in 2019, and looks to grow annual lending to c. £59m at the end of five years.

3.3 Lending Products

3.3.1 Existing Lending Product Lines

The bank proposes to have the following business lines. All of the business lines are currently being originated and administered by Orchard:

1. Orchard provides finance to limited companies ("Broker Finance Companies"), which are owned and operated by insurance brokers. Broker Finance Companies provide finance to the clients of the related insurance broker to finance the insurance premiums of those clients. Orchard provides its finance to Broker Finance Companies, based upon and secured by the credit agreements between each Broker Finance Company and its client. Orchard takes a debenture from the Broker Finance Company and also a guarantee from the related insurance broker for all the obligations of the Broker Finance Company. Orchard's lending is for a maximum term of 12 months and is repaid on a fully amortising basis. Broker Finance Companies assign the benefit of all their credit agreements to Orchard and Orchard undertakes the collection and administration of the credit agreements;
2. Orchard provides finance to the clients of insurance brokers. The clients of insurance brokers are introduced to Orchard by the insurance broker. The clients can be consumers and non-consumers. A guarantee of the obligations of the clients is obtained from the introducing insurance broker;
3. Orchard provides finance to the clients of professional services firms, which are mainly accountancy practices. The clients of professional services firms are introduced to Orchard by the firms. The clients can be consumers and non-consumers. Orchard's lending is for a term of 12 months or less and is repaid on a fully amortising basis. A guarantee of the obligations of the clients is obtained from the introducing professional firm;
4. Orchard provides finance to professional services firms directly. This is all non-consumer business. The lending is for a term of 12 months or less and is repaid on a fully amortising basis. Guarantees are also provided by the partners of the professional firm;
5. Orchard provides a nominal amount of finance in adjacent markets to its core markets, such as golf fees, school fees, caravan pitch fees and football season ticket fees. These are relatively embryonic markets and the current lending is very small. Orchard's core focus as a bank will continue to be the insurance premium finance market and professions finance market.

3.3.2 Lending Product Features

Structure

Bexhill – Insurance Premium Financing

Bexhill is currently a wholly owned subsidiary of Orchard. The Bexhill business will be folded into the new bank. Bexhill was established in 2002 and has achieved consistent revenue growth between 2002 and 2019. However, due to the global financial crisis, Bexhill's funding became significantly restricted in 2008. Bexhill continued to trade through the difficult period and supported its client base despite scarcity of available funding. Currently Bexhill has over 100 insurance broker clients.

Bexhill typically lends through a finance company owned and operated by an insurance broker (corporate insurance) for the purpose of providing finance to the clients of the insurance broker. All Bexhill's lending is guaranteed by the insurance broker and all credit agreements entered into by the finance company are assigned to Bexhill and Bexhill undertakes the collection and administration of those credit agreements.

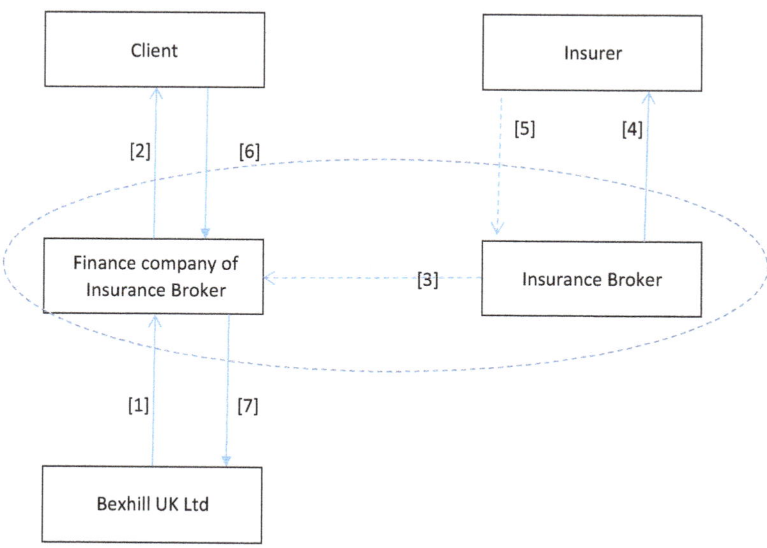

[1] Funding to financing company
[2] White-labeled finance agreement
[3] Guarantee from insurance broker
[4] Premium paid to the insurer
[5] Unearned premium on cancellation
[6] Monthly instalments
[7] Loan repayment

Figure 3: Corporate insurance structure.

Orchard – Professions Financing and Direct Insurance Lending
Orchard Funding Limited (OFL) is currently a wholly owned subsidiary of Orchard. The OFL business will be merged into the new bank. OFL was established in 2010 in order to take advantage of the withdrawal of one of the largest funders in the market for smaller professional practices. OFL's lending book has grown since its launch, despite its funding being relatively expensive and constrained. OFL has over 400 professional firm clients as at July 2019, most of which are accountancy firms. OFL's professional firm clients introduce their clients to OFL to finance their professional fees. OFL also provides facilities to a number of professional firms directly. OFL's insurance broker clients introduce their clients to OFL to finance their insurance premiums. OFL's client list has grown consistently year-on-year.

OFL typically lends directly to the client of the insurance broker (direct insurance), client of the professional firm; or the professional firm directly.

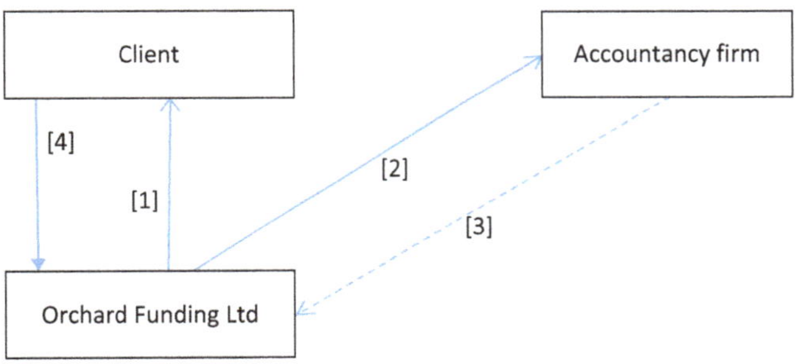

[1] Funding agreement
[2] Fees paid to the accountancy firm
[3] Guarantee from accountancy firm
[4] Monthly instalments

Figure 4: Accountancy fee funding structure.

Product Terms
Orchard's lending products will have the following terms, which replicate the terms of the products currently originated and administered by the group:
- APR – target 15–18%;
- Maximum term – 12 months;
- Fully amortising over the term of the credit;
- Full agreement to pay from the introducing insurance broker or professional firm.

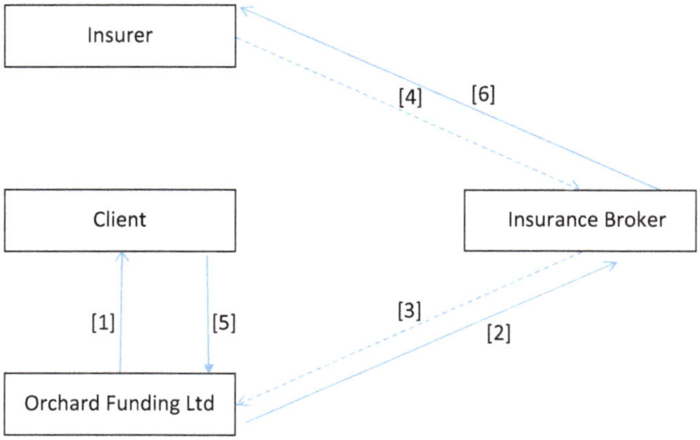

[1] Funding agreement
[2] Premium paid to the broker
[3] Guarantee from insurance broker
[4] Unearned premium
[5] Monthly instalments
[6] Premium paid to insurer

Figure 5: Direct insurance structure.

Although in isolation an APR of 15–18% appears relatively high, there are a number of factors, which suggest the rate is sustainable and fair to the borrower, including inter-alia:

- There are very limited sub-12 month amortising credit products available in the market. The larger financial institutions, including the banking market find the short-term nature and relatively small ticket size of this type of credit product unattractive;
- Unsecured overdrafts from banks can be over 20% APR and often over 30% APR;
- Credit card rates for borrowing are generally over 20% APR;
- Non-bank short-term credit terms can be punitively expensive;
- The rate paid by the Customer is often less than 10% APR, but Orchard is able to increase its IRR to over 15% by managing its settlement dates to the Introducer.

Financing through Orchard enables a borrower to still have the option of using its other credit providers for alternative spending.

Delivery Channels

Orchard currently uses a relationship-based model for lending origination which it plans to continue after authorisation.

Origination

Orchard has over 18 years of experience in its lending markets. The senior members of the sales team have decades of experience in the short-term financing market working with Orchard and previously with the leading competitors in the market. They have long-standing relationships with key players in the insurance brokerage sector and accountancy/law firms. The in-house solution offered by Bexhill allows insurance brokers to white-label the financing of insurance premiums to their clients, which is particularly attractive to a number of larger insurance brokers and may potentially lead to opportunities to scale up the lending business further in the future. Ongoing communication with the borrowers about loan administration is carried out over phone/email.

3.3.3 Lending Products – Conduct Risk

All new products are assessed for conduct risks, to ensure fair customer outcomes, and are signed off in accordance with the product approval policy. This includes:
- Product Characteristics
- Incentives/Income
- Pricing Structure
- Barriers to Exit
- Product Complexity
- Target Market
- Customer risk (performance metrics)
- Staff Competency
- Soft launch
- Monitoring
- Financial Promotions

All financial promotions require sign off from senior management and Compliance prior to publication.

3.3.4 Future Lending Products

Orchard has, in line with its key competitors, conducted test marketing in adjacent markets to its core insurance premium finance and accountancy fee funding market. The test marketing is currently at its peak because of the seasonality of caravan site fees and represents c.20% of Orchard's lending book. The adjacent markets are in service fee markets with similar characteristics, documentation and system requirements to its core markets, i.e., short-term credit where there is recourse to the introducer or a there are compelling reasons for the customer to ensure that its payments are made. Currently adjacent markets that are being tested are school fees, club fees and site fees. Orchard will continue to focus on the insurance premium market and accountancy fee funding market and consider adjacent markets where it can use its existing documentation, systems and expertise to ensure effective, profitable and controlled lending.

3.4 Competitive Advantages

The directors believe Orchard has the following key differentiators vis-à-vis its competitors:

- Orchard has been operating in the insurance premium finance market and professions finance market since 2002. In that time its senior management team has remained in place and developed strong and trusted relationships with its existing clients and with other key parties in its markets. The length of time that Orchard has operated in the market provides confidence to insurance brokers and professional firms that Orchard is a constant and reliable player in the market. This is very important as a number of companies have entered and exited the market since Orchard commenced its business.
- Orchard's senior management team has unparalleled experience in the premium finance and professions finance market. Unlike the management teams in the other leading competitors in the market, the management team has been exclusively focused on its markets since 2002 and in the case of some of the team since the late 1990s. Again, this depth of expertise provides a high level of confidence to insurance brokers and professional firms seeking a funding partner.
- The group understands the needs and requirements of insurance broker firms and professional firms and offers a fully tailored solution to the target market. The larger dominant market players are less focused on the smaller end of the lending market creating an opportunity for the group.
- Orchard is in regular contact with all its clients and strives to ensure that a high-quality service is consistently delivered. The larger players in both the insurance premium finance and professions finance market have in the past provided limited services to certain parts of the market allowing the group to build up a loyal customer base.
- The group's in-house premium finance product is unique and enables insurance brokers to take greater control and provide unparalleled service in the provision of premium finance to their clients. This product is very attractive to well capitalised insurance brokers who wish to ensure the highest levels of service are provided to their clients. No other company offers this product to insurance brokers and the product is attractive to some of the largest insurance brokers in the UK.
- The group does not impose any fees or require minimum levels of business for the availability of its facility to insurance brokers or professional firms.
- The group's online platform has the functionality to support white-label and direct financing and is simple to navigate and use. The system enables quick and efficient data entry for its insurance broker and professional firm clients, effective credit and affordability assessment and efficient production of compliant legal documentation for a client to sign either by hand or electronically.
- Senior management of the group is involved in all aspects of the business and in particular maintain close and strong relationships with the group's clients. The personal involvement of senior management in the needs and concerns of the group's

client base is very important to the clients of the group. The group has always regarded itself as an SME and is therefore sympathetic to the needs and aspirations of insurance brokers and professional firms, many of which are themselves SMEs.
- The ability, given the pricing of its lending, to offer consistently attractive rates on a simple and transparent deposit range to raise and retain the requisite deposit base to develop its business.

Due to the simplicity of its lending products Orchard will provide transparency and openness to depositors and all other stakeholders on all aspects of its business.

4 Capital and Funding

4.1 Capital Allocation and Mobility

The credit risk weight of the loan assets is calculated assuming lending is split between retail and SME on a 64% and 36% basis throughout the projection period as forecast from the firm's current actual experience. Although the loss experience over a number of years is very small, a higher than historic 1% impairment charge has been assumed for the financial plan. The financial model assumes a maximum cash balance of £1m is maintained in the nostro account, with all remaining surplus cash being held in the reserve account with the Bank of England. The Pillar I capital requirement is calculated as the sum of capital required in respect of credit risk on the loan assets, bank balances, fixed assets and operational risk where the operational risk charge is the average of the net income over the past three years. Orchard does not have any trading book and FX exposures and therefore does not have any Pillar 1 market risk. Detailed calculations, with risk weight percentages, are presented in the ICAAP.

Table 2: Pillar 1 Capital Requirements.

					£'000
Base	**Plan Year 1**	**Plan Year 2**	**Plan Year 3**	**Plan Year 4**	**Plan Year 5**
Pillar 1					
Credit risk on loan assets	1,833	2,265	2,883	3,800	5,201
Credit risk on bank balances	16	16	16	16	16
Fixed assets	2	3	4	4	5
Credit risk on HQLA	0	0	0	0	0
Total credit risk	**1,851**	**2,284**	**2,903**	**3,820**	**5,221**
Operational risk (Basic Indicator Approach)	718	806	1,005	1,284	1,696
Pillar 1 capital requirements	**2,569**	**3,090**	**3,908**	**5,104**	**6,917**

For Pillar 2A the bank intends to hold capital against:

1. Residual operational risk arising from the risk register after deducting the amount of capital provided under Pillar 1 for operational risk;
2. Credit concentration risk for single-name, sector and geographic concentration risk; and
3. Interest rate risk in the banking book (IRRBB) with a 200bps shift in the interest rate.

Table 3: Pillar 2A Capital Requirements.

					£'000
Base	**Plan Year 1**	**Plan Year 2**	**Plan Year 3**	**Plan Year 4**	**Plan Year 5**
Pillar 2A capital requirements					
Operational risk	101	54	0	0	0
Business risk	0	0	0	0	0
Reputational risk	0	0	0	0	0
Credit concentration risk	318	390	493	645	878
Interest rate risk in the banking book (IRRBB)	158	135	332	320	320
Residual operational risk from risk register	0	0	0	0	0
Pillar 2A capital requirements	**577**	**578**	**825**	**965**	**1,197**

The PRA have stated their intention to set Orchard's Pillar 2B capital (post-mobilisation) using the full stress testing approach. Beyond the mobilisation year the Pillar 2B capital is therefore set at values equal to the impact on capital surplus in a combined (market plus idiosyncratic) stress event.

The stress tests are described in detail in the ICAAP document, and the Pillar 2B capital requirements are summarised below:

Table 4: Pillar 2B Capital Requirements.

					£'000
	Year 1	**Year 2**	**Year 3**	**Year 4**	**Year 5**
CRD IV Pillar 2B (X)	1,124	1,352	1,710	2,233	3,026
Stress testing Pillar 2B (Y)	1,913	2,035	2,111	1,875	992
Max (X,Y)	**1,913**	**2,035**	**2,111**	**2,233**	**3,026**

Table 5: Summary Capital Requirements.

					£'000
Base	**Plan**	**Plan**	**Plan**	**Plan**	**Plan**
	Year 1	**Year 2**	**Year 3**	**Year 4**	**Year 5**
Pillar 1 capital requirements	2,569	3,090	3,908	5,104	6,917
Pillar 2A capital requirements	577	578	825	965	1,197
Total capital requirement (Pillar 1 + Pillar 2A)	**3,146**	**3,669**	**4,733**	**6,069**	**8,115**
Pillar 2B	1,913	2,035	2,111	2,233	3,026
TCR plus P2B	**5,059**	**5,704**	**6,844**	**8,302**	**11,141**
Total Capital resources	**16,370**	**17,579**	**19,250**	**21,792**	**25,646**
Risk weighted assets	32,117	38,626	48,853	63,802	86,464
Total Capital requirement % of RWAs	9.8%	9.5%	9.7%	9.5%	9.4%
TCR + Pillar 2B % of RWAs	15.8%	14.8%	14.0%	13.0%	12.9%
CET1 % of RWAs	53.5%	47.6%	41.0%	35.4%	30.6%
Surplus / (deficit) capital	11,310	11,875	12,405	13,491	14,505

The group intends to grow the balance sheet of the bank by leveraging on internally generated capital resources rather than introducing any additional capital over the plan period and in the three years projects to increase capital by £4.2m, a 30% increase.

4.1.1 Capital Related Risk Appetite

The bank intends to have a number of explicit capital risk metrics:

- CET 1 ratio;
- Surplus capital over TCR plus Pillar 2B; and
- Leverage ratio

The capital risk metrics will be monitored regularly and presented to the Executive Committee and Board by the CFO at least monthly as part of the monthly management information. While the bank anticipates adequate capital throughout its plan period, it is confident of raising further capital from institutional shareholders to supplement the current capital resources if the asset origination growth significantly exceeds expectation.

If the forecast earnings fall well short of plan the bank will have a number of options available to it including to:

1. Revise planned lending numbers and re-forecast the plan;
2. Consider carrying out a rights issue, even at a discounted price, taking advantage of Orchard's AIM listing and the quality of the shareholder base;
3. Consider revision to the dividend policy;
4. Reduce operational costs, without compromising customer service or risk management.

Orchard considers that it has sufficient capital for its 5 year plan and therefore has not approached shareholders for further capital. Orchard shareholders include some substantial institutions, which have the capacity to introduce further capital to Orchard but have not, at this stage, been tested to determine whether they have the appetite for such investment.

4.2 Treasury Function

Orchard is a small organisation with the Treasury function embedded in its Finance department and the Head of Finance acting as Treasurer.

4.3 Funding

All of Orchard's funding will be through its core tier 1 capital base and deposits raised from retail customers. Post authorisation and mobilisation, no intra group funding will exist as the authorised bank will be the only trading entity.

4.4 Intra-Group Guarantees

Not applicable to Orchard.

4.5 Other Financial Dependencies

Not applicable to Orchard.

4.6 Encumbrances

Immediately after exiting mobilisation, the majority of funding will still be through warehouse facilities with Barclays and Conister which are secured on Orchard's receivables. These borrowings will be paid down as the deposits book is grown.

4.7 Deposits Analysis

4.7.1 Deposit Target Market

Deposits Market

The total deposit base in the UK is over £2.9trn[10] of which the share of notice accounts is 12% (£350bn) and the share of fixed rate deposits is 7% (£200bn). The rate-sensitive share of the deposit market that is prone to switching is about 10% or £35bn and £20bn respectively for notice and fixed rate deposits according to market estimates of PBF Solutions (an outsourced deposit management provider). Assuming the average behavioural maturity of fixed term deposits is 2 years (realistic as most of the fixed term deposits are of 1 year maturity), £10bn of fixed rate deposits migrate looking for attractive rates in the market. By all measures, the market is vast and Orchard's share (projected to be c. £76m even after five years of operation) will be a very small fraction of the total available market.

Orchard intends to raise liabilities in the retail deposits market and understands it is difficult to offer a deposit proposition which is significantly differentiated from that of the competition. However, Orchard will offer a simple set of deposit products with attractive interest rates and a simple postal application process, through conventional best-buy tables.

Details in respect of the projected deposits to be raised by Orchard are set out in the base financial operating plan. Our deposit raising numbers (amounts and customers) are extremely conservative. We are confident that such deposit levels will be capable of being raised through a prominent exposure on best buy tables.

In the context of Orchard's conservative deposit raising aspirations, we believe the following research we have undertaken is sufficient to determine whether there is a market for our deposit taking plans. We have reviewed a number of publicly available research documents on the subject, including the FCA's Cash Savings Market Study of the UK deposit market and believe that such research enables us to conclude that there is a deep enough deposit market for the numbers set out in our Plan.

The current rates offered in the market place have been studied through the best buy tables to assess the margins above the bank base rates for the top ten providers. The base plan has assumed similar margins above the base rate, which is presented below. The time period in the chart is the period post mobilisation and authorisation as a bank.

---

10 Cash Savings – An International Comparison, A Study for the FCA, PwC, Sep 2014

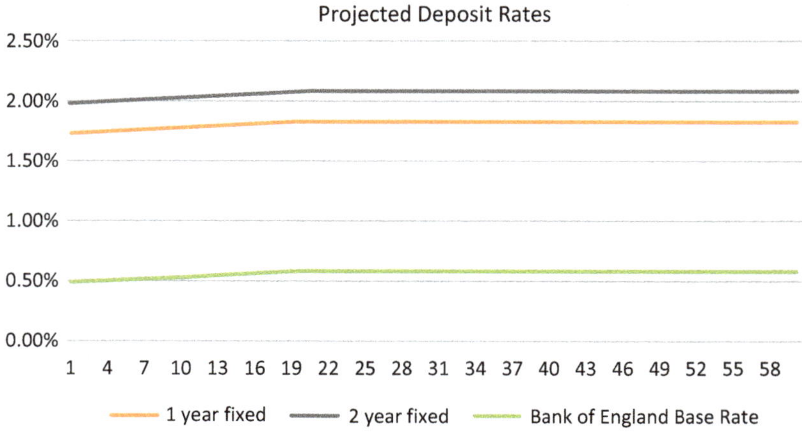

Figure 6: Deposit Rates.

4.7.2 New Deposit Products

Orchard will initially have 2 deposit products:

1. 1 year fixed rate deposit
2. 2 year fixed rate deposit.

The proposed new bank will operate nationally across the UK from its base in Luton. Staff with relevant experience will be recruited to run the new retail deposits operation. As noted above, the markets in which the group currently lends are very large and provide ample opportunities for growth over the time horizon envisaged in this plan. The group's proposed new deposit taking activities will similarly form an even smaller share of the target market.

Orchard plans to have a low-risk liability strategy focusing on a limited product set (1 year and 2 year fixed rate deposit accounts) initially offered in tranches to retail customers, combined with a simple postal application process, attractive and consistently fair rates and targeted customer retention schemes. There are no plans to offer instant access or current accounts. Initially the bank will develop brand awareness through prominence on the best-buy tables. Given the modest deposit raising plans in the projection (Orchard plans to have just over £76m in its deposit book at the end of year 5) these marketing efforts are considered to be adequate and proportionate.

Orchard will utilise the savings module of a proven software house, Mutual Vision Limited, for its deposit business. This software is used by a number of small building societies and banks.

4.7.3 Deposit Product Features

Structure

The fixed rate, fixed term deposits will have a minimum of £1K to cover operational costs and a maximum set to stay within the FSCS guarantee limit. Money will only be returned to the UK bank account where the deposit was credited from, with the option to roll over. Fixed term deposits will not be withdrawable before contractual maturity except in hardship conditions.

Product Terms

1-Year Fixed Rate Deposit

We have assumed a margin above base rate of 1.25% and average deposit size of £24,000. In year 1 we will therefore have approximately 525 depositors and this will increase to 1,900 over the 5-year life of the plan.

2-Year Fixed Rate Deposit

We have assumed a margin above base rate of 1.5% and average deposit size of £24,000. In year 1 we will therefore have approximately 336 depositors and this will increase to 1,216 over the 5-year life of the plan.

Deposit Delivery Channels, Origination and Retention

Orchard initially intends to raise deposits through postal applications. It plans to offer simple deposit products with market-leading rates and a simple postal application process. Orchard will be a new entrant into the deposits market and intends to market its products through the best-buy tables. This will help build brand recognition among the target market of depositors (high net worth, cash-rich individuals such as pensioners) and will result in lower costs of customer acquisition, higher retention and lower deposit rates over time given the modest deposit requirements planned in the projections.

Monthly tranche limits will be set by ALCO in order to avoid peaks in funds inflows and, therefore, funds outflows at maturity. Deposit applications will be made by filling out a form downloaded from the Orchard website. The number of downloads will be monitored automatically in order to estimate the expected inflow of funds and flag where run-rates exceed or fall short of preset parameters. This will prompt adjustment to pricing or temporary withdrawal of products where necessary. Orchard recognises that the appearance of deposit products in the best buy tables could lead to increases in inflows of deposits in excess of the levels required leading to excess liquidity and thereby creating a negative carry cost and spikes in outgoing funds at maturity. Orchard will carefully manage this risk by closely monitoring the application activity by number of downloads of the application forms from the website to project expected volume and amend the interest rates on the deposit products to reduce new business levels if required.

Orchard recognises that the cost of acquiring new deposits is significantly higher than the cost of retaining existing deposits, and will design tailored retention schemes (depositors contacted 4–6 weeks prior to deposit maturity, offered market leading rates that are the same as what is offered to new customers) to preserve them. Orchard will also work to build a brand that reflects partnership with the SME sector that over time will help it attract/retain deposits without paying market-leading interest rates.

In the event that customers are met with financial difficulties leading them to want to withdraw their deposit, Orchard will review each application to withdraw deposits prior to the contractual maturity date. As Orchard's assets are amortising and the liquidity buffers are extremely conservative throughout the term of the plan, Orchard will act in the manner of a reasonably prudent financial institution to determine whether a contractual deposit term can be broken. Our Deposit Hardship Policy sets out the basis on which each case will be determined, ensuring a fair and equitable outcome for the customer. It is anticipated that less than 1% (by value) of depositors will request a withdrawal of deposits prior to the contractual term date. An outline customer journey for Deposit customers with Orchard is attached in the Appendix.

Redemption Profile of Deposits

All deposit stock will be up to the FSCS limit lowering the risk of large-scale outflow in a stress scenario. Liability origination will be spread across the year by flexing the rate relative to competition to ensure no more than 12% of the existing liability stock contractually matures in a given month. Daily applications and new business will be tracked to manage the future maturity profile. At maturity, tailored retention schemes focused on a simple experience and consistently fair rates will help retain deposits and result in lower behavioural outflows. The terms of the deposit will clearly state that upon redemption a deposit will be rolled over for the same term at a rate that will be communicated to the depositor 4–6 weeks before the maturity of the deposit, and the depositor will be given an option to either switch to another deposit product or withdraw the proceeds altogether.

SCV File Generation

Orchard plans to use an outsourced software solution for deposits – 'Mutual Vision' which will contain up to 3k live records over the 5 year planning horizon. Lending data, consisting of up to 100k records over the 5 year planning horizon, will be on Orchard's in-house LendXP system. Output from the two systems will be merged manually.

4.8 Access to Financial Market Infrastructure

Orchard will set up an agency banking relationship to support deposit taking and get access to additional payment mechanisms to provide back-up. Application will be made to the Bank of England during the mobilisation phase to get membership of the Sterling Monetary Framework (SMF) to enable the deposit of excess cash in the reserve account, with accompanying access to BoE EnquiryLink either directly through SWIFT or via Bottomline.

Orchard will not provide banking services to any third parties and will not undertake any trading in securities.

4.9 Cash Services

Orchard will not provide any cash services (note circulation, cash supply, cash processing or commercial note issuance).

4.10 Risk Management Practices

Orchard operates within a risk management framework signed off by the Board and reviewed at least annually. Compliance with the framework and adherence to the agreed risk appetite is monitored by the Chief Risk Officer and the Risk Committee with Key Risk Indicators reported within the firm's management information packs.

4.11 Counterparty Risk Management

Orchard will not have a trading book.

4.12 Critical Shared Services

Orchard will be an independent stand-alone bank and therefore does not share services across legal entities.

The following table describes Orchard's current key outsourcing relationships. These cover the IT infrastructure as well as bespoke IT platforms.

Table 6: Outsourced Functions.

Function	Company	Description	Control/Mitigants
Servers + Infrastructure	Assign-IT	Assign IT manage OFG's general IT infrastructure, such as file storage and system security. All the data is stored on servers maintained in the office.	Service Level Agreements are in place with Assign IT. The relationship is regularly reviewed by the Head of Operations and the Audit Committee.
Bexhill Email	Assign-IT	Hosted on Microsoft Exchange, maintained by Assign IT.	See above.
Orchard Funding Email	Assign-IT	Hosted on Microsoft Exchange, maintained by Assign IT.	See above.
Loan management system – software development and maintenance	Brucode	Development of loan management software, both the back-end data management/ calculations and the user interface for use by Orchard staff and brokers.	Brucode recruits staff to a dedicated Orchard team who take direction from the Head of IT at Orchard via daily emails and twice- weekly conference calls.

In addition to the existing vendor relationships Orchard will establish the following outsourcing arrangements to deliver end-to-end banking services to its depositors and borrowers:

- Agency banking relationship with Orchard's existing GBP clearing bank to enable deposit account creation and administration;
- An outsourced provider to provide deposit taking software after full due diligence assessment;
- An outsourced provider to assist Orchard in the preparation of its regulatory reports, subject to due diligence and approval by CFO;
- Bottomline for payment mechanisms (SWIFT for RTGS, and deposit integration); and
- Professional accounting firms for internal audit and external audit through formal tender process, with appointment approved by Audit Committee
- Company secretarial services to deal with the increased governance workload in the form of minute-taking and tracking actions from the Board and management committees.

All outsourcing arrangements will comply with Orchard's Outsourcing Policy, which will be finalised during Mobilisation.

Phase 1 Part B: Economic Functions

5 Economic Functions

The table below presents the organisation's economic functions. Given the small scale of the planned business, no activities are deemed critical to the financial system. Figures are based on the plan numbers at the end of the first year of operation as a bank.

Economic Function	Economic Scale Metric		
Deposit Taking and Savings	Retail Current Accounts		None
	SME current accounts		None
	Retail Savings Accounts/ Time Accounts	Total liabilities	£21m
		Number of customers	875
		Market share	0.001%
	SME Savings Accounts		None
	Corporate Deposits		None
Lending & Loan Servicing	Retail Mortgages/Other Secured (Auto)		None
	Retail Personal Lending	Total Assets	£21.5m
		Total Committed Facilities	0
		Total Customers	12274
		RWA's	£15.9m
	Retail Credit Cards		None
	SME Lending	Total Assets	£11.6m
		Total Committed Facilities	0
		Total Customers	113
		RWA's	£6.6m
	Corporate Lending		None
	Trade Finance		None
	Infrastructure Lending		None
	Credit Card Merchant Services		None
Capital Markets & Investment	No activity		
Wholesale Funding Markets	No activity		
Payments, clearing, custody and settlement	No activity		

Table A Derivatives
Not applicable, as the firm will not have any derivatives
Table B Trading portfolio
Not applicable, as the firm will not have a trading portfolio
Table C Securities Financing
Not applicable, as the firm will not undertake any Securities Financing Transactions (Repurchase or Reverse Repurchase agreement).
Table D Note flow statistics
Not applicable, as the firm will not provide any cash services
Table E
The firm will have no cash centres, ATMs, or Branches.
Table of economic functions split by legal entities
The firm will only be one legal entity and no further split is required

5.1 The Inter-Relationship of Economic Functions, Legal Entities and Business Units

Orchard Bank will operate as a standalone legal entity.

5.2 Impact of Cessation of Economic Functions

The impact of Orchard's cessation of economic functions on the wider financial market is very limited due to the insignificant market share of lending and as well as deposit taking.

5.3 Ownership of Resolution Plan and review

The Resolution Plan preparation is the responsibility of the CFO. It will be updated annually, reviewed by the Risk Committee and approved by the Board.

7 Senior Managers and Certification Regime

7.1 Outline of SMCR Regime

The SMCR is designed to enhance individual accountability, clarifying specific responsibilities of senior managers and expanding the range of persons who are subject to standards of conduct so as to impact individual behaviour and culture within firms as a whole. It implements the recommendations of the 2012 report of the Parliamentary Commission on Banking Standards, using the legislative framework introduced by the Financial Services (Banking Reform) Act 2013.

The regime comprises of the Senior Managers Regime ('SMR'), the Certification Regime ('CR') and the Conduct Rules. All three are designed to embed principles of accountability and good conduct at all levels of a bank. Table 20 sets out a summary of the SMR and the CR.

Table 20: Senior Managers Regime/Certification Regime.

Senior Managers Regime	Focuses on individuals holding key roles (e.g., CEO, CFO, Chairman) or having overall responsibility for management functions or business areas within the Group (CRO, business heads, Operations, IT, HR). A bank is required to identify these individuals as 'senior management function holders' ('SMs'). There must be no gaps in accountability to these SMs. A bank must allocate specific prescribed responsibilities to these SMs. A bank is required to set out each SM's responsibilities in a regulatory Statement of Responsibilities which must be filed with the regulators and kept up to date. A bank must document its management and governance arrangements in a Responsibilities Map SMs are subject to regulatory pre-approval by the PRA/FCA and a bank is required to assess their Fitness and Proprietary at least annually. A bank should take reasonable steps to ensure that new SMs and SMs with changed responsibilities have the information and material they could reasonably expect to perform their responsibilities effectively.
Certification Regime	The CR covers staff who could pose a risk of significant harm to a bank or any of its customers A number of 'Certification Functions' have been identified who would previously have been Approved Persons but who fall outside the SMR CR staff are not subject to regulatory approval by the PRA/FCA but a bank will be accountable for assessing Fitness and Propriety prior to appointment and, on at least an annual basis thereafter. A bank must issue a 'Certificate' recording the assessment and the function(s) being performed.

https://doi.org/10.1515/9783111101545-007

Table 20 (continued)

Conduct Rules	High-level standards designed to hold individuals to account and facilitate cultural change within a bank. They are intended to promote a common understanding of acceptable/unacceptable behaviour at all levels and are therefore applicable to (and regulators could commence enforcement action against) all staff other than 'ancillary staff'. SMR-specific conduct rules set out additional expectations of SMs Enhanced breach reporting requirements.

7.2 Senior Management Function Holders

An example of the management function holders in a new bank applicant is set out in Table 21.

Table 21: Management Function Holders.

		Chairman	**CEO**	**CRO**	**CFO**	**Inde-pendent NED**	**Inde-pendent NED**
SMF1	Chief Executive function		✓				
SMF2	Chief Finance function				✓		
SMF3	Executive Director		✓		✓		
SMF4	Chief Risk function			✓			
SMF5	Head of Internal Audit	***Outsourced to Internal Audtior***					
SMF6	Head of Key Business Area	NA					
SMF7	Group Entity Senior Manager	NA					
SMF8	Credit Union SMF (small Credit Unions only)	NA					
SMF9	Chairman	✓					
SMF10	Chair of the Risk Committee						✓
SMF11	Chair of the Audit Committee					✓	
SMF12	Chair of the Remuneration Committee	✓					
SMF13	Chair of the Nominations Committee	✓					
SMF14	Senior Independent Director	NA					
SMF16	Compliance Oversight			✓			
SMF17	Money Laundering Reporting			✓			
SMF18	Other Overall Responsibility function	NA					
SMF24	Chief Operations function		✓				
a	Responsibility for the firm's performance of its obligations under the senior management regime		✓				
b	Responsibility for the firm's performance of its obligations under the employee certification regime		✓				

Table 21 (continued)

		Chairman	CEO	CRO	CFO	Inde-pendent NED	Inde-pendent NED
b1	Responsibility for the firm's obligations in relation to individual conduct rules for training and reporting		✓				
c	Responsibility for compliance with the requirements of the regulatory system about the management responsibilities map		✓				
d	Overall responsibility for the firm's policies and procedures for countering the risk that the firm might be used to further financial crime			✓			
e	Responsibility for the allocation of all prescribed responsibilities		✓				
v	Proprietary trading	NA					
w	No Chief Risk function	NA					
x	If the firm outsources its internal audit function taking reasonable steps to ensure that every person involved in the performance of the service is independent from the persons who perform external audit, including (a) Supervision and management of the work of outsourced internal auditors and (b)Management of potential conflicts of interest between the provision of external audit and internal audit services		✓				
y	Ring fenced	NA					
z	Overall responsibility for the firm's compliance with CASS			✓			
aa	Responsibility for implementing and management of the firm's risk management policies and procedures			✓			
bb	Responsibility for managing the systems and controls of the firm			✓			
cc	Responsibility for managing the firm's financial resources.				✓		
dd	Responsibility for ensuring the governing body is informed of its legal and regulatory obligations			✓			

The Systems and Controls Rules also require the allocation of responsibilities to the relevant members of the board. Table 22 sets out an example of allocations by a bank.

Table 22: Allocation of Systems and Controls Responsibilities to Senior Managers.

Payment Services				✓
Settlement				✓
Investment Management				✓
Financial or Investment advice	NA			
Mortgage advice	NA			
Corporate investments	NA			
Wholesale sales	NA			
Retail sales		✓		
Trading for clients	NA			
Market making	NA			
Investment Research	NA			
Origination/syndication and underwtng	NA			
Retail lending decisions		✓		
Wholesale lending decisions	NA			
Design and manufacture products – whsle	NA			
Design and manufacture products – retail		✓		
Production/distribn marketing materials		✓		
Customer service		✓		
Customer complaints handling			✓	
Collection and recovery from clients			✓	
Middle office			✓	
IT		✓		
Business continuity planning		✓		
Human resources		✓		
Incentives for staff			✓	
Input data BMR benchmark	NA			
Administering benchmark	NA			

The senior management function holders are required to understand the SMR rules, their roles and responsibilities under the responsibilities map and have a comprehensive training plan to address any skills or knowledge gaps to evidence they have met their obligations under the SMR, in order to prevent regulatory breaches from occurring or continuing in their area of accountability. If found guilty of misconduct, SMs may be subject to disciplinary action by the bank and/or the FCA/PRA, including the imposition of potentially unlimited fines, approval being suspended, withdrawn or made subject to conditions, or the imposition of a prohibition order preventing the individual from working in financial services or within certain roles.

The Roles and Responsibilities of each of the Senior Managers should be clearly defined. Examples are set out in Tables 23 and 24.

Table 23: Senior Management Roles & Responsibilities – NEDs.
Non-Executive Roles & Responsibilities

Role	Key Responsibilities
Chairman (Board) & Chairman of Nominations and Remuneration INED SMF 9 SMF 12 SMF 13	Responsible for leading the Board and ensuring effective direction and challenge for Management Setting Board Agenda (in consultation with Management) Chair of Noms and Rems Committee Setting tone from the top in terms of the culture of the organisation Board training agenda Board evaluation (annual) Appraisal of performance of Board members and CEO Ensuring appropriate balance of skills and diversity of Board
Chair of Audit INED SMF 10	Responsible for ensuring an effective Audit Committee operating in the interests of all stakeholders Ensuring regulatory and listing responsibilities are discharged effectively Audit Committee Agenda (in consultation with Management) Oversight of Internal Audit (including assessing performance in conjunction with CEO) Liaising with External Auditors Audit Committee Evaluation (annual)
Chair of Risk INED SMF 11	Responsible for ensuring an effective Risk Committee in accordance with its terms of reference Setting Risk Committee agenda Oversight of CRO (including assessing performance in conjunction with CEO) Risk Committee evaluation (Annual) Responsible for the maintenance of an appropriate Whistleblowing process for customers, staff and other stakeholders of the business.

7.3 Executive Roles & Responsibilities

Table 24: Senior Management Roles & Responsibilities – Executive.

Role	Principal Responsibilities
Chief Executive Officer and Board Director SMF1, SMF 3, SMF 24	The CEO is responsible for: – effective day-to-day management of the business – operating the business in accordance with board approved strategies, plans and policies – ensuring an effective systems and control environment – managing overall enterprise risk and returns – setting the corporate culture – primarily responsible for the relationship with the relevant regulatory bodies and for all other stakeholders in the business – compliance with Board Risk Appetite Statement

Table 24 (continued)

Role	Principal Responsibilities
	The CEO is Chairman of the Executive Committee and member of ALCO and Credit Committee. The CEO is also responsible for ensuring that the board members are: – able to sufficiently challenge the executive and understand the business model – provided with a full understanding of higher risk activities and products – in receipt of appropriate management information to be able to carry out their oversight role The CEO will have oversight responsibility for HR and marketing. The CEO also has oversight responsibility for: – the effective development of the bank's retail savings business in terms of its administration functions, ensuring that high standards of performance and service are achieved at all times and that the bank operates at all times within the policies and parameters set by the board. – ensuring that all staff members within the retail savings business act at all times in compliance with the letter and the spirit of all laws and regulations applying to the bank The CEO also holds primary responsibility for: – management, stability, security and effectiveness of the systems and communications used in the bank – operating within parameters and budgets set by the Board and the Executive Committee – ensuring the bank remains appropriately positioned to address its business needs, provide operational resilience, security risks and to respond to identified opportunities and threats relevant to IT and Communications – managing the secure delivery of the bank's website and email communications. – Business Continuity and Disaster Recovery Plan, maintaining it up to date at all times and ensuring it is subject to appropriate and regular testing – Bank-wide project management – Outsourcing arrangements – Facilities management
Chief Financial Officer and Board Director SMF2, SMF3	The CFO has overall responsibility for: – overseeing the Finance and Treasury functions of the bank and ensuring that each operates within the parameters and policies set by the Board and Executive Committee – primary accountability for the quality of the business-wide financial and management information – all statutory and regulatory reporting – oversight of the principal financial systems and controls of the business – the preparation of the ILAAP, ICAAP, Recovery Plan and Resolution Plan – the financial and treasury-related risks of the bank on a day-to-day basis including capital management, liquidity management and compliance with IFRS. – managing the production of and present the medium-term financial plan for approval to the Board – compliance with Board Risk Appetite Statement

Table 24 (continued)

Role	Principal Responsibilities
	As a member of the Executive Committee the CFO is responsible for contributing to overall direction of the business in terms of its strategies, performance, systems and controls. The CFO is a member of the Executive Committee and Credit Committee and Chair of ALCO. Working with the CEO, the CFO will take primary responsibility for the delivery of the bank's deposit strategy, ensuring that the bank achieves the right mix of funding across its target customer segments and at an acceptable cost of funds. The CFO is also responsible for: the production of all financially related statutory and regulatory returns in accordance with prescribed timetables – production of timely management information, pulling this together from across all areas of the Group – operation of the payments and reconciliations of the bank which is a key area of control – ensuring that finance operations function within Board and Executive Committee-approved parameters and policies
Chief Risk Officer SMF4, SMF 16, SMF 17	The CRO has primary responsibility to the Board on the quality of the bank's overall risk management framework. He is a key link between the Board and the business with the ability to translate what is at times highly technical and often detailed reporting of risk into high level information for the Board to understand and interpret at a strategic level. The CRO attends all the executive committees of the bank providing internal challenge and is a Member of ALCO and Credit Committee. As a member of the Executive Committee the CRO is responsible for contributing to the overall direction of the business in terms of its strategies, performance, systems and controls. In addition to enterprise-wide risk management, the CRO has primary oversight responsibility for: – legal and compliance (including conduct risk) – financial crime prevention – fraud management – credit risk and credit systems Operational risk – compliance with Board Risk Appetite Statement The CRO will be responsible for: – ensuring the bank meets all its statutory and regulatory requirements relating to the operation of the bank other than the financial ones undertaken by the Finance Director and CFO – ensuring compliant procedures are in place to enable the business operations to comply with current legislation and regulations – taking responsibility for the effective management, measurement and monitoring of exposure to Conduct Risk

Table 24 (continued)

Role	Principal Responsibilities
	– monitoring compliance with Complaints Handling and Treating Customers Fairly – documenting and reporting results of legal and compliance monitoring to the Board, Audit& Risk and Executive Committees as appropriate – compliance with Board Risk Appetite Statement He also acts as Money Laundering Reporting Officer (MLRO). As MLRO he has responsibility for: – ensuring all statutory and regulatory responsibilities are discharged on behalf of the bank – the implementation of and compliance with anti-money laundering procedures and policies – receiving and reviewing suspicious transaction reports and advising SOCA as necessary He is responsible for developing and delivering all compliance training requirements. His legal responsibilities relate to taking primary responsibility for: – reviewing all terms and conditions of products, third-party contracts for services and business relationships – and ensuring that they are appropriate within the context of the board-approved policies and parameters and applicable laws and regulations.
Head of Savings	Develop and grow robust savings functions to ensure that the bank manages its business effectively and efficiently, providing excellent customer service and meeting all business and regulatory requirements Develop and maintain written policies and procedures to deliver excellent customer service and positive customer outcomes Identify, promote and implement innovative methods of service delivery and continuously develop the service provided to ensure it meets and exceeds customer expectations Ensure that customer feedback and root cause analysis are utilised to improve processes and services to increase satisfaction Ensure attainment of key performance indicators from all channel contacts, e.g., service level response times, abandon rates, first contact resolution customer satisfaction, retention and quality Ensure effective resource management to optimise the use of staff and outsource service providers for cyclical peaks and troughs and develop effective call overflow strategies Ensure Savings functions are managed with robust governance, controls, protocols and frameworks in place to effectively manage all conduct and operational risks Contribute to the creation and implementation of bank's strategic plans Ensure all complaints are dealt with in a timely manner Implement a competitor monitoring service to inform pricing decisions and provide information to inform decision making on opportunities to improve margin for the bank Review product set performance and identify trends to drive future product decision making

Table 24 (continued)

Role	Principal Responsibilities
	Investigate expansion of product set in to new areas, e.g., ISAs, regular savings, offshore savings Develop a marketing and PR strategy for the savings business Develop the product strategy that delights customers while driving profitable revenue for the business The ongoing development and refinement of the bank's deposit product portfolio to anticipate/respond to customer/market demand, industry trends and regulatory change Develop introducer channels, affinity partnerships and white label products Finance function liaison, working closely with Finance to define and agree funding targets and associated product requirements/volumes, deploying products to meet these Product operational performance, maintaining regular tracking of product performance relative to other market players, developing initiatives where appropriate Produce forecasting/capacity planning, developing and maintaining product forecasting and planning tools to ensure the bankp establishes a satisfactory level of customer services Responsible for managing supplier relationships with third-party providers.
Chief Internal Auditor	The bank will have an outsourced independent Internal Audit team which will report to the Board through the Audit Committee. It will adopt a risk-based approach in order to independently assess the effectiveness and appropriateness of the internal control systems and ensure that MB's activities and processes comply with the appropriate regulations. The role of the internal audit function is based on a risk-based audit plan which will be updated on an annual basis and approved by the Audit & Risk Committee. Activities and processes of the bank will be audited at appropriate intervals, at least every 3 years. Internal audit will also have a responsibility to review the activities and processes which have been outsourced to third parties. To fulfil its role, the internal audit function will: Develop an audit plan, to be agreed with the Audit Committee, focusing on key areas of risk. Perform assessments of the bank's activities, focusing on the design and operation of processes and controls. Prepare written audit reports which will be submitted and reviewed by the Audit Committee and senior management. Reports will include a description of the audit and findings, any planned measures, and any major deficiencies. The Audit Committee will review audit reports to demonstrate whether or not the audit plan has been adhered to. Perform appropriate assessments to ensure that any deficiencies discovered are remedied within the required period and report to the Audit Committee on any outstanding actions. Internal audit will be informed of any management directives, resolutions and material changes to risk management that could be relevant to its activities, and update its audit plan appropriately.

Each member of the Board will undertake an assessment of his current abilities to perform his defined responsibilities.

An example Table of a Board Assessment for a bank is set out in Table 25:

Table 25: Board Assessment.

Code: **1-Experienced** **2- Reasonable knowledge** **3- Capable of development with support/training** **4- Not considered essential as sufficiently covered by others**	**CEO**	**CFO**	**CRO**	**INED**	**Chairman**
Lending	1	2	2	1	1
Credit Risk	1	1	2	1	1
Lending market	1	2	2	2	2
Operations/Change Risk	1	1	2	1	1
Market/Competition Risk	1	2	2	2	2
Compliance & Risk	1	1	1	1	2
Prudential Risk	1	1	1	1	2
Conduct Risk	1	1	1	1	2
Information Technology	1	2	2	1	2
IT Security Risk/Cyber Risk	1	2	2	1	2
Capital Planning, Funding, Liquidity	1	1	1	1	1
Financial Risk & Analysis	1	1	1	1	1
Regulatory Reporting	2	1	1	1	1
Deposit Product Management	3	1	2	1	1
Remuneration/People Risk	1	1	2	1	1
Financial Services (Banking) Experience	1	1	1	1	1
Understanding of Bank Strategy and Key Risks	1	1	1	1	2
Customer Focus	1	1	1	1	2
Challenges Executives	NA	NA	NA	1	1
Actively Participates in Debates	1	1	1	1	1
Prepares Properly for Meeting and Reads Papers	1	1	1	1	1
Up-to-date in Own Area of Expertise	1	1	1	1	1
Board Committees Chairman – Leadership Qualities/Effectiveness/Potential	1	1	2	1	1

Another example of an Experience Matrix for a Chief Executive Officer is set out in Table 26.

Table 26: Example Experience Matrix for a CEO.

Area of Expertise	**Score**	***CEO***
Risk Management and setting risk appetite	1	Involved in all aspects of Risk Management for the bank since its commencement in business. Directly involved in creation of the Enterprise Risk Management and Governance Framework including various risk policy approvals for the bank and its refinement and evolution. Key part of bank team responsible for the preparation of ICAAP, ILAAP and RRP and Board approval. (Rated 1, as roles have been direct responsibility roles)

Table 26 (continued)

Technology including business continuity, resilience and security	1	Directly responsible for the creation, operation, maintenance and upgrading of the IT systems utilised by the bank. The role has involved making decisions on the purchase and implementation of technology (IT hardware, IT systems and software, IT development, IT Infrastructure, IT security, IT resilience, BCP, IT business support and outsourcing). (Rated 1 as roles have been direct responsibility roles)
Treasury management including asset and liability management	2	Key part of bank team responsible for ICAAP, ILAAP and RRP. Experience in residential mortgage securitisation as banking solicitor and investment banker. (Rated 2 as will not be directly responsible for the bank's Treasury function)
Operations and project management	1	Many years' experience of operations and project management at the bank, from the introduction of implementation of IT systems, to the building up of an operational platform. Also key in the project management of entry into new markets, building the team, IT and liquidity for new markets. (Rated 1 as roles have been direct responsibility roles)
Financial statements and reporting, including regulatory	2	Considerable experience as the CEO of the bank with responsibility for assistance in the preparation of statutory financial statements under UK GAAP and IFRS, management reporting and regulatory reporting. (Rated 2, as has not been directly responsible for Financial Statements at the bank)
Prudential and Conduct regulation, including conduct, Sysc, threshold conditions (PRA and FCA), SMCR	1	Extensive experience of Conduct regulation gained as CEO of the bank. Detailed experience of Prudential regulation accumulated through being a key member of bank team preparing the ICAAP, ILAAP and RRP.
Business strategy, including for the bank's chosen markets	1	CEO of the bank with detailed experience in the bank's lending and deposit taking markets in a variety of market conditions.
Retail deposits marketing and operations	3	Limited experience in retail deposits. Extensive experience of managing third-party liquidity for the bank.

List of Tables

https://doi.org/10.1515/9783111101545-008

About the Author

Mr Ravi Takhar has over 35 years' experience in the creation, acquisition, growth, financing and disposal of financial businesses and banks. Mr Takhar is CEO of London Stock Exchange listed Orchard Funding Group PLC, a company he founded in 2002. He was an investment banker and Head of Financial Services Investment at Nikko, the Japanese investment bank, from 1998 to 2002, as well as Chairman of Mortgages PLC, the mortgage lender. Ravi was also Head of Mortgage Principal Finance at Investec Bank PLC from 2005 to 2008 and Chairman and Chief Risk Officer of Urban Exposure PLC, the development finance lender, from 2009 to 2020. He qualified as a banking solicitor at Clifford Chance, a leading international law firm, and has an MA from the University of Oxford.

https://doi.org/10.1515/9783111101545-009

About the Series Editor

Moorad Choudhry is an independent non-executive director at Recognise Bank Limited, a non-executive director at the Loughborough Building Society and a non-executive director at the Wandle Housing Association. He is Honorary Professor at University of Kent Business School. He was latterly Treasurer, Corporate Banking Division at The Royal Bank of Scotland.

Moorad is a Fellow of the Chartered Institute for Securities & Investment, a Fellow of the London Institute of Banking and Finance, a Fellow of the Global Association of Risk Professionals, a Fellow of the Institute of Directors and a Freeman of The Worshipful Company of International Bankers. He is author of *The Principles of Banking* (John Wiley & Sons 2012, 2022).

Moorad was educated at Claremont Fan Court school, University of Westminster and University of Reading. He obtained his MBA from Henley Business School and his PhD from Birkbeck, University of London. He was born in Bangladesh and lives in Surrey, England.

https://doi.org/10.1515/9783111101545-010

Index

https://doi.org/10.1515/9783111101545-011

The Moorad Choudhry Global Banking Series

Principles of Green Banking: Managing Environmental Risk and Sustainability
by Suborna Barua

Reverse Stress Testing in Banking: A Comprehensive Guide
by Michael Eichhorn, Tiziano Bellini, and Daniel Mayenberger (eds.)

Bank Asset Liability Management Best Practice: Yesterday, Today and Tomorrow
by Polina Bardaeva

Random Walks in Fixed Income and Foreign Exchange: Unexpected Discoveries in Issuance, Investment and Hedging of Yield Curve Instruments
by Jessica James, Michael Leister, and Christoph Rieger

Banking Associations: Their Role and Impact in a Time of Market Change,
by Sladjana Sredojevic and Milan Brkovic

Inflation-Linked Bonds and Derivatives: Investing, Hedging and Valuation Principles for Practitioners
by Jessica James, Michael Leister, and Christoph Rieger

Banking in the Age of the Platform Economy: Digital Acceleration Through Strategies of Interdependence
by Giorgio Bou-Daher

ALM Modeling and Balance Sheet Optimization: A Mathematical Approach to Banking
by Diogo Gobira and Lucas Processi

Climate Change Risk Management in Banks: The Next Paradigm
by Saloni P. Ramakrishna

How to Build a Bank: A Guide to Key Bank Regulations, the License Application Process and Bank Risk Management
by Ravi Takhar

www.ingramcontent.com/pod-product-compliance
Lightning Source LLC
Chambersburg PA
CBHW080936240926
51849CB00004BA/472
9783111100555